Essential SNMP

Essential SNMP

Douglas R. Mauro and Kevin J. Schmidt

O'REILLY®

Beijing · Cambridge · Farnham · Köln · Paris · Sebastopol · Taipei · Tokyo

Essential SNMP

by Douglas R. Mauro and Kevin J. Schmidt

Published by O'Reilly & Associates, Inc., 101 Morris Street, Sebastopol, CA 95472.

Editor: Mike Loukides

Production Editor: Rachel Wheeler

Cover Designer: Ellie Volckhausen

Printing History:

July 2001:   First Edition.

ISBN: 0-596-00020-0

[M]

[12/01]

Table of Contents

Preface

The Simple Network Management Protocol (SNMP) is an Internet-standard protocol for managing devices on IP networks. Many kinds of devices support SNMP, including routers, switches, servers, workstations, printers, modem racks, and uninterruptible power supplies (UPSs). The ways you can use SNMP range from the mundane to the exotic: it's fairly simple to use SNMP to monitor the health of your routers, servers, and other pieces of network hardware, but you can also use it to control your network devices and even send pages or take other automatic action if problems arise. The information you can monitor ranges from relatively simple and standardized items, like the amount of traffic flowing into or out of an interface, to more esoteric hardware- and vendor-specific items, like the air temperature inside a router.

Given that there are already a number of books about SNMP in print, why write another one? Although there are many books on SNMP, there's a lack of books aimed at the practicing network or system administrator. Many books cover how to implement SNMP or discuss the protocol at a fairly abstract level, but none really answers the network administrator's most basic questions: How can I best put SNMP to work on my network? How can I make managing my network easier?

We provide a brief overview of the SNMP protocol in Chapter 2, then spend a few chapters discussing issues such as hardware requirements and the sorts of tools that are available for use with SNMP. However, the bulk of this book is devoted to discussing, with real examples, how to use SNMP for system and network administration tasks.

Most newcomers to SNMP ask some or all of the following questions:

* What exactly is SNMP?

* How can I, as a system or network administrator, benefit from SNMP?

- What is a MIB?

- What is an OID?

- What is a community string?

- What is a trap?

- I've heard that SNMP is insecure. Is this true?

- Do any of my devices support SNMP? If so, how can I tell if they are configured properly?

- How do I go about gathering SNMP information from a device?

- I have a limited budget for purchasing network-management software. What sort of free/open source software is available?

- Is there an SNMP Perl module that I can use to write cool scripts?

This book answers all these questions and more. Our goal is to demystify SNMP and make it more accessible to a wider range of users.

Audience for This Book

This book is intended for system and network administrators who could benefit from using SNMP to manage their equipment but who have little or no experience with SNMP or SNMP applications. In our experience almost any network, no matter how small, can benefit from using SNMP. If you're a Perl programmer, this book will give you some ideas about how to write scripts that use SNMP to help manage your network. If you're not a Perl user you can use many of the other tools we present, ranging from Net-SNMP (an open source collection of command-line tools) to Hewlett Packard's OpenView (a high-end, high-priced network-management platform).

Organization

Chapter 1, *What Is SNMP?*, provides a nontechnical overview of network management with SNMP. We introduce the different versions of SNMP as well as the concepts of managers and agents.

Chapter 2, *A Closer Look at SNMP*, discusses the technical details of SNMP. We look at the Structure of Management Information (SMI) and the Management Information Base (MIB) and discuss how SNMP actually works; i.e., how management information is sent and received over the network.

Chapter 3, *NMS Architectures*, helps you to think about strategies for deploying SNMP.

Chapter 4, *SNMP-Compatible Hardware*, discusses what it means when a vendor says that its equipment is "SNMP-compatible."

Chapter 5, *Network-Management Software*, introduces some of the available network-management software. We discuss the pros and cons of each package and provide pointers to vendors' web sites. We include both commercial and open source packages in the discussion.

Chapter 6, *Configuring Your NMS*, provides a basic understanding of what to expect when installing NMS software by looking at two NMS packages, HP's OpenView and Castle Rock's SNMPc.

Chapter 7, *Configuring SNMP Agents*, describes how to configure the Windows SNMP agent and several SNMP agents for Unix, including the Net-SNMP agent. To round the chapter out, we discuss how to configure the embedded agents on two network devices: the Cisco SNMP agent and the APC Symetra SNMP agent.

Chapter 8, *Polling and Setting*, shows how you can use command-line tools and Perl to gather (poll) SNMP information and change (set) the state of a managed device.

Chapter 9, *Polling and Thresholds*, discusses how to configure OpenView and SNMPc to gather SNMP information via polling. This chapter also discusses RMON configuration on a Cisco router.

Chapter 10, *Traps*, examines how to send and receive traps using command-line tools, Perl, OpenView, and other management applications.

Chapter 11, *Extensible SNMP Agents*, shows how several popular SNMP agents can be extended. Extensible agents provide end users with a means to extend the operation of an agent without having access to the agent's source code.

Chapter 12, *Adapting SNMP to Fit Your Environment*, is geared toward Perl-savvy system administrators. We provide Perl scripts that demonstrate how to perform some common system-administration tasks with SNMP.

Chapter 13, *MRTG*, introduces one of the most widely used open source SNMP applications, the Multi Router Traffic Grapher (MRTG). MRTG provides network administrators with web-based usage graphs of router interfaces and can be configured to graph many other kinds of data.

Appendix A, *Using Input and Output Octets*, discusses how to use OpenView to graph input and output octets.

Appendix B, *More on OpenView's NNM*, discusses how to graph external data with Network Node Manager (NNM), add menu items to NNM, configure user profiles, and use NNM as a centralized communication interface.

Appendix C, *Net-SNMP Tools*, summarizes the usage of the Net-SNMP command-line tools.

Appendix D, *SNMP RFCs*, provides an authoritative list of the various RFC numbers that pertain to SNMP.

Appendix E, *SNMP Support for Perl*, is a good summary of the SNMP Perl module used throughout the book.

Appendix F, *SNMPv3*, provides a brief introduction to SNMPv3. Two configuration examples are provided: configuring SNMPv3 on a Cisco router and configuring SNMPv3 for Net-SNMP.

Example Programs

All the example programs in this book are available at *http://www.oreilly.com/ catalog/esnmp/*.

Conventions Used in This Book

The following typographical conventions are used in this book:

Italic
> Used for commands, object IDs, URLs, filenames, and directory names. It is also used for emphasis and for the first use of technical terms.

Constant width
> Used for examples, object definitions, literal values, and datatypes. It is also used to show source code, the contents of files, and the output of commands.

Constant width bold
> Used in interactive examples to show commands or text that would be typed literally by the user. It is also used to emphasize when something, usually in source code or file-contents examples, has been added to or changed from a previous example.

Constant width italic
> Used for replaceable parameter names in command syntax.

     Indicates a tip, suggestion, or general note.

Indicates a warning or caution.

Comments and Questions

Please address comments and questions concerning this book to the publisher:

O'Reilly & Associates, Inc.
101 Morris Street
Sebastopol, CA 95472
(800) 998-9938 (in the United States or Canada)
(707) 829-0515 (international/local)
(707) 829-0104 (fax)

There is a web page for this book, which lists errata, the text of several helpful technical papers, and any additional information. You can access this page at:

http://www.oreilly.com/catalog/esnmp/

To comment or ask technical questions about this book, send email to:

bookquestions@oreilly.com

For more information about books, conferences, software, Resource Centers, and the O'Reilly Network, see the O'Reilly web site at:

http://www.oreilly.com

Acknowledgments

It would be an understatement to say that this book was a long time in the making. It would never have been published without the patience and support of Michael Loukides. Thanks Mike! We would also like to thank the individuals who provided us with valuable technical review feedback and general help and guidance: Mike DeGraw-Bertsch at O'Reilly & Associates; Donald Cooley at Global Crossing; Jacob Kirsch at Sun Microsystems, Inc.; Bobby Krupczak, Ph.D., at Concord Communications; John Reinhardt at Road Runner; Patrick Bailey and Rob Sweet at Netrail; and Jürgen Schönwälder at the Technical University of Braunschweig. Rob Romano, O'Reilly & Associates graphic artist, deserves a thank you for making the figures throughout the book look great. Finally, thanks to Jim Sumser, who took the project over in its final stages, and to Rachel Wheeler, the production editor, for putting this book together.

Douglas

For years I worked as a system and network administrator and often faced the question, "How are things running?" This is what led me to SNMP and eventually the idea for this book. Of course I would like to thank Kevin for his hard work and dedication. Special thanks go to the two special girls in my life: my wife, Amy, and our daughter, Kari, for putting up with my long absences while I was writing in the computer room. Thanks also go to my family and friends, who provided support and encouragement.

Kevin

While at MindSpring Enterprises (now Earthlink) I was fortunate enough to work for Allen Thomas, who gave me the freedom to explore my technical interests, including SNMP. I would like to thank Bobby Krupczak for providing me with valuable feedback on the SystemEDGE agent. Thanks also to my colleagues Patrick Bailey and Rob Sweet at Netrail, who provided some general Perl code feedback. I'm very fortunate to have worked with Douglas on this book; thanks for allowing me to help out. My parents deserve a thank you for buying me my first computer all those years ago. And finally, I would like to thank Callie, my significant other, for allowing me to use our nights and weekends to work on this book.

1

What Is SNMP?

In today's complex network of routers, switches, and servers, it can seem like a daunting task to manage all the devices on your network and make sure they're not only up and running but performing optimally. This is where the *Simple Network Management Protocol* (SNMP) can help. SNMP was introduced in 1988 to meet the growing need for a standard for managing *Internet Protocol* (IP) devices. SNMP provides its users with a "simple" set of operations that allows these devices to be managed remotely.

This book is aimed toward system administrators who would like to begin using SNMP to manage their servers or routers, but who lack the knowledge or understanding to do so. We try to give you a basic understanding of what SNMP is and how it works; beyond that, we show you how to put SNMP into practice, using a number of widely available tools. Above all, we want this to be a practical book— a book that helps you keep track of what your network is doing.

Network Management and Monitoring

The core of SNMP is a simple set of operations (and the information these operations gather) that gives administrators the ability to change the state of some SNMP-based device. For example, you can use SNMP to shut down an interface on your router or check the speed at which your Ethernet interface is operating. SNMP can even monitor the temperature on your switch and warn you when it is too high.

SNMP usually is associated with managing routers, but it's important to understand that it can be used to manage many types of devices. While SNMP's predecessor, the *Simple Gateway Management Protocol* (SGMP), was developed to manage Internet routers, SNMP can be used to manage Unix systems, Windows systems, printers, modem racks, power supplies, and more. Any device running software that allows the retrieval of SNMP information can be managed. This includes not only physical devices but also software, such as web servers and databases.

Another aspect of network management is *network* monitoring; that is, monitoring an entire network as opposed to individual routers, hosts, and other devices. *Remote Network Monitoring* (RMON) was developed to help us understand how the network itself is functioning, as well as how individual devices on the network are affecting the network as a whole. It can be used to monitor not only LAN traffic, but WAN interfaces as well. We discuss RMON in more detail later in this chapter and in Chapter 2.

Before going any further, let's look at a before-and-after scenario that shows how SNMP can make a difference in an organization.

Before and After SNMP

Let's say that you have a network of 100 machines running various operating systems. Several machines are file servers, a few others are print servers, another is running software that verifies credit card transactions (presumably from a web-based ordering system), and the rest are personal workstations. In addition, there are various switches and routers that help keep the actual network going. A T1 circuit connects the company to the global Internet, and there is a private connection to the credit card verification system.

What happens when one of the file servers crashes? If it happens in the middle of the workweek, it is likely that the people using it will notice and the appropriate administrator will be called to fix it. But what if it happens after everyone has gone home, including the administrators, or over the weekend?

What if the private connection to the credit card verification system goes down at 10 p.m. on Friday and isn't restored until Monday morning? If the problem was faulty hardware and could have been fixed by swapping out a card or replacing a router, thousands of dollars in web site sales could have been lost for no reason. Likewise, if the T1 circuit to the Internet goes down, it could adversely affect the amount of sales generated by individuals accessing your web site and placing orders.

These are obviously serious problems—problems that can conceivably affect the survival of your business. This is where SNMP comes in. Instead of waiting for someone to notice that something is wrong and locate the person responsible for fixing the problem (which may not happen until Monday morning, if the problem occurs over the weekend), SNMP allows you to monitor your network constantly, even when you're not there. For example, it will notice if the number of bad packets coming through one of your router's interfaces is gradually increasing, suggesting that the router is about to fail. You can arrange to be notified automatically when failure seems imminent, so you can fix the router before it actually breaks.

You can also arrange to be notified if the credit card processor appears to get hung—you may even be able to fix it from home. And if nothing goes wrong, you can return to the office on Monday morning knowing there won't be any surprises.

There might not be quite as much glory in fixing problems before they occur, but you and your management will rest more easily. We can't tell you how to translate that into a higher salary—sometimes it's better to be the guy who rushes in and fixes things in the middle of a crisis, rather than the guy who makes sure the crisis never occurs. But SNMP does enable you to keep logs that prove your network is running reliably and show when you took action to avert an impending crisis.

Human Considerations

Implementing a network-management system can mean adding more staff to handle the increased load of maintaining and operating such an environment. At the same time, adding this type of monitoring should, in most cases, reduce the workload of your system-administration staff. You will need:

- Staff to maintain the management station. This includes ensuring the management station is configured to properly handle events from SNMP-capable devices.

- Staff to maintain the SNMP-capable devices. This includes making sure that workstations and servers can communicate with the management station.

- Staff to watch and fix the network. This group is usually called a *Network Operations Center* (NOC) and is staffed 24/7. An alternative to 24/7 staffing is to implement rotating pager duty, where one person is on call at all times, but not necessarily present in the office. Pager duty works only in smaller networked environments, in which a network outage can wait for someone to drive into the office and fix the problem.

There is no way to predetermine how many staff members you will need to maintain a management system. The size of the staff will vary depending on the size and complexity of the network you're managing. Some of the larger Internet backbone providers have 70 or more people in their NOCs, while others have only one.

RFCs and SNMP Versions

The *Internet Engineering Task Force* (IETF) is responsible for defining the standard protocols that govern Internet traffic, including SNMP. The IETF publishes *Requests for Comments* (RFCs), which are specifications for many protocols that exist in the IP realm. Documents enter the standards track first as *proposed* standards, then move to *draft* status. When a final draft is eventually approved, the RFC is given *standard* status—although there are fewer completely approved standards than you might think. Two other standards-track designations, *historical* and *experimental*, define (respectively) a document that has been replaced by a newer RFC and a document that is not yet ready to become a standard. The following list includes all the current SNMP versions and the IETF status of each (see Appendix D for a full list of the SNMP RFCs):

- *SNMP Version 1* (SNMPv1) is the current standard version of the SNMP protocol. It's defined in RFC 1157 and is a full IETF standard. SNMPv1's security is based on *communities*, which are nothing more than passwords: plain-text strings that allow any SNMP-based application that knows the strings to gain access to a device's management information. There are typically three communities in SNMPv1: *read-only*, *read-write*, and *trap*.

- *SNMP Version 2* (SNMPv2) is often referred to as community string–based SNMPv2. This version of SNMP is technically called SNMPv2c, but we will refer to it throughout this book simply as SNMPv2. It's defined in RFC 1905, RFC 1906, and RFC 1907, and is an experimental IETF. Even though it's experimental, some vendors have started supporting it in practice.

- *SNMP Version 3* (SNMPv3) will be the next version of the protocol to reach full IETF status. It's currently a proposed standard, defined in RFC 1905, RFC 1906, RFC 1907, RFC 2571, RFC 2572, RFC 2573, RFC 2574, and RFC 2575. It adds support for strong authentication and private communication between managed entities. Appendix F provides an introduction to SNMPv3 and goes through the SNMPv3 agent configuration for Net-SNMP and Cisco. The information in this appendix provides any system or network administrator with the practical knowledge needed to begin using SNMPv3 as it gains acceptance in the network-management world.

The official site for RFCs is *http://www.ietf.org/rfc.html*. One of the biggest problems with RFCs, however, is finding the one you want. It is a little easier to navigate the RFC index at Ohio State University (*http://www.cis.ohio-state.edu/services/rfc/index.html*).

Managers and Agents

In the previous sections we've vaguely referred to SNMP-capable devices and network-management stations. Now it's time to describe what these two things really are. In the world of SNMP there are two kind of entities: *managers* and *agents*. A manager is a server running some kind of software system that can handle management tasks for a network. Managers are often referred to as *Network Management Stations* (NMSs).* An NMS is responsible for polling and receiving traps

---

* See Chapter 5 for a pro-and-con discussion of some popular NMS applications.

from agents in the network. A *poll*, in the context of network management, is the act of querying an agent (router, switch, Unix server, etc.) for some piece of information. This information can later be used to determine if some sort of catastrophic event has occurred. A *trap* is a way for the agent to tell the NMS that something has happened. Traps are sent asynchronously, not in response to queries from the NMS. The NMS is further responsible for performing an action* based upon the information it receives from the agent. For example, when your T1 circuit to the Internet goes down, your router can send a trap to your NMS. In turn, the NMS can take some action, perhaps paging you to let you know that something has happened.

The second entity, the *agent*, is a piece of software that runs on the network devices you are managing. It can be a separate program (a daemon, in Unix language), or it can be incorporated into the operating system (for example, Cisco's IOS on a router, or the low-level operating system that controls a UPS). Today, most IP devices come with some kind of SNMP agent built in. The fact that vendors are willing to implement agents in many of their products makes the system administrator's or network manager's job easier. The agent provides management information to the NMS by keeping track of various operational aspects of the device. For example, the agent on a router is able to keep track of the state of each of its interfaces: which ones are up, which ones are down, etc. The NMS can query the status of each interface on a router, and take appropriate action if any of them are down. When the agent notices that something bad has happened, it can send a trap to the NMS. This trap originates from the agent and is sent to the NMS, where it is handled appropriately. Some devices will send a corresponding "all clear" trap when there is a transition from a bad state to a good state. This can be useful in determining when a problem situation has been resolved. Figure 1-1 shows the relationship between the NMS and an agent.

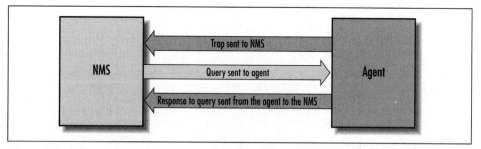

Figure 1-1. Relationship between an NMS and an agent

It's important to keep in mind that polls and traps can happen at the same time. There are no restrictions on when the NMS can query the agent or when the agent can send a trap.

---

* Note that the NMS is preconfigured to perform this action.

The Structure of Management Information and MIBS

The *Structure of Management Information* (SMI) provides a way to define managed objects and their behavior. An agent has in its possession a list of the objects that it tracks. One such object is the operational status of a router interface (for example, *up*, *down*, or *testing*). This list collectively defines the information the NMS can use to determine the overall health of the device on which the agent resides.

The *Management Information Base* (MIB) can be thought of as a database of managed objects that the agent tracks. Any sort of status or statistical information that can be accessed by the NMS is defined in a MIB. The SMI provides a way to define managed objects, while the MIB is the definition (using the SMI syntax) of the objects themselves. Like a dictionary, which shows how to spell a word and then gives its meaning or definition, a MIB defines a textual name for a managed object and explains its meaning. Chapter 2 goes into more technical detail about MIBs and the SMI.

An agent may implement many MIBs, but all agents implement a particular MIB called *MIB-II** (RFC 1213). This standard defines variables for things such as interface statistics (interface speeds, MTU, octets† sent, octets received, etc.) as well as various other things pertaining to the system itself (system location, system contact, etc.). The main goal of MIB-II is to provide general TCP/IP management information. It doesn't cover every possible item a vendor may want to manage within its particular device.

What other kinds of information might be useful to collect? First, there are many draft and proposed standards developed to help manage things such as frame relay, ATM, FDDI, and services (mail, DNS, etc.). A sampling of these MIBs and their RFC numbers includes:

- ATM MIB (RFC 2515)
- Frame Relay DTE Interface Type MIB (RFC 2115)
- BGP Version 4 MIB (RFC 1657)
- RDBMS MIB (RFC 1697)
- RADIUS Authentication Server MIB (RFC 2619)
- Mail Monitoring MIB (RFC 2249)
- DNS Server MIB (RFC 1611)

---

* MIB-I is the original version of this MIB, but it is no longer referred to since MIB-II enhances it.

† An octet is an 8-bit quantity, which is the fundamental unit of transfer in TCP/IP networks.

But that's far from the entire story, which is why vendors, and individuals, are allowed to define MIB variables for their own use.* For example, consider a vendor that is bringing a new router to market. The agent built into the router will respond to NMS requests (or send traps to the NMS) for the variables defined by the MIB-II standard; it probably also implements MIBs for the interface types it provides (e.g., RFC 2515 for ATM and RFC 2115 for Frame Relay). In addition, the router may have some significant new features that are worth monitoring but are not covered by any standard MIB. So, the vendor defines its own MIB (sometimes referred to as a proprietary MIB) that implements managed objects for the status and statistical information of their new router.

 Simply loading a new MIB into your NMS does not necessarily allow you to retrieve the data/values/objects, etc. defined within that MIB. You need to load only those MIBs supported by the agents from which you're requesting queries (e.g., *snmpget, snmpwalk*). Feel free to load additional MIBs for future device support, but don't panic when your device doesn't answer (and possibly returns errors for) these unsupported MIBs.

Host Management

Managing host resources (disk space, memory usage, etc.) is an important part of network management. The distinction between traditional system administration and network management has been disappearing over the last decade, and is now all but gone. As Sun Microsystems puts it, "The network is the computer." If your web server or mail server is down, it doesn't matter whether your routers are running correctly—you're still going to get calls. The *Host Resources MIB* (RFC 2790) defines a set of objects to help manage critical aspects of Unix and Windows systems.†

Some of the objects supported by the Host Resources MIB include disk capacity, number of system users, number of running processes, and software currently installed. In today's e-commerce world, more and more people are relying on service-oriented web sites. Making sure your backend servers are functioning properly is as important as monitoring your routers and other communications devices.

Unfortunately, some agent implementations for these platforms do not implement this MIB, since it's not required.

---

* This topic is discussed further in the next chapter.

† Any operating system running an SNMP agent can implement Host Resources; it's not confined to agents running on Unix and Windows systems.

A Brief Introduction to Remote Monitoring (RMON)

Remote Monitoring Version 1 (RMONv1, or RMON) is defined in RFC 2819; an enhanced version of the standard, called RMON Version 2 (RMONv2), is defined in RFC 2021. RMONv1 provides the NMS with packet-level statistics about an entire LAN or WAN. RMONv2 builds on RMONv1 by providing network- and application-level statistics. These statistics can be gathered in several ways. One way is to place an RMON probe on every network segment you want to monitor. Some Cisco routers have limited RMON capabilities built in, so you can use their functionality to perform minor RMON duties. Likewise, some 3Com switches implement the full RMON specification and can be used as full-blown RMON probes.

The RMON MIB was designed to allow an actual RMON probe to run in an offline mode that allows the probe to gather statistics about the network it's watching without requiring an NMS to query it constantly. At some later time, the NMS can query the probe for the statistics it has been gathering. Another feature that most probes implement is the ability to set thresholds for various error conditions and, when a threshold is crossed, alert the NMS with an SNMP trap. You can find a little more technical detail about RMON in the next chapter.

Getting More Information

Getting a handle on SNMP may seem like a daunting task. The RFCs provide the official definition of the protocol, but they were written for software developers, not network administrators, so it can be difficult to extract the information you need from them. Fortunately, many online resources are available. The most notable web site is the Network Management Server at the University at Buffalo (*http://netman.cit.buffalo.edu*). It contains useful links to other sites that provide similar information, as well as a network-management product list (*http://netman.cit.buffalo.edu/Products.html*) that includes both software and hardware vendors; it even has product reviews. This site is a great starting point in the search for network-management information and can be an extremely useful tool for determining what kinds of hardware and software are currently out there. Two more great web sites are the SimpleWeb (*http://wwwsnmp.cs.utwente.nl*) and SNMP Link (*http://www.SNMPLink.org*). *The Simple Times*, an online publication devoted to SNMP and network management, is also useful. You can find the current edition, and all the previous ones, at *http://www.simple-times.org*.

Another great resource is Usenet news. The newsgroup most people frequent is *comp.dcom.net-management*. Another good newsgroup is *comp.protocols.snmp*. Groups such as these promote a community of information sharing, allowing seasoned professionals to interact with individuals who are not as knowledge-able about SNMP or network management.

If you would like to know if a particular vendor has SNMP-compatible equipment, the *Internet Assigned Numbers Authority* (IANA) has compiled a list of the proprietary MIB files various vendors supply. The list can be found at *ftp://ftp.iana.org/mib/*. There is also an SNMP FAQ, available in two parts at *http://www.faqs.org/faqs/snmp-faq/part1/* and *http://www.faqs.org/faqs/snmp-faq/part2/*.

2

A Closer Look at SNMP

In this chapter, we start to look at SNMP in detail. By the time you finish this chapter, you should understand how SNMP sends and receives information, what exactly SNMP communities are, and how to read MIB files. We'll also look in more detail at the three MIBs that were introduced in Chapter 1, namely MIB-II, Host Resources, and RMON.

SNMP and UDP

SNMP uses the *User Datagram Protocol* (UDP) as the transport protocol for passing data between managers and agents. UDP, defined in RFC 768, was chosen over the *Transmission Control Protocol* (TCP) because it is connectionless; that is, no end-to-end connection is made between the agent and the NMS when *datagrams* (packets) are sent back and forth. This aspect of UDP makes it unreliable, since there is no acknowledgment of lost datagrams at the protocol level. It's up to the SNMP application to determine if datagrams are lost and retransmit them if it so desires. This is typically accomplished with a simple timeout. The NMS sends a UDP request to an agent and waits for a response. The length of time the NMS waits depends on how it's configured. If the timeout is reached and the NMS has not heard back from the agent, it assumes the packet was lost and retransmits the request. The number of times the NMS retransmits packets is also configurable.

At least as far as regular information requests are concerned, the unreliable nature of UDP isn't a real problem. At worst, the management station issues a request and never receives a response. For traps, the situation is somewhat different. If an agent sends a trap and the trap never arrives, the NMS has no way of knowing that it was ever sent. The agent doesn't even know that it needs to resend the trap, because the NMS is not required to send a response back to the agent acknowledging receipt of the trap.

The upside to the unreliable nature of UDP is that it requires low overhead, so the impact on your network's performance is reduced. SNMP has been implemented over TCP, but this is more for special-case situations in which someone is developing an agent for a proprietary piece of equipment. In a heavily congested and managed network, SNMP over TCP is a bad idea. It's also worth realizing that TCP isn't magic, and that SNMP is designed for working with networks that are in trouble—if your network never failed, you wouldn't need to monitor it. When a network is failing, a protocol that tries to get the data through but gives up if it can't is almost certainly a better design choice than a protocol that will flood the network with retransmissions in its attempt to achieve reliability.

SNMP uses the UDP port 161 for sending and receiving requests, and port 162 for receiving traps from managed devices. Every device that implements SNMP must use these port numbers as the defaults, but some vendors allow you to change the default ports in the agent's configuration. If these defaults are changed, the NMS must be made aware of the changes so it can query the device on the correct ports.

Figure 2-1 shows the TCP/IP protocol suite, which is the basis for all TCP/IP communication. Today, any device that wishes to communicate on the Internet (e.g., Windows NT systems, Unix servers, Cisco routers, etc.) must use this protocol suite. This model is often referred to as a protocol stack, since each layer uses the information from the layer directly below it and provides a service to the layer directly above it.

When either an NMS or an agent wishes to perform an SNMP function (e.g., a request or trap), the following events occur in the protocol stack:

Application

First, the actual SNMP application (NMS or agent) decides what it's going to do. For example, it can send an SNMP request to an agent, send a response to an SNMP request (this would be sent from the agent), or send a trap to an NMS. The application layer provides services to an end user, such as an operator requesting status information for a port on an Ethernet switch.

UDP

The next layer, UDP, allows two hosts to communicate with one another. The UDP header contains, among other things, the destination port of the device to which it's sending the request or trap. The destination port will either be 161 (query) or 162 (trap).

IP

The IP layer tries to deliver the SNMP packet to its intended destination, as specified by its IP address.

Medium Access Control (MAC)

The final event that must occur for an SNMP packet to reach its destination is for it to be handed off to the physical network, where it can be routed to its

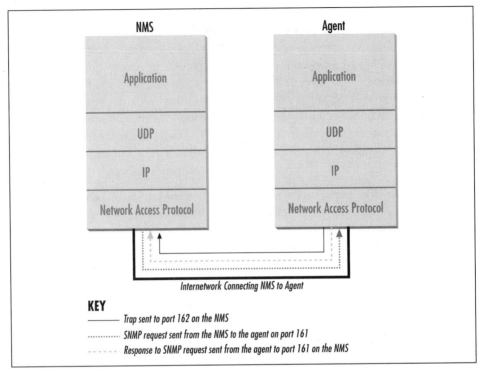

Figure 2-1. TCP/IP communication model and SNMP

final destination. The MAC layer is comprised of the actual hardware and device drivers that put your data onto a physical piece of wire, such as an Ethernet card. The MAC layer also is responsible for receiving packets from the physical network and sending them back up the protocol stack so they can be processed by the application layer (SNMP, in this case).

This interaction between SNMP applications and the network is not unlike that between two pen pals. Both have messages that need to be sent back and forth to one another. Let's say you decide to write your pen pal a letter asking if she would like to visit you over the summer. By deciding to send the invitation, you've acted as the SNMP application. Filling out the envelope with your pen pal's address is equivalent to the function of the UDP layer, which records the packet's destination port in the UDP header; in this case it's your pen pal's address. Placing a stamp on the envelope and putting it in the mailbox for the mailman to pick up is equivalent to the IP layer's function. The final act occurs when the mailman comes to your house and picks up the letter. From here the letter will be routed to its final destination, your pen pal's mailbox. The MAC layer of a computer network is equivalent to the mail trucks and airplanes that carry your letter on its way. When your pen pal receives the letter, she will go through the same process to send you a reply.

SNMP Communities

SNMPv1 and SNMPv2 use the notion of communities to establish trust between managers and agents. An agent is configured with three community names: read-only, read-write, and trap. The community names are essentially passwords; there's no real difference between a community string and the password you use to access your account on the computer. The three community strings control different kinds of activities. As its name implies, the read-only community string lets you read data values, but doesn't let you modify the data. For example, it allows you to read the number of packets that have been transferred through the ports on your router, but doesn't let you reset the counters. The read-write community is allowed to read and modify data values; with the read-write community string, you can read the counters, reset their values, and even reset the interfaces or do other things that change the router's configuration. Finally, the trap community string allows you to receive traps (asynchronous notifications) from the agent.

Most vendors ship their equipment with default community strings, typically *public* for the read-only community and *private* for the read-write community. It's important to change these defaults before your device goes live on the network. (You may get tired of hearing this because we say it many times, but it's absolutely essential.) When setting up an SNMP agent, you will want to configure its trap destination, which is the address to which it will send any traps it generates. In addition, since SNMP community strings are sent in clear text, you can configure an agent to send an SNMP authentication-failure trap when someone attempts to query your device with an incorrect community string. Among other things, authentication-failure traps can be very useful in determining when an intruder might be trying to gain access to your network.

Because community strings are essentially passwords, you should use the same rules for selecting them as you use for Unix or NT user passwords: no dictionary words, spouse names, etc. An alphanumeric string with mixed upper- and lower-case letters is generally a good idea. As mentioned earlier, the problem with SNMP's authentication is that community strings are sent in plain text, which makes it easy for people to intercept them and use them against you. SNMPv3 addresses this by allowing, among other things, secure authentication and communication between SNMP devices.

There are ways to reduce your risk of attack. IP firewalls or filters minimize the chance that someone can harm any managed device on your network by attacking it through SNMP. You can configure your firewall to allow UDP traffic from only a list of known hosts. For example, you can allow UDP traffic on port 161 (SNMP requests) into your network only if it comes from one of your network-management stations. The same goes for traps; you can configure your router so it allows

UDP traffic on port 162 to your NMS only if it originates from one of the hosts you are monitoring. Firewalls aren't 100% effective, but simple precautions such as these do a lot to reduce your risk.

 It is important to realize that if someone has read-write access to any of your SNMP devices, he can gain control of those devices by using SNMP (for example, he can set router interfaces, switch ports down, or even modify your routing tables). One way to protect your community strings is to use a *Virtual Private Network* (VPN) to make sure your network traffic is encrypted. Another way is to change your community strings often. Changing community strings isn't difficult for a small network, but for a network that spans city blocks or more and has dozens (or hundreds or thousands) of managed hosts, changing community strings can be a problem. An easy solution is to write a simple Perl script that uses SNMP to change the community strings on your devices.

The Structure of Management Information

So far, we have used the term "management information" to refer to the operational parameters of SNMP-capable devices. However, we've said very little about what management information actually contains or how it is represented. The first step toward understanding what kind of information a device can provide is to understand how this data itself is represented within the context of SNMP. The *Structure of Management Information Version 1* (SMIv1, RFC 1155) does exactly that: it defines precisely how managed objects* are named and specifies their associated datatypes. The *Structure of Management Information Version 2* (SMIv2, RFC 2578) provides enhancements for SNMPv2. We'll start by discussing SMIv1 and will discuss SMIv2 in the next section.

The definition of managed objects can be broken down into three attributes:

Name
> The name, or *object identifier* (OID), uniquely defines a managed object. Names commonly appear in two forms: numeric and "human readable." In either case, the names are long and inconvenient. In SNMP applications, a lot of work goes into helping you navigate through the namespace conveniently.

---

* For the remainder of this book "management information" will be referred to as "managed objects." Similarly, a single piece of management information (such as the operational status of a router interface) will be known as a "managed object."

Type and syntax

> A managed object's datatype is defined using a subset of
> *tion One* (ASN.1). ASN.1 is a way of specifying how d
> transmitted between managers and agents, within the
> nice thing about ASN.1 is that the notation is m
> means that a PC running Windows NT can comm
> machine and not have to worry about things such

Encoding

> A single instance of a managed object is enco
> the *Basic Encoding Rules* (BER). BER defines
> decoded so they can be transmitted over a t

Naming OIDs

Managed objects are organized into a tree-like hierarchy. This sis for SNMP's naming scheme. An object ID is made up of a series of ased on the nodes in the tree, separated by dots (.). Although there's a human- dable form that's more friendly than a string of numbers, this form is nothing more than a series of names separated by dots, each of which represents a node of the tree. So you can use the numbers themselves, or you can use a sequence of names that represent the numbers. Figure 2-2 shows the top few levels of this tree. (We have intentionally left out some branches of the tree that don't concern us here.)

In the object tree, the node at the top of the tree is called the *root*, anything with children is called a *subtree*, and anything without children is called a *leaf node*. For example, Figure 2-2's root, the starting point for the tree, is called "Root-Node." Its subtree is made up of *ccitt(0)*, *iso(1)*, and *joint(2)*. In this illustration, *iso(1)* is the only node that contains a subtree; the other two nodes are both leaf nodes. *ccitt(0)* and *joint(2)* do not pertain to SNMP, so they will not be discussed in this book.*

For the remainder of this book we will focus on the *iso(1).org(3).dod(6). internet(1)* subtree,† which is represented in OID form as *1.3.6.1* or as *iso.org.dod. internet*. Each managed object has a numerical OID and an associated textual name. The dotted-decimal notation is how a managed object is represented internally within an agent; the textual name, like an IP domain name, saves humans from having to remember long, tedious strings of integers.

The *directory* branch currently is not used. The *management* branch, or *mgmt*, defines a standard set of Internet management objects. The *experimental* branch is

---

* The *ccitt* subtree is administered by the International Telegraph and Telephone Consultative Committee (CCITT); the *joint* subtree is administered jointly by the International Organization for Standardization (ISO) and CCITT. As we said, neither branch has anything to do with SNMP.

† Note that the term "branch" is sometimes used interchangeably with "subtree."

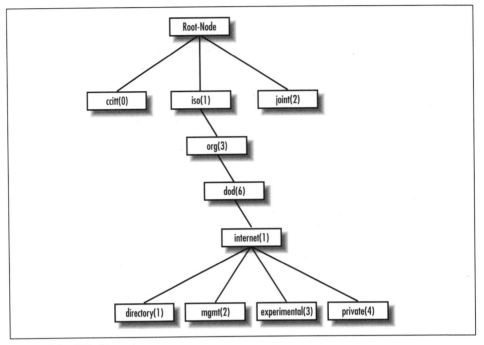

Figure 2-2. SMI object tree

reserved for testing and research purposes. Objects under the *private* branch are defined unilaterally, which means that individuals and organizations are responsible for defining the objects under this branch. Here is the definition of the *internet* subtree, as well as all four of its subtrees:

```
internet       OBJECT IDENTIFIER ::= { iso org(3) dod(6) 1 }
directory      OBJECT IDENTIFIER ::= { internet 1 }
mgmt           OBJECT IDENTIFIER ::= { internet 2 }
experimental   OBJECT IDENTIFIER ::= { internet 3 }
private        OBJECT IDENTIFIER ::= { internet 4 }
```

The first line declares *internet* as the OID *1.3.6.1*, which is defined as a subtree of *iso.org.dod*, or *1.3.6* (the ::= is a definition operator). The last four declarations are similar, but they define the other branches that belong to *internet*. For the *directory* branch, the notation { internet 1 } tells us that it is part of the *internet* subtree, and that its OID is *1.3.6.1.1*. The OID for *mgmt* is *1.3.6.1.2*, and so on.

There is currently one branch under the *private* subtree. It's used to give hardware and software vendors the ability to define their own private objects for any type of hardware or software they want managed by SNMP. Its SMI definition is:

```
enterprises   OBJECT IDENTIFIER ::= { private 1 }
```

The Internet Assigned Numbers Authority (IANA) currently manages all the private enterprise number assignments for individuals, institutions, organizations, companies, etc.* A list of all the current private enterprise numbers can be obtained from *ftp://ftp.isi.edu/in-notes/iana/assignments/enterprise-numbers*. As an example, Cisco Systems's private enterprise number is 9, so the base OID for its private object space is defined as *iso.org.dod.internet.private.enterprises.cisco*, or *1.3.6.1.4.1.9*. Cisco is free to do as it wishes with this private branch. It's typical for companies such as Cisco that manufacture networking equipment to define their own private enterprise objects. This allows for a richer set of management information than can be gathered from the standard set of managed objects defined under the *mgmt* branch.

Companies aren't the only ones who can register their own private enterprise numbers. Anyone can do so, and it's free. The web-based form for registering private enterprise numbers can be found at *http://www.isi.edu/cgi-bin/iana/ enterprise.pl*. After you fill in the form, which asks for information such as your organization's name and contact information, your request should be approved in about a week. Why would you want to register your own number? When you become more conversant in SNMP, you'll find things you want to monitor that aren't covered by any MIB, public or private. With your own enterprise number, you can create your own private MIB that allows you to monitor exactly what you want. You'll need to be somewhat clever in extending your agents so that they can look up the information you want, but it's very doable.

Defining OIDs

The SYNTAX attribute provides for definitions of managed objects through a subset of ASN.1. SMIv1 defines several datatypes that are paramount to the management of networks and network devices. It's important to keep in mind that these datatypes are simply a way to define what kind of information a managed object can hold. The types we'll be discussing are similar to those that you'd find in a computer programming language like C. Table 2-1 lists the supported datatypes for SMIv1.

Table 2-1. SMIv1 Datatypes

Datatype	Description
INTEGER	A 32-bit number often used to specify enumerated types within the context of a single managed object. For example, the operational status of a router interface can be *up*, *down*, or *testing*. With enumerated types, 1 would represent up, 2 down, and 3 testing. The value zero (0) must not be used as an enumerated type, according to RFC 1155.
OCTET STRING	A string of zero or more octets (more commonly known as bytes) generally used to represent text strings, but also sometimes used to represent physical addresses.

---

* The term "private enterprise" will be used throughout this book to refer to the *enterprises* branch.

Table 2-1. SMIv1 Datatypes (continued)

Datatype	Description
Counter	A 32-bit number with minimum value 0 and maximum value $2^{32} - 1$ (4,294,967,295). When the maximum value is reached, it wraps back to zero and starts over. It's primarily used to track information such as the number of octets sent and received on an interface or the number of errors and discards seen on an interface. A Counter is monotonically increasing, in that its values should never decrease during normal operation. When an agent is rebooted, all Counter values should be set to zero. Deltas are used to determine if anything useful can be said for successive queries of Counter values. A delta is computed by querying a Counter at least twice in a row, and taking the difference between the query results over some time interval.
OBJECT IDENTIFIER	A dotted-decimal string that represents a managed object within the object tree. For example, *1.3.6.1.4.1.9* represents Cisco Systems's private enterprise OID.
NULL	Not currently used in SNMP.
SEQUENCE	Defines lists that contain zero or more other ASN.1 datatypes.
SEQUENCE OF	Defines a managed object that is made up of a SEQUENCE of ASN.1 types.
IpAddress	Represents a 32-bit IPv4 address. Neither SMIv1 nor SMIv2 discusses 128-bit IPv6 addresses; this problem will be addressed by the IETF's SMI Next Generation (SMING) working group (see *http:// www.ietf.org/html.charters/sming-charter.html*).
NetworkAddress	Same as the IpAddress type, but can represent different network address types.
Gauge	A 32-bit number with minimum value 0 and maximum value $2^{32} - 1$ (4,294,967,295). Unlike a Counter, a Gauge can increase and decrease at will, but it can never exceed its maximum value. The interface speed on a router is measured with a Gauge.
TimeTicks	A 32-bit number with minimum value 0 and maximum value $2^{32} - 1$ (4,294,967,295). TimeTicks measures time in hundredths of a second. Uptime on a device is measured using this datatype.
Opaque	Allows any other ASN.1 encoding to be stuffed into an OCTET STRING.

The goal of all these object types is to define managed objects. In Chapter 1, we said that a MIB is a logical grouping of managed objects as they pertain to a specific management task, vendor, etc. The MIB can be thought of as a specification that defines the managed objects a vendor or device supports. Cisco, for instance, has literally hundreds of MIBs defined for its vast product line. For example, its Catalyst device has a separate MIB from its 7000 series router. Both devices have different characteristics that require different management capabilities. Vendor-specific MIBs typically are distributed as human-readable text files that can be inspected (or even modified) with a standard text editor such as *vi*.

Most modern NMS products maintain a compact form of all the MIBs that define the set of managed objects for all the different types of devices they're responsible for managing. NMS administrators will typically compile a vendor's MIB into a format the NMS can use. Once a MIB has been loaded or compiled, administrators can refer to managed objects using either the numeric or human-readable object ID.

It's important to know how to read and understand MIB files. The following example is a stripped-down version of MIB-II (anything preceded by -- is a comment):

```
RFC1213-MIB DEFINITIONS ::= BEGIN

        IMPORTS
                mgmt, NetworkAddress, IpAddress, Counter, Gauge,
                TimeTicks
                        FROM RFC1155-SMI
                OBJECT-TYPE
                        FROM RFC 1212;

        mib-2      OBJECT IDENTIFIER ::= { mgmt 1 }

-- groups in MIB-II

        system       OBJECT IDENTIFIER ::= { mib-2 1 }
        interfaces   OBJECT IDENTIFIER ::= { mib-2 2 }
        at           OBJECT IDENTIFIER ::= { mib-2 3 }
        ip           OBJECT IDENTIFIER ::= { mib-2 4 }
        icmp         OBJECT IDENTIFIER ::= { mib-2 5 }
        tcp          OBJECT IDENTIFIER ::= { mib-2 6 }
        udp          OBJECT IDENTIFIER ::= { mib-2 7 }
        egp          OBJECT IDENTIFIER ::= { mib-2 8 }
        transmission OBJECT IDENTIFIER ::= { mib-2 10 }
        snmp         OBJECT IDENTIFIER ::= { mib-2 11 }

        -- the Interfaces table

        -- The Interfaces table contains information on the entity's
        -- interfaces. Each interface is thought of as being
        -- attached to a 'subnetwork.' Note that this term should
        -- not be confused with 'subnet,' which refers to an
        -- addressing-partitioning scheme used in the Internet
        -- suite of protocols.

        ifTable OBJECT-TYPE
            SYNTAX  SEQUENCE OF IfEntry
            ACCESS  not-accessible
            STATUS  mandatory
```

```
            DESCRIPTION
                "A list of interface entries. The number of entries is
                given by the value of ifNumber."
            ::= { interfaces 2 }

    ifEntry OBJECT-TYPE
        SYNTAX  IfEntry
        ACCESS  not-accessible
        STATUS  mandatory
        DESCRIPTION
            "An interface entry containing objects at the subnetwork
            layer and below for a particular interface."
        INDEX   { ifIndex }
        ::= { ifTable 1 }

    IfEntry ::=
        SEQUENCE {
            ifIndex
                INTEGER,
            ifDescr
                DisplayString,
            ifType
                INTEGER,
            ifMtu
                INTEGER,
            ifSpeed
                Gauge,
            ifPhysAddress
                PhysAddress,
            ifAdminStatus
                INTEGER,
            ifOperStatus
                INTEGER,
            ifLastChange
                TimeTicks,
            ifInOctets
                Counter,
            ifInUcastPkts
                Counter,
            ifInNUcastPkts
                Counter,
            ifInDiscards
                Counter,
            ifInErrors
                Counter,
            ifInUnknownProtos
                Counter,
            ifOutOctets
                Counter,
            ifOutUcastPkts
                Counter,
            ifOutNUcastPkts
                Counter,
            ifOutDiscards
```

```
                              Counter,
                        ifOutErrors
                              Counter,
                        ifOutQLen
                              Gauge,
                        ifSpecific
                              OBJECT IDENTIFIER
                  }


        ifIndex OBJECT-TYPE
              SYNTAX   INTEGER
              ACCESS   read-only
              STATUS   mandatory
              DESCRIPTION
                    "A unique value for each interface. Its value ranges
                    between 1 and the value of ifNumber. The value for each
                    each interface must remain constant at least from one
                    reinitialization of the entity's network-management
                    system to the next reinitialization."

              ::= { ifEntry 1 }

        ifDescr OBJECT-TYPE
              SYNTAX   DisplayString (SIZE (0..255))
              ACCESS   read-only
              STATUS   mandatory
              DESCRIPTION
                    "A textual string containing information about the
                    interface. This string should include the name of
                    the manufacturer, the product name, and the version
                    of the hardware interface."
              ::= { ifEntry 2 }


        END
```

The first line of this file defines the name of the MIB, in this case **RFC1213-MIB**. (RFC 1213 is the RFC that defines MIB-II; many of the MIBs we refer to are defined by RFCs). The format of this definition is always the same. The **IMPORTS** section of the MIB is sometimes referred to as the *linkage* section. It allows you to import datatypes and OIDs from other MIB files using the **IMPORTS** clause. This MIB imports the following items from **RFC1155-SMI** (RFC 1155 defines SMIv1, which we discussed earlier in this chapter):

- **mgmt**
- **NetworkAddress**
- **IpAddress**
- **Counter**
- **Gauge**
- **TimeTicks**

It also imports **OBJECT-TYPE** from RFC 1212, the *Concise MIB Definition*, which defines how MIB files are written. Each group of items imported using the **IMPORTS** clause uses a **FROM** clause to define the MIB file from which the objects are taken.

The OIDs that will be used throughout the remainder of the MIB follow the linkage section. This group of lines sets up the top level of the *mib-2* subtree. *mib-2* is defined as *mgmt* followed by *.1*. We saw earlier that *mgmt* was equivalent to *1.3.6.1.2*. Therefore, *mib-2* is equivalent to *1.3.6.1.2.1*. Likewise, the *interfaces* group under *mib-2* is defined as { **mib-2 2** }, or *1.3.6.1.2.1.2*.

After the OIDs are defined, we get to the actual object definitions. Every object definition has the following format:

```
<name> OBJECT-TYPE
    SYNTAX <datatype>
    ACCESS <either read-only, read-write, write-only, or not-accessible>
    STATUS <either mandatory, optional, or obsolete>
    DESCRIPTION
        "Textual description describing this particular managed object."
    ::= { <Unique OID that defines this object> }
```

The first managed object in our subset of the MIB-II definition is *ifTable*, which represents a table of network interfaces on a managed device (note that object names are defined using mixed case, with the first letter in lowercase). Here is its definition using ASN.1 notation:

```
ifTable OBJECT-TYPE
    SYNTAX  SEQUENCE OF IfEntry
    ACCESS  not-accessible
    STATUS  mandatory
    DESCRIPTION
        "A list of interface entries. The number of entries is given by
        the value of ifNumber."
    ::= { interfaces 2 }
```

The **SYNTAX** of *ifTable* is **SEQUENCE OF IfEntry**. This means that *ifTable* is a table containing the columns defined in *IfEntry*. The object is **not-accessible**, which means that there is no way to query an agent for this object's value. Its status is **mandatory**, which means an agent must implement this object in order to comply with the MIB-II specification. The **DESCRIPTION** describes what exactly this object is. The unique OID is *1.3.6.1.2.1.2.2*, or *iso.org.dod.internet.mgmt.interfaces.2*.

Let's now look at the **SEQUENCE** definition from the MIB file earlier in this section, which is used with the **SEQUENCE OF** type in the *ifTable* definition:

```
IfEntry ::=
    SEQUENCE {
        ifIndex
            INTEGER,
```

```
ifDescr
    DisplayString,
ifType
    INTEGER,
ifMtu
    INTEGER,
        .
        .
        .
ifSpecific
    OBJECT IDENTIFIER
}
```

Note that the name of the sequence (*IfEntry*) is mixed-case, but the first letter is capitalized, unlike the object definition for *ifTable*. This is how a sequence name is defined. A sequence is simply a list of columnar objects and their SMI datatypes, which defines a conceptual table. In this case, we expect to find variables defined by *ifIndex*, *ifDescr*, *ifType*, etc. This table can contain any number of rows; it's up to the agent to manage the rows that reside in the table. It is possible for an NMS to add rows to a table. This operation is covered later, in the section "The set Operation."

Now that we have *IfEntry* to specify what we'll find in any row of the table, we can look back to the definition of *ifEntry* (the actual rows of the table) itself:

```
ifEntry OBJECT-TYPE
    SYNTAX   IfEntry
    ACCESS   not-accessible
    STATUS   mandatory
    DESCRIPTION
        "An interface entry containing objects at the subnetwork layer
         and below for a particular interface."
    INDEX    { ifIndex }
    ::= { ifTable 1 }
```

ifEntry defines a particular row in the *ifTable*. Its definition is almost identical to that of *ifTable*, except we have introduced a new clause, **INDEX**. The index is a unique key used to define a single row in the *ifTable*. It's up to the agent to make sure the index is unique within the context of the table. If a router has six interfaces, *ifTable* will have six rows in it. *ifEntry*'s OID is *1.3.6.1.2.1.2.2.1*, or *iso.org. dod.internet.mgmt.interfaces.ifTable.ifEntry*. The index for *ifEntry* is *ifIndex*, which is defined as:

```
ifIndex OBJECT-TYPE
    SYNTAX   INTEGER
    ACCESS   read-only
    STATUS   mandatory
    DESCRIPTION
        "A unique value for each interface. Its value ranges between
         1 and the value of ifNumber. The value for each interface
         must remain constant at least from one reinitialization of the
```

```
        entity's network-management system to the next reinitialization."
        ::= { ifEntry 1 }
```

The *ifIndex* object is **read-only**, which means we can see its value, but we
cannot change it. The final object our MIB defines is *ifDescr*, which is a textual
description for the interface represented by that particular row in the *ifTable*. Our
MIB example ends with the **END** clause, which marks the end of the MIB. In the
actual MIB-II files, each object listed in the *IfEntry* sequence has its own object
definition. In this version of the MIB we list only two of them, in the interest of
conserving space.

Extensions to the SMI in Version 2

SMIv2 extends the SMI object tree by adding the *snmpV2* branch to the *internet*
subtree, adding several new datatypes, and making a number of other changes.
Figure 2-3 shows how the *snmpV2* objects fit into the bigger picture; the OID for
this new branch is *1.3.6.1.6.3.1.1*, or *iso.org.dod.internet.snmpV2.snmpModules.*
snmpMIB.snmpMIBObjects. SMIv2 also defines some new datatypes, which are
summarized in Table 2-2.

Table 2-2. New Datatypes for SMIv2

Datatype	Description
Integer32	Same as an INTEGER.
Counter32	Same as a Counter.
Gauge32	Same as a Gauge.
Unsigned32	Represents decimal values in the range of 0 to $2^{32} - 1$ inclusive.
Counter64	Similar to Counter32, but its maximum value is 18,446,744,073,709,551,615. Counter64 is ideal for situations in which a Counter32 may wrap back to 0 in a short amount of time.
BITS	An enumeration of nonnegative named bits.

The definition of an object in SMIv2 has changed slightly from SMIv1. There are
some new optional fields, giving you more control over how an object is accessed,
allowing you to augment a table by adding more columns, and letting you give
better descriptions. Here's the syntax of an object definition for SMIv2. The
changed parts are in bold:

```
<name> OBJECT-TYPE
    SYNTAX <datatype>
    UnitsParts <Optional, see below>
    MAX-ACCESS <See below>
    STATUS <See below>
    DESCRIPTION
        "Textual description describing this particular managed object."
    AUGMENTS { <name of table> }
    ::= { <Unique OID that defines this object> }
```

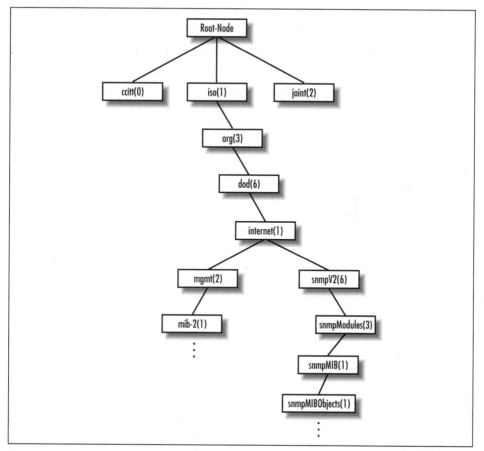

Figure 2-3. SMIv2 registration tree for SNMPv2

Table 2-3 briefly describes the object definition enhancements made in SMIv2.

Table 2-3. SMIv2 Object Definition Enhancements

Object Definition Enhancement	Description
UnitsParts	A textual description of the units (i.e., seconds, milliseconds, etc.) used to represent the object.
MAX-ACCESS	An OBJECT-TYPE's ACCESS can be MAX-ACCESS in SNMPv2. The valid options for MAX-ACCESS are read-only, read-write, read-create, not-accessible, and accessible-for-notify.
STATUS	This clause has been extended to allow the current, obsolete, and deprecated keywords. current in SNMPv2 is the same as mandatory in an SNMPv1 MIB.
AUGMENTS	In some cases it is useful to add a column to an existing table. The AUGMENTS clause allows you to extend a table by adding one or more columns, represented by some other object. This clause requires the name of the table the object will augment.

SMIv2 defines a new trap type called NOTIFICATION-TYPE, which we will discuss later in the section "SNMP Notification." SMIv2 also introduces new textual conventions that allow managed objects to be created in more abstract ways. RFC 2579 defines the textual conventions used by SNMPv2, which are listed in Table 2-4.

Table 2-4. Textual Conventions for SMIv2

Textual Convention	Description
DisplayString	A string of NVT ASCII characters. A DisplayString can be no more than 255 characters in length.
PhysAddress	A media- or physical-level address, represented as an OCTET STRING.
MacAddress	Defines the media-access address for IEEE 802 (the standard for local area networks) in canonical[a] order. (In everyday language, this means the Ethernet address.) This address is represented as six octets.
TruthValue	Defines both true and false Boolean values.
TestAndIncr	Used to keep two management stations from modifying the same managed object at the same time.
AutonomousType	An OID used to define a subtree with additional MIB-related definitions.
VariablePointer	A pointer to a particular object instance, such as the *ifDescr* for interface *3*. In this case, the VariablePointer would be the OID *ifDescr.3*.
RowPointer	A pointer to a row in a table. For example, *ifIndex.3* points to the third row in the *ifTable*.
RowStatus	Used to manage the creation and deletion of rows in a table, since SNMP has no way of doing this via the protocol itself. RowStatus can keep track of the state of a row in a table, as well as receive commands for creation and deletion of rows. This textual convention is designed to promote table integrity when more than one manager is updating rows. The following enumerated types define the commands and state variables: active(1), notInService(2), notReady(3), createAndGo(4), createAndWait(5), and destroy(6).
TimeStamp	Measures the amount of time elapsed between the device's system uptime and some event or occurrence.
TimeInterval	Measures a period of time in hundredths of a second. TimeInterval can take any integer value from 0–2147483647.
DateAndTime	An OCTET STRING used to represent date-and-time information.
StorageType	Defines the type of memory an agent uses. The possible values are other(1), volatile(2), nonVolatile(3), permanent(4), and readOnly(5).
TDomain	Denotes a kind of transport service.
TAddress	Denotes the transport service address. TAddress is defined to be from 1–255 octets in length.

[a] Canonical order means that the address should be represented with the least-significant bit first.

A Closer Look at MIB-II

MIB-II is a very important management group, because every device that supports SNMP must also support MIB-II. Therefore, we will use objects from MIB-II in our examples throughout this book. We won't go into detail about every object in the MIB; we'll simply define the subtrees. The section of *RFC1213-MIB* that defines the base OIDs for the *mib-2* subtree looks like this:

```
mib-2        OBJECT IDENTIFIER ::= { mgmt 1 }
system       OBJECT IDENTIFIER ::= { mib-2 1 }
interfaces   OBJECT IDENTIFIER ::= { mib-2 2 }
at           OBJECT IDENTIFIER ::= { mib-2 3 }
ip           OBJECT IDENTIFIER ::= { mib-2 4 }
icmp         OBJECT IDENTIFIER ::= { mib-2 5 }
tcp          OBJECT IDENTIFIER ::= { mib-2 6 }
udp          OBJECT IDENTIFIER ::= { mib-2 7 }
egp          OBJECT IDENTIFIER ::= { mib-2 8 }
transmission OBJECT IDENTIFIER ::= { mib-2 10 }
snmp         OBJECT IDENTIFIER ::= { mib-2 11 }
```

mib-2 is defined as *iso.org.dod.internet.mgmt.1*, or *1.3.6.1.2.1*. From here, we can see that the *system* group is mib-2 1, or *1.3.6.1.2.1.1*, and so on. Figure 2-4 shows the MIB-II subtree of the *mgmt* branch.

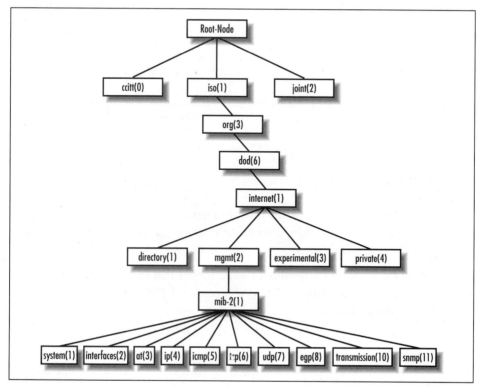

Figure 2-4. MIB-II subtree

Table 2-5 briefly describes each of the management groups defined in MIB-II. We don't go into great detail about each group, since you can pull down RFC 1213 and read the MIB yourself.

Table 2-5. Brief Description of the MIB-II Groups

Subtree Name	OID	Description
system	*1.3.6.1.2.1.1*	Defines a list of objects that pertain to system operation, such as the system uptime, system contact, and system name.
interfaces	*1.3.6.1.2.1.2*	Keeps track of the status of each interface on a managed entity. The *interfaces* group monitors which interfaces are up or down and tracks such things as octets sent and received, errors and discards, etc.
at	*1.3.6.1.2.1.3*	The address translation (*at*) group is deprecated and is provided only for backward compatibility. It will probably be dropped from MIB-III.
ip	*1.3.6.1.2.1.4*	Keeps track of many aspects of IP, including IP routing.
icmp	*1.3.6.1.2.1.5*	Tracks things such as ICMP errors, discards, etc.
tcp	*1.3.6.1.2.1.6*	Tracks, among other things, the state of the TCP connection (e.g., *closed*, *listen*, *synSent*, etc.).
udp	*1.3.6.1.2.1.7*	Tracks UDP statistics, datagrams in and out, etc.
egp	*1.3.6.1.2.1.8*	Tracks various statistics about EGP and keeps an EGP neighbor table.
transmission	*1.3.6.1.2.1.10*	There are currently no objects defined for this group, but other media-specific MIBs are defined using this subtree.
snmp	*1.3.6.1.2.1.11*	Measures the performance of the underlying SNMP implementation on the managed entity and tracks things such as the number of SNMP packets sent and received.

SNMP Operations

We've discussed how SNMP organizes information, but we've left out how we actually go about gathering management information. Now, we're going to take a look under the hood to see how SNMP does its thing.

The *Protocol Data Unit* (PDU) is the message format that managers and agents use to send and receive information. There is a standard PDU format for each of the following SNMP operations:

- *get*
- *get-next*
- *get-bulk* (SNMPv2 and SNMPv3)

- *set*

- *get-response*

- *trap*

- *notification* (SNMPv2 and SNMPv3)

- *inform* (SNMPv2 and SNMPv3)

- *report* (SNMPv2 and SNMPv3)

Let's take a look at each of these operations.

The get Operation

The *get* request is initiated by the NMS, which sends the request to the agent. The agent receives the request and processes it to best of its ability. Some devices that are under heavy load, such as routers, may not be able to respond to the request and will have to drop it. If the agent is successful in gathering the requested information, it sends a *get-response* back to the NMS, where it is processed. This process is illustrated in Figure 2-5.

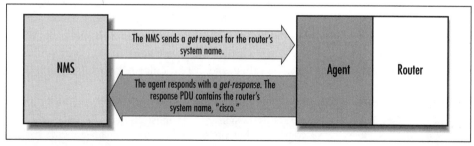

Figure 2-5. get request sequence

How did the agent know what the NMS was looking for? One of the items in the *get* request is a *variable binding*. A variable binding, or varbind, is a list of MIB objects that allows a request's recipient to see what the originator wants to know. Variable bindings can be thought of as *OID=value* pairs that make it easy for the originator (the NMS, in this case) to pick out the information it needs when the recipient fills the request and sends back a response. Let's look at this operation in action:

```
$ snmpget cisco.ora.com public .1.3.6.1.2.1.1.6.0
system.sysLocation.0 = ""
```

All the Unix commands presented in this chapter come from the Net-SNMP agent package (formerly the UCD-SNMP project), a freely available Unix and Windows NT agent. Chapter 5 provides a URL from which you can download the package. The commands in this package are summarized in Appendix C.

Several things are going on in this example. First, we're running a command on a Unix host. The command is called *snmpget*. Its main job is to facilitate the gathering of management data using a *get* request. We've given it three arguments on the command line: the name of the device we would like to query (*cisco.ora.com*), the read-only community string (*public*), and the OID we would like gathered (*.1.3.6.1.2.1.1.6.0*). If we look back at Table 2-5 we see that *1.3.6.1.2.1.1* is the *system* group, but there are two more integers at the end of the OID: *.6* and *.0*. The *.6* is actually the MIB variable that we wish to query; its human-readable name is *sysLocation*. In this case, we would like to see what the system location is set to on the Cisco router. As you can see by the response (`system.sysLocation.0 = ""`), the system location on this router currently is not set to anything. Also note that the response from *snmpget* is in variable binding format, *OID=value*.

There is one more thing to look at. Why does the MIB variable have a *.0* tacked on the end? In SNMP, MIB objects are defined by the convention *x.y*, where *x* is the actual OID of the managed object (in our example, *1.3.6.1.2.1.1.6*) and *y* is the instance identifier. For scalar objects (that is, objects that aren't defined as a row in a table) *y* is always 0. In the case of a table, the instance identifier lets you select a specific row of the table; 1 is the first row, 2 is the second row, etc. For example, consider the *ifTable* object we looked at earlier in this chapter. When looking up values in the *ifTable*, we would use a nonzero instance identifier to select a particular row in the table (in this case, a particular network interface).

Graphical NMS applications, which include most commercial packages, do not use command-line programs to retrieve management information. We use these commands to give you a feel for how the retrieval commands work and what they typically return. The information a graphical NMS retrieves and its retrieval process are identical to these command-line programs; the NMS just lets you formulate queries and displays the results using a more convenient GUI.

The *get* command is useful for retrieving a single MIB object at a time. Trying to manage anything in this manner can be a waste of time, though. This is where the *get-next* command comes in. It allows you to retrieve more than one object from a device, over a period of time.

The get-next Operation

The *get-next* operation lets you issue a sequence of commands to retrieve a group of values from a MIB. In other words, for each MIB object we want to retrieve, a separate *get-next* request and *get-response* are generated. The *get-next* command traverses a subtree in lexicographic order. Since an OID is a sequence of integers, it's easy for an agent to start at the root of its SMI object tree and work its way down until it finds the OID it is looking for. When the NMS receives a response from the agent for the *get-next* command it just issued, it issues another *get-next* command. It keeps doing this until the agent returns an error, signifying that the end of the MIB has been reached and there are no more objects left to get.

If we look at another example, we can see this behavior in action. This time we'll use a command called *snmpwalk*. This command simply facilitates the *get-next* procedure for us. It's invoked just like the *snmpget* command, except this time we specify which branch to start at (in this case, the *system* group):

```
$ snmpwalk cisco.ora.com public system
system.sysDescr.0 = "Cisco Internetwork Operating System Software
..IOS (tm) 2500 Software (C2500-I-L), Version 11.2(5), RELEASE
SOFTWARE (fc1)..Copyright (c) 1986-1997 by cisco Systems, Inc...
Compiled Mon 31-Mar-97 19:53 by ckralik"
system.sysObjectID.0 = OID: enterprises.9.1.19
system.sysUpTime.0 = Timeticks: (27210723) 3 days, 3:35:07.23
system.sysContact.0 = ""
system.sysName.0 = "cisco.ora.com"
system.sysLocation.0 = ""
system.sysServices.0 = 6
```

The *get-next* sequence returns seven MIB variables. Each of these objects is part of the *system* group as it's defined in RFC 1213. We see a system object ID, the amount of time the system has been up, the contact person, etc.

Given that you've just looked up some object, how does *get-next* figure out which object to look up next? *get-next* is based on the concept of the lexicographic ordering of the MIB's object tree. This order is made much simpler because every node in the tree is assigned a number. To understand what this means, let's start at the root of the tree and walk down to the *system* node.

To get to the *system* group (OID *1.3.6.1.2.1.1*), we start at the root of the object tree and work our way down. Figure 2-6 shows the logical progression from the root of the tree all the way to the *system* group. At each node in the tree, we visit the lowest-numbered branch. Thus, when we're at the root node, we start by visiting *ccitt*. This node has no nodes underneath it, so we move to the *iso* node. Since *iso* does have a child we move to that node, *org*. The process continues until we reach the *system* node. Since each branch is made up of ascending integers (*ccitt(0) iso(1) join(2)*, for example), the agent has no problem traversing this tree structure all the way down to the *system(1)* group. If we were to continue this walk, we'd proceed to *system.1* (*system.sysLocation*), *system.2*, and the other objects in the *system* group. Next, we'd go to *interfaces(2)*, and so on.

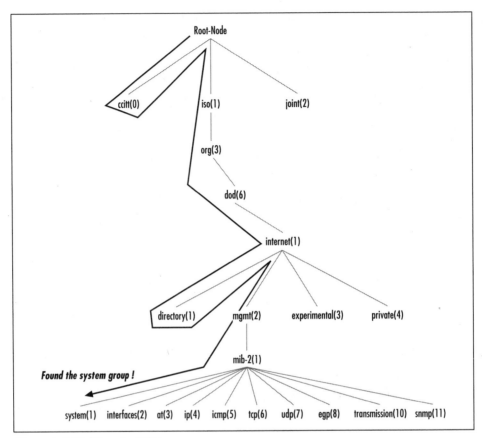

Figure 2-6. Walking the MIB tree

The get-bulk Operation

SNMPv2 defines the *get-bulk* operation, which allows a management application to retrieve a large section of a table at once. The standard *get* operation can attempt to retrieve more than one MIB object at once, but message sizes are limited by the agent's capabilities. If the agent can't return all the requested responses, it returns an error message with no data. The *get-bulk* operation, on the other hand, tells the agent to send as much of the response back as it can. This means that incomplete responses are possible. Two fields must be set when issuing a *get-bulk* command: nonrepeaters and max-repetitions. Nonrepeaters tells the *get-bulk* command that the first N objects can be retrieved with a simple *get-next* operation. Max-repetitions tells the *get-bulk* command to attempt up to M *get-next* operations to retrieve the remaining objects. Figure 2-7 shows the *get-bulk* command sequence.

In Figure 2-7, we're requesting three bindings: *sysDescr*, *ifInOctets*, and *ifOutOctets*. The total number of variable bindings that we've requested is given by the formula

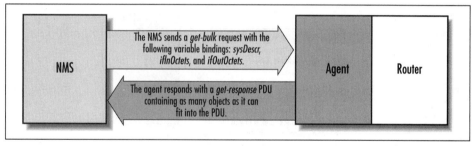

Figure 2-7. get-bulk request sequence

$N + (M * R)$, where N is the number of nonrepeaters (i.e., scalar objects in the request—in this case 1, because *sysDescr* is the only scalar object), M is max-repetitions (in this case, we've set it arbitrarily to 3), and R is the number of nonscalar objects in the request (in this case 2, because *ifInOctets* and *ifOutOctets* are both nonscalar). Plugging in the numbers from this example, we get $1 + (3 * 2) = 7$, which is the total number of variable bindings that can be returned by this *get-bulk* request.

The Net-SNMP package comes with a command for issuing *get-bulk* queries. If we execute this command using all the parameters previously discussed, it will look like the following:

```
$ snmpbulkget -v2c -B 1 3 linux.ora.com public sysDescr ifInOctets ifOutOctets
system.sysDescr.0 = "Linux linux 2.2.5-15 #3 Thu May 27 19:33:18 EDT 1999 i686"
interfaces.ifTable.ifEntry.ifInOctets.1 = 70840
interfaces.ifTable.ifEntry.ifOutOctets.1 = 70840
interfaces.ifTable.ifEntry.ifInOctets.2 = 143548020
interfaces.ifTable.ifEntry.ifOutOctets.2 = 111725152
interfaces.ifTable.ifEntry.ifInOctets.3 = 0
interfaces.ifTable.ifEntry.ifOutOctets.3 = 0
```

Since *get-bulk* is an SNMPv2 command, you have to tell *snmpgetbulk* to use an SNMPv2 PDU with the *–v2c* option. The nonrepeaters and max-repetitions are set with the *–B 1 3* option. This sets nonrepeaters to 1 and max-repetitions to 3. Notice that the command returned seven variable bindings: one for *sysDescr* and three each for *ifInOctets* and *ifOutOctets*.

The set Operation

The *set* command is used to change the value of a managed object or to create a new row in a table. Objects that are defined in the MIB as read-write or write-only can be altered or created using this command. It is possible for an NMS to set more than one object at a time.

Figure 2-8 shows the *set* request sequence. It's similar to the other commands we've seen so far, but it is actually changing something in the device's configuration, as

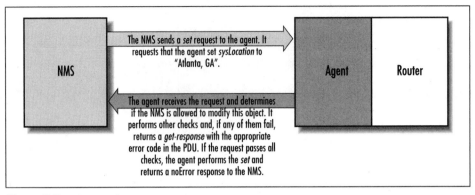

Figure 2-8. set request sequence

opposed to just retrieving a response to a query. If we look at an example of an actual *set*, you will see the command take place. The following example queries the *sysLocation* variable, then sets it to a value:

```
$ snmpget cisco.ora.com public system.sysLocation.0
system.sysLocation.0 = ""
$ snmpset cisco.ora.com private system.sysLocation.0 s "Atlanta, GA"
system.sysLocation.0 = "Atlanta, GA"
$ snmpget cisco.ora.com public system.sysLocation.0
system.sysLocation.0 = "Atlanta, GA"
```

The first command is the familiar *get* command, which displays the current value of *sysLocation*. In one of the previous examples we saw that it was undefined; this is still the case. The second command is *snmpset*. For this command, we supply the hostname, the read-write community string (*private*), and the variable we want to set (*system.sysLocation.0*), together with its new value (s "Atlanta, GA"). The s tells *snmpset* that we want to set the value of *sysLocation* to a string; and "Atlanta, GA" is the new value itself. How do we know that *sysLocation* requires a string value? The definition of *sysLocation* in RFC 1213 looks like this:

```
sysLocation OBJECT-TYPE
    SYNTAX  DisplayString (SIZE (0..255))
    ACCESS  read-write
    STATUS  mandatory
    DESCRIPTION
        "The physical location of this node (e.g., 'telephone closet,
        3rd floor')."
    ::= { system 6 }
```

The SYNTAX for *sysLocation* is DisplayString (SIZE (0..255)), which means that it's a string with a maximum length of 255 characters. The *snmpset* command succeeds and reports the new value of *sysLocation*. But just to confirm, we run a final *snmpget*, which tells us that the *set* actually took effect. It is possible to set more than one object at a time, but if any of the sets fail, they all fail (i.e., no values are changed). This behavior is intended.

get, get-next, get-bulk, and set Error Responses

Error responses help you determine wether your *get* or *set* request was processed correctly by the agent. The *get*, *get-next*, and *set* operations can return the error responses shown in Table 2-6. The error status for each error is show in parentheses.

Table 2-6. SNMPv1 Error Messages

SNMPv1 Error Message	Description
noError(0)	There was no problem performing the request.
tooBig(1)	The response to your request was too big to fit into one response.
noSuchName(2)	An agent was asked to get or set an OID that it can't find; i.e., the OID doesn't exist.
badValue(3)	A read-write or write-only object was set to an inconsistent value.
readOnly(4)	This error is generally not used. The noSuchName error is equivalent to this one.
genErr(5)	This is a catch-all error. If an error occurs for which none of the previous messages is appropriate, a genError is issued.

The SNMPv1 error messages are not very robust. In an attempt to fix this problem, SNMPv2 defines additional error responses that are valid for *get*, *set*, *get-next*, and *get-bulk* operations, provided that both the agent and NMS support SNMPv2. These responses are listed in Table 2-7.

Table 2-7. SNMPv2 Error Messages

SNMPv2 Error Message	Description
noAccess(6)	A *set* to an inaccessible variable was attempted. This typically occurs when the variable has an ACCESS type of not-accessible.
wrongType(7)	An object was set to a type that is different from its definition. This error will occur if you try to set an object that is of type INTEGER to a string, for example.
wrongLength(8)	An object's value was set to something other than what it calls for. For instance, a string can be defined to have a maximum character size. This error occurs if you try to set a string object to a value that exceeds its maximum length.
wrongEncoding(9)	A *set* operation was attempted using the wrong encoding for the object being set.
wrongValue(10)	A variable was set to a value it doesn't understand. This can occur when a read-write is defined as an enumeration, and you try to set it to a value that is not one of the enumerated types.

Table 2-7. SNMPv2 Error Messages (continued)

SNMPv2 Error Message	Description
noCreation(11)	You tried to set a nonexistent variable or create a variable that doesn't exist in the MIB.
inconsistentValue	A MIB variable is in an inconsistent state, and is not accepting any *set* requests.
resourceUnavailable(13)	No system resources are available to perform a *set*.
commitFailed(14)	This is a catch-all error for *set* failures.
undoFailed(15)	A *set* failed and the agent was unable to roll back all the previous *sets* up until the point of failure.
authorizationError(16)	An SNMP command could not be authenticated; in other words, someone has supplied an incorrect community string.
notWritable(17)	A variable will not accept a *set*, even though it is supposed to.
inconsistentName(18)	You attempted to set a variable, but that attempt failed because the variable was in some kind of inconsistent state.

SNMP Traps

A trap is a way for an agent to tell the NMS that something bad has happened. In the "Managers and Agents" section of Chapter 1 we explored the notion of traps at a general level; now we'll look at them in a bit more detail. Figure 2-9 shows the trap-generation sequence.

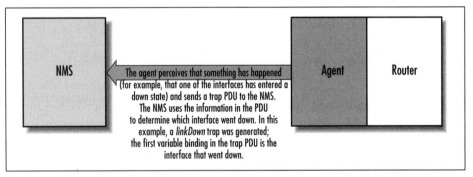

Figure 2-9. Trap generation

The trap originates from the agent and is sent to the trap destination, as configured within the agent itself. The trap destination is typically the IP address of the NMS. No acknowledgment is sent from the NMS to the agent, so the agent has no way of knowing if the trap makes it to the NMS. Since SNMP uses UDP, and since traps are designed to report problems with your network, traps are especially prone to getting lost and not making it to their destinations. However, the fact that traps can get lost doesn't make them any less useful; in a well-planned environment, they are an integral part of network management. It's better for your equipment to try to tell you that something is wrong, even if the message may never reach you, than simply to give up and let you guess what happened. Here are a few situations that a trap might report:

- A network interface on the device (where the agent is running) has gone down.

- A network interface on the device (where the agent is running) has come back up.

- An incoming call to a modem rack was unable to establish a connection to a modem.

- The fan on a switch or router has failed.

When an NMS receives a trap, it needs to know how to interpret it; that is, it needs to know what the trap means and how to interpret the information it carries. A trap is first identified by its generic trap number. There are seven generic trap numbers (0–6), shown in Table 2-8. Generic trap 6 is a special catch-all category for "enterprise-specific" traps, which are traps defined by vendors or users that fall outside of the six generic trap categories. Enterprise-specific traps are further identified by an enterprise ID (i.e., an object ID somewhere in the *enterprises* branch of the MIB tree, *iso.org.dod.internet.private.enterprises*) and a specific trap number chosen by the enterprise that defined the trap. Thus, the object ID of an enterprise-specific trap is *enterprise-id.specific-trap-number*. For example, when Cisco defines special traps for its private MIBs, it places them all in its enterprise-specific MIB tree (*iso.org.dod.internet.private.enterprises.cisco*). As we'll see in Chapter 10, you are free to define your own enterprise-specific traps; the only requirement is that you register your own enterprise number with IANA.

A trap is usually packed with information. As you'd expect, this information is in the form of MIB objects and their values; as mentioned earlier, these object-value pairs are known as variable bindings. For the generic traps 0 through 5, knowledge of what the trap contains is generally built into the NMS software or trap receiver. The variable bindings contained by an enterprise-specific trap are determined by whomever defined the trap. For example, if a modem in a modem rack fails, the rack's agent may send a trap to the NMS informing it of the failure. The trap will most likely be an enterprise-specific trap defined by the rack's manufacturer; the trap's contents are up to the manufacturer, but it will probably contain enough information to let you determine exactly what failed (for example, the position of the modem card in the rack and the channel on the modem card).

Table 2-8. Generic Traps

Generic Trap Name and Number	Definition
coldStart (0)	Indicates that the agent has rebooted. All management variables will be reset; specifically, `Counters` and `Gauges` will be reset to zero (0). One nice thing about the *coldStart* trap is that it can be used to determine when new hardware is added to the network. When a device is powered on, it sends this trap to its trap destination. If the trap destination is set correctly (i.e., to the IP address of your NMS) the NMS can receive the trap and determine whether it needs to manage the device.
warmStart (1)	Indicates that the agent has reinitialized itself. None of the management variables will be reset.
linkDown (2)	Sent when an interface on a device goes down. The first variable binding identifies which interface went down.
linkUp (3)	Sent when an interface on a device comes back up. The first variable binding identifies which interface came back up.
authenticationFailure (4)	Indicates that someone has tried to query your agent with an incorrect community string; useful in determining if someone is trying to gain unauthorized access to one of your devices.
egpNeighborLoss (5)	Indicates that an *Exterior Gateway Protocol* (EGP) neighbor has gone down.
enterpriseSpecific (6)	Indicates that the trap is enterprise-specific. SNMP vendors and users define their own traps under the private-enterprise branch of the SMI object tree. To process this trap properly, the NMS has to decode the specific trap number that is part of the SNMP message.

In Chapter 1 we mentioned that RFC 1697 is the RDBMS MIB. One of traps defined by this MIB is *rdbmsOutOfSpace*:

```
rdbmsOutOfSpace TRAP-TYPE
    ENTERPRISE  rdbmsTraps
    VARIABLES   { rdbmsSrvInfoDiskOutOfSpaces }
    DESCRIPTION
        "An rdbmsOutOfSpace trap signifies that one of the database
         servers managed by this agent has been unable to allocate
         space for one of the databases managed by this agent. Care
         should be taken to avoid flooding the network with these traps."
    ::= 2
```

The enterprise is *rdbmsTraps* and the specific trap number is 2. This trap has one variable binding, *rdbmsSrvInfoDiskOutOfSpaces*. If we look elsewhere in the MIB, we will find that this variable is a scalar object. Its definition is:

```
rdbmsSrvInfoDiskOutOfSpaces OBJECT-TYPE
    SYNTAX  Counter
    ACCESS  read-only
```

```
STATUS  mandatory
DESCRIPTION
    "The total number of times the server has been unable to obtain
     disk space that it wanted, since server startup. This would be
     inspected by an agent on receipt of an rdbmsOutOfSpace trap."
::= { rdbmsSrvInfoEntry 9 }
```

The DESCRIPTION for this object indicates why the note about taking care to avoid flooding the network (in the DESCRIPTION text for the TRAP-TYPE) is so important. Every time the RDBMS is unable to allocate space for the database, the agent will send a trap. A busy (and full) database could end up sending this trap thousands of times a day.

Some commercial RDBMS vendors, such as Oracle, provide an SNMP agent with their database engines. Agents such as these typically have functionality above and beyond that found in the RDBMS MIB.

SNMP Notification

In an effort to standardize the PDU format of SNMPv1 traps (recall that SNMPv1 traps have a different PDU format from *get* and *set*), SNMPv2 defines a NOTIFICATION-TYPE. The PDU format for NOTIFICATION-TYPE is identical to that for *get* and *set*. RFC 2863 redefines the *linkDown* generic notification type like so:

```
linkDown NOTIFICATION-TYPE
    OBJECTS { ifIndex, ifAdminStatus, ifOperStatus }
    STATUS  current
    DESCRIPTION
        "A linkDown trap signifies that the SNMPv2 entity, acting in an
         agent role, has detected that the ifOperStatus object for one
         of its communication links left the down state and transitioned
         into some other state (but not into the notPresent state). This
         other state is indicated by the included value of ifOperStatus."
    ::= { snmpTraps 3 }
```

The list of bindings is called OBJECTS rather than VARIABLES, but little else has changed. The first object is the specific interface (*ifIndex*) that transitioned from the *linkDown* condition to some other condition. The OID for this trap is *1.3.6.1.6. 3.1.1.5.3*, or *iso.org.dod.internet.snmpV2.snmpModules.snmpMIB.snmpMIBObjects. snmpTraps.linkDown*.

SNMP inform

Finally, SNMPv2 provides an *inform* mechanism, which allows for manager-to-manager communication. This operation can be useful when the need arises for more than one NMS in the network. When an *inform* is sent from one NMS to another, the receiver sends a response to the sender acknowledging receipt of the event. This behavior is similar to that of the *get* and *set* requests. Note that an

SNMP *inform* can be used to send SNMPv2 traps to an NMS. If you use an *inform* for this purpose, the agent will be notified when the NMS receives the trap.

SNMP report

The *report* operation was defined in the draft version SNMPv2 but never implemented. It is now part of the SNMPv3 specification and is intended to allow SNMP engines to communicate with each other (mainly to report problems with processing SNMP messages).

Host Management Revisited

Managing your hosts is an important part of network management. You would think that the Host Resources MIB would be part of every host-based SNMP agent, but this isn't the case. Some SNMP agents implement this MIB, but many don't. A few agents go further and implement proprietary extensions based upon this MIB. This is mainly due to the fact that this MIB was intended to serve as a basic, watered-down framework for host management, designed mainly to foster wide deployment.

The Host Resources MIB defines the following seven groups:

```
host            OBJECT IDENTIFIER ::= { mib-2 25 }

hrSystem        OBJECT IDENTIFIER ::= { host 1 }
hrStorage       OBJECT IDENTIFIER ::= { host 2 }
hrDevice        OBJECT IDENTIFIER ::= { host 3 }
hrSWRun         OBJECT IDENTIFIER ::= { host 4 }
hrSWRunPerf     OBJECT IDENTIFIER ::= { host 5 }
hrSWInstalled   OBJECT IDENTIFIER ::= { host 6 }
```

The *host* OID is *1.3.6.1.2.1.25* (*iso.org.dod.internet.mgmt.mib-2.host*). The remaining six groups define various objects that provide information about the system.

The *hrSystem* (*1.3.6.1.2.1.25.1*) group defines objects that pertain to the system itself. These objects include uptime, system date, system users, and system processes.

The *hrDevice* (*1.3.6.1.2.1.25.3*) and *hrStorage* (*1.3.6.1.2.1.25.2*) groups define objects pertaining to filesystems and system storage, such as total system memory, disk utilization, and CPU nonidle percentage. They are particularly helpful, since they can be used to manage the disk partitions on your host. You can even use them to check for errors on a given disk device.

The *hrSWRun* (*1.3.6.1.2.1.25.4*), *hrSWRunPerf* (*1.3.6.1.2.1.25.5*), and *hrSW-Installed* (*1.3.6.1.2.1.25.6*) groups define objects that represent various aspects of software running or installed on the system. From these groups, you can determine what operating system is running on the host, as well as what programs the host is currently running. The *hrSWInstalled* group can be used to track which software packages are installed.

As you can see, the Host Resources MIB provides some necessary system-management objects that can be utilized by almost anyone who needs to manage critical systems.

Remote Monitoring Revisited

A thorough treatment of RMON is beyond the scope of this book, but it's worth discussing the groups that make up RMONv1. RMON probes are typically stand-alone devices that watch traffic on the network segments to which they are attached. Some vendors implement at least some kind of RMON probe in their routers, hubs, or switches. Chapter 9 provides an example of how to configure RMON on a Cisco router.

The RMON MIB defines the following 10 groups:

```
rmon          OBJECT IDENTIFIER ::= { mib-2 16 }
statistics    OBJECT IDENTIFIER ::= { rmon 1 }
history       OBJECT IDENTIFIER ::= { rmon 2 }
alarm         OBJECT IDENTIFIER ::= { rmon 3 }
hosts         OBJECT IDENTIFIER ::= { rmon 4 }
hostTopN      OBJECT IDENTIFIER ::= { rmon 5 }
matrix        OBJECT IDENTIFIER ::= { rmon 6 }
filter        OBJECT IDENTIFIER ::= { rmon 7 }
capture       OBJECT IDENTIFIER ::= { rmon 8 }
event         OBJECT IDENTIFIER ::= { rmon 9 }
```

RMONv1 provides packet-level statistics about an entire LAN or WAN. The *rmon* OID is *1.3.6.1.2.1.16 (iso.org.dod.internet.mgmt.mib-2.rmon)*. RMONv1 is made up of nine groups:

statistics (1.3.6.1.2.1.16.1)

Contains statistics about all the Ethernet interfaces monitored by the probe

history (1.3.6.1.2.1.16.2)

Records periodic statistical samples from the statistics group

alarm (1.3.6.1.2.1.16.3)

Allows a user to configure a polling interval and a threshold for any object the RMON probe records

hosts (1.3.6.1.2.1.16.4)

Records traffic statistics for each host on the network

hostTopN (1.3.6.1.2.1.16.5)

Contains host statistics used to generate reports on hosts that top a list ordered by a parameter in the *host* table *matrix (1.3.6.1.2.1.16.6)*

Stores error and utilization information for sets of two addresses

filter (1.3.6.1.2.1.16.7)

Matches packets based on a filter equation; when a packet matches the filter, it may be captured or an event may be generated

capture (1.3.6.1.2.1.16.8)

Allows packets to be captured if they match a filter in the filter group

event (1.3.6.1.2.1.16.9)

Controls the definition of RMON events

RMONv2 enhances RMONv1 by providing network- and application-level statistical gathering. Since the only example of RMON in this book uses RMONv1, we will stop here and not go into RMONv2. However, we encourage you to read RFC 2021 to get a feel for what enhancements this version of RMON brings to network monitoring.

3

NMS Architectures

Now that you understand the basic concepts behind how management stations (NMSs) and agents communicate, it's time to introduce the concept of a network-management architecture. Before rushing out to deploy SNMP management, you owe it to yourself to put some effort into developing a coherent plan. If you simply drop NMS software on a few of your favorite desktop machines, you're likely to end up with something that doesn't work very well. By NMS architecture, we mean a plan that helps you use NMSs effectively to manage your network. A key component of network management is selecting the proper hardware (i.e., an appropriate platform on which to run your NMS) and making sure that your management stations are located in such a way that they can observe the devices on your network effectively.

Hardware Considerations

Managing a reasonably large network requires an NMS with substantial computing power. In today's complex networked environments, networks can range in size from a few nodes to thousands of nodes. The process of polling and receiving traps from hundreds or thousands of managed entities can be taxing on the best of hardware. Your NMS vendor will be able to help you determine what kind of hardware is appropriate for managing your network. Most vendors have formulas for determining how much RAM you will need to achieve the level of performance you want, given the requirements of your network. It usually boils down to the number of devices you want to poll, the amount of information you will request from each device, and the interval at which you want to poll them. The software you want to run is also a consideration. NMS products such as OpenView are large, heavyweight applications; if you want to run your own scripts with Perl, you can get away with a much smaller management platform.

Is it possible to say something more helpful than "ask your vendor"? Yes. First, although we've become accustomed to thinking of NMS software as requiring a midrange workstation or high-end PC, desktop hardware has advanced so much in the past year or two that running this software is within the range of any modern PC. Specifically, surveying the recommendations of a number of vendors, we have found that they suggest a PC with at least a 300 MHz CPU, 128 MB of memory, and 500 MB of disk space. Requirements for Sun SPARC and HP workstations are similar.

Let's look at each of these requirements:

300 MHz CPU

> This is well within the range of any modern desktop system, but you probably can't bring your older equipment out of retirement to use as a management station.

128 MB of memory

> You'll probably have to add memory to any off-the-shelf PC; Sun and HP workstations come with more generous memory configurations. Frankly, vendors tend to underestimate memory requirements anyway, so it won't hurt to upgrade to 256 MB. Fortunately, RAM is cheap these days. (Memory prices fluctuate from day to day, but we recently found 256 MB DIMMs for under $100.)

500 MB of disk space

> This recommendation is probably based on the amount of space you'll need to store the software, and not on the space you'll need for log files, long-term trend data, etc. But again, disk space is cheap these days, and skimping is counterproductive.

Let's think a bit more about how long-term data collection affects your disk requirements. First, you should recognize that some products have only minimal data-collection facilities, while others exist purely for the purpose of collecting data (for example, MRTG). Whether or not you can do data collection effectively depends to some extent on the NMS product you've selected. Therefore, before deciding on a software product, you should think about your data-collection requirements. Do you want to do long-term trend analysis? If so, that will affect both the software you choose and the hardware on which you run it.

For a starting point, let's say that you have 1,000 nodes, you want to collect data every minute, and you're collecting 1 KB of data per node. That's 1 MB per minute, 1.4 GB per day—you'd fill a 40 GB disk in about a month. That's bordering on extravagant. But let's look at the assumptions:

- Collecting data every minute is certainly excessive; every 10 minutes should do. Now your 40 GB disk will store almost a year's worth of data.

- 1,000 nodes isn't that big a network. But do you really want to store trend data for all your users' PCs? Much of this book is devoted to showing you how to control the amount of data you collect. Instead of 1,000 nodes, let's first count interfaces. And let's forget about desktop systems—we really care only about trend data for our network backbone: key servers, routers, switches, etc. Even on a midsize network, we're probably talking about 100 or 200 interfaces.

- The amount of data you collect per interface depends on many factors, not the least of which is the format of the data. An interface's status may be up or down—that's a single bit. If it's being stored in a binary data structure, it may be represented by a single bit. But if you're using *syslog* to store your log data and writing Perl scripts to do trend analysis, your *syslog* records are going to be 80 bytes or so even if you are storing only one bit of information. Data-storage mechanisms range from *syslog* to fancy database schemes—you obviously need to understand what you're using, and how it will affect your storage requirements. Furthermore, you need to understand how much information you really want to keep per interface. If you want to track only the number of octets going in and out of each interface and you're storing this data efficiently, your 40 GB disk could easily last the better part of a century.

Seriously, it's hard to talk about what your storage requirements will be when they vary over two or three orders of magnitude. But the lesson is that no vendor can tell you what your storage requirements will be. A gigabyte should be plenty for log data on a moderately large network, if you're storing data only for a reasonable subset of that network, not polling too often, and not saving too much data. But that's a lot of variables, and you're the only one in control of them. Keep in mind, though, that the more data you collect, the more time and CPU power will be required to grind through all that data and produce meaningful results. It doesn't matter whether you're using expensive trend-analysis software or some homegrown scripts—processing lots of data is expensive. At least in terms of long-term data collection, it's probably better to err by keeping too little data around than by keeping too much.

NMS Architectures

Before going out and buying all your equipment, it's worth spending some time coming up with an architecture for your network that will make it more manageable. The simplest architecture has a single management station that is responsible for the entire network, as shown in Figure 3-1.

The network depicted in Figure 3-1 has three sites: New York, Atlanta, and San Jose. The NMS in New York is responsible for managing not only the portion of the network in New York, but also those in Atlanta and San Jose. Traps sent from

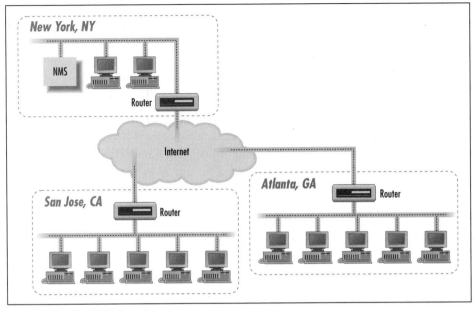

Figure 3-1. Single NMS architecture

any device in Atlanta or San Jose must travel over the Internet to get to the NMS in New York. The same thing goes for polling devices in San Jose and Atlanta: the NMS in New York must send its requests over the Internet to reach these remote sites. For small networks, an architecture like this can work well. However, when the network grows to the point that a single NMS can no longer manage everything, this architecture becomes a real problem. The NMS in New York can get behind in its polling of the remote sites, mainly because it has so much to manage. The result is that when problems arise at a remote site, they may not get noticed for some time. In the worst case, they might not get noticed at all.

It's also worth thinking about staffing. With a single NMS, your primary operations staff would be in New York, watching the health of the network. But problems frequently require somebody onsite to intervene. This requires someone in Atlanta and San Jose, plus the coordination that entails. You may not need a full-time network administrator, but you will need someone who knows what to do when a router fails.

When your network grows to a point where one NMS can no longer manage everything, it's time to move to a distributed NMS architecture. The idea behind this architecture is simple: use two or more management stations and locate them as close as possible to the nodes they are managing. In the case of our three-site network, we would have an NMS at each site. Figure 3-2 shows the addition of two NMSs to the network.

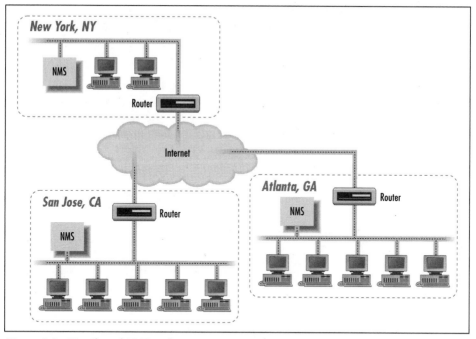

Figure 3-2. Distributed NMS architecture

This architecture has several advantages, not the least of which is flexibility. With the new architecture, the NMSs in Atlanta and San Jose can act as standalone management stations, each with a fully self-sufficient staff, or they can forward events to the NMS in New York. If the remote NMSs forward all events to the NMS in New York, there is no need to put additional operations staff in Atlanta and San Jose. At first glance this looks like we've returned to the situation of Figure 3-1, but that isn't quite true. Most NMS products provide some kind of client interface to viewing the events currently in the NMS (traps received, responses to polls, etc.). Since the NMS that forwards events to New York has already discovered the problem, we're simply letting the NMS in New York know about it so it can be dealt with appropriately. The New York NMS didn't have to use valuable resources to poll the remote network to discover that there was a problem.

The other advantage is that if the need arises you can put operations staff in Atlanta and San Jose to manage each of these remote locations. If New York loses connectivity to the Internet, events forwarded from Atlanta or San Jose will not make it to New York. With operations staff in Atlanta and San Jose, and the NMSs at these locations acting in standalone mode, a network outage in New York won't matter. The remote-location staff will continue on as if nothing has happened.

Another possibility with this architecture is a hybrid mode: you staff the operations center in New York 24 hours a day, 7 days a week, but you staff Atlanta and

San Jose only during business hours. During off-hours, they rely on the NMS and operations staff in New York to notice and handle problems that arise. But during the critical (and busiest) hours of the day, Atlanta and San Jose don't have to burden the New York operators.

Both of the architectures we have discussed use the Internet to send and receive management traffic. This poses several problems, mainly dealing with security and overall reliability. A better solution is to use private links to perform all your network-management functions. Figure 3-3 shows how the distributed NMS architecture can be extended to make use of such links.

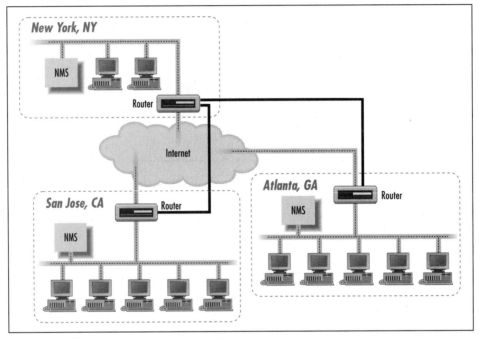

Figure 3-3. Using private links for network management

Let's say that New York's router is the core router for the network. We establish private (but not necessarily high-speed) links between San Jose and New York, and between New York and Atlanta. This means that San Jose will not only be able to reach New York, but it will also be able to reach Atlanta via New York. Atlanta will use New York to reach San Jose, too. The private links (denoted by thicker router-to-router connections) are primarily devoted to management traffic, though we could put them to other uses. Using private links has the added benefit that our community strings are never sent out over the Internet. The use of private network links for network management works equally well with the single NMS architecture, too. Of course, if your corporate network consists entirely of private links and your Internet connections are devoted to external traffic only, using private links for your management traffic is the proverbial "no-brainer."

One final item worth mentioning is the notion of trap-directed polling. This doesn't really have anything to do with NMS architecture, but it can help to alleviate an NMS's management strain. The idea behind trap-directed polling is simple: the NMS receives a trap and initiates a poll to the device that generated the trap. The goal of this scenario is to determine if there is indeed a problem with the device, while allowing the NMS to ignore (or devote few resources to) the device in normal operation. If an organization relies on this form of management, it should implement it in such a way that non-trap-directed polling is almost done away with. That is, it should avoid polling devices at regular intervals for status information. Instead, the management stations should simply wait to receive a trap before polling a device. This form of management can significantly reduce the resources needed by an NMS to manage a network. However, it has an important disadvantage: traps can get lost in the network and never make it to the NMS. This is a reality of the connectionless nature of UDP and the imperfect nature of networks.

A Look Ahead

Web-based network management entails the use of the *HyperText Transport Protocol* (HTTP) and the *Common Gateway Interface* (CGI) to manage networked entities. It works by embedding a web server in an SNMP-compatible device, along with a CGI engine to convert SNMP-like requests (from a web-based NMS) to actual SNMP operations, and vice versa. Web servers can be embedded into such devices at very low monetary and operating cost.

Figure 3-4 is a simplified diagram of the interaction between a web-based NMS and a managed device. The CGI application bridges the gap between the management application and the SNMP engine. In some cases, the management application can be a collection of Java applets that are downloaded to the web browser and executed on the web-based manager. Current versions of OpenView ship with a web-based GUI.

Web-based network management could eliminate, or at least reduce, the need for traditional NMS software. NMS software can be expensive to purchase, set up, and maintain. Most of today's major NMS vendors support only a few popular versions of Unix, and have only recently begun to support Windows 9x/NT/2000, thus limiting your operating-system choices. With a web-based NMS, however, these two concerns are moot. For the most part web-browser technology is free, and Netscape Communications (now AOL Time Warner) supports many flavors of Unix, as well as the Wintel and Apple platforms.

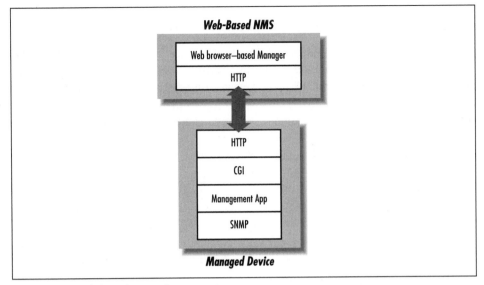

Figure 3-4. Web-based network management

Web-based network management should not be viewed as a panacea, though. It is a good idea, but it will take some time for vendors to embrace this technology and move toward web-integration of their existing products. There is also the issue of standardization, or the lack of it. The *Web-Based Enterprise Management* (WBEM) consortium addresses this by defining a standard for web-based management. Industry leaders such as Cisco and BMC Software are among the original founders of WBEM. You can learn more about this initiative at the Distributed Management Task Force's web page, *http://www.dmtf.org/wbem/*.

4

SNMP-Compatible Hardware

Determining if you have devices that are manageable by SNMP is a good place to start down the path to network-management Zen. Before we get into how to determine if what you already have is manageable, we will briefly discuss what makes a device SNMP-compatible.

Vendors do not have to implement all the MIBs SNMP provides,* but SNMP-manageable devices must support at least MIB-II. It also behooves the vendors to implement some of the more useful MIBs, as well as their own private MIBs, since the ability to manage a product effectively using SNMP is an increasingly important selling point.

What Does SNMP-Compatible Really Mean?

Many vendors claim that their products are SNMP-compatible or compliant. For the most part this is true. What they actually mean is that their product supports a set of SNMP operations, as well as MIB-II. For SNMPv1 compatibility, the supported operations include:

- *get*
- *get-next*
- *set*
- *get-response*
- *trap*

---

* You can find a few examples of these standard MIBs in Chapter 1.

Additionally, if the product is SNMPv2 and SNMPv3 compatible, it must support the following operations:

- *get-bulk*
- *inform*
- *notification*
- *report*

Vendors can choose to support SNMPv1, SNMPv2, SNMPv2, or all three. An SNMP agent that supports two versions of SNMP is called "bilingual." In recent years, this was restricted to devices supporting SNMPv1 and SNMPv2. Now a device can support all three versions, which technically makes it trilingual. It is possible for an agent to speak all versions of SNMP because SMIv2 is a superset of SMIv1, and SMIv2 is used, for the most part, with SNMPv3.

Supporting these operations, however, is only one piece to the puzzle of providing a manageable product. The other piece is providing a private MIB that is comprehensive enough to give network managers the information they need to manage their networks intelligently. In today's complex network environments, it does not pay to purchase equipment that has a minimal or poorly implemented private MIB. For instance, it is important to measure ambient temperature inside devices such as routers, hubs, and switches. Cisco and others provide this information via their private MIBs; other vendors do not. If you're in the process of purchasing a high-end router, you might want to look into the vendors' private MIBs to see which vendors provide more relevant information.

Another factor that affects vendor MIB support is product definition. Concord Communications (vendors of an SNMP agent for Unix and Windows) will probably not support the RS-232 MIB (RFC 1659), since their product is geared toward providing system- and application-management information. 3Com, on the other hand, implemented this MIB for their line of Dual Speed Hubs, since these hubs have RS-232 ports.

Is My Device SNMP-Compatible?

Your product documentation should be helpful in determining hardware or software compatibility with SNMP. You can also consult your sales representative, or customer support, if applicable. Another way to tell if a product is SNMP-compatible is to perform an *snmpget* query against the device in question.* Issuing a

---

* With this method, we can try to guess what the community string is. In our case, we try *public* or *private*. If we don't get a response, it might mean either that we guessed wrong or that the agent isn't set up/ configured.

diagnostic *get* against any device is easy. The most common way to accomplish this is to find a Unix host that has the *snmpget* binary command installed.* There are several varieties of this command, so consult your manpage or system administrator for help. The easiest variable to query for is *sysDescr*, which provides a description of the system being queried. Here's what happens when you use the Net-SNMP *snmpget* command to look at *sysDescr* on a typical Linux host:

```
$ snmpget linuxserver.ora.com public system.sysDescr.0
system.sysDescr.0 = "Linux version 2.0.34 (root@porky.redhat.com)
(gcc version 2.7.2.3) #1 Fri May 8 16:05:57 EDT 1998"
```

The response from *linuxserver.ora.com* is typical of most managed devices. Note, however, that there's nothing sacred about the actual description; the text you retrieve will vary from vendor to vendor. Issuing an *snmpget* against a Cisco 2503 router should return something like this:

```
$ snmpget orarouter.ora.com public system.sysDescr.0
system.sysDescr.0 = "Cisco Internetwork Operating System Software
..IOS (tm) 2500 Software (C2500-I-L), Version 11.2(5), RELEASE
SOFTWARE (fc1)..Copyright (c) 1986-1997 by cisco Systems, Inc...
Compiled Mon 31-Mar-97 19:53 by ckralik"
```

This router's system description tells us that it is running Version 11.2(5) of the Cisco IOS. This sort of information is generally useless, but it does tell us that the device is running an SNMP agent. Here's what happens when something goes wrong:

```
$ snmpget linuxserver.ora.com public system.sysDescr.0
Timeout: No Response from linuxserver.ora.com.
```

This message means that the Net-SNMP *snmpget* command did not receive a response from *linuxserver.ora.com*. A number of things could be wrong, one of which is that there is no SNMP agent running on the target host. But it's also possible that *linuxserver* has crashed, that there's some sort of network problem, or that everything is running correctly but you aren't using the correct community string. It's even possible that the device you're querying has SNMP capabilities, but the SNMP agent won't be enabled until you explicitly configure it.

If you suspect you have manageable equipment but are not sure, it is good to know that most vendors ship their products with the read and write community strings set to *public* and *private*, respectively. (The Net-SNMP tools we're using here use *private* as the default for both community strings.†)

---

* Chapter 7 discusses installing the Net-SNMP agent and toolkit, which comes with utilities such as *snmpget*.

† Since our agents use *public* for the community string and Net-SNMP defaults to *private*, we needed to specify the community string *public* on the command line.

Once you verify that the device you're testing is SNMP-manageable, you should immediately change the community strings. Leaving the community strings set to well-known values like *public* and *private* is a serious security problem.

Once you've established that your device supports SNMP, you can go further to check if it supports Version 2. A good way to do that is to make a request that can be answered only by a Version 2 agent, such as the *bulk-get* request. You can use the *snmpbulkget* command we demonstrated in Chapter 2 to make such a request:

```
$ snmpbulkget -v2c -B 1 3 linux.ora.com public sysDescr ifInOctets ifOutOctets
system.sysDescr.0 = "Linux linux 2.2.5-15 #3 Thu May 27 19:33:18 EDT 1999 i686"
interfaces.ifTable.ifEntry.ifInOctets.1 = 70840
interfaces.ifTable.ifEntry.ifOutOctets.1 = 70840
interfaces.ifTable.ifEntry.ifInOctets.2 = 143548020
interfaces.ifTable.ifEntry.ifOutOctets.2 = 111725152
interfaces.ifTable.ifEntry.ifInOctets.3 = 0
interfaces.ifTable.ifEntry.ifOutOctets.3 = 0
```

Now we know that *linux.ora.com* supports SNMPv2—in particular, v2c. Can we go further, and check for Version 3 support? For Version 3, you're better off checking your vendor's documentation. Most vendors don't support Version 3 yet, and we expect adoption to be fairly slow—many vendors still support only Version 1.

Upgrading Your Hardware

Now that you know whether or not you have SNMP devices on your network, it might be time to upgrade! You may find that some of the devices you would like to manage don't support SNMP. There are two ways to upgrade: you can retire your existing equipment and buy newer, more manageable hardware, or you can upgrade your equipment's firmware (if provided by the vendor) to a version that supports SNMP. Some vendors, however, will offer to buy back older equipment, or even give a discount for turning in a competitor's equipment.

Of course, updating your equipment may not be necessary. If you have software applications that are used to manage non-SNMP equipment and they work, there is no need to upgrade. If you're reasonably handy with scripts and want to learn about SNMP in some depth, you may find that it's possible to write scripts that allow you to use SNMP to monitor applications that doesn't support SNMP using wrapper/scripts. For an example of this, see the section "Veritas Disk Check" in Chapter 12.

Whatever approach you take, realize that SNMP exists to provide a consistent way to manage networked equipment. If you're currently managing your network using a number of legacy management tools, each supporting a few devices from a particular vendor, SNMP provides a way out. You may be comfortable with your old tools—but it will become increasingly convenient to use SNMP to provide a uniform network-management approach.

In the End

You may have been purchasing SNMP-compatible devices for years without knowing it. As SNMP has become more popular, it has been incorporated into more and more devices. SNMP compatibility has become a true selling point for most vendors.

It goes without saying that most network devices support SNMP, including routers, bridges, hubs, servers, and desktop PCs.* However, many other kinds of equipment are also manageable via SNMP, including uninterruptible power supplies (UPSs), air-conditioning units, and other important pieces of your infrastructure. After you identify which routers and hubs are SNMP-compatible, keep your eyes open for other devices that may need to be managed. While SNMP is very good at managing your network, hosts, hubs, and routers, it's not limited to only your networking environment.

A Look Ahead

The Internet Engineering Task Force (IETF) is in the process of defining a standards-track technology for SNMP *agent extensibility* (AgentX). As we defined it earlier, an SNMP agent is software that resides on a managed device, replying to SNMP requests and generating asynchronous traps. Information about agent extensibility can be found in RFC 2741, as well as at the AgentX web site, *http://www.scguild.com/agentx/*. The need for AgentX arises from the inability to add and remove MIB objects while an agent is running; in other words, the lack of a standard way to extend an agent's functionality. The *SNMP Multiplexing Protocol* (SMUX, RFC 1227) was an early attempt to provide standardization for agent extensibility, but the protocol was found to be flawed and has since been abandoned.

Figure 4-1 is an overview of the AgentX architecture. With AgentX, the agent consists of a single processing entity called a *master agent* and zero or more processing entities called *subagents*. The master agent and subagents can reside on the same device or communicate via a proxy device. The master agent communicates with the NMS, much like a traditional SNMP agent. The subagents have direct access to the MIB, whereas the master agent does not. Consequently, the subagents perform management functions on managed variables, then communicate this information to the master agent via the AgentX protocol, which is not SNMP-based.

---

* Low-end hubs, switches, and routers designed for home use probably won't support SNMP. Hubs and switches that support SNMP usually are advertised as "manageable" and usually cost significantly more. For routers, you'll have to read the literature carefully.

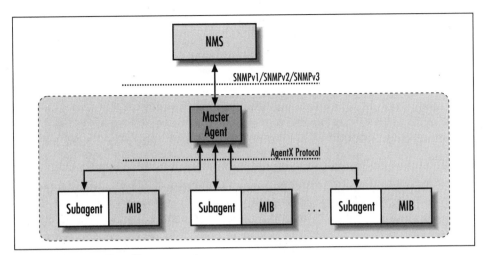

Figure 4-1. AgentX architecture

Without a standardized approach to extensibility, it is very difficult for vendors to keep track of extensions to agents for the various platforms they support. AgentX tries to address this by giving vendors a consistent interface for extending agents. It also establishes the notion of MIB regions, or sets of managed variables. A subagent is responsible for registering these MIBs with a single master agent. In practice this means that vendors will have a subagent for each MIB they implement; for example, an RMON subagent, a MIB-II subagent, a Host Resources subagent, and others. This helps vendors because it gives them a way to add and remove MIB instances from an agent without disturbing the actual operation between an NMS and the agent.

5

Network-Management Software

Many SNMP software packages are available, ranging from programming libraries that let you build your own utilities (using Perl, C/C++ or Java) to expensive, complete network-management platforms. This chapter presents some pros and cons for many of the most commonly used packages. This will not only give you an idea of what packages are out there, but also help you decide what might be right for you (keep in mind, though, that these pros and cons are merely our opinions). Whenever possible, we present both open source solutions and commercial products.

Management software falls into five categories:

- SNMP agents
- NMS suites
- Element managers (vendor-specific management)
- Trend-analysis software
- Supporting software

Unfortunately, deciding what you need isn't as simple as picking one program from each category. If you have a small network and are interested in building your own tools, you probably don't need a complex NMS suite. Whether or not you need trend-analysis software depends, obviously, on if you're interested in analyzing trends in your network usage. The products available depend in part on the platforms in which you're interested. The minimum you can get by with is an SNMP agent on a device and some software that can retrieve a value from that device (using an SNMP *get*). Although this is minimal, it's enough to start working, and you can get the software for free.

This chapter presents a broad survey of some of the leading products in each of these categories. Since there are more packages than we can cover in this book, be sure to check the Network Management Server (*http://netman.cit.buffalo.edu/ Products.html*) for network-management product listings.

SNMP Agents

As we explained in Chapter 1, the agent is the software that controls all the SNMP communication to and from any SNMP-compatible device. In some devices, such as Cisco routers, the agent software is built into the device itself and requires no installation. On other platforms, such as Windows NT, you may have to install the agent as part of an additional software package.

Before you can look at what types of agents you need, you must research what types of devices you have on your network and what types of information you would like to receive from each. Some agents are very basic and return only a limited amount of information, while others can return a wealth of information. To start, determine whether you need to receive information from servers (Unix, Windows NT, etc.) or network devices (routers, switches, etc.). Generally, out-of-the-box network-type devices provide more information than their server counterparts. On the other hand, network devices do not extend very easily, if at all, in part because network hardware usually doesn't have a disk-based operating environment.* This keeps the end user from accessing the agent to make modifications or extend it. The rest of this section provides information about some of the software packages that are currently available for use as SNMP agents.

 Make sure that you understand what kind of software is running on your servers (email systems, accounting packages, etc.). Many applications will not listen or respond to SNMP requests, but will send out traps. Traps can be very useful for monitoring some of these applications. Also, there are applications for virus scanners, remote logins (pcAnywhere), and UPSs that will send informative traps when an error has been found. Look for this feature the next time you purchase any package or software suite.

HP Extensible SNMP Agent   *http://www.openview.hp.com*

Platforms	Solaris, HP-UX
Pros	Includes an *snmptrap* program and an HP agent that gives some additional functionality (mostly for HP systems). The agent is extensible using a subset of ASN.1.
Cons	Cost is per device. You have to keep track of multiple daemons.

---

* See Chapter 11 for a discussion of extensible agents.

Sun Microsystems   *http://www.sun.com*

Platforms   Solaris

Pros   Available free for most recent versions of Solaris. Comes bundled with Solaris (Versions 2.6 and up). The agent is extensible.

Cons   Very minimal; supports only MIB-II.

Concord SystemEDGE   *http://www.empire.com*

Platforms   Many flavors of Unix, Windows NT

Pros   Provides very detailed information about the system (CPU, disk space, filesystems, installed apps, etc.). Integrates with the Windows NT SNMP service. Log watcher for Unix and NT. The agent is fully extensible. Works with Concord's Network Health package and Trinagy's TREND suite.

Cons   Can be expensive unless you purchase in quantity.

Microsoft   *http://www.microsoft.com*

Platforms   Windows 9x/NT/2000

Pros   Built into the operating-system kernel. Can be controlled by NT services.

Cons   Meets only the minimal requirements of an SNMP-compatible agent. You must install the latest service pack after you install the software.

Net-SNMP*   *http://net-snmp.sourceforge.net*

Platforms   Many flavors of Unix, Windows 9x/NT

Pros   Free and fairly robust. Easily extensible using shell or Perl scripts. Includes a trap daemon.

Cons   Documentation is minimal, which means it can be difficult for first-time users to get it running the way they want.

SNMP Research   *http://www.int.snmp.com*

Platforms   Unix, Windows NT

Pros   Good toolkit for writing an agent, if this is the functionality you're looking for.

Cons   Does not integrate with Windows SNMP Service. Mostly a toolkit product; requires extensive work to make it useful.

NMS Suites

We use the term "suite" to mean a software package that bundles multiple applications into one convenient product. In this section, we discuss NMS software, which

---

* Formerly the UCD-SNMP project.

is one of the more important pieces of the network-management picture. Without it, the agent software in the previous section is virtually useless. NMS products allow you to have a total network view of your servers, routers, switches, etc. In most cases, this view is a graphical representation of your network, with lots of neat labels and icons. These packages are very configurable and work in almost any network environment. With this freedom, however, often comes a big price tag and a confusing setup process. Some of the products focus more on the network side of management (i.e., devices such as routers, hubs, and switches). Others go a step beyond this and allow you to customize server and workstation agents to integrate nicely into your NMSs. Keep in mind that the bigger packages are for larger, more complicated networks and require extensive training. Be sure to take some time to research the packages before purchasing; if at all possible, get trial versions. The rest of this section lists some of the more common NMS packages.

HP OpenView NNM   *http://www.openview.hp.com*

Platforms	Solaris, HP-UX, Windows NT/2000
Pros	Great mid- to large-business SNMP suite. While it can be complicated, it is manageable with a little help from OpenView support. Has a nice graphical map and event-monitoring system. Can do some historical trend analysis. Price seems right and can be trimmed by obtaining a license for a limited number of managed nodes.
Cons	Not many third-party application plug-ins available.

HP OpenView ITO   *http://www.openview.hp.com*

Platforms	Solaris, HP-UX, Windows NT/2000
Pros	If you're a Fortune 500 company looking to implement OpenView on steroids, ITO is your product. It is very user-centered. Maps, events, and more can be displayed or hidden based on a user's profile. The event system is more like a ticket center. A wealth of third-party "smart plug-ins" are available.
Cons	Price can be very high. Made for serious enterprise companies. Not many people can properly implement this without training or outside consulting help.

Tivoli Netview   *http://www.tivoli.com/products/index/netview/*

Platforms	OS/390, Solaris, AIX, Digital UNIX, Windows NT (Intel and Alpha)
Pros	A truly distributed network-management solution. It has the ability to detect problems at the source before they affect users.
Cons	This is a heavyweight management system that requires extensive investment and resources to implement and operate.

Castle Rock SNMPc   *http://www.castlerock.com*

Platforms   Windows 98/NT/2000

Pros   Great for small to midsize companies. Contains everything you need to get an
                NMS up and running in your environment. Price is very reasonable, and it's
                loaded with features.

Cons   Network map could use a little work. Doesn't give a realistic representation of
                your network.

BMC   *http://www.bmc.com*

Platforms   Many platforms, including Unix and Windows NT

Pros   BMC has developed knowledge bases for managing most aspects of the enter-
                prise, including networks, databases, and servers.

Cons   The knowledge modules are useful, but proprietary. The cost tends to be on
                the high side. Does not use SNMP as its native language.

Computer Associates Unicenter TNG Framework   *http://www.cai.com*

Platforms   Unix, Windows NT/2000

Pros   Can help you manage your entire IT business—everything from traditional
                network management to your Oracle database system.

Cons   This is another heavyweight management system that can take substantial
                time, resources, and money to implement.

Veritas NerveCenter   *http://www.veritas.com*

Platforms   Solaris, HP-UX, Windows NT

Pros   Uses behavior models (finite state machines) to model real-world network
                situations. NerveCenter is designed to be a standalone polling engine, or to be
                used in conjunction with OpenView's graphical map. Perl subroutines can be
                compiled into the polling engine for later use.

Cons   Takes more effort to maintain than OpenView, and tends to be more compli-
                cated to operate.

OpenRiver   *http://www.riversoft.com*

Platforms   Solaris

Pros   RiverSoft, the company behind OpenRiver, boasts that their NMS provides
                "interventionless network management." They also provide true layer 2 and 3
                network discovery. Despite the product's impressive abilities, it is priced very
                reasonably.

Cons   Currently available only for Solaris (although RiverSoft is planning a Windows
                NT release).

GxSNMP   *http://www.gxsnmp.org*

Platforms	Any Unix platform with an ANSI C compiler and the GTK/GDK toolkit installed
Pros	This free NMS comes with several nice features, such as a mapping tool (not auto discovery) and integration with SQL.
Cons	This project is still in its infancy (but there are many planned features that will make it a robust NMS solution).

Tkined   *http://wwwhome.cs.utwente.nl/~schoenw/scotty/*

Platforms	Most Unix platforms, Windows NT
Pros	Tkined is a free extensible network management platform. It provides a network map and tools to perform discovery of IP networks. It can also perform management of devices with SNMP and non-SNMP standards (*ping*, *traceroute*, etc.). Tcl is used to extend and add functionality to Tkined.
Cons	You must be familiar with Tcl to extend this package.

OpenNMS   *http://www.opennms.org*

Platforms	Any platform that supports Java
Pros	OpenNMS is an attempt to provide users with a truly open service and network-management product. It is written in Java and is released under the GNU Public License (GPL). It supports network discovery and distributed polling, among other things.
Cons	This project is still in its infancy.

Element Managers (Vendor-Specific Management)

These software packages are geared toward a certain type of vendor or function; for example, an element manager might be a product that focuses on managing a modem rack. Before purchasing such a package, take a good look at your present environment, how it's likely to grow, and what vendors you are currently using or are likely to use in the future. Because many of these products are vendor-specific, it's easy to buy something that turns out to be less useful than you expect. For example, CiscoView (part of the CiscoWorks suite) is a great piece of software; it does lots of fancy things, such as showing you the backs of your routers. However, if you purchase a number of Nortel devices a few months after installing this product, it won't be able to give you a unified view of your network. Some packages do allow you to manage their competitor's equipment; for example, an element manager that monitors switches may be able to handle switches from competing vendors. Before buying any of these products, research where your network is headed, and be sure to ask hard questions about the products' capabilities. The remainder of this section lists some of the available element managers.

Sun Management Center   *http://www.sun.com/symon/*

Platforms   Solaris, Windows (Console layer)

Pros   Provides a single point of management for all Sun servers, desktops, storage systems, the Solaris operating environment, applications, and datacenter services. This product scales to thousands of systems on a single, unified management platform and integrates easily with leading third-party platforms for added flexibility. It also has the ability to get real-time system performance and offers a free hardware diagnostic suite (plug-in) that detects hardware faults.

Cons   While it can manage and monitor other vendors, this ability doesn't come easily.

CiscoWorks 2000   *http://www.cisco.com*

Platforms   Solaris, HP-UX, AIX, Windows NT for some

Pros   This suite allows you to do everything from version control on your configuration files to latency graphs and detailed pictures of the backs of your devices. If you have a Cisco shop, stop everything and get this package!

Cons   The maps are a bit hokey. Doesn't produce a very friendly snapshot of your network, and has a hard time returning configurations to the devices. Would be nice if it could restore as easily as it backs up.

3Com Total Control   *http://www.3com.com*

Platforms   Solaris, Windows 9x

Pros   Allows the user to view the status of a modem rack by displaying an image of how the modem rack physically looks—everything down to the bolts and logo. The user can proceed to reset individual cards or reset the entire chassis, among other things. This is a very slick product and can be very useful when trying to track down equipment problems.

Cons   Since newer 3Com Total Control chassis can have up to 336 modems, this can be a bear to start (it has to query the status of all the modems in the rack). The startup time can be greatly affected by the speed of the network between you and the chassis in question.

Aprisma*   *http://www.spectrummgmt.com*

Platforms   Unix, Windows NT

Pros   Very good tool for managing Cabletron equipment, and is starting to add the ability to manage equipment from other vendors.

Cons   Complicated to set up and maintain. Meant for shops that need a high-end platform.

---

* Formerly Spectrum for Cabletron hardware.

Trend Analysis

When faced with most network problems, it's nice to have some kind of historical record to give you an idea of when things started going wrong. This allows you to go back and review what happened before a problem appeared, and possibly prevent it from recurring. If you want to be proactive about diagnosing problems before they appear, it is essential to know what "normal" means for your network—you need a set of baseline statistics that show you how your network normally behaves. While many of the bigger packages do some trend reporting, they can be clunky and hard to use. They might not even provide you with the kind of information you need. Once you see what a dedicated trend-analysis system can do, you will see why it might be worth the time, energy, and money to integrate one into your network-monitoring scheme.

If your environment calls for some serious monitoring, you should look into getting RMON probes. RMON probes are a great addition to trend-analysis packages, since most trend packages can make use of the kind of data these probes gather. The rest of this section lists some trend-analysis packages.

Concord eHealth   *http://www.concord.com*

Platforms   Solaris, HP-UX, Windows NT

Pros   Very professional, web-based graphs. Gives the user the ability to download and view reports in PDF. You can drill down in the web for more detailed reports. Great user management, allowing you to restrict users so that they see only what they need to see. Concord gives a free "Network Health Checkup." This is a great try-before-you-buy program. This program can also interact with probes and server-based devices to give a full trend analysis of your network and servers.

Cons   Some people may get sticker-shock when they see the price. Licensing is done on a per-element basis.

Trinagy* TREND   *http://www.desktalk.com*

Platforms   Unix, Windows 9x/NT

Pros   An excellent product for use in capacity planning. Out of the box, Trinagy supports 30, 60, and 90-day forecasts, among other calculations. Its report viewer is written in Java, so it is usable on most platforms. The report architecture is open, in that you can build your own reports.

Cons   Requires two weeks of training to run and administer. The pricing scheme is somewhat similar to eHealth's, since the size of the database depends on how many devices you query, how long you keep rate data around, etc. You can get more for less by tweaking polling intervals and retention times.

---

* Formerly DeskTalk Systems, Inc.

MRTG

http://www.mrtg.org

Platforms   Most Unix platforms, Windows NT

Pros   Free, easy to set up and use, very well documented. In addition to polling devices on your network, MRTG can receive input from non-SNMP sources.

Cons   Have to install multiple packages, which may be difficult to do on some platforms. For example, MRTG needs a specific SNMP Perl module to perform all of its polling duties. Not very scalable.

Cricket

http://cricket.sourceforge.net

Platforms   Most Unix platforms

Pros   Great tool that picks up where MRTG leaves off. It uses RRDTool, the next-generation version of MRTG.

Cons   Cricket is single-threaded, so collecting data from a good-sized network can take a while, especially if you gather usage data frequently. Having said that, it is fairly efficient, so you should not see any problem for quite some time.

InfoVista

http://www.infovista.com

Platforms   Unix, Windows NT

Pros   Very flexible and comes with some great reporting right out of the box.

Cons   Requires in-depth knowledge of network management and programming (Perl) in order to customize it to do anything beyond its out-of-the-box capabilities.

Supporting Software

Supporting software is a grab-bag that includes all sorts of things that are used in conjunction with the software packages listed earlier. Some of these packages can be used to write standalone SNMP applications. The rest of this section outlines several supporting software packages. Most of these are freely available and can be used with little or no previous experience.

Perl

http://www.perl.com
http://www.perl.org

Platforms   Unix, Windows NT, Mac OS

Pros   The *Practical Extraction and Report Language* (Perl) is a versatile, all-purpose scripting language that is the tool of choice for system administrators and network engineers, among others. Both MRTG and Cricket make use of Perl to perform their behind-the-scenes work.

Cons   Some people say that there are no cons to Perl. The most common complaint about the language is that it's interpreted and not compiled, like the C programming language.

SNMP Support for Perl

http://www.switch.ch/misc/leinen/snmp/perl/
http://www.cpan.org

Platforms	Unix, Windows NT, Mac OS
Pros	Supplies easy-to-use subroutines that give access to the core SNMP functions. Widely tested, as it's the fundamental SNMP engine for the MRTG package.
Cons	Doesn't seem to have a lot of market exposure.

WILMA

ftp://ftp.ldv.e-technik.tu-muenchen.de/dist/WILMA/INDEX.html

Platforms	Most Unix platforms
Pros	Contains the core SNMP functions as well as a MIB compiler and browser.
Cons	Functions could be a bit more streamlined and user-friendly.

Net-SNMP C Library

http://net-snmp.sourceforge.net

Platforms	Unix, Windows 9x/NT
Pros	This library can be used to develop your own SNMP applications. The library is very easy to use, once you figure it out. The nice thing about the package is that it comes with the source code to commands such as *snmpget, snmpset,* and *snmpwalk,* which can be used to see how these sorts of operations are accomplished.
Cons	The documentation on how to use the library is poor to the point of nonexistence.

Net-SNMP Perl Module

http://www.cpan.org/authors/id/GSM/

Platforms	Unix, Windows 9x/NT
Pros	This library provides identical functionality to the Net-SNMP C library, except in Perl.
Cons	During installation, this module needs to have access to the Net-SNMP C library in order to work properly.

A3Com

http://www.kernel.org/software/A3Com/

Platforms	Unix, Windows NT
Pros	A simple set of modules that can be used to manage 3Com SuperStack II 3900/9300 and CoreBuilder 3500 LAN switches. This can be a good start for management on a budget.
Cons	The functionality is limited.

SNMP++   *http://rosegarden.external.hp.com/snmp++/*

Platforms   Unix (Linux, HP-UX, and Solaris), Windows

Pros   If you need to use C++ for SNMP application development, this is the package to get. You can create powerful applications with minimal programming. This library has been released into the open source community and is freely available.

Cons   Requires knowledge of C++.

Netcool   *http://www.micromuse.com*

Platforms   Unix, Windows NT

Pros   An event-correlation and deduplication engine, used to cut down on the management events that traditional NMS platforms tend to generate by showing the end user only what she needs to know to fix network problems. It is designed to receive events from NMSs such as OpenView or Nerve-Center, but it can receive events from almost any kind of management source. Micromuse sells probes that can interface with everything from popular NMS platforms to telephone switch equipment.

Cons   Requires a bit of initial setup (but after that it's easy to use and maintain).

Network Computing Technologies Trap Receiver   *http://www.ncomtech.com*

Platforms   Windows 95/NT

Pros   Easy to use and can be configured to perform actions on received traps.

Cons   Doesn't run on any flavor of Unix.

6

Configuring Your NMS

Now that you have picked out some software to use in your environment, it's time to talk about installing and running it. In this chapter we will look at a few NMS packages in detail. While we listed several packages in Chapter 5, we will dig into only a few packages here, and we'll use these packages in examples throughout the rest of the book. These examples should allow you to get most other SNMP-based network-management packages up and running with very little effort.

HP's OpenView Network Node Manager

Network Node Manager (NNM) is a licensed software product. The package includes a feature called "Instant-On" that allows you to use the product for a limited time (60 days) while you are waiting for your real license to arrive. During this period, you are restricted to a 250-managed-node license, but the product's capabilities aren't limited in any other way. When you install the product, the Instant-On license is enabled by default.

 Check out the OpenView scripts located in OpenView's *bin* directory (normally */opt/OV/bin*). One particularly important group of scripts sets environment variables that allow you to traverse Open-View's directory structure much more easily. These scripts are named *ov.envvars.csh*, *ov.envvars.sh*, etc. (that is, *ov.envvars* followed by the name of the shell you're using). When you run the appropriate script for your shell, it defines environment variables such as $OV_BIN, $OV_MAN, and $OV_TMP, which point to the OpenView *bin*, *man*, and *tmp* directories. Thus, you can easily go to the directory containing OpenView's manual pages with the command *cd $OV_MAN*. These environment variables are used throughout this book and in all of OpenView's documentation.

Running NNM

To start the OpenView GUI on a Unix machine, define your DISPLAY environment variable and run the command *$OV_BIN/ovw*. This starts OpenView's NNM. If your NNM has performed any discovery, the nodes it has found should appear under your Internet (top-level) icon. If you have problems starting NNM, run the command *$OV_BIN/ovstatus −c* and then *$OV_BIN/ovstart* or *$OV_BIN/ovstop*, respectively, to start or stop it. By default, NNM installs the necessary scripts to start its daemons when the machine boots. OpenView will perform all of its functions in the background, even when you aren't running any maps. This means that you do not have to keep a copy of NNM running on your console at all times and you don't have to start it explicitly when your machine reboots.

When the GUI starts, it presents you with a clickable high-level map. This map, called the Root map, provides a top-level view of your network. The map gives you the ability to see your network without having to see every detail at once. If you want more information about any item in the display, whether it's a subnet or an individual node, click on it. You can drill down to see any level of detail you want—for example, you can look at an interface card on a particular node. The more detail you want, the more you click. Figure 6-1 shows a typical NNM map.

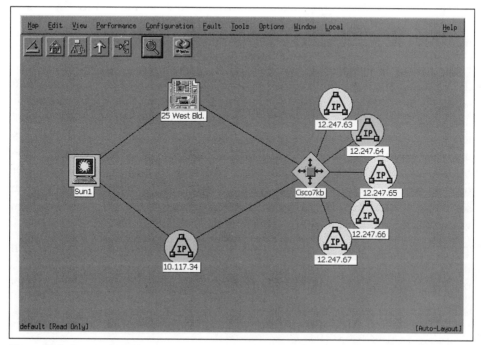

Figure 6-1. A typical NNM map

The menu bar (see Figure 6-2) allows you to traverse the map with a bit more ease. You have options such as closing NNM (the leftmost button), going straight to the Home map (second from the left),* the Root map (third-left), the parent or previous map (fourth-left), or the quick navigator.† There is also a button that lets you pan through the map or zoom in on a portion of it.

Figure 6-2. OpenView NNM menu bar

 Before you get sick looking at your newly discovered network, keep in mind that you can add some quick and easy customizations that will transform your hodgepodge of names, numbers, and icons into a coordinated picture of your network.

The netmon Process

NNM's daemon process (*netmon*) starts automatically when the system boots and is responsible for discovering nodes on your network, in addition to a few other tasks. In NNM's menu, go to "Options → Network Polling Configurations: IP." A window should appear that looks similar to Figure 6-3.

Figure 6-3 shows the General area of the configuration wizard. The other areas are IP Discovery, Status Polling, and Secondary Failures. The General area allows us to specify a filter (in this example, NOUSERS) that controls the discovery process—we might not want to see every device on the network. We discuss the creation of filters later in this chapter, in the section "Using OpenView Filters." We elected to discover beyond the license limit, which means that NNM will discover more objects on our network than our license allows us to manage. "Excess" objects (objects past the license's limit) are placed in an unmanaged state, so that you can see them on your maps but can't control them through NNM. This option is useful when your license limits you to a specific number of managed nodes.

The IP Discovery area (Figure 6-4) lets us enable or disable the discovery of IP nodes. Using the "auto adjust" discovery feature allows NNM to figure out how often to probe the network for new devices. The more new devices it finds, the

---

* You can set any map as your Home map. When you've found the map you'd like to use, go to "Map → Submap → Set This Submap as Home."

† This is a special map in which you can place objects that you need to watch frequently. It allows you to access them quickly without having to find them by searching through the network map.

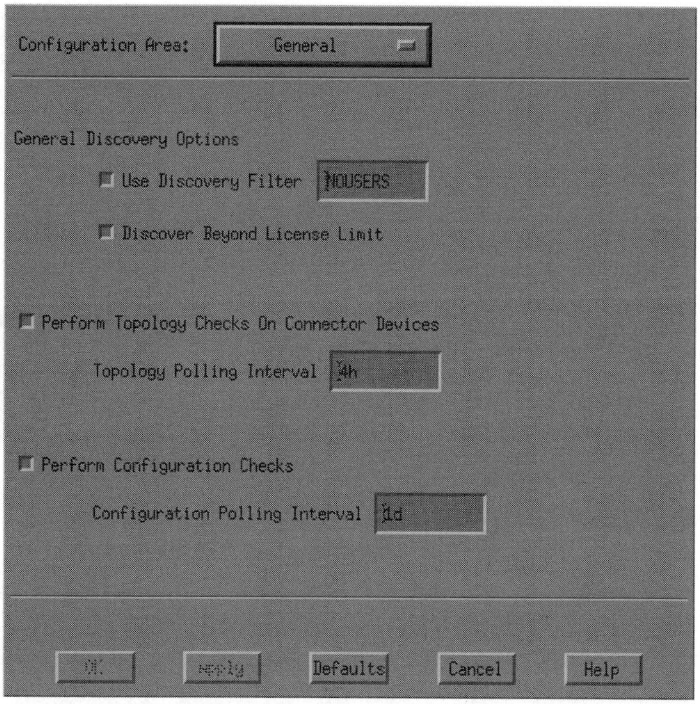

Figure 6-3. OpenView's General network polling configuration options

more often it polls; if it doesn't find any new devices it slows down, eventually waiting one day (1d) before checking for any new devices. If you don't like the idea that the discovery interval varies (or perhaps more realistically, if you think that probing the network to find new devices will consume more resources than you like, either on your network-management station or the network itself), you can specify a fixed discovery interval. Finally, the "Discover Level-2 Objects" button tells NNM to discover and report devices that are at the second layer of the OSI network model. This category includes things such as unmanaged hubs and switches, many AppleTalk devices, and so on.

Figure 6-5 shows the Status Polling configuration area. Here you can turn status polling on or off, and delete nodes that have been down or unreachable for a specified length of time. This example is configured to delete nodes after they've been down for one week (1w).

The DHCP polling options are, obviously, especially useful in environments that use DHCP. They allow you to establish a relationship between polling behavior and IP addresses. You can specify a filter that selects addresses that are assigned by DHCP. Then you can specify a time after which *netmon* will delete non-responding DHCP addresses from its map of your network. If a device is down for

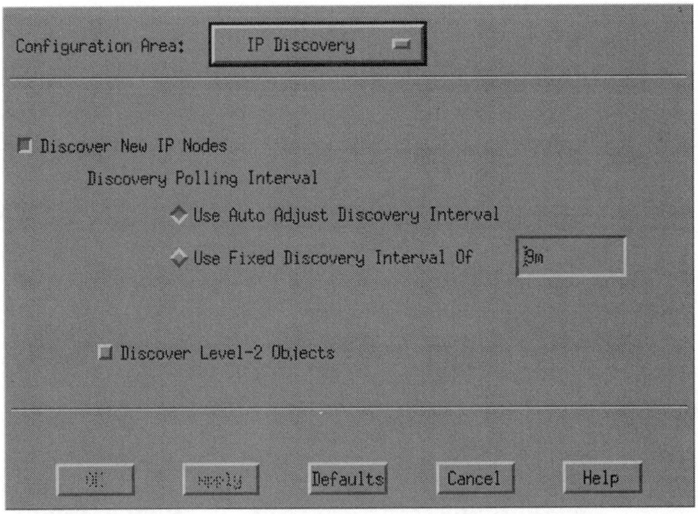

Figure 6-4. OpenView's IP Discovery network polling configuration options

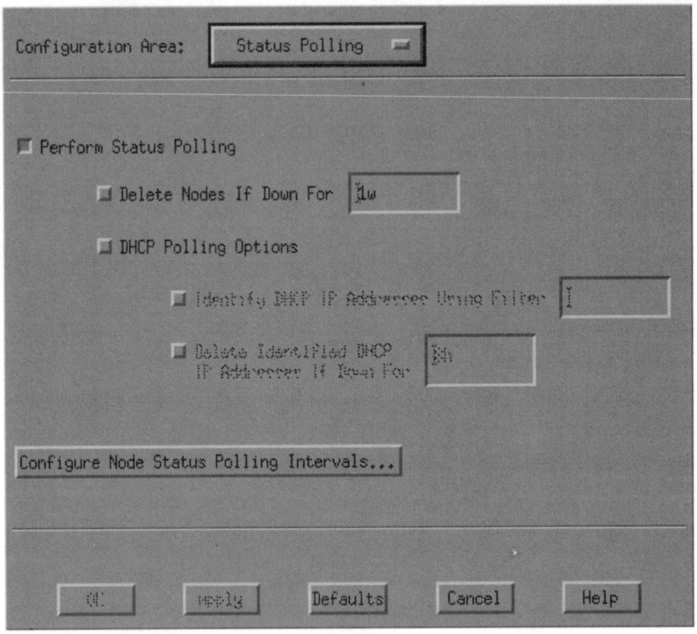

Figure 6-5. OpenView's Status Polling network polling configuration options

the given amount of time, *netmon* disassociates the node and IP address. The rationale for this behavior is simple: in a DHCP environment, the disappearance of an IP address often means that the node has received a new IP address from a

DHCP server. In that case, continuing to poll the old address is a waste of effort and is possibly even misleading, since the address may be reassigned to a different host.

Finally, the Secondary Failures configuration area shown in Figure 6-6 allows you to tell the poller how to react when it sees a secondary failure. This occurs when a node beyond a failed device is unreachable; for example, when a router goes down, making the file server that is connected via one of the router's interfaces unreachable. In this configuration area, you can state whether to show alarms for the secondary failures or suppress them. If you choose to suppress them, you can set up a filter that identifies important nodes in your network that won't get suppressed even if they are deemed secondary failures.

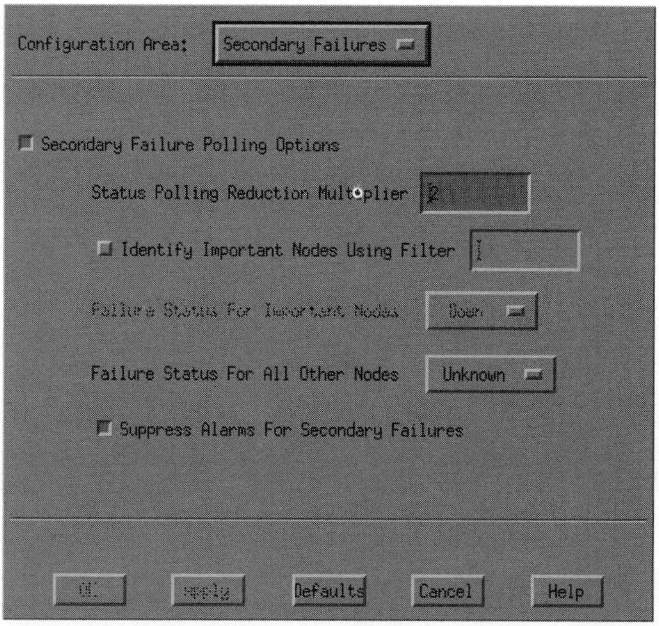

Figure 6-6. OpenView's Secondary Failures network polling configuration options

Once your map is up, you may notice that nothing is getting discovered. Initially, *netmon* won't discover anything beyond the network segment to which your NMS is attached. If your NMS has an IP address of 24.92.32.12, you will not discover your devices on 123.67.34.0. NNM finds adjacent routers and their segments, as long as they are SNMP-compatible, and places them in an unmanaged (tan colored) state on the map.* This means that anything in and under that icon will not be polled or

---

* In NNM, go to "Help → Display Legend" for a list of icons and their colors.

discovered. Selecting the icon and going to "Edit → Manage Objects" tells NNM to begin managing this network and allows *netmon* to start discovering nodes within it. You can quit managing nodes at any time by clicking on UnManage instead of Manage.

If your routers do not show any adjacent networks, you should try testing them with "Fault → Test IP/TCP/SNMP." Add the name of your router, click "Restart," and see what kind of results you get back. If you get "OK except for SNMP," review Chapter 7 and read the next section, "Configuring Polling Intervals," on setting up the default community names within OpenView.

netmon also allows you to specify a seed file that helps it to discover objects faster. The seed file contains individual IP addresses, IP address ranges, or domain names that narrow the scope of hosts that are discovered. You can create the seed file with any text editor—just put one address or hostname on each line. Placing the addresses of your gateways in the seed file sometimes makes the most sense, since gateways maintain ARP tables for your network. *netmon* will subsequently discover all the other nodes on your network, thus freeing you from having to add all your hosts to the seed file. For more useful information, see the documentation for the *-s* switch to *netmon* and the Local Registration Files (LRF).

NNM has another utility, called *loadhosts*, that lets you add nodes to the map one at a time. Here is an example of how you can add hosts, in a sort of freeform mode, to the OpenView map. Note the use of the *-m* option, which sets the subnet to 255.255.255.0:

```
$ loadhosts -m 255.255.255.0
10.1.1.12 gwrouter1
```

Once you have finished adding as many nodes as you'd like, press Ctrl-d to exit the command.

Configuring Polling Intervals

The SNMP Configuration page is located off of the main screen in "Options → SNMP Configuration." A window similar to the one in Figure 6-7 should appear. This window has four sections: Specific Nodes, IP Address Wildcards, Default, and the entry area (chopped off for viewing purposes). Each section contains the same general areas: Node or IP Address, Get Community, Set Community, Proxy (if any), Timeout, Retry, Port, and Polling. The Default area, which unfortunately is at the bottom of the screen, sets up the default behavior for SNMP on your network—that is, the behavior (community strings, etc.) for all hosts that aren't listed as "specific nodes" or that match one of the wildcards. The Specific Nodes section allows you to specify exceptions, on a per node basis. IP Address Wildcards allows you to configure properties for a range of addresses. This is especially useful if you have networks that have different *get* and *set* community names.* All areas allow you to specify a Timeout in seconds and a Retry value. The Port field gives you the option of inserting a different port number (the default port is 161). Polling is the frequency at which you would like to poll your nodes.

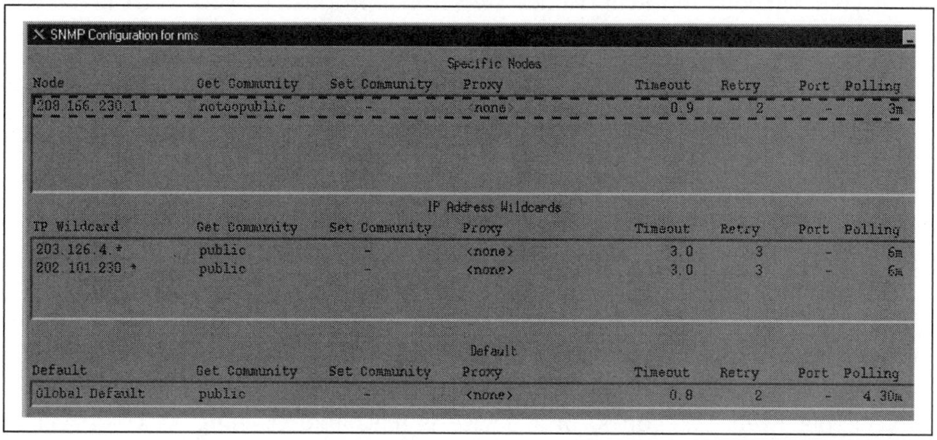

			Specific Nodes				
Node	Get Community	Set Community	Proxy	Timeout	Retry	Port	Polling
208.166.230.1	notsopublic	-	<none>	0.9	2	-	3m

			IP Address Wildcards				
IP Wildcard	Get Community	Set Community	Proxy	Timeout	Retry	Port	Polling
203.126.4.*	public	-	<none>	3.0	3	-	6m
202.101.230.*	public	-	<none>	3.0	3	-	6m

			Default				
Default	Get Community	Set Community	Proxy	Timeout	Retry	Port	Polling
Global Default	public	-	<none>	0.8	2	-	4.30m

Figure 6-7. OpenView's SNMP Configuration page

It's important to understand how timeouts and retries work. If we look at Specific Nodes, we see a Timeout of .9 seconds and a Retry of 2 for 208.166.230.1. If OpenView doesn't get a response within .9 seconds, it tries again (the first retry) and waits 1.8 seconds. If it still doesn't get anything back, it doubles the timeout period again to 3.6 seconds (the second retry); if it still doesn't get anything back it declares the node unreachable and paints it red on the NNM's map. With these Timeout and Retry values, it takes about 6 seconds to identify an unreachable node.

Imagine what would happen if we had a Timeout of 4 seconds and a Retry of 5. By the fifth try we would be waiting 128 seconds, and the total process would take 252 seconds. That's over four minutes! For a mission-critical device, four minutes can be a long time for a failure to go unnoticed.

This example shows that you must be very careful about your Timeout and Retry settings—particularly in the Default area, because these settings apply to most of your network. Setting your Timeout and Retry too high and your Polling periods too low will make *netmon* fall behind; it will be time to start over before the

---

* These community names are used in different parts throughout NNM. For example, when polling an object with *xnmbrowser*, you won't need to enter (or remember) the community string if it (or its network) is defined in the SNMP configurations.

poller has worked through all your devices.* This is a frequent problem when you have many nodes, slow networks, small polling times, and high numbers for Timeout and Retry.† Once a system falls behind, it will take a long time to discover problems with the devices it is currently monitoring, as well as to discover new devices. In some cases, NNM may not discover problems with downed devices at all! If your Timeout and Retry values are set inappropriately, you won't be able to find problems and will be unable to respond to outages.

Falling behind can be very frustrating. We recommend starting your Polling period very high and working your way down until you feel comfortable. Ten to twenty minutes is a good starting point for the Polling period. During your initial testing phase, you can always set a wildcard range for your test servers, etc.

A Few Words About NNM Map Colors

By now discovery should be taking place, and you should be starting to see some new objects appear on your map. You should see a correlation between the colors of these objects and the colors in NNM's Event Categories (see Chapter 10 for more about Event Categories). If a device is reachable via *ping*, its color will be green. If the device cannot be reached, it will turn red. If something "underneath" the device fails, the device will become off-green, indicating that the device itself is okay, but something underneath it has reached a nonnormal status. For example, a router may be working, but a web server on the LAN behind it may have failed. The status source for an object like this is Compound or Propagated. (The other types of status source are Symbol and Object.) The Compound status source is a great way to see if there is a problem at a lower level while still keeping an eye on the big picture. It alerts you to the problem and allows you to start drilling down until you reach the object that is under duress.

It's always fun to shut off or unplug a machine and watch its icon turn red on the map. This can be a great way to demonstrate the value of the new management system to your boss. You can also learn how to cheat and make OpenView miss a device, even though it was unplugged. With a relatively long polling interval, it's easy to unplug a device and plug it back in before OpenView has a chance to notice that the device isn't there. By the time OpenView gets around to it, the node is back up and looks fine. Long polling intervals make it easy to miss such temporary failures. Lower polling intervals make it less likely that OpenView will miss something, but more likely that *netmon* will fall behind, and in turn miss other failures. Take small steps so as not to crash or overload *netmon* or your network.

---

* Keep in mind that most of NNM's map is polled using regular *ping*s and not SNMP.

† Check the manpage for *netmon* for the *−a* switch, especially around *−a12*. You can try to execute *net-mon* with an *−a \ ?*, which will list all the valid *−a* options. If you see any negative numbers in *netmon. trace* after running *netmon −a12*, your system is running behind.

Using OpenView Filters

Your map may include some devices you don't need, want, or care about. For example, you may not want to poll or manage users' PCs, particularly if you have many users and a limited license. It may be worthwhile for you to ignore these user devices to open more slots for managing servers, routers, switches, and other more important devices. *netmon* has a filtering mechanism that allows you to control precisely which devices you manage. It lets you filter out unwanted devices, cleans up your maps, and can reduce the amount of management traffic on your network.

In this book, we warn you repeatedly that polling your network the wrong way can generate huge amounts of management traffic. This happens when people or programs use default polling intervals that are too fast for the network or the devices on the network to handle. For example, a management system might poll every node in your 10.1.0.0 network—conceivably thousands of them—every two minutes. The poll may consist of SNMP *get* or *set* requests, simple *ping*s, or both. OpenView's NNM uses a combination of these to determine if a node is up and running. Filtering saves you (and your management) the trouble of having to pick through a lot of useless nodes and reduces the load on your network. Using a filter allows you to keep the critical nodes on your network in view. It allows you to poll the devices you care about and ignore the devices you don't care about. The last thing you want is to receive notification each time a user turns off his PC when he leaves for the night.

Filters also help network management by letting you exclude DHCP users from network discovery and polling. DHCP and BOOTP are used in many environments to manage large IP address pools. While these protocols are useful, they can make network management a nightmare, since it's often hard to figure out what's going on when addresses are being assigned, deallocated, and recycled.

In my environment we use DHCP only for our users. All servers and printers have hardcoded IP addresses. With our setup, we can specify all the DHCP clients and then state that we want everything *but* these clients in our discovery, maps, etc. The following example should get most users up and running with some pretty good filtering. Take some time to review OpenView's "A Guide to Scalability and Distribution for Network Node Manager" manual for more in-depth information on filtering.

The default filter file, which is located in *$OV_CONF/C*, is broken up into three sections:

- Sets
- Filters
- FilterExpressions

In addition, lines that begin with // are comments. // comments can appear anywhere; some of the other statements have their own comment fields built in.

Sets allow you to place individual nodes into a group. This can be useful if you want to separate users based on their geographic locations, for example. You can then use these groups or any combination of IP addresses to specify your Filters, which are also grouped by name. You then can take all of these groupings and combine them into FilterExpressions. If this seems a bit confusing, it is! Filters can be very confusing, especially when you add complex syntax and not so logical logic (&&, ||, etc.). The basic syntax for defining Sets, Filters, and FilterExpressions looks like this:

```
name "comments or description" { contents }
```

Every definition contains a name, followed by comments that appear in double quotes, and then the command surrounded by brackets. Our default filter,[*] named **filters**, is located in *$OV_CONF/C* and looks like this:

```
// lines that begin with // are considered COMMENTS and are ignored!
// Begin of MyCompanyName Filters

Sets {

    dialupusers "DialUp Users" { "dialup100", " dialup101", \
                " dialup102" }
}

Filters {

    ALLIPRouters "All IP Routers" { isRouter }

    SinatraUsers "All Users in the Sinatra Plant" { \
        ("IP Address" ~ 199.127.4.50-254) || \
        ("IP Address" ~ 199.127.5.50-254) || \
        ("IP Address" ~ 199.127.6.50-254) }

    MarkelUsers "All Users in the Markel Plant" { \
        ("IP Address" ~ 172.247.63.17-42) }

    DialAccess "All DialAccess Users" { "IP Hostname" in dialupusers }
}

FilterExpressions
{
    ALLUSERS "All Users" { SinatraUsers || MarkelUsers || DialAccess }

    NOUSERS "No Users " { !ALLUSERS }
}
```

---

[*] Your filter, if right out of the box, will look much different. The one shown here is trimmed to ease the pains of writing a filter.

Now let's break this file down into pieces to see what it does.

Sets

First, we defined a Set* called `dialupusers` containing the hostnames (from DNS) that our dial-up users will receive when they dial into our facility. These are perfect examples of things we don't want to manage or monitor in our OpenView environment.

Filters

The Filters section is the only nonoptional section. We defined four filters: `ALLIPRouters`, `SinatraUsers`, `MarkelUsers`, and `DialAccess`. The first filter says to discover nodes that have field value `isRouter`. OpenView can set the object attribute for a managed device to values such as `isRouter`, `isHub`, `isNode`, etc.† These attributes can be used in Filter expressions to make it easier to filter on groups of managed objects, as opposed to IP address ranges, for example.

The next two filters specify IP address ranges. The `SinatraUsers` filter is the more complex of the two. In it, we specify three IP address ranges, each separated by logical OR symbols (`||`). The first range (`("IP Address" ~ 199.127.6.50-254)`) says that if the IP address is in the range 199.127.6.50–199.127.6.254, then filter it and ignore it. If it's not in this range, the filter looks at the next range to see if it's in that one. If it's not, the filter looks at the final IP range. If the IP address isn't in any of the three ranges, the filter allows it to be discovered and subsequently managed by NNM. Other logical operators should be familiar to most programmers: && represents a logical AND, and ! represents a logical NOT.

The final filter, `DialAccess`, allows us to exclude all systems that have a hostname listed in the `dialupusers` set, which was defined at the beginning of the file.

FilterExpressions

The next section, FilterExpressions, allows us to combine the filters we have previously defined with additional logic. You can use a FilterExpression anywhere you would use a Filter. Think of it like this: you create complex expressions using Filters, which in turn can use Sets in the `contents` parts of their expressions. You can then use FilterExpressions to create simpler yet more robust expressions. In our case, we take all the filters from above and place them into a FilterExpression called `ALLUSERS`. Since we want our NNM map to contain nonuser devices, we then define a group called `NOUSERS` and tell it to ignore all user-type devices with

---

* These Sets have nothing to do with the *snmpset* operation with which we have become familiar.

† Check out the $OV_FIELDS area for a list of fields.

the command !ALLUSERS. As you can see, FilterExpressions can also aid in making things more readable. When you have finished setting up your filter file, use the *$OV_BIN/ovfiltercheck* program to check your new filters' syntax. If there are any problems, it will let you know so you can fix them.

Now that we have our filters defined, we can apply them by using the *ovtopofix* command or the polling configuration menu shown in Figure 6-3.

If you want to remove nodes from your map, use *$OV_BIN/ovtopofix –f FILTER_ NAME*. Let's say that someone created a new DHCP scope without telling you and suddenly all the new users are now on the map. You can edit the filters file, create a new group with the IP address range of the new DHCP scope, add it to the ALLUSERS FilterExpression, run *ovfiltercheck*, and, if there are no errors, run *$OV_ BIN/ovtopofix –f NOUSERS* to update the map on the fly. Then stop and restart *netmon*—otherwise it will keep discovering these unwanted nodes using the old filter. I find myself running *ovtopofix* every month or so to take out some random nodes.

Loading MIBs into OpenView

Before you continue exploring OpenView's NNM, take time to load some vendor-specific MIBs.[*] This will help you later on when you start interacting (polling, graphing, etc.) more with SNMP-compatible devices. Go to "Options → Load/ Unload MIBs: SNMP." This presents you with a window in which you can add vendor-specific MIBs to your database. Alternatively, you can run the command *$OV_BIN/xnmloadmib* and bypass having to go through NNM directly.

That's the end of our brief tour of OpenView configuration. It's impossible to provide a complete introduction to configuring OpenView in this chapter, so we tried to provide a survey of the most important aspects of getting it running. There can be no substitute for the documentation and manual pages that come with the product itself.

Castle Rock's SNMPc Enterprise Edition

We'll end the chapter with a brief discussion of Castle Rock's SNMPc, Version 5.0, which runs on Windows NT/2000. SNMPc is a simpler product than OpenView in many respects. However, even though it's simpler, it's far from featureless. It's also cheaper than OpenView, which makes it ideal for shops that don't have a lot of money to spend on an NMS platform but need the support and backing that a commercial product provides.

---

[*] Some platforms and environments refer to loading a MIB as compiling it.

Installation of SNMPc is straightforward. The installer asks for the license number and a discovery seed device. The seed device is similar to a seed file for Open-View's *netmon*. In the case of SNMPc, we recommend giving it the IP address (or hostname) of your gateway, since this device can be used to discover other segments of your network. Omitting the discovery seed device will not keep SNMPc from performing discovery but will limit it to the devices on the network to which it's directly connected.

SNMPc's Map

Once SNMPc is up and running, you will see any devices it has discovered in the Root map view. Figure 6-8 shows the main button bar. The far right button (the house) gets you to the highest level on the map. The zooming tools allow you to pan in and out of the map, increasing or decreasing the amount of detail it shows. You can also reach the Root submap by selecting "Map View → Root submap" from the View menu.

Figure 6-8. SNMPc main button bar

Discovery and Filters

Once you are done playing around with your maps, it's time to start tuning your polling parameters. Go to "Config → Discovery Agents." This should bring up a menu that looks like Figure 6-9. Looking at the menu tabs, it's easy to tell that you will be able to configure your Seeds, Communities, and Filters here. SNMPc filters are equivalent to OpenView filters, but much simpler.

The General tab lets you control SNMPc's polling and discovery behavior. The checkbox for enabling and disabling discovery is self-explanatory. The "Enable Status Polling" checkbox determines if SNMPc will *ping* the nodes on your network periodically to determine whether or not they are responding. By default, all nodes are polled every 10 to 30 seconds. To change these default values, you can either edit the properties of each device (one by one), select and highlight multiple devices (using your Ctrl key), or use the object selection tool. You can bring up this tool by using the third button from the left on the main button bar or by going to "View → Selection Tool." The "Discover Ping Nodes" checkbox lets you specify if you want to discover devices that have an IP or IPX entity but do not have an SNMP agent. "Discover IPX Nodes" gives you the option of discovering IPX devices. SNMPc will also check if a device supports various protocols such as SMTP, HTTP, etc. This feature allows you to set up custom menu items based on

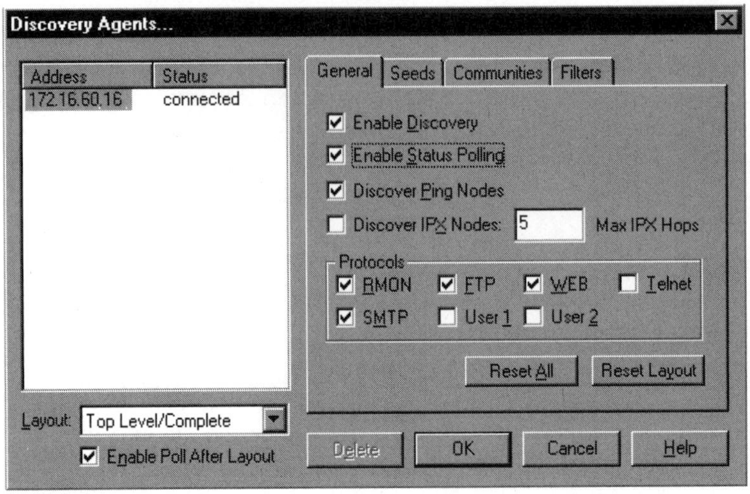

Figure 6-9. SNMPc Discovery Agents menu

what services the device is running. The Protocols section of the General tab lets you specify the protocols for which SNMPc will test.

The Seeds tab allows you to specify SNMP devices that will help the discovery process along. This tab allows you to specify more than one seed IP address. (Remember that you're asked for a seed address device when you install the product.)

The Communities tab lets you specify the community strings for your network. You can specify multiple community names; SNMPc will try the different community names when discovering your nodes. Once SNMPc figures out which community is correct for a given device, it inserts the community string in the "Get Community" attribute for that particular device. This simply means the newly discovered device will be saved with its community string.

The final tab, Filters, allows you to exclude certain IP addresses from being discovered. You can specify individual addresses, or use an asterisk (*) as a wildcard to specify entire networks.

Loading MIBs into SNMPc

Like any reasonably comprehensive network-management product, SNMPc can load and compile new MIBs. To do so, select "Config → MIB Database" from the main menu bar. This window lets you specify the path to the MIB file and gives you full feedback about the status of the compilation, etc. Click on the "Help" button for more information about MIB compilation.

SNMPc is a compact NMS that provides some added features, such as trend reporting. A thorough treatment of its installation is beyond the scope of this book. The online help system that comes with SNMPc is very good, and we recommend you take full advantage of it.

7

Configuring SNMP Agents

By this time you should understand what an SNMP agent is: it's nothing more than software that lives on the device you want to monitor. It responds to requests from the NMS and generates traps. This chapter discusses how to configure agents. It starts by defining some standard configuration parameters that are common to all SNMP agents, then goes into some advanced parameters you might run into when configuring your equipment. The bulk of this chapter walks through the configuration for a number of common devices, paying attention to security issues.

Parameter Settings

All SNMP devices share the following common configurable parameters:

- *sysLocation*
- *sysContact*
- *sysName*
- Read-write and read-only access community strings (and frequently, a trap community string)
- Trap destination

sysLocation is the physical location for the device being monitored. Its definition in RFC 1213 is:

```
sysLocation OBJECT-TYPE
    SYNTAX  DisplayString (SIZE (0..255))
    ACCESS  read-write
    STATUS  mandatory
    DESCRIPTION
        "The physical location of this node (e.g., 'telephone closet,
        3rd floor')."
    ::= { system 6 }
```

As you can see, its **SYNTAX** is **DisplayString**, which means it can be an ASCII string of characters; its size is declared to be at most 255 characters. This particular object is useful for determining where a device is located. This kind of practical information is essential in a large network, particularly if it's spread over a wide area. If you have a misbehaving switch, it's very convenient to be able to look up the switch's physical location. Unfortunately, *sysLocation* frequently isn't set when the device is installed and even more often isn't changed when the device is moved. Unreliable information is worse than no information, so use some discipline and keep your devices up to date.

RFC 1213's definition of *sysContact* is similar to that of *sysLocation*:

```
sysContact OBJECT-TYPE
    SYNTAX  DisplayString (SIZE (0..255))
    ACCESS  read-write
    STATUS  mandatory
    DESCRIPTION
        "The textual identification of the contact person for this managed
        node, together with information on how to contact this person."
    ::= { system 4 }
```

sysContact is a **DisplayString**. It's fairly obvious what it's used for: it identifies the primary contact for the device in question. It is important to set this object with an appropriate value, as it can help your operations staff determine who needs to be contacted in the event of some catastrophic failure. You can also use it to make sure you're notified, if you're responsible for a given device, when someone needs to take your device down for maintenance or repairs. As with *sysLocation*, make sure to keep this information up to date as your staff changes. It's not uncommon to find devices for which the *sysContact* is someone who left the company several years ago.

sysName should be set to the *fully-qualified domain name* (FQDN) for the managed device. In other words, it's the hostname associated with the managed device's IP address. The RFC 1213 definition follows:

```
sysName OBJECT-TYPE
    SYNTAX  DisplayString (SIZE (0..255))
    ACCESS  read-write
    STATUS  mandatory
    DESCRIPTION
        "An administratively-assigned name for this managed node. By
        convention, this is the node's fully-qualified domain name."
    ::= { system 5 }
```

The read-only and read-write parameters are the community strings for read-only and read-write access. Notice that *sysLocation*, *sysContact*, and *sysName* all have **ACCESS** values of **read-write**. With the appropriate read-write community string, anyone can change the definition of these objects and many more objects of significantly greater importance. Ultimately, it's not a huge problem if somebody maliciously makes your router lie about its location—you probably already know that it isn't located in Antarctica. But someone who can do this can also fiddle with your routing tables and do other kinds of much more serious damage. Someone who has only the read-only community string can certainly find out more information about your network than you would like to reveal to an outsider. Setting the community strings is extremely important to maintaining a secure environment. Most devices are shipped with default community strings that are well known. Don't assume that you can put off setting your community strings until later.

The trap destination parameters specify the addresses to which traps are sent. There's nothing really magical here—since traps are asynchronous notifications generated by your devices, the agent needs to know who should receive notification. Many devices support authentication-failure traps, which are generated if someone attempts to access them using incorrect community strings. This feature is extremely useful, as it allows you to detect attempts to break into your devices. Many devices also support the ability to include a community string with traps; you can configure the network-management station to respond only to traps that contain the proper community string.

Many devices have additional twists on the access and trap parameters. For example, Cisco devices allow you to create different community strings for different parts of the MIB—you can use this to allow people to set some variables, but not others. Many vendors allow you to place restrictions on the hosts that are allowed to make SNMP requests. That is, the device will respond only to requests from certain IP addresses, regardless of the community string.

The range of configuration options you're likely to run into is limited only by the imagination of the vendors, so it's obviously impossible for us to describe everything you might encounter. The "Agent Configuration Walkthroughs" section later in this chapter will give you an idea of how some agents implement the standard configuration parameters and a little insight into what other features might be available.

Security Concerns

Chapter 2 discussed the security issues with SNMPv1 and SNMPv2. The biggest problem, of course, is that the read-only and read-write community strings are sent as clear-text strings; the agent or the NMS performs no encryption. Therefore, the community strings are available to anyone with access to a packet sniffer. That certainly means almost anyone on your network with a PC and the ability to download widely available software. Does that make you uncomfortable? It should.

Obviously, you need to take the same precautions with the community strings that you would with your superuser or administrator passwords. Choose community strings that are hard to guess. Mixed-case alphanumeric strings are good choices for community strings; don't use dictionary words. Although someone with the read-only community string can't do as much damage as someone with the read-write string, you might as well take the same precautions for both. Don't forget to change your community strings—most devices ship with preconfigured community strings that are extremely easy to guess.

That doesn't solve the problems with packet sniffers. When you're configuring an agent, it's a good idea to limit the devices that can make SNMP requests (assuming that your agent allows you to make this restriction). That way, even if someone gets the community strings, he'll have to spoof the IP address of one of your management stations to do any damage.

Of course, many people know how to spoof IP addresses these days, and it's not a really good idea to assume that you can trust your employees. A better solution to the problem is to prevent the SNMP packets from being visible on your external network connections and parts of your network where you don't want them to appear. This requires configuring your routers and firewalls with access lists that block SNMP packets from the outside world (which may include parts of your own network). If you don't trust the users of your network, you may want to set up a separate administrative network to be used for SNMP queries and other management operations. This is expensive and inflexible—it's hard to imagine extending such a network beyond your core routers and servers—but it may be what your situation requires.

If you want to use SNMP to monitor your network from home, be extremely careful. You do not want your community strings traveling over the public Internet in an unencrypted form. If you plan to use SNMP tools directly from home, make sure to install VPN software, or some form of tunneling, to keep your SNMP traffic private. A better approach to home monitoring is to use a web interface; by using SSL, you can prevent others from seeing your usage graphs. (No network-management products that we're aware of support SSL out of the box; but they do allow you to integrate with external servers, such as Apache, which do support SSL).

SNMPv3 (discussed in Appendix F) fixes most of the security problems; in particular, it makes sure that the community strings are always encrypted. Unfortunately, there are very few implementations of SNMPv3 out there. It's clear what direction you want to head in, but you can't get there yet.

Agent Configuration Walkthroughs

In the following sections we will walk through the configurations of some typical SNMP agents. We have chosen devices that are found on almost every modern network (x86 PCs, Unix Servers, routers, UPSs, etc.). The point of this discussion isn't to show you how your particular agent is configured—that would not be practical, given the hundreds of devices and vendors out there. Our intent is to give you a feel for what the common options are, and what steps you'll typically go through to configure an agent.

Windows 95/98 Agent

In this section, we'll walk through the SNMP configuration for the Windows 95/98 agent, using the Windows System Policy Editor. The settings are all stored in the registry, so you can also make changes to the configuration using *regedit*, but there's less chance of error if you use the System Policy Editor. It's worth noting that Windows 95, 98, and NT all have the same SNMP entries in the registry, so configuration for these operating systems is similar. It's also worth noting that Microsoft's SNMP agent isn't terribly robust, although it's adequate if you want only basic SNMP functionality. Other agents are available; Concord's SystemEDGE and Castle Rock's SNMPc support the Microsoft operating systems.

Unless you are completely comfortable taking the registry editing leap, we strongly recommend that you use the System Policy Editor to make agent configuration changes. Incorrect settings in the registry can result in serious system problems. Consider yourself warned.

The Windows System Policy Editor comes with the Windows 95/98 Resource Kit, and must be installed before you can configure the SNMP agent. The first time you run the System Policy Editor it will ask you for an *.adm* file. Select *C:\WINDOWS\ INF\ADMIN.ADM* as this file. Select "File → Open Registry," then double-click the Local Computer icon. In the Policies tab, click down the plus signs until you reach Network and then SNMP. This should leave you with four SNMP agent configuration items. Figure 7-1 shows what your window should look like. To enable an option, place a check next to it. When you are finished, click "OK," then "File → Save" at the main screen. If you don't follow these steps, your configuration won't be saved to the registry.

The "Communities" settings allow you to define your community strings. Check the box and then click "Show" in the lower section. This brings up another window showing your community strings. To create a new community, click "Add" and then enter the string. Repeat the steps, if appropriate, for your site. If this option is left unchecked, or if it is checked but no community names are listed, the agent will answer all SNMP requests it receives. The next checkbox item, "Permitted managers," specifies what NMSs can access this agent. You can identify your management stations by IPX addresses, IP addresses, or DNS names. For example, you can use this item to restrict SNMP access to a particular NMS. If

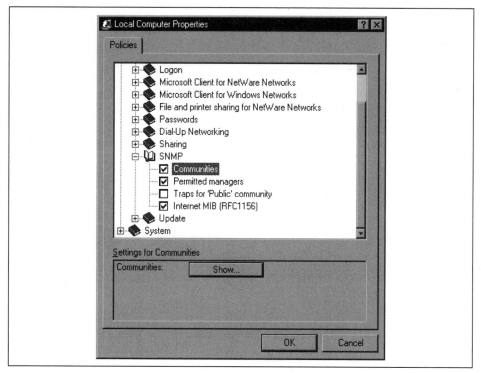

Figure 7-1. Windows 95/98 System Policy Editor

the "Permitted managers" box is unchecked or is checked but has no entries, the agent will answer all requests, no matter where they come from. Checking "Traps for 'Public' community" allows you to designate up to five NMSs to receive traps. The last setting, "Internet MIB (RFC1156)," allows you to set the Contact Name (*sysContact*) and Location (*sysLocation*) objects.

Remember to save your changes using "File → Save" at the main menu of the System Policy Editor. Figure 7-2 shows what the 'entries look like in the Registry Editor, after you've used the Policy Editor to set them.

Windows NT 4.0 and Windows 2000 Agent

To configure the SNMP service in Windows NT 4.0 and 2000, start in the Control Panel and double-click on the Network icon. Click on the Services tab, select "SNMP Service," and click on the "Properties" button. If "SNMP Service" isn't listed, you need to add it. Press the "Add" button and select "SNMP Service" from the list of services. It will prompt you for your Windows NT system disk, so be sure to have it ready. For Windows 2000, go to the Control Panel and click on "Add/ Remove Programs." When the window pops up click on "Add/Remove Windows Components," then select "Management and Monitoring Tools." This should bring

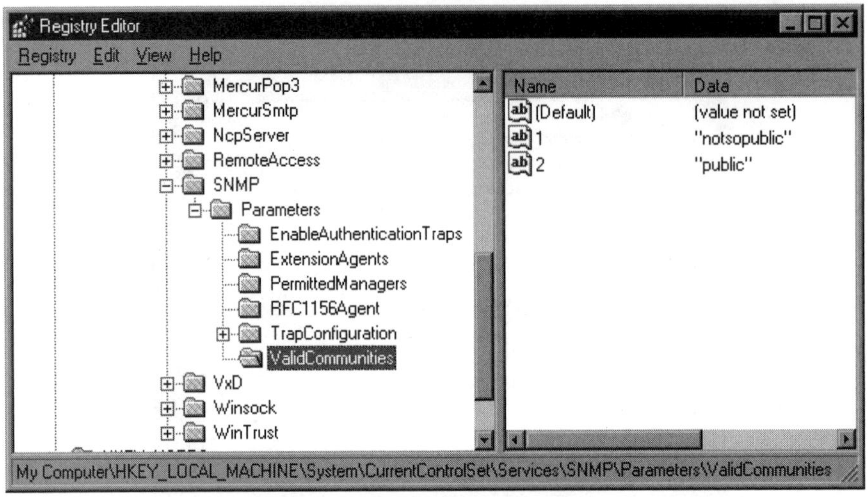

Figure 7-2. Windows 95/98 Registry Editor

up a window with one item in it, "Simple Network Management Protocol." Check the box next to it and press "OK." This will take you back to the Components Wizard window. Click "Next" to begin the installation of the SNMP service. You will probably need your Windows 2000 CD-ROM.

Once you have installed the SNMP service or selected it from the list of installed services, a new window should appear. This window is broken up into three tabs: Agent, Traps, and Security. In the Agent tab, you should configure the Contact (*sysContact*), Location (*sysLocation*), and Service (*sysServices*). We haven't mentioned the *sysServices* object yet; RFC 1213 defines it like this:

```
sysServices OBJECT-TYPE
     SYNTAX   INTEGER (0..127)
     ACCESS   read-only
     STATUS   mandatory
     DESCRIPTION
        "A value which indicates the set of services that this entity
        primarily offers.

        The value is a sum. This sum initially takes the value zero.
        Then, for each layer, L, in the range 1 through 7, that this node
        performs transactions for, 2 raised to (L - 1) is added to the sum.
        For example, a node which performs primarily routing functions
        would have a value of 4 (2^(3-1)). In contrast, a node which is a
        host offering application services would have a value of 72
        (2^(4-1) + 2^(7-1)). Note that in the context of the Internet
        suite of protocols, values should be calculated accordingly:

           layer  functionality
             1    physical (e.g., repeaters)
```

```
2  datalink/subnetwork (e.g., bridges)
3  internet (e.g., IP gateways)
4  end-to-end  (e.g., IP hosts)
7  applications (e.g., mail relays)

     For systems including OSI protocols, layers 5 and 6 may also
     be counted."
::= { system 7 }
```

The Agent tab provides a checkbox for each of the seven ISO layers *sysServices* represents. The DESCRIPTION text in the RFC gives a brief definition for each layer. If you so desire, check each service that is offered by your NT machine.

Once you're finished with the Agent tab, select the Traps tab; this allows you to configure the community in which the SNMP agent sends traps. In the "Community Name" box, enter the case-sensitive community name of your choice. Click the "Add" button to the left and then add up to five trap destinations for this community name. The trap destinations can be IPX addresses, IP addresses, or DNS names.

Now click on the Security tab. The top of this tab gives you the option to send authentication-error traps. It's a good idea to check this box, since it can help you detect intruders. The "Accepted Community Names" box lists all the community names to which the agent will respond. Click "Add" and enter your community name of choice. Configuring these communities is important, since someone with the correct community string can wreak havoc on your system. If you leave this box blank, the agent will respond to all requests. The bottom half of the Security menu allows you to specify whether the agent will accept SNMP packets from any host or only from a specified list. To create a list, which we strongly recommend, click "Only Accept SNMP Packets from These Hosts" and then use the "Add" button to add the hostnames or addresses of your monitoring stations. The options for the hosts are the same as for trap destinations; IPX addresses, IP addresses, and DNS names are acceptable.

Finally, click "OK" to save your changes and update the Windows registry. If at any time you make a mistake, click "Cancel." This aborts the configuration process; no changes will be made to your registry.

HP OpenView Agent for HP-UX and Solaris

One text-configuration file controls the parameters for this agent; the file is typically named */etc/SnmpAgent.d/snmpd.conf,* or */etc/snmpd.conf* on older systems. You don't need to edit this file for the agent to function normally. If you do edit it, you must stop and restart the master agent by executing the *SnmpMaster* script, first with a *stop* and then a *start*:

```
$ /sbin/init.d/SnmpMaster stop
$ /sbin/init.d/SnmpMaster start
```

Simple configuration

The following configuration file configures the agent to respond to *get* requests using the community name *public* and *set* requests using the community name *private*. There are no restrictions on which MIBs can be queried, or which hosts can make the queries. This configuration has no security, since the community strings are set to commonly used defaults and are widely known. The OpenView agent sends authentication-failure traps by default, so you don't have to enable these traps in the configuration file.

```
get-community-name:     public
set-community-name:     private
trap-dest:              127.0.0.1
contact:                B.Gates
location:               12 Pyramid - Egypt
```

The simplest configuration is to edit the file and place more reasonable community names in the first two lines. We can't say it too much: community names are essentially passwords. Use the same rules for picking community names that you would for choosing the root password. You should always set the destination trap host (**trap-dest**) to the IP address of the host that will receive the trap.

The next example configures several different community names:

```
get-community-name:     public
get-community-name:     media
set-community-name:     hushed
set-community-name:     veryprivate
set-community-name:     shhhh
```

We have created two *get* (read-only) communities and three *set* (read-write) communities. These communities can be used as you see fit. (In real life, we would have chosen more obscure names.) For example, you might give your operations group in New York *public* community access and your operations group in Atlanta *media* community access. The remaining *set* communities can further be subdivided among various administrators and other staff who need read-write access.

Advanced configuration

Setting up multiple community strings doesn't sound very useful, and by itself, it isn't. But you can take the concept a step further and create different communities, each of which consists of a few particular hosts and can access only some of the objects SNMP manages. The next example allows the host 10.123.56.25 to issue *gets* using the community name *comname* and *sets* using the community name *private*. The host 10.123.46.101 can issue *gets* using only the community name *comname*. You cannot use hostnames after the IP: directive; you must use IP addresses.

```
get-community-name      comname IP: 10.123.56.25 10.123.46.101
set-community-name      private IP: 10.123.56.25
```

You can also configure the agent to restrict access to MIB subtrees based on IP addresses. The next example allows any host to get any object under *iso.org.dod. internet.mgmt.mib-2*, except for objects in the *interfaces* subtree. The minus sign (-) in front of *interfaces* instructs the agent to disallow access to this subtree.

```
get-community-name      public VIEW: mib-2 -interfaces
```

The final example sets up multiple community names for both *sets* and *gets*. An administrator who is located at host 10.123.46.25 and knows the *admin* community string has read access to the entire MIB tree; with the *adminset* community string, he has write access to the entire tree. Someone with the *operator* community string can sit anywhere and access everything in *mib-2* except for the *interfaces* subtree, but must be sitting at his desk (10.123.56.101) to issue *sets* and is not allowed to set anything in the *mib-2* subtree.

```
get-community-name      operator VIEW: mib-2 -interfaces
get-community-name      admin    IP: 10.123.56.25
set-community-name      operset  IP: 10.123.46.101 VIEW: -mib-2
set-community-name      adminset IP: 10.123.56.25
```

Net-SNMP (Formerly UCD-SNMP)

Net-SNMP is an open source agent that is freely available from *http://net-snmp. sourceforge.net*. We will focus on Net-SNMP Version 4.2, which is the most recent as of this publication. Once you have downloaded and unpacked the distribution, *cd* into the directory in which you unpacked Net-SNMP and read the *README* and *INSTALL* files. These files provide general information on installing the agent and don't require much explanation here.

Net-SNMP uses a *configure* script to make sure your environment has some key utilities and libraries installed, so it can be compiled successfully. Many configuration options are settable when you run this script. To see a list of them, run the following command:

```
ucd-snmp-4.2/> ./configure --help
```

One common option is *—-prefix=PATH*. This specifies an alternate installation directory. By default, Net-SNMP will install in */usr/local/bin*, */usr/local/man*, etc.

We'll be running *configure* without any options, which means our Net-SNMP build will have default values assigned for various options. For example, the agent binary will be placed in */usr/local/sbin*. Run the following command to begin the configuration process:

```
ucd-snmp-4.2/> ./configure
```

You will see various messages about what features *configure* is looking for and whether or not they're found.

After running for a while, *configure* will ask for some basic SNMP information:

```
************** Configuration Section **************

     You are about to be prompted by a series of questions. Answer
them carefully, as they determine how the snmp agent and related
applications are to function.

     After the configure script finishes, you can browse the newly
created config.h file for further - less important - parameters to
modify. Be careful if you re-run configure though since config.h will
be over written.

-Press return to continue-
```

When you type Return, you'll be prompted for the system contact information:

```
disabling above prompt for future runs...  yes
checking System Contact Information...

*** System Contact Information:

     Describes who should be contacted about the host the agent is
running on. This information is available in the MIB-II tree. This
can also be over-ridden using the "syscontact" syntax in the agent's
configuration files.

System Contact Information (root@): snmpadmin@ora.com
setting System Contact Information to...  snmpadmin@ora.com
checking System Location...
```

We've decided to set our contact information to something useful, but we could have left it blank. The next item you're asked to configure is system location. We've chosen an informative value, but again could have left it blank:

```
*** System Location:

     Describes the location of the system. This information is
available in the MIB-II tree. This can also be over-ridden using the
"syslocation" syntax in the agent's configuration files.

System Location (Unknown): FTP Server #1, O'Reilly Data Center
setting System Location to...  FTP Server #1, O'Reilly Data Center
checking Location to write logfile...
```

The final option you need to configure is the *snmpd* log file location:

```
*** Logfile location:

     Enter the default location for the snmpd agent to dump
information & errors to. If not defined (enter the keyword "none"
at the prompt below) the agent will use stdout and stderr instead.
(Note: This value can be over-ridden using command line options.)

Location to write logfile (/var/log/snmpd.log):
setting Location to write logfile to...  /var/log/snmpd.log
```

```
*** snmpd persistent storage location:

    Enter a directory for the snmp library to store persistent
data in the form of a configuration file.

Location to write persistent information (/var/ucd-snmp):
setting Location to write persistent information to...  /var/ucd-snmp
updating cache ./config.cache
creating ./config.status
creating Makefile
creating MakefileMakefile
creating snmplib/Makefile
creating agent/Makefile
creating apps/Makefile
creating apps/snmpnetstat/Makefile
creating agent/mibgroup/Makefile
creating agent/dlmods/Makefile
creating local/Makefile
creating testing/Makefile
creating man/Makefile
creating ov/Makefile
creating mibs/Makefile
creating config.h
```

The default value is */var/log/snmpd.log*, which should work on most Unix systems.

When the *configure* script finishes, it creates a system-specific file named *config.h*. Before you continue, take a look through this file. It houses many local configuration variables that you may want to change before you start compiling. Here are some snippets from my *config.h* file:

```
/* default list of mibs to load */

#define DEFAULT_MIBS "IP-MIB:IF-MIB:TCP-MIB:UDP-MIB:SNMPv2-MIB: \
RFC1213-MIB:UCD-SNMP-MIB:SNMPv2-PARTY-MIB:SNMPv2-M2M-MIB: \
SNMP-VIEW-BASED-ACM-MIB"

/* default location to look for mibs to load using the above tokens
   and/or those in the MIBS environment variable */

#define DEFAULT_MIBDIRS "/usr/local/share/snmp/mibs"

/* LOGFILE: If defined it closes stdout/err/in and opens this in out/err's
   place. (stdin is closed so that sh scripts won't wait for it) */

#define LOGFILE "/var/log/snmpd.log"

/* default system contact */
#define SYS_CONTACT "snmpadmin@ora.com"

/* system location */
#define SYS_LOC "FTP Server #1, O'Reilly Data Center"
```

You can now compile your new package with the *make* command. The compilation process displays many messages, most of which you can ignore. In short, if it completes, you've succeeded and can proceed to installation. If not, you will see errors and should investigate what went wrong. If you tweaked the *config.h* file and your build failed, try recreating *config.h*. Without modifying this new *config.h*, try another build. This will weed out any problems you created within that file.

Install your new package with the command *make install*. By default, this command installs various executables in */usr/local/bin* and other important information in */usr/local/share/snmp*.

At this point, you can configure the agent further by using one of two approaches:

- Running the program */usr/local/bin/snmpconf*, which asks you a lot of questions and creates a configuration file. The configuration script is surprisingly confusing, though, so it's hard to recommend this approach.

- Crafting a configuration by hand. If you're not interested in SNMPv3, this is fairly easy.

Running the configuration script

The configuration script is rather long and complex. Here are a few pointers:

- It starts by asking whether you want to create *snmp.conf* or *snmpd.conf*. To configure the agent, select *snmpd.conf*. *snmp.conf* sets up some defaults for command-line tools such as *snmpget*. Strictly speaking, creating *snmp.conf* isn't necessary.

- Most of the configurable options have to do with SNMPv3. Although Version 3 is an important step forward, you can almost certainly ignore this; very few vendors support v3. Version 3 is discussed in Appendix F.

- When you're finished configuring, the script leaves the configuration file in your current directory. You can either place the files in *~/.snmp*, if they're for your own use, or in */usr/local/share/snmp*, if you want this configuration to be used by everyone on the system.

Creating a configuration by hand

If you don't want to do anything complex, creating your own configuration file is easy. Here's a very simple configuration file:

```
syslocation      "O'Reilly Data Center"
syscontact       snmpadmin@oreilly.com
rwcommunity      private
rocommunity      public
authtrapenable   1
trapcommunity    trapsRus
trapsink         nmshost.oreilly.com
trap2sink        nmshost.oreilly.com
```

The configuration items should be familiar: we're setting up the system location; the system contact; the read-write, read-only, and trap community strings; and the destination to which traps should be sent. We're also enabling authentication traps. Note that we configured destinations for both SNMP Version 1 and Version 2 traps. The trap destination lines (`trapsink` and `trap2sink`) can also have a trap community string, if the NMS at the given host requires a different community name.

The `rwcommunity` and `rocommunity` lines allow us to be a bit more sophisticated than the example indicates. We're allowed to specify the network or subnet to which the community strings apply, and an object ID that restricts queries to MIB objects that are underneath that OID. For example, if you want to restrict read-write access to management stations on the subnetwork 10.0.15.0/24, you could use the line:

```
rwcommunity    private 10.0.15.0
```

If you take this route, you should certainly look at the *EXAMPLE.conf* file in the directory in which you built Net-SNMP. You can modify this file and install it in the appropriate location (either *~/.snmp/snmpd.conf* or */usr/local/share/snmp/snmpd.conf*), or you can take ideas from it and use them in your own configuration. It includes some particularly clever tricks that we'll discuss in Chapter 11 but that are well beyond the simple configuration we're discussing here.

Concord SystemEDGE Agent for Unix and NT

Concord SystemEDGE is a commercial product that can be used as a subagent to the standard Windows NT agent. On Unix systems, this agent can be used either as a standalone agent or side-by-side with an existing agent. It runs on Linux, Solaris, and other operating systems. The CD on which the product is shipped includes agents for all the platforms SystemEDGE supports. Whenever possible, SystemEDGE uses the platform's native package manager to make installation easier. Each architecture-dependent version of the agent comes with an easy-to-follow *README* file for installation. See Chapter 11 for a discussion of this agent's capabilities.

Simple configuration

The SystemEDGE configuration file is located in */etc/sysedge.cf*. Use your editor of choice to make changes to this file. You must stop and restart SystemEDGE for your changes to take effect. The configuration file format is the same for all the versions of SystemEDGE.

For a typical SNMP configuration, *sysedge.cf* looks like this:

```
community public read-only
community veryprivate read-write 127.0.0.1 10.123.56.25
community traps 127.0.0.1
```

Comment lines begin with a # character. The first parameter sets the read-only community to `public`. The read-write community is defined to be `veryprivate`. The two IP addresses following the read-write community string are an access list that tells the agent to allow *set* operations from *localhost* (127.0.0.1) and 10. 123.56.25 only. Always use an access list if possible; without this security feature, any host can execute *set* operations. Note that there is a space between the two addresses, not a Tab character. The third option tells the agent where to send traps; in this case, to *localhost* (127.0.0.1).

The agent sends authentication-failure traps by default, and we strongly recommend using them. If you don't want authentication-failure traps, include the following line in your configuration file:

```
no_authen_traps
```

Advanced configuration

SystemEDGE provides some powerful self-monitoring capabilities. These extensions (found only in Concord's Empire private enterprise MIB) are similar to the Remote Network Monitoring (RMON) MIB, which is discussed in Chapter 9. Empire's extensions can reduce network load by allowing the agent, instead of an NMS, to perform monitoring (polling) of important system objects. For example, the agent can be instructed to make sure the free space available in the root filesystem stays above some predefined threshold. When this threshold is crossed, the agent sends a trap to the NMS so the condition can be dealt with appropriately.

The following line shows how you can monitor and restart *sendmail* if it dies:

```
watch process procAlive 'sendmail' 1 0x100 60 'Watch Sendmail' '/etc/init.d/sendmail start'
```

This monitor sends a trap to the NMS, defined earlier as `community traps 127.0. 0.1`, when the *sendmail* process dies. The agent then executes */etc/init.d/sendmail start* to restart the process. The general form of this command is:

```
watch process procAlive 'procname' index flags interv 'description' 'action'
```

The *procname* parameter is a regular expression that SystemEDGE uses to select the processes that it is monitoring; in this case, we're watching processes with the name *sendmail*. Each entry in the process-monitoring table must have a unique *index*; in this example, we used the value 1. We could have picked any integer, as long as that integer was not already in use in the table. The *flag* parameter is a hexadecimal* flag that changes the behavior of the monitor. We specified a flag of 0x100, which tells the monitor that the process it's watching spawns child processes; this flag ensures that SystemEDGE will take action only when the parent

---

* Generally speaking, there are several ways to represent hexadecimal numbers. SystemEDGE uses the notion of a number prefixed with *0x*, which should be familiar to C and Perl programmers.

sendmail process dies, not when any of the children die. The use of process-monitor flags is beyond the scope of this chapter; see the manual that comes with SystemEDGE for more information. The *interv* parameter specifies how often (in seconds) the agent checks the process's status. We have set the interval to 60 seconds. The *description* parameter contains information about the process being monitored; it can be up to 128 characters in length. It is a good idea to use a description that indicates what is being monitored, since the agent stores this value in the monitor table for retrieval by an NMS and includes it in the variable bindings when a trap is sent. The final parameter is the action the monitor will take when the process dies; we chose to restart the daemon.

SystemEDGE can be extended by using plug-ins. These plug-ins manage and monitor applications such as Apache (web server), Exchange (Microsoft mail), and Oracle (database), to name a few. A "top processes" plug-in named *topprocs* comes with every distribution. The following statement tells SystemEDGE to load this plug-in for 64-bit Solaris (this statement is similar for NT and other Unix platforms):

```
sysedge_plugin /opt/EMPsysedge/plugins/topprocs/topprocs-sol64bit.so
```

The folks at Concord have taken great care to add useful comments to the *sysedge.cf* file. The comments are often all you need to configure the agent.

Cisco Devices

Cisco Systems produces a wide range of routers, switches, and other networking equipment. The configuration process is virtually the same on all Cisco devices, because they share the IOS operating system.[*] There are some minor differences in the parameters that can be configured on every device; these generally have to do with the capabilities of the device, rather than the SNMP implementation.

To configure the SNMP parameters, you must be in *enable* mode. You can use the following commands to see what traps are available:

```
router> enable
Password: mypassword
router# config terminal
router(config)#snmp-server enable traps ?
  bgp          Enable BGP state change traps
  envmon       Enable SNMP environmental monitor traps
  frame-relay  Enable SNMP frame-relay traps
  isdn         Enable SNMP isdn traps
  <cr>
```

The question mark tells the router to respond with the possible completions for the command you're typing. You can use this feature throughout the entire command-

---

[*] There are some exceptions to this rule, such as the PIX firewalls. These exceptions usually mean that the product is made by a company that Cisco acquired.

line interface. If the part of the command you have already typed has a syntax error, the router will give you the "Unrecognized command" message when you type the question mark. <cr> tells you that you can exit without configuring the command (snmp-server enable traps in this case) by typing a carriage return.

Simple configuration

Here's a simple configuration that lets you start using the SNMP agent:

```
router(config)#snmp-server community private RW
router(config)#snmp-server community public RO
router(config)#snmp-server trap-authentication
router(config)#snmp-server location Delta Building - 1st Floor
router(config)#snmp-server contact J Jones
router(config)#snmp-server host 10.123.135.25 public
```

Most of these commands set parameters with which you should be familiar by now. We define two communities, public and private, with read-only (RO) and read-write (RW) permissions, respectively. snmp-server trap-authentication turns on authentication-failure traps. The command snmp-server host 10.123. 135.25 public configures the destination to which traps should be sent. The IP address is set to the address of our NMS. The community string public will be included in the traps.

Advanced configuration

The following configuration item tells the device what interface it should use when sending out SNMP traps:

```
router(config)#snmp-server trap-source VLAN1
```

Configuring the trap source is useful because routers, by definition, have multiple interfaces. This command allows you to send all your traps out through a particular interface.

There may be times when you want to send only certain traps to your NMS. The next item sends only environmental monitor traps to the specified host, 172.16.52.25 (the *envmon* option is not available on all Cisco devices):

```
router(config)#snmp-server host 172.16.52.25 public envmon
```

One of the most frightening SNMP *sets* is the Cisco shutdown, which lets you shut down the router from the NMS. The good news is that you have to include a switch in the configuration before the router will respond to shutdown commands. Issuing the following command disables shutdowns:

```
router(config)#no snmp-server system-shutdown
```

To receive traps about authentication failures (something trying to poll your device with the wrong community name) add the following line:

```
router(config)#snmp-server trap-authentication
```

The final advanced configuration parameter is an access list. The first line sets up access list 15. It states that the IP address 10.123.56.25 is permitted to access the agent. The second line says that anyone that passes access list 15 (i.e., a host with IP address 10.123.56.25) and gives the community name *notsopublic* has read-only (RO) access to the agent. Access lists are a very powerful tool for controlling access to your network. They're beyond the scope of this book, but if you're not familiar with them, you should be.

```
router(config)#access-list 15 permit 10.123.56.25
router(config)#snmp-server community notsopublic RO 15
```

That's it! You now have a working SNMP configuration for your Cisco router.

APC Symetra

APC's uninterruptible power supplies (UPSs) are typical of a large class of products that aren't usually considered network devices, but that have incorporated a network interface for the purpose of management.

To configure an APC UPS, you can use its management port (a familiar serial port to which you can connect a console terminal) or, assuming that you've performed basic network configuration, *telnet* to the UPS's IP address. SNMP configuration is the same regardless of the method you use. Either way, you get a Text User Interface (TUI) that presents you with rather old-fashioned menus—you type your menu selection (usually a number) followed by Enter to navigate through the menus.

We'll assume that you've already performed basic network configuration, such as assigning an IP address for the UPS. To configure SNMP, go to the Network menu and select "5" to go into the SNMP submenu. You should get a menu like this:

```
------- SNMP -------------------------------------------------------

        1- Access Control 1
        2- Access Control 2
        3- Access Control 3
        4- Access Control 4
        5- Trap Receiver 1
        6- Trap Receiver 2
        7- Trap Receiver 3
        8- Trap Receiver 4
        9- System
        10- Summary

        ?- Help
 <ENTER> Redisplay Menu
    <ESC> Return To Previous Menu

    >
```

You need to configure three distinct sections: Access Control, Trap Receiver, and System. To see a summary of the current SNMP settings, use the Summary submenu.

This particular device allows us to specify four IP addresses for access control and four IP addresses to receive traps. The access control items allow you to configure the IP addresses of your management stations—this is similar to the access lists we've seen in other devices, and is obviously basic to security. The UPS will reply only to queries from the IP addresses you have listed. Configuration is a bit awkward—you need to go to a separate menu to configure each IP address. Here's what you'll see when configuring the Access Control 1 submenu:

```
------- Access Control 1 --------------------------------------------

        Access Control Summary
        #  Community  Access     NMS IP
        --------------------------------------------------------------
        1  public     Read       10.123.56.25
        2  private    Write      10.123.56.25
        3  public2    Disabled   0.0.0.0
        4  private2   Disabled   0.0.0.0

    1- Community      : public
    2- Access Type    : Read
    3- NMS IP Address  : 10.123.56.25
    4- Accept Changes  :

    ?- Help
<ENTER> Redisplay Menu
  <ESC> Return To Previous Menu


    >
```

The first part of the menu summarizes the state of access control. On this menu, we can change only the first item on the list. The special address 0.0.0.0 is a wildcard—it means that the UPS will respond to queries from any IP address. Although addresses 3 and 4 are set to 0.0.0.0, these addresses are currently disabled, and that's how we want to keep them. We want the UPS to respond only to the management stations we explicitly list.

On this menu, we've configured items 1 (the community string), 2 (the access type), and 3 (the IP address). We've set the community string to `public` (not a choice you'd want in a real configuration), the access type to `Read` (allowing various SNMP *get* operations, but no *set* operations), and the NMS IP address to `10.123.56.25`. The net effect is that the UPS's SNMP agent will accept *get* requests from IP address 10.123.56.25 with the community name *public*. When you are satisfied with the configuration, enter a 4 to accept your changes.

To configure the second access control item, press Esc to return to the previous menu; then select 2. As you can see, we allow 10.123.56.25 to perform *set* operations. We don't have any other management stations, so we've left items 3 and 4 disabled.

Once the Access Control section is complete, you can start configuring traps. The Trap Receivers section is simply a list of NMSs that receive traps. As with Access Control, four trap receivers can be configured. To get to the first trap receiver, return to the SNMP menu and select menu 5. A typical trap receiver setup looks like this:

```
------- Trap Receiver 1 -------------------------------------------------

        Trap Receiver Summary
        #  Community  Generation  Authentication  Receiver NMS IP
        ----------------------------------------------------------------
        1  public     Enabled     Enabled         10.123.56.25
        2  public     Enabled     Enabled         0.0.0.0
        3  public     Enabled     Enabled         0.0.0.0
        4  public     Enabled     Enabled         0.0.0.0

     1- Trap Community Name : public
     2- Trap Generation      : Enabled
     3- Authentication Traps: Enabled
     4- Receiver NMS IP      : 10.123.56.25
     5- Accept Changes       :

      ?- Help
 <ENTER> Redisplay Menu
   <ESC> Return To Previous Menu


   >
```

Once again, the first part of the menu is a summary of the trap receiver configuration. We've already set the first trap receiver to the address of our NMS, enabled trap generation, and enabled the generation of authentication traps—as always, a good idea. The traps we generate will include the community string *public*. Note that trap receivers 2, 3, and 4 are set to 0.0.0.0. On this menu, 0.0.0.0 is not a wildcard; it's just an invalid address that means you haven't yet configured the trap receiver's IP address. It's basically the same as leaving the entry disabled.

The final configuration items that should be set are on the System submenu, found under the SNMP main menu:

```
------- System -------------------------------------------------

     1- sysName       : ups1.ora.com
     2- sysContact    : Douglas Mauro
     3- sysLocation   : Apache Hilo Deck
     4- Accept Changes :

      ?- Help
 <ENTER> Redisplay Menu
   <ESC> Return To Previous Menu


   >
```

After you have finished configuring all your SNMP parameters, use the Summary submenu for a quick look at what you have done. A typical setup will look something like this:

```
-------------------------------------------------------------------------
          SNMP Configuration Summary

          sysName             : ups1.ora.com
          sysLocation         : Apache Hilo Deck
          sysContact          : Douglas Mauro

          Access Control Summary
          #  Community  Access       NMS IP
          -----------------------------------------------------------------
          1  public     Read         10.123.56.25
          2  private    Write        10.123.56.25
          3  public2    Disabled     0.0.0.0
          4  private2   Disabled     0.0.0.0

          Trap Receiver Summary
          #  Community  Generation   Authentication  Receiver NMS IP
          ----------------------------------------------------------
          1  public     Enabled      Enabled          10.123.56.25
          2  public     Enabled      Enabled          0.0.0.0
          3  public     Enabled      Enabled          0.0.0.0
          4  public     Enabled      Enabled          0.0.0.0

          Press <ENTER> to continue...
```

Upon completion and verification, use the Esc key to take you all the way out to the Logout menu.

8

Polling and Setting

We've put a lot of work into getting things set up so that we can use SNMP effectively. But now that we've installed a fancy node manager and configured agents on all our devices, what can we do? How can we interact with the devices that are out there?

The three basic SNMP operations are *snmpget, snmpset,* and *snmpwalk.* They are fairly self-explanatory: *snmpget* reads a value from a managed device, *snmpset* sets a value on a device, and *snmpwalk* reads a portion of the MIB tree from a device. For example, you can use *snmpget* to query a router and find out its administrative contact (i.e., the person to call if the router appears to be broken), *snmpset* to change this contact information, and *snmpwalk* to traverse a MIB to get an idea of which objects the router has implemented or to retrieve status information on all the router's interfaces.

This chapter shows you how to use these operations in day-to-day network management. First, we will use Perl to demonstrate how you can *set*, *get*, and *walk* objects in a script (the nice thing about using Perl is that you can easily extend the simple scripts in this chapter to fit your needs and environment). We will then use HP OpenView and Net-SNMP to perform the same operations, but from the command line. Finally, as an alternative to the command line, we will demonstrate OpenView's graphical MIB Browser, which has a nice interface for getting, setting and walking MIB data.

Retrieving a Single MIB Value

Let's start by querying a router for the name of its administrative contact. This operation, called polling, is accomplished with the SNMP *get* command. The following

Perl script, *snmpget.pl*, uses an SNMP Perl module to retrieve the information we want (Chapter 5 contains the URL for this module):

```perl
#!/usr/local/bin/perl
#filename: /opt/local/perl_scripts/snmpget.pl
use BER;
use SNMP_util;
use SNMP_Session;
$MIB1 = ".1.3.6.1.2.1.1.4.0";
$HOST = "orarouter1";
($value) = &snmpget("public\@$HOST","$MIB1");
if ($value) { print "Results :$MIB1: :$value:\n"; }
else { warn "No response from host :$HOST:\n"; }
```

This script is obviously very primitive, but it is also easy to understand, even if you're not an experienced Perl user. It's importance isn't in what it does, which is very little, but as a template you can use to insert SNMP operations into other programs. (If you are not used to writing quick Perl programs, or are unfamiliar with the language, a good starting point is the official Perl web site, *http://www.perl.com.*) The script starts with three use statements, which are similar to #include statements in C. The use statements load Perl modules containing functions and definitions for working with SNMP. The three modules we use are:

BER

> Describes how to encode management data into bit patterns for transmission. *Basic Encoding Rules* (BER) is an ISO standard.

SNMP_util

> Defines a set of functions that use the SNMP_Session module to make it much more programmer-friendly. SNMP_util itself uses BER and SNMP_Session, but in this first script we chose to reference these other modules explicitly. In future programs, we'll just use SNMP_util.

SNMP_Session

> Provides Perl with core SNMP functionality.

The next two lines specify the data we want to get. We have hardcoded the object ID of a particular piece of data defined by the MIB and the hostname from which we want to retrieve this MIB data. In a more flexible program, you might want to get these values from the command line, or build a user interface to help users specify exactly what they are interested in retrieving. For the time being, however, this will get us started. It is easy enough to replace orarouter1 with the hostname or IP address of the device you want to poll. The OID we are requesting is stored in the variable $MIB1. The value .1.3.6.1.2.1.1.4.0 requests the device's administrative contact. Again, you can replace this with any OID of your choice. We used the numeric form of this object, but you can also use the textual form for the OID, which is *.org.dod.internet.mgmt.mib-2.system.sysContact.0.* You can abbreviate this further to *sysContact* because SNMP_util defines some parts of the OID string for us (for example, `SNMP_util` defines *sysContact* as *1.3.6.1.2.1.1.4.0*), but it's often safer to be explicit and use the entire OID. Don't forget to include the *.0*, which states that we want the first (0) and only instance of *iso.org.dod.internetmgmt.mib-2.system.sysContact.0*, at the end of your OID.

The next line polls the device. The `snmpget` function retrieves the data from the device specified by the variable $HOST. Notice the two arguments to the function. The first is the device we want to poll, preceded by the community name `public`. (If you need to use another community name—you did change the community names when you configured the device, didn't you?—you'll have to modify this line and insert your community name in place of it.) The second argument to *snmpget* is the OID in which we are interested. If you type the code in yourself, do not forget the parentheses around $value. If you omit the parentheses, $value will be set to the number of items in the array *snmpget* returns.

Once we have polled the device, we print either the output or an error message. I put a colon before and after any output that I print; this makes it easy to see if there are any hidden characters in the output. The decimal integer "16" is *very* different from "16\n", which is the decimal integer 16 followed by a newline character.

Now let's run the program:

```
$ /opt/local/perl_scripts/snmpget.pl
Results :.1.3.6.1.2.1.1.4.0: :ORA IT Group:
```

snmpget.pl prints the OID we requested, followed by the actual value of that object, which is `ORA IT Group`. Don't worry if the return value for *sysContact* is wrong or blank. (The trick of putting colons before and after the output will make it clear if *sysContact* is blank or empty.) This probably means that no one has configured an administrative contact, or that it was configured incorrectly. We'll show you how to fix that when we discuss the *set* operation. If you get an error, skip to the end of this chapter to see a list of some errors and their appropriate fixes.

We will now modify *snmpget.pl* to poll any host and any OID we want. This is accomplished by passing the host and OID as command-line arguments to the Perl script:

```
#!/usr/local/bin/perl
#filename: /opt/local/perl_scripts/snmpget.pl
use SNMP_util;
$MIB1 = shift;
$HOST = shift;
($MIB1) && ($HOST) || die "Usage: $0 MIB_OID HOSTNAME";
($value) = &snmpget("$HOST","$MIB1");
if ($value) { print "Results :$MIB1: :$value:\n"; }
else { warn "No response from host :$HOST:\n"; }
```

Now that this program is a little more flexible, it is possible to look up different kinds of information on different hosts. We even left out the community string, which allows us to poll hosts with different community names. Here's how to run the new version of *snmpget.pl*:

```
$ /opt/local/perl_scripts/snmpget.pl .1.3.6.1.2.1.1.1.0 public@orarouter1
Results ::1.3.6.1.2.1.1.1.0: :Cisco Internetwork Operating System Software
IOS (tm) 3000 Software (IGS-I-L), Version 11.0(16), RELEASE SOFTWARE (fc1)
Copyright (c) 1986-1997 by cisco Systems, Inc.
Compiled Tue 24-Jun-97 12:20 by jaturner:
```

In this example, we asked the router to describe itself by looking up the OID .1.3. 6.1.2.1.1.1.0 (*system.sysDesc.0*). The result tells us that orarouter1 is a Cisco router running Version 11.0(16) of the IOS operating system, along with some other useful information.

Using HP OpenView to Retrieve Values

Let's start by looking up our router's administrative contact (*system.sysContact.0*) and see if we get the same result as we did with our previous Perl script. The arguments to OpenView's *snmpget*[*] are the community name, the hostname of the device we want to poll, and the OID of the data we are requesting; we gave the OID in numeric form, but again, we could have given it as a text string:

```
$ /opt/OV/bin/snmpget -c public orarouter1 .1.3.6.1.2.1.1.4.0
system.sysContact.0 : DISPLAY STRING- (ascii):  ORA IT Group
```

Although this looks a little different from the output of the Perl script, it tells us the same thing. *snmpget* prints the OID we requested on the command line, making it easy to verify that we polled the right object. Again, note that the trailing *.0* is important. The output also tells us the object's datatype: DISPLAY STRING- (ascii). Back in Chapter 2, we discussed the datatypes that SNMP uses; some of the common types are INTEGER, OCTET STRING, Counter, and IpAddress. Finally, the output gives us the information we asked for: the router is administered by the ORA IT Group, which is the value returned from the SNMP *get* request.

Now let's do the same thing using OpenView's GUI interface. From the Network Node Manager's display, select "Misc → SNMP MIB Browser."[†] If you don't have NNM running, you can start the MIB Browser from the command line: */opt/OV/bin/ xnmbrowser.* Figure 8-1 shows the GUI. Its input fields are similar to the variables we have been setting in our Perl scripts: Name or IP Address, Community Name, MIB Object ID, MIB Instance, SNMP Set Value, and MIB Values.

Let's use this browser to run an *snmpget.* Start by inserting a Name or IP Address and Community Name in the input boxes provided. To enter the object you want

---

[*] Most OpenView executable files are located in */opt/OV/bin.*

[†] If you find that the SNMP MIB Browser menu item is grayed out and cannot be clicked on, click on an SNMP object on your NNM map. You should then be able to click on the menu item to start your GUI.

to retrieve, use the MIB Object ID field and the text box below it. MIB Object ID shows us that we are currently in the subtree *.iso.org.dod.internet.* The text area shows the objects at the next level of the tree: *directory, mgmt,* etc. (To see the numeric OIDs for these objects, click on their names and then on the "Describe" button.) Then browse down through the MIB by double-clicking *mgmt,* then *mib-2, system,* and finally *sysContact.* Click on *sysContact* and then on "Start Query." The result that appears in the "MIB Values" field (as shown in Figure 8-2) should look very similar to the value that was returned in the command-line example.

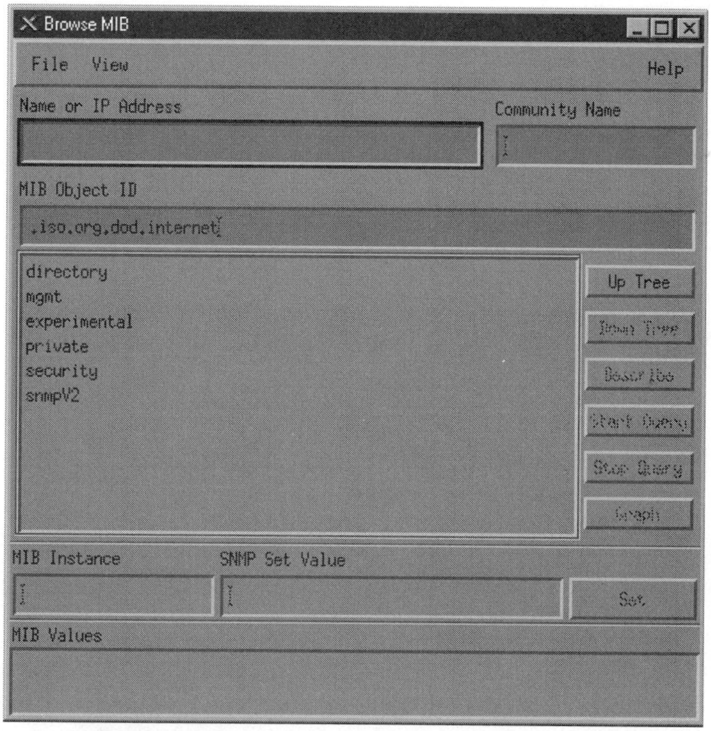

Figure 8-1. OpenView xnmbrowser default

Let's go back to the command line and poll for *sysDesc* again:

```
$ /opt/OV/bin/snmpget orarouter1 .1.3.6.1.2.1.1.1.0
system.sysDescr.0 : DISPLAY STRING- (ascii):  Cisco Internetwork Operating
System Software IOS (tm) 3000 Software (IGS-I-L), Version 11.0(16), RELEASE
SOFTWARE (fc1)Copyright (c) 1986-1997 by cisco Systems, Inc. Compiled Tue
24-Jun-97 12:20 by jaturner
```

Looks the same, right? Notice that we left out the community string. We can do this because the default *get* community string is *public,* which is the correct community string for the target host, orarouter1. You can change your default community

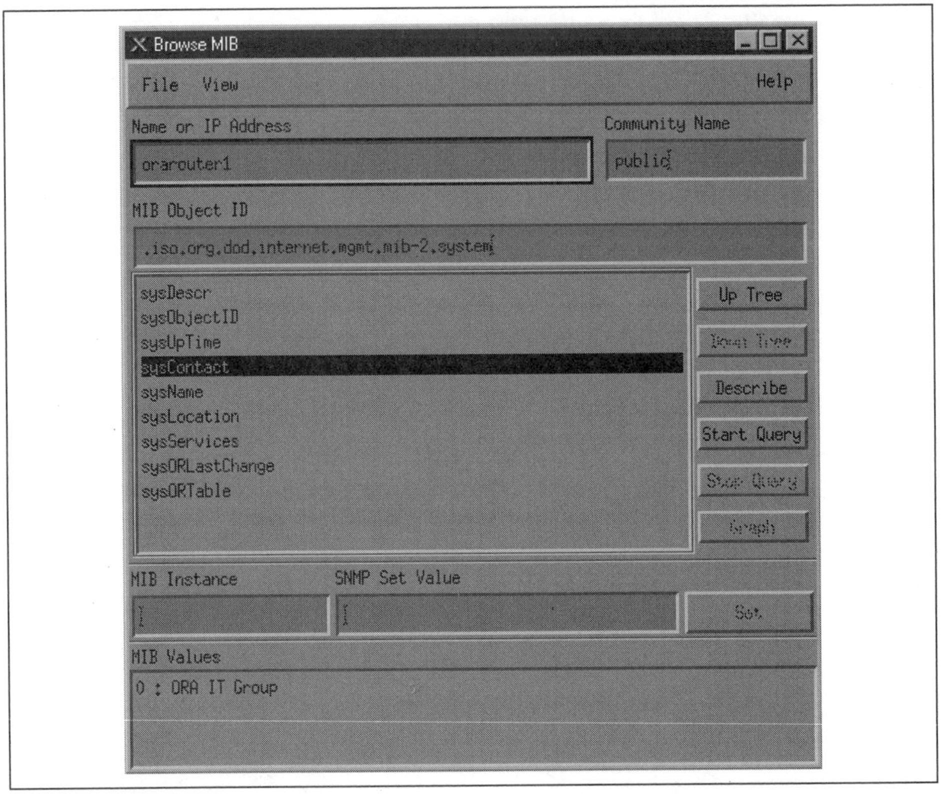

Figure 8-2. OpenView xnmbrowser response

strings in OpenView's global settings. Let's see if we can get an object with a different datatype:

```
$ /opt/OV/bin/snmpget  orarouter1 .1.3.6.1.2.1.1.3.0
system.sysUpTime.0 : Timeticks: (159857288) 18 days, 12:02:52.88
```

This command returns the system uptime, which is of type `TimeTicks`. `TimeTicks` (RFC 1155) represents a nonnegative integer, which counts the time in hundredths of a second since some epoch. Ignoring the number in parentheses, this shows me that my router has been up and operational for 18 days, 12 hours, 02 minutes, and so on. The big number in parentheses is the exact amount of time the machine has been up, in hundredths of seconds. If you do the math, you will see this adds up to 18.501 days, or 18 days, 12 hours, and a little bit: exactly what we expect.

Using Net-SNMP

The Net-SNMP tools provide an excellent command-line interface to SNMP operations. These tools are also commonly known as UCD-SNMP—you'll still find this older name in many references, and even in the code itself.

Chapter 7 discussed how to compile, install, and configure the Net-SNMP agent. If you've done that, you've already compiled and installed the SNMP tools. They're shipped in the same package as the SNMP agent, and no real configuration is necessary for them. There is a configuration program, called *snmpconf,* which can be used to generate an *snmp.conf* file that provides default values for some of the options to the commands.* Unless you're using SNMPv3, though, it isn't really necessary. It might be handy to set up a default community string but, in practice, this is of only limited use: you probably have different community strings on different devices, anyway. If you decide to use *snmpconf* to create the tool configuration file, make sure that you place *snmp.conf* in the *.snmp* subdirectory of your home directory or (if you want the options to apply to all users) in */usr/local/share/snmp.*

We'll assume that you won't do any configuration and will simply use the tools "out of the box." Here's a simple poll that asks a router for its location:

```
$ snmpget orarouter1 public .1.3.6.1.2.1.1.6.0
system.sysLocation.0 = Sebastopol CA
```

It's fairly simple: we provided the hostname of the router we wanted to poll, a community string, and the OID of the object we wanted to retrieve. Instead of using the numeric OID, you can use the lengthy human-readable form. To save typing, *snmpget* assumes everything up to the object name and instance ID. Therefore, the following command is exactly equivalent to the previous one:

```
$ snmpget orarouter1 public sysLocation.0
system.sysLocation.0 = Sebastopol CA
```

We'll take a look at the *snmpwalk* and *snmpset* commands that come with the Net-SNMP package later in this chapter, but the package contains many tools and is well worth a more detailed explanation. One tool that's particularly useful is *snmptranslate,* which converts between the numeric and textual names of MIB objects and can do things such as look up the definition of an object in a MIB file. The software distribution comes with a number of standard MIBs; you can place additional MIB files in */usr/local/share/snmp/mibs.* Appendix C gives an overview of the Net-SNMP package.

Retrieving Multiple MIB Values

The syntax for *snmpwalk* is similar to the syntax for its cousin, *snmpget.* As discussed in Chapter 2, *snmpwalk* traverses a MIB starting with some object, continuously returning values until it gets to the end of that object's branch. For example,

---

* This is the same command used to create *snmpd.conf,* which configures the Net-SNMP agent. The *snmp.conf* configuration file is similar in form to *snmpd.conf.*

the upcoming Perl script begins walking the *.iso.org.dod.internet.mgmt.mib-2.
interfaces.ifTable.ifEntry.ifDescr* object and provides a description of each Ethernet
interface on the device it polls.

This new script is a minor modification of *snmpget.pl*. We turned the scalar
$value into the array @values;* we need an array because we expect to get mul-
tiple values back. We also called the function *snmpwalk* instead of *snmpget* (syn-
tactically, the two functions are the same):

```perl
#!/usr/local/bin/perl
#filename: /opt/local/perl_scripts/snmpwalk.pl
use SNMP_util;
$MIB1 = shift;
$HOST = shift;
($MIB1) && ($HOST) || die "Usage: $0 MIB_OID HOSTNAME";
(@values) = &snmpwalk("$HOST","$MIB1");
if (@values) { print "Results :$MIB1: :@values:\n"; }
else { warn "No response from host :$HOST:\n"; }
```

Here's how to run the script:

```
$ /opt/local/perl_scripts/snmpwalk.pl .1.3.6.1.2.1.2.2.1.2 orarouter1
```

This command walks down the *.iso.org.dod.internet.mgmt.mib-2.interfaces.ifTable.
ifEntry.ifDescr* object, returning information about the interfaces that are on the
router. The results look something like this:

```
Results :.1.3.6.1.2.1.2.2.1.2: :1:Ethernet0 2:Serial0 3:Serial1:
```

The output depends on the interfaces on the host or router you are polling. To
give some examples, I've run this script against some of the machines on my network. Here are the results.

Cisco 7000 router:

```
Results :.1.3.6.1.2.1.2.2.1.2: :1:Ethernet0/0 2:Ethernet0/1 3:TokenRing1/0
4:TokenRing1/1 5:TokenRing1/2 6:TokenRing1/3 7:Serial2/0 8:Serial2/1
9:Serial2/2 10:Serial2/3 11:Serial2/4 12:Serial2/5 13:Serial2/6 14:Serial2/7
15:FastEthernet3/0 16:FastEthernet3/1 17:TokenRing4/0 18:TokenRing4/1:
```

Sun workstation:

```
Results :.1.3.6.1.2.1.2.2.1.2: :1:lo0 2:hme0:
```

Windows NT PC:

```
Results :.1.3.6.1.2.1.2.2.1.2: :1:MS TCP Loopback interface
2:PCI2 Token-Ring Network 16/4 Adapter          :
```

---

* The Perl program we used earlier could have used the array instead of the scalar as well. This is possible because Perl's version of *snmpget* allows for multiple OIDs, not just one. To specify multiple
OIDs, place a comma (,) between each OID. Remember to enclose each OID within its own double
quotes.

APC uninterruptible power supply:

```
Results :.1.3.6.1.2.1.2.2.1.2: :1:peda:
```

For each device, we see at least one interface. As you'd expect, the router has many interfaces. The first interface on the router is listed as `1:Ethernet0/0`, the second is listed as `2:Ethernet0/1`, and so on, up through interface 18. SNMP keeps track of interfaces as a table, which can have many entries. Even single-homed devices usually have two entries in the table: one for the network interface and one for the loopback interface. The only device in the example above that really has a single interface is the APC UPS—but even in this case, SNMP keeps track of the interface through a table that is indexed by an instance number.

This feature allows you to append an instance number to an OID to look up a particular table element. For example, we would use the OID *.1.3.6.1.2.1.2.2.1.2.1* to look at the first interface of the Cisco router, *.1.3.6.1.2.1.2.2.1.2.2* to look at the second, and so on. In a more human-readable form, *ifDescr.1* is the first device in the interface description table, *ifDescr.2* is the second device, and so on.

Walking the MIB Tree with OpenView

Switching over to OpenView's *snmpwalk*, let's try to get every object in the *.iso. org.dod.internet.mgmt.mib-2.system* subtree:

```
$ /opt/OV/bin/snmpwalk oraswitch2 .1.3.6.1.2.1.1
system.sysDescr.0 : DISPLAY STRING- (ascii):  Cisco Internetwork Operating
System Software IOS (tm) C2900XL Software (C2900XL-H-M), Version 11.2(8)
SA1,RELEASE SOFTWARE (fc1)Copyright (c) 1986-1998 by cisco Systems, Inc.
Compiled Tue 03-Feb-98 14:59 by rheaton
system.sysObjectID.0: OBJECT IDENTIFIER:
.iso.org.dod.internet.private.enterprises.cisco.ciscoProducts.cisco2509
system.sysUpTime.0 : Timeticks: (168113316) 19 days, 10:58:53.16
system.sysContact.0 : DISPLAY STRING- (ascii):  J.C.M. Pager 555-1212
system.sysName.0 : DISPLAY STRING- (ascii):  oraswitch2.ora.com
system.sysLocation.0 : DISPLAY STRING- (ascii): Sebastopol CA
system.sysServices.0 : INTEGER: 6
```

Let's go to the GUI MIB Browser and try that same walk. Repeat the steps you took for the *snmpget* using the GUI. This time insert the OID *.1.3.6.1.2.1.1* and hit the "Start Query" button. Check out the results.

> The GUI figures out whether it needs to perform an *snmpwalk* or *snmpget*. If you give an instance value (being specific), the browser performs an *snmpget*. Otherwise, it does an *snmpwalk*. If you are looking for more speed and less cost to your network, include the instance value.

What will happen if you walk the entire *.iso* subtree? It may hurt or even crash your machine, because in most cases the device can return several thousand values. Each interface on a router can add thousands of values to its MIB tables. If each object takes .0001 seconds to compute and return, and there are 60,000 values to return, it will take your device 6 seconds to return all the values—not counting the load on the network or on the monitoring station. If possible, it is always a good idea to perform an *snmpwalk* starting at the MIB subtree that will provide you with the specific information you are looking for, as opposed to walking the entire MIB.

It might be useful to get a feel for how many MIB objects a given device has implemented. One way to do this is to count the number of objects each *snmp-walk* returns. This can be accomplished with the Unix *grep* command. The *−c* switch to *grep* tells it to return the number of lines that matched. The period (.) tells *grep* to match everything. Starting from the *.system* object (*.1.3.6.1.2.1.1*), let's go back one and see how many objects are implemented in the *mib-2* subtree. Take off the last *.1* off the object ID and run the *snmpwalk* command again, this time piping the results into *grep −c*:

```
$ /opt/OV/bin/snmpwalk oraswitch2 .1.3.6.1.2.1 | grep -c .
```

The number of objects you see will depend on the type of device and the software running on it. When I tried several different devices, I got results ranging from 164 to 5193.

This command is great when you want to walk a MIB to see all the types of values that a device is capable of returning. When I am trying out a new device or MIB, I often walk some decent-sized portion of the MIB and read through all the returned values, looking for any info that may be of interest. When something catches my eye, I go to the MIB definition and read its description. Many GUI MIB Browsers allow you to check the description with the click of a button. In OpenView's GUI, click on the OID and then on "Describe."

Walking the Tree with Net-SNMP

Net-SNMP's *snmpwalk* is very similar in form and function to OpenView's. Here's how you use it:

```
$ snmpwalk orarouter1 public .1.3.6.1.2.1.1
system.sysDescr.0 = Cisco Internetwork Operating System Software
IOS (tm) C820 Software (C820-Y6-M), Version 12.1(3)XG3, EARLY DEPLOYMENT RELEASE
SOFTWARE (fc1)
TAC:Home:SW:IOS:Specials for info
Copyright (c) 1986-2000 by cisco Systems, Inc.
Compiled Wed 20-Dec-00 16:21
system.sysObjectID.0 = OID: enterprises.9.1.284
system.sysUpTime.0 = Timeticks: (100946413) 11 days, 16:24:24.13
```

```
system.sysContact.0 = thenetworkadministrator@oreilly.com
system.sysName.0 = orarouter1@oreilly.com
system.sysLocation.0 = Sebastopol CA
system.sysServices.0 = 6
system.sysORLastChange.0 = Timeticks: (0) 0:00:00.00
```

There aren't any real surprises. Again, you can use an object name instead of a numerical ID; because you're walking a tree, you don't need to specify an instance number.

Setting a MIB Value

With *snmpget* and *snmpwalk*, we have retrieved management information only from devices. The next logical step is to change the value of a MIB object via SNMP. This operation is known as *snmpset*, or *set*. In this section we'll read the value of an object, use *snmpset* to change its value, then read the value again to prove that it's been changed.

There's obviously some danger here: what happens if you change a variable that's critical to the state of the system you're monitoring? In this chapter, we'll deal only with some simple objects, such as the administrative contact, that won't damage anything if they're changed incorrectly. Therefore, if you keep the OIDs correct, you shouldn't worry about hurting any of your devices. All the objects we set in this chapter have an ACCESS of read-write. It's a good idea to get a feel for which objects are writable by reading the MIB in which the object is defined— either one of the RFCs or a MIB file provided by your vendor.

Let's get started. Run the following OpenView command (or use one of the other programs we've discussed) to find out the *sysContact* for your chosen device:

```
$ /opt/OV/bin/snmpget -c public orarouter1 .1.3.6.1.2.1.1.4.0
system.sysContact.0 : DISPLAY STRING- (ascii): ORA IT Group
```

The -c public switch passes the community string *public* to the *snmpget* command.

 Keep in mind that your devices shouldn't use the same (default) community strings that are used within this book. In addition, using the same string for the read-only (*snmpget*) and read-write (*snmpset*) communities is a poor idea.

Now let's run the OpenView *snmpset* command. This command takes the value specified in quotes on the command line and uses it to set the object indicated by the given OID. Use the same OID (*system.sysContact.0*). Since the new value for *sysContact* contains words and possibly numbers, we must also specify the variable type `octetstring`.* Run the OpenView *snmpset* command with the following parameters:

```
$ /opt/OV/bin/snmpset -c private orarouter1 .1.3.6.1.2.1.1.4.0 \
octetstring "Meg A. Byte  555-1212"
system.sysContact.0 : DISPLAY STRING- (ascii):  Meg A. Byte  555-1212
```

The result shows that *snmpset* successfully changed the router's contact person to `Meg A. Byte 555-1212`. If you don't see this result, the *set* was not successful. Table 8-2 shows some of the common error messages you might receive, and steps you can take to correct the problems. To confirm the value the device has stored in *sysContact*, we can repeat the *snmpget* command.

If we use OpenView's GUI, things start to get a bit easier to see, set, and confirm. Use the GUI to get the value of *sysContact*. Once you have confirmed that a value is there, type a description in the SNMP Set Value text box. Since there is only one instance for *sysContact*, you have to insert a 0 (zero) for the MIB Instance. After you have completed all the required input items, click on the "Set" button located to the right of the "SNMP Set Value" text box. You should see a pop-up window that reads "Set has completed successfully." To verify that the *set* actually occurred, click on "Start Query." (It should be apparent to you by now that using a GUI such as OpenView's MIB Browser program makes getting and setting MIB objects much easier.)

To show how this can be done programmatically, we will write another small Perl script, named *snmpset.pl*:

```
#!/usr/local/bin/perl
#filename: /opt/local/perl_scripts/snmpset.pl
use SNMP_util;
$MIB1 = ".1.3.6.1.2.1.1.6.0";
$HOST = "oraswitch2";
$LOC  = "@ARGV";
($value) = &snmpset("private\@$HOST","$MIB1",'string',"$LOC");
if ($value) { print "Results :$MIB1: :$value:\n"; }
else { warn "No response from host :$HOST:\n"; }
```

Let's run this script:

```
$ /opt/local/perl_scripts/snmpset.pl A bld JM-10119 floor 7
Results :.1.3.6.1.2.1.1.6.0: :A bld JM-10119 floor 7:
```

Using the *snmpget.pl* script, we can verify that the *set* took place:

```
$ /opt/local/perl_scripts/snmpget.pl .1.3.6.1.2.1.1.6.0 public@oraswitch2
Results :.1.3.6.1.2.1.1.1.0: :A bld JM-10119 floor 7:
```

Now we'll use the Net-SNMP *snmpset* utility to change the system contact:

```
$ snmpset oraswitch2 private sysContact.0 s myself
system.sysContact.0 = myself
```

---

* If you read RFC 1213 (MIB-II) you will note that *sysLocation* has a SYNTAX of DisplayString. This is really a textual convention of type OCTET STRING with a size of 0..255 octets.

```
$ snmpget oraswitch2 public sysContact.0
system.sysContact.0 = myself
```

There's nothing really confusing here. We supplied a community string, a hostname, and an object ID, followed by a datatype (`s` for `String`) and the new value of *sysContact*. Just to convince ourselves that the *set* actually took place, we followed it with an *snmpget*. The only additional thing you need to know is the mechanism for specifying datatypes. Net-SNMP uses the single-character abbreviations shown in Table 8-1.

Table 8-1. Net-SNMP Datatype Abbreviations

Abbreviation	Meaning
a	IP address
b[a]	Bits
d	Decimal string
D	Double
F	Float
i	Integer
I	Signed int64
n	Null
o	Object ID
s	String
t	Time ticks
u	Unsigned integer
U	Unsigned int64
x	Hexadecimal string

[a] While the manpages show this as a valid datatype, the help output from the command does not.

Error Responses

Table 8-2 shows the error responses that a device might return while executing the commands presented in this chapter. Consult your local documentation if these explanations do not cover your exact problem.

Table 8-2. Error Response Table

Server Responded with	Explanation
Contained under subtree	*snmpwalk* returns this error if you have tried going down a MIB and are already at the end, or if the tree doesn't exist on the client.
No response arrived before timeout	Possible causes include invalid community name, agent is not running, or the node is inaccessible.

Table 8-2. Error Response Table (continued)

Server Responded with	Explanation
Agent reported error with variable	You are trying to set to an object with a datatype that is not the same as (or close to) the variable's specified type. For example, if the variable wants a `DisplayString`, you'll get this error if you send it an `INTEGER`. Read through the MIB to see what `SYNTAX` type the variable needs.
Missing instance value for . . .	When you are setting a value, you must supply the entire OID and instance. A scalar object will end with zero (0) and a tabular object will end with the instance number of the object in a table. Verify that the instance number you're using with *snmpget* is correct and retry your *set*.
Access is denied for variable	This may happen if you are trying to set a value on a read-only object. Review the MIB to see what the object's `ACCESS` setting is.

9

Polling and Thresholds

SNMP gives you the ability to poll your devices regularly, collecting their management information. Furthermore, you can tell the NMS that there are certain thresholds that, if crossed, require some sort of action. For example, you might want to be notified if the traffic at an interface jumps to an extremely high (or low) value; that event might signal a problem with the interface, or insufficient capacity, or even a hostile attack on your network. When such a condition occurs, the NMS can forward an alarm to an event-correlation engine or have an icon on an OpenView map flash. To make this more concrete, let's say that the NMS is polling the status of an interface on a router. If the interface goes down, the NMS reports what has happened so the problem can be quickly resolved.

SNMP can perform either internal or external polling. *Internal* polling is typically used in conjunction with an application that runs as a daemon or a facility such as *cron* that periodically runs a local application. *External* polling is done by the NMS. The OpenView NMS provides a great implementation of external polling; it can graph and save your data for later retrieval or notify you if it looks like something has gone wrong. Many software packages make good NMSs, and if you're clever about scripting you can throw together an NMS that's fine-tuned to your needs. In this chapter, we will look at a few of the available packages.

Polling is like checking the oil in a car; this analogy may help you to think about appropriate polling strategies. Three distinct items concern us when checking the oil: the physical process (opening the hood, pulling out the dipstick, and putting it back in); the preset gauge that tells us if we have a problem (is the level too high, too low, or just right?); and the frequency with which we check it (once an hour, week, month, or year?).

Let's assume that you ask your mechanic to go to the car and check the oil level. This is like an NMS sending a packet to a router to perform an *snmpget* on some piece of information. When the mechanic is finished, you pay him $30 and go on your way. Because a low oil level may result in real engine damage, you want to check the oil regularly. So how long should you wait until you send the mechanic out to the car again? Checking the oil has a cost: in this scenario, you paid $30. In networks, you pay with bandwidth. Like money, you have only so much bandwidth, and you can't spend it frivolously. So the real question is, how long can you wait before checking the oil again without killing your budget?

The answer lies within the car itself. A finely tuned racing car needs to have its fluids at perfect levels. A VW Beetle,* unlike a racecar, can have plus or minus a quart at any time without seriously hindering its performance. You're probably not driving a Beetle, but you're probably not driving a racecar either. So you decide that you can check the oil level about every three weeks. But how will you know what is low, high, or just right?

The car's dipstick tells you. Your mechanic doesn't need to know the car model, engine type, or even the amount of oil in the car; he only needs to know what value he gets when he reads the dipstick. On a network, a device's dipstick is called an agent, and the dipstick reading is the SNMP response packet. All SNMP-compatible devices contain standardized agents (dipsticks) that can be read by any mechanic (NMS). It is important to keep in mind that the data gathered is only as good as the agent, or mechanic, that generated it.

In both cases, some predefined threshold determines the appropriate action. In the oil example, the threshold is "low oil," which triggers an automatic response: add oil. (Crossing the "high oil" threshold might trigger a different kind of response.) If we're talking about a router interface, the possible values we might receive are "up" and "down." Imagine that your company's gateway to the Internet, a port on a router, must stay up 24 hours a day, 7 days a week. If that port goes down, you could lose $10,000 for each second it stays down. Would you check that port often? Most organizations won't pay someone to check router interfaces every hour, let alone every second. Even if you had the time, that wouldn't be fun, right? This is where SNMP polling comes in. It allows network managers to guarantee that mission-critical devices are up and functioning properly, without having to pay someone to constantly monitor routers, servers, etc.

Once you determine your monitoring needs, you can specify at what interval you would like to poll a device or set of devices. This is typically referred to as the *poll interval*, and can be as granular as you like (e.g., every second, every hour, etc.). The threshold value at which you take action doesn't need to be binary: you might decide that something's obviously wrong if the number of packets leaving your Internet connection falls below a certain level.

---

* The old ones from the 1960s, not the fancy modern ones.

Whenever you are figuring out how often to poll a device, remember to keep three things in mind: the device's agent/CPU, bandwidth consumption, and the types of values you are requesting. Some values you receive may be 10-minute averages. If this is the case, it is a waste to poll every few seconds. Review the MIBs surrounding the data for which you are polling. My preference is to start polling fairly often. Once I see the trends and peak values, I back off. This can add congestion to the network but ensures that I don't miss any important information.

Whatever the frequency at which you poll, keep in mind other things that may be happening on the network. Be sure to stagger your polling times to avoid other events if possible. Keep in mind backups, data loads, routing updates, and other events that can cause stress on your networks or CPUs.

Internal Polling

It may seem like a waste of bandwidth to poll a device just to find out that everything is okay. On a typical day, you may poll dozens of devices hundreds or thousands of times without discovering any failures or outages. Of course, that's really what you want to find out—and you'll probably conclude that SNMP has served its purpose the first time you discover a failed device and get the device back online before users have had a chance to start complaining. However, in the best of all possible worlds, you'd get the benefits of polling without the cost: that is, without devoting a significant chunk of your network's bandwidth to monitoring its health.

This is where internal polling comes in. As its name implies, internal polling is performed by an agent that is internal, or built in, to the device you want to manage. Since polling is internal to the device, it doesn't require traffic between the agent and your NMS. Furthermore, the agent doing the polling does not have to be an actual SNMP agent, which can allow you to monitor systems (either machines or software) that do not support SNMP. For example, some industrial-strength air-conditioning-equipment vendors provide operational status information via a serial port. If the air-conditioning unit is attached to a terminal server or similar device, it becomes easy to use scripting languages to monitor the unit and generate traps if the temperature exceeds a certain threshold. This internal program can be written in your favorite scripting language, and it can check any status information to which you can get access. All you need is a way to get data from the script to the management station.

One strategy for writing a polling program is to use "hooks" within a program to extract information that can then be fed into an SNMP trap and sent to the NMS. We will cover traps more in Chapter 10. Another way to do internal polling is to use a program (e.g., *sh*, Perl, or C) that is run at set intervals. (On Unix, you would use *cron* to run a program at fixed intervals; there are similar services on other operating systems.) Hooks and *cron*-driven scripts both allow you to check internal variables and report errors as they are found. Here is a Perl script that checks for the existence of a file and sends a trap if the file is not found:

```
#!/usr/local/bin/perl
# Filename: /opt/local/perl_scripts/check4file.pl

use SNMP_util "0.54";  # This will load the BER and SNMP_Session modules for us

$FILENAME = "/etc/passwd";

#
# if the /etc/passwd file does not exist, send a trap!
#
if(!(-e $FILENAME)) {
    snmptrap("public\@nms:162", ".1.3.6.1.4.1.2789", "sunserver1", 6, 1547, \
            ".1.3.6.1.4.1.2789.1547.1", "string", "File \:$FILENAME\: Could\
            NOT Be Found");
}
```

Here is what the Sun-style *crontab* looks like:

```
$ crontab -l

# Check for this file every 15 minutes and report trap if not found
4,19,34,49 * * * * /opt/local/perl_scripts/check4file.pl
```

Notice that we poll four minutes after each quarter hour, rather than on the quarter hour. The next poll we insert into the *crontab* file may run five minutes after the quarter hour (5,20,35,50). This practice prevents us from starting a huge number of programs at the same time. It's a particularly good idea to avoid polling on the hour—that's a popular time for random programs and *cron* jobs to start up. Consult the *cron* manpage if you are unfamiliar with its operation.

Remote Monitoring (RMON)

RMON is a supplement to the MIB-II group. This group, if supported by the device's SNMP agent, allows us to do both internal and external polling. We can poll devices through a remote NMS (external polling) or have the local RMON agent check itself periodically and report any errors (internal polling). The RMON agent will send traps when error conditions are found.

Many devices support RMON, making it an effective mechanism for internal polling. For example, Cisco supports the Events and Alarms RMON categories. You can configure the Alarms category to poll MIBs internally and react in different ways when a rising or falling threshold occurs. Each threshold has the option of calling an internal Event. Figure 9-1 shows the flow that these two RMON categories take.

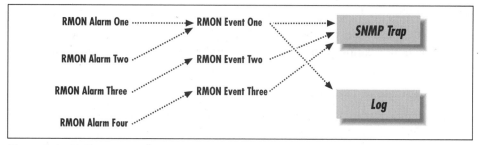

Figure 9-1. RMON process flow

The distinction between alarms and events is important. Each alarm is tied to a specific event, which defines what action to perform when the alarm goes off. Once a threshold is met, triggering an alarm, the alarm calls the event, which can perform additional functions, including sending traps to the NMS and writing a record in a log. Standard SNMP traps are preconfigured by the agent's vendor, which gives network managers no control over setting any kind of thresholds; however, RMON allows a network manager to set rising and falling thresholds. Figure 9-2 represents the interaction between a router's RMON agent and an NMS.

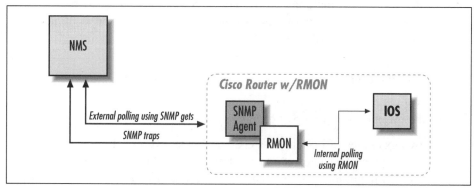

Figure 9-2. RMON and NMS interaction

In Figure 9-2, the Cisco router's SNMP agent forwards a trap to the NMS. Notice the direction of communication: RMON trap transmission is unidirectional. The NMS receives the trap from the Cisco router and decides what action to take, if any.

In addition to sending traps, we can also log events; if we so choose, we can even log the event without generating a trap. Logging can be particularly useful when you are initially configuring RMON alarms and events. If you make your alarm conditions too sensitive, you can clog your NMS with trigger-happy RMON events. Logging can help you fine-tune your RMON alarms before they are released into production.

RMON configuration

As a practical example of how to configure RMON, we will use Cisco's RMON implementation, starting with events. The following IOS command defines an RMON event:

```
rmon event number [log] [trap community] [description string] [owner string]
```

If you're familiar with IOS, you should be expecting a corresponding *no* command that discards an RMON event:

```
no rmon event number
```

The parameters to these IOS commands are:

number

Specifies the unique identification number for the event. This value must be greater than 0; a value of 0 is not allowed.

log

Tells the agent to log the entry when triggered. This argument is optional.

trap *community*

Specifies the trap community string; i.e., a community string to be included with the trap. Many network-management programs can be configured to respond only to traps with a particular community string.

description *string*

Describes the event.

owner *string*

Ties the event or item to a particular person.

Here are two examples of how to create Cisco RMON events. The first line creates a rising alarm, which facilitates sending a trap to the NMS. The second creates a falling alarm that might indicate that traffic has returned to an acceptable level (this alarm is logged, but doesn't generate a trap):

```
(config)#rmon event 1 log trap public description "High ifInOctets" owner dmauro
(config)#rmon event 2 log description "Low ifInOctets" owner dmauro
```

You can also use logging to keep track of when the events were called. Though you can configure traps without logging, what happens if the line to your NMS goes down? Logging ensures that you don't lose information when the NMS is disabled. We suggest using both log and trap on all your events. You can view the logs of your RMON events by issuing the following command on the router:

```
orarouter1# show rmon event

Event 1 is active, owned by dmauro
 Description is High ifInOctets
 Event firing causes log and trap to community public, last fired 00:05:04
```

```
Current log entries:
     index        time     description
         1    00:00:31     High ifInOctets
         2    00:05:04     High ifInOctets
Event 2 is active, owned by dmauro
Description is Low ifInOctets
Event firing causes log, last fired 00:00:11
Current log entries:
     index        time     description
         1    00:00:11     Low ifInOctets
```

The following command walks the *rmon* event table, which displays the values we just set:

```
$ snmpwalk orarouter1 .iso.org.dod.internet.mgmt.mib-2.rmon.event.eventTable
rmon.event.eventTable.eventEntry.eventIndex.1 : INTEGER: 1
rmon.event.eventTable.eventEntry.eventIndex.2 : INTEGER: 2
rmon.event.eventTable.eventEntry.eventDescription.1
                          : DISPLAY STRING- (ascii): High ifInOctets
rmon.event.eventTable.eventEntry.eventDescription.2
                          : DISPLAY STRING- (ascii): Low ifInOctets
rmon.event.eventTable.eventEntry.eventType.1 : INTEGER: log-and-trap
rmon.event.eventTable.eventEntry.eventType.2 : INTEGER: log
rmon.event.eventTable.eventEntry.eventCommunity.1 : OCTET STRING- (ascii): public
rmon.event.eventTable.eventEntry.eventCommunity.2 : OCTET STRING- (ascii):
rmon.event.eventTable.eventEntry.eventLastTimeSent.1 : Timeticks: (0) 0:00:00.00
rmon.event.eventTable.eventEntry.eventLastTimeSent.2 : Timeticks: (0) 0:00:00.00
rmon.event.eventTable.eventEntry.eventOwner.1 : DISPLAY STRING- (ascii): dmauro
rmon.event.eventTable.eventEntry.eventOwner.2 : DISPLAY STRING- (ascii): dmauro
rmon.event.eventTable.eventEntry.eventStatus.1 : INTEGER: valid
rmon.event.eventTable.eventEntry.eventStatus.2 : INTEGER: valid
```

Most of the information we set on the command line is available through SNMP. We see two events, with indexes 1 and 2. The first event has the description `High ifInOctets`; it is logged and a trap is generated; the community string for the event is `public`; the event's owner is `dmauro`; the event is `valid`, which essentially means that it is enabled; and we also see that the event has not yet occurred. Instead of using the command line to define these events, we could have used *snmpset* either to create new events or to modify events we already have. If you take this route, keep in mind that you must set the *eventEntry.eventStatus* to 1, for "valid," for the event to work properly.

 You can poll the objects *ifDescr* and *ifType* in the *mgmt.interfaces.ifEntry* subtree to help you identify which instance number you should use for your devices. If you are using a device with multiple ports, you may need to search the *ifType*, *ifAdminStatus*, and *ifOperStatus* to help you identify what's what. In the next section, "External Polling," we will see that it is not necessary to keep track of these MIB variables (the external polling software takes care of this for us).

Now that we have our events configured, let's start configuring alarms to do some internal polling. We need to know what we are going to poll, what type of data is returned, and how often we should poll. Assume that the router is our default gateway to the Internet. We want to poll the router's second interface, which is a serial interface. Therefore, we want to poll *mgmt.interfaces.ifEntry.ifInOctets.2* to get the number of outbound octets on that interface, which is an INTEGER type.*
To be precise, the *ifInOctets* MIB object is defined as "The total number of octets received on the interface, including framing characters." (The *.2* at the end of the OID indicates the second entry in the *ifEntry* table. On our router, this denotes the second interface, which is the one we want to poll.) We want to be notified if the traffic on this interface exceeds 90,000 octets/second; we'll assume things are back to normal when the traffic falls back under 85,000 octets/second. This gives us the rising and falling thresholds for our alarm. Next, we need to figure out the interval at which we are going to poll this object. Let's start by polling every 60 seconds.

Now we need to put all this information into a Cisco RMON *alarm* command. Here is the command to create an alarm:

```
rmon alarm number variable interval {delta | absolute}
    rising-threshold value [event-number]
    falling-threshold value [event-number]
    [owner string]
```

The following command discards the alarm:

```
no rmon alarm number
```

The parameters to these commands are:

number
Specifies the unique identification number assigned to the alarm.

variable
Specifies which MIB object to monitor.

interval
Specifies the frequency at which the alarm monitors the MIB variable.

delta
Indicates that the threshold values given in the command should be interpreted in terms of the difference between successive readings.

absolute
Indicates that the threshold values given in the command should be interpreted as absolute values; i.e., the difference between the current value and preceding values is irrelevant.

---

* From RFC 1757, the *alarmVariable* (the object/MIB we are going to poll) needs to resolve to an ASN.1 primitive type of INTEGER, Counter, Gauge, or TimeTicks.

`rising-threshold` *value event-number*

> Specifies the value at which the alarm should be triggered, calling the event, when the value is rising. *event-number* is the event that should be called when the alarm occurs. The event number is optional because the threshold doesn't have to be assigned an event. If either of the two thresholds is left blank the event number will be set to 0, which does nothing.

`falling-threshold` *value event-number*

> Specifies the value at which the alarm should be triggered, calling the event, when the value is falling. *event-number* is the event that should be called when the alarm occurs. The event number is optional because the threshold doesn't have to be assigned an event. If either of the two thresholds is left blank the event number will be set to 0, which does nothing.

`owner` *string*

> Ties this alarm to a particular person.

To configure the alarm settings we just described, enter the following command, in *configuration* mode, on a Cisco console:

```
orarouter1(config)#rmon alarm 25 ifEntry.10.2 60 absolute \
rising-threshold 90000 1 falling-threshold 85000 2 owner dmauro
```

This command configures alarm number 25, which monitors the object in *ifEntry. 10.2* (instance 2 of *ifEntry.ifInOctets*, or the input octets on interface 2) every 60 seconds. It has a rising threshold of 90,000 octets, which has event number 1 tied to it: event 1 is called when traffic on this interface exceeds 90,000 octets/second. The falling threshold is set to 85,000 octets and has event number 2 tied to it. Here's how the alarm looks in the router's internal tables:

```
orarouter1#show rmon alarm

Alarm 1 is active, owned by dmauro
 Monitors ifEntry.10.2 every 60 second(s)
 Taking absolute samples, last value was 87051
 Rising threshold is 90000, assigned to event 1
 Falling threshold is 85000, assigned to event 2
 On startup enable rising or falling alarm
```

The last line of output says that the router will enable the alarm upon reboot. As you'd expect, you can also look at the alarm settings through the RMON MIB, beginning with the subtree *1.3.6.1.2.1.16*. As with the events themselves, we can create, change, edit, and delete entries using *snmpset*.

One problem with internal polling is that getting trends and seeing the data in a graph or table is difficult. Even if you develop the backend systems to gather MIB objects and display them graphically, retrieving data is sometimes painful. The Multi Router Traffic Grapher (MRTG) is a great program that allows you to do both internal and external polling. Furthermore, it is designed to generate graphs of your data in HTML format. MRTG is covered in Chapter 13.

External Polling

It is often impossible to poll a device internally, for technical, security, or political reasons. For example, the System Administration group may not be in the habit of giving out the root password, making it difficult for you to install and maintain internal polling scripts. However, they may have no problem with installing and maintaining an SNMP agent such as Concord's SystemEDGE or Net-SNMP. It's also possible that you will find yourself in an environment in which you lack the knowledge to build the tools necessary to poll internally. Despite the situation, if an SNMP agent is present on a machine that has objects worth polling, you can use an external device to poll the machine and read the objects' values.* This external device can be one or more NMSs or other machines or devices. For instance, when you have a decent-sized network it is sometimes convenient, and possibly necessary, to distribute polling among several NMSs.

Each of the external polling engines we will look at uses the same polling methods, although some NMSs implement external polling differently. We'll start with the OpenView *xnmgraph* program, which can be used to collect and display data graphically. You can even use OpenView to save the data for later retrieval and analysis. We'll include some examples that show how you can collect data and store it automatically and how you can retrieve that data for display. Castle Rock's SNMPc also has an excellent data-collection facility that we will use to collect and graph data.

Collecting and Displaying Data with OpenView

One of the easiest ways to get some interesting graphs with OpenView is to use the *xnmgraph* program. You can run *xnmgraph* from the command line and from some of NNM's menus. One practical way to graph is to use OpenView's *xnmbrowser†* to collect some data and then click "Graph." It's as easy as that. If the node you are polling has more than one instance (say, multiple interfaces), OpenView will graph all known instances. When an NMS queries a device such as a router, it determines how many instances are in the *ifTable* and retrieves management data for each entry in the table.

---

* Many devices say they are SNMP-compatible but support only a few MIBs. This makes polling nearly impossible. If you don't have the object(s) to poll there is nothing you can do, unless there are hooks for an extensible agent. Even with extensible agents, unless you know how to program, the Simple in SNMP goes away fast.

† Review Chapter 8 for an explanation of starting the *xnmbrowser.*

OpenView Graphing

Figure 9-3 shows the sort of graph you can create with NNM. To create this graph, we started the browser (Figure 8-2) and clicked down through the MIB tree until we found the *.iso.org.dod.internet.mgmt.mib-2.interfaces.ifTable.ifEntry* list. Once there, we clicked on *ifInOctets*; then, while holding down the Ctrl key, we clicked on *ifOutOctets*. After both were selected and we verified that the "Name or IP Address" field displayed the node we wanted to poll, we clicked on the "Graph" button.

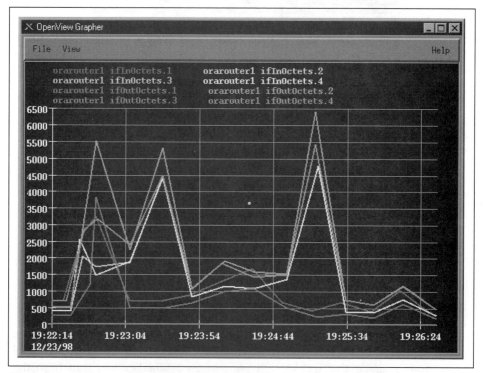

Figure 9-3. OpenView xnmgraph of octets in/out

Once the graph has started, you can change the polling interval and the colors used to display different objects. You can also turn off the display of some or all of the object instances. The menu item "View → Line Configuration" lets you specify which objects you would like to display; it can also set multipliers for different items. For example, to display everything in K, multiply the data by .001. There is also an option ("View → Statistics") that shows a statistical summary of your graph. Figure 9-4 shows some statistics from the graph in Figure 9-3. While the statistics menu is up, you can left-click on the graph; the statistics window will display the values for the specific date and time to which you are pointing with the mouse.

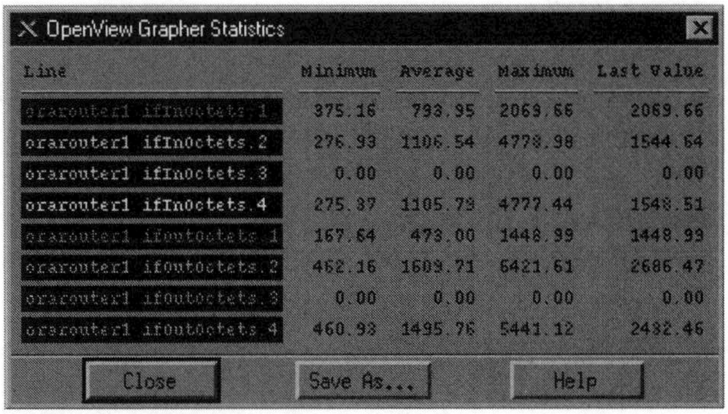

Line	Minimum	Average	Maximum	Last Value
orarouter1 ifInOctets.1	375.16	793.95	2069.66	2069.66
orarouter1 ifInOctets.2	276.93	1106.54	4778.98	1544.64
orarouter1 ifInOctets.3	0.00	0.00	0.00	0.00
orarouter1 ifInOctets.4	275.87	1105.73	4777.44	1548.51
orarouter1 ifOutOctets.1	167.64	473.00	1448.99	1448.99
orarouter1 ifOutOctets.2	462.16	1609.71	6421.61	2686.47
orarouter1 ifOutOctets.3	0.00	0.00	0.00	0.00
orarouter1 ifOutOctets.4	460.93	1495.76	5441.12	2432.46

OpenView Grapher Statistics

Close   Save As...   Help

Figure 9-4. xnmgraph statistics

Starting *xnmgraph* from the command line allows you to start the grapher at a specific polling period and gives you several other options. By default, OpenView polls at 10-second intervals. In most cases this is fine, but if you are polling a multiport router to check if some ports are congested, a 10-second polling interval may be too quick and could cause operational problems. For example, if the CPU is busy answering SNMP queries every 10 seconds, the router might get bogged down and become very slow, especially if the router is responsible for OSPF or other CPU-intensive tasks. You may also see messages from OpenView complaining that another poll has come along while it is still waiting for the previous poll to return. Increasing the polling interval usually gets rid of these messages.

Some of NNM's default menus let you use the grapher to poll devices depending on their type. For example, you can select the object type "router" on the NNM and generate a graph that includes all your routers. Whether you start from the command line or from the menu, there are times when you will get a message back that reads "Requesting more lines than number of colors (25). Reducing number of lines." This message means that there aren't enough colors available to display the objects you are trying to graph. The only good ways to avoid this problem are to break up your graphs so that they poll fewer objects or to eliminate object instances you don't want. For example, you probably don't want to graph router interfaces that are down (for whatever reason) and other "dead" objects. We will soon see how you can use a regular expression as one of the arguments to the *xnmgraph* command to graph only those interfaces that are up and running.

Although the graphical interface is very convenient, the command-line interface gives you much more flexibility. The following script displays the graph in Figure 9-3 (i.e., the graph we generated through the browser):

```
#!/bin/sh
# filename: /opt/OV/local/scripts/graphOctets
# syntax: graphOctets <hostname>
/opt/OV/bin/xnmgraph -c public -mib \
".iso.org.dod.internet.mgmt.mib-2.interfaces.ifTable.ifEntry.ifInOctets:::::::,\
.iso.org.dod.internet.mgmt.mib-2.interfaces.ifTable.ifEntry.ifOutOctets:::::::" \
$1
```

You can run this script with the command:

$ **/opt/OV/local/scripts/graphOctets orarouter1**

The worst part of writing the script is figuring out what command-line options you want—particularly the long strings of nine colon-separated options. All these options give you the ability to refine what you want to graph, how often you want to poll the objects, and how you want to display the data. (We'll discuss the syntax of these options as we go along, but for the complete story, see the *xnmgraph*(1) manpage.) In this script, we're graphing the values of two MIB objects, *ifInOctets* and *ifOutOctets*. Each OID we want to graph is the first (and in this case, the only) option in the string of colon-separated options. On our network, this command produces eight traces: input and output octets for each of our four interfaces. You can add other OIDs to the graph by adding sets of options, but at some point the graph will become too confusing to be useful. It will take some experimenting to use the *xnmgraph* command efficiently, but once you learn how to generate useful graphs you'll wonder how you ever got along without it.

Keeping your scripts neat is not only good practice, but also aesthetically pleasing. Using a "\" at the end of a line indicates that the next line is a continuation of the current line. Breaking your lines intelligently makes your scripts more readable. Be warned that the Unix shells do *not* like extra whitespace after the "\". The only character after each "\" should be one carriage return.

Now, let's modify the script to include more reasonable labels—in particular, we'd like the graph to show which interface is which, rather than just showing the index number. In our modified script, we've used numerical object IDs, mostly for formatting convenience, and we've added a sixth option to the ugly sequence of colon-separated options: *.1.3.6.1.2.1.2.2.1.2* (this is the *ifDescr*, or interface description, object in the interface table). This option says to poll each instance and use the return value of *snmpget .1.3.6.1.2.1.2.2.1.2.INSTANCE* as the label. This should give us meaningful labels. Here's the new script:

```
#!/bin/sh
# filename: /opt/OV/local/scripts/graphOctets
# syntax: graphOctets <hostname>
/opt/OV/bin/xnmgraph -c public -title Bits_In_n_Out -mib \
".1.3.6.1.4.1.9.2.2.1.1.6:::::.1.3.6.1.2.1.2.2.1.2:::,\
.1.3.6.1.4.1.9.2.2.1.1.8:::::.1.3.6.1.2.1.2.2.1.2:::" $1
```

To see what we'll get for labels, here's the result of walking *.1.3.6.1.2.1.2.2.1.2*:

```
$ snmpwalk orarouter1 .1.3.6.1.2.1.2.2.1.2
interfaces.ifTable.ifEntry.ifDescr.1 : DISPLAY STRING- (ascii): Ethernet0
interfaces.ifTable.ifEntry.ifDescr.2 : DISPLAY STRING- (ascii): Serial0
interfaces.ifTable.ifEntry.ifDescr.3 : DISPLAY STRING- (ascii): Serial1
```

Figure 9-5 shows our new graph. With the addition of this sixth option, the names and labels are much easier to read.

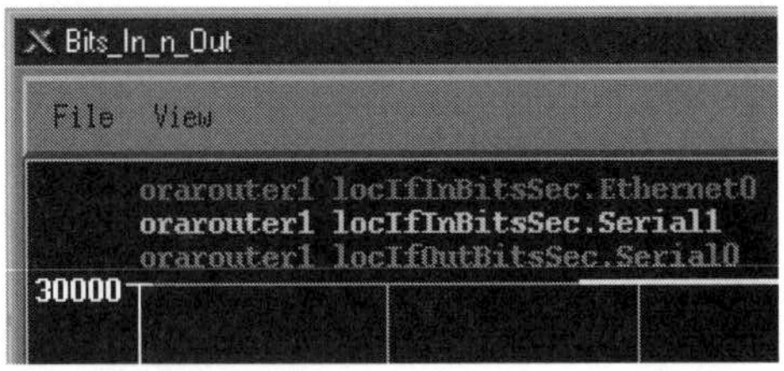

Figure 9-5. OpenView xnmgraph with new labels

Meaningful labels and titles are important, especially if management is interested in seeing the graphs. A label that contains an OID and not a textual description is of no use. Some objects that are useful in building labels are *ifType (.1.3.6.1.2.1.2. 2.1.3)* and *ifOperStatus (.1.3.6.1.2.1.2.2.1.8)*. Be careful when using *ifOperStatus*; if the status of the interface changes during a poll, the label does not change. The label is evaluated only once.

One of the most wasteful things you can do is poll a useless object. This often happens when an interface is administratively down or not configured. Imagine that you have 20 serial interfaces, but only one is actually in use. If you are looking for octets in and out of your serial interfaces, you'll be polling 40 times and 38 of the polls will always read 0. OpenView's *xnmgraph* allows you to specify an OID and regular expression to select what should be graphed. To put this feature to use, let's walk the MIB to see what information is available:

```
$ snmpwalk orarouter1 .1.3.6.1.2.1.2.2.1.8
interfaces.ifTable.ifEntry.ifOperStatus.1 : INTEGER: up
interfaces.ifTable.ifEntry.ifOperStatus.2 : INTEGER: up
interfaces.ifTable.ifEntry.ifOperStatus.3 : INTEGER: down
```

This tells us that only two interfaces are currently up. By looking at *ifDescr*, we see that the live interfaces are *Ethernet0* and *Serial0*; *Serial1* is down. Notice that the type of *ifOperStatus* is INTEGER, but the return value looks like a string. How is this? RFC 1213 defines string values for each possible return value:

```
ifOperStatus OBJECT-TYPE
    SYNTAX   INTEGER {
                up(1),         -- ready to pass packets
                down(2),
                testing(3)     -- in some test mode
             }
    ACCESS   read-only
    STATUS   mandatory
    DESCRIPTION
        "The current operational state of the interface. The testing(3)
         state indicates that no operational packets can be passed."
    ::= { ifEntry 8 }
```

It's fairly obvious how to read this: the integer value 1 is converted to the string up. We can therefore use the value 1 in a regular expression that tests *ifOper-Status*. For every instance we will check the value of *ifOperStatus*; we will poll that instance and graph the result only if the status returns 1. In pseudocode, the operation would look something like this:

```
if (ifOperStatus == 1) {
    pollForMIBData;
    graphOctets;
}
```

Here's the next version of our graphing script. To put this logic into a graph, we use the OID for *ifOperStatus* as the fourth colon option, and the regular expression (1) as the fifth option:

```
#!/bin/sh
# filename: /opt/OV/local/scripts/graphOctets
# syntax: graphOctets <hostname>
/opt/OV/bin/xnmgraph -c public \
-title Octets_In_and_Out_For_All_Up_Interfaces \
-mib ".1.3.6.1.2.1.2.2.1.10:::.1.3.6.1.2.1.2.2.1.8:1::::, \
.1.3.6.1.2.1.2.2.1.16:::.1.3.6.1.2.1.2.2.1.8:1::::" $1
```

This command graphs the *ifInOctets* and *ifOutOctets* of any interface that has a current operational state equal to 1, or up. It therefore polls and graphs only the ports that are important, saving on network bandwidth and simplifying the graph. Furthermore, we're less likely to run out of colors while making the graph because we won't assign them to useless objects. Note, however, that this selection happens only during the first poll and stays effective throughout the entire life of the graphing process. If the status of any interface changes after the graph has been started, nothing in the graph will change. The only way to discover any changes in interface status is to restart *xnmgraph*.

Finally, let's look at:

- How to add a label to each of the OIDs we graph
- How to multiply each value by a constant
- How to specify the polling interval

The cropped graph in Figure 9-6 shows how the labels change when we run the following script:

```
#!/bin/sh
# filename: /opt/OV/local/scripts/graphOctets
# syntax: graphOctets <hostname>
/opt/OV/bin/xnmgraph -c public -title Internet_Traffic_In_K -poll 68 -mib \
".1.3.6.1.4.1.9.2.2.1.1.6:Incoming_Traffic:::::.1.3.6.1.2.1.2.2.1.2::.001:,\
.1.3.6.1.4.1.9.2.2.1.1.8:Outgoing_Traffic:::::.1.3.6.1.2.1.2.2.1.2::.001:" \
$1
```

The labels are given by the second and sixth fields in the colon-separated options (the second field provides a textual label to identify the objects we're graphing and the sixth uses the *ifDescr* field to identify the particular interface); the constant multiplier (.001) is given by the eighth field; and the polling interval (in seconds) is given by the *–poll* option.

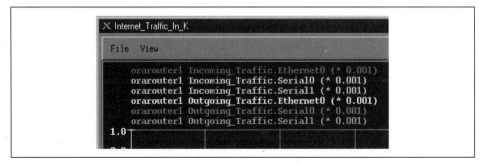

Figure 9-6. xnmgraph with labels and multipliers

By now it should be apparent how flexible OpenView's *xnmgraph* program really is. These graphs can be important tools for troubleshooting your network. When a network manager receives complaints from customers regarding slow connections, he can look at the graph of *ifInOctets* generated by *xnmgraph* to see if any router interfaces have unusually high traffic spikes.

Graphs like these are also useful when you're setting thresholds for alarms and other kinds of traps. The last thing you want is a threshold that is too triggery (one that goes off too many times) or a threshold that won't go off until the entire building burns to the ground. It's often useful to look at a few graphs to get a feel for your network's behavior before you start setting any thresholds. These graphs will give you a baseline from which to work. For example, say you want to be notified when the battery on your UPS is low (which means it is being used) and when it is back to normal (fully charged). The obvious way to implement this is to generate an alarm when the battery falls below some percentage of full charge, and another alarm when it returns to full charge. So the question is: what value can we set for the threshold? Should we use 10% to indicate that the battery is being used and 100% to indicate that it's back to normal? We can find the baseline by graphing the device's MIBs.* For example, with a few days' worth of graphs, we can see that our UPS's battery stays right around 94–97% when it is not in use. There was a brief period when the battery dropped down to 89%, when it was performing a self-test. Based on these numbers, we may want to set the "in use" threshold at 85% and the "back to normal" threshold at 94%. This pair of thresholds gives us plenty of notification when the battery's in use, but won't generate useless alarms when the device is in self-test mode. The appropriate thresholds depend on the type of devices you are polling, as well as the MIB data that is gathered. Doing some initial testing and polling to get a baseline (normal numbers) will help you set thresholds that are meaningful and useful.

Before leaving *xnmgraph*, we'll take a final look at the nastiest aspect of this program: the sequence of nine colon-separated options. In the examples, we've demonstrated the most useful combinations of options. In more detail, here's the syntax of the graph specification:

> *object:label:instances:match:expression:instance-label:truncator:multiplier:nodes*

The parameters are:

object

> The OID of the object whose values you want to graph. This can be in either numeric or human-readable form, but it should *not* have an instance number at the end. It can also be the name of an expression (expressions are discussed in Appendix A).

label

> A string to use in making the label for all instances of this object. This can be a literal string or the OID of some object with a string value. The label used on the graph is made by combining this label (for all instances of the object) with *instance-label*, which identifies individual instances of an object in a table. For example, in Figure 9-6, the labels are *Incoming_Traffic* and *Outgoing_Traffic*; *instance-label* is *1.3.6.1.2.1.2.2.1.2*, or the *ifDescr* field for each object being graphed.

---

* Different vendors have different UPS MIBs. Refer to your particular vendor's MIB to find out which object represents low battery power.

instances

> A regular expression that specifies which instances of *object* to graph. If this is omitted, all instances are graphed. For example, the regular expression 1 limits the graph to instance 1 of *object*; the regular expression [4-7] limits the graph to instances 4 through 7. You can use the *match* and *expression* fields to further specify which objects to match.

match

> The OID of an object (not including the instance ID) to match against a regular expression (the match-expression), to determine which instances of the object to display in the graph.

expression

> A regular expression; for each instance, the object given by *match* is compared to this regular expression. If the two match, the instance is graphed.

instance-label

> A label to use to identify particular instances of the object you are graphing. This is used in combination with the *label* and *truncator* fields to create a label for each instance of each object being graphed.

truncator

> A string that will be removed from the initial portion of the instance label, to make it shorter.

multiplier

> A number that's used to scale the values being graphed.

nodes

> The nodes to poll to create the graph. You can list any number of nodes, separated by spaces. The wildcard "*" polls all the nodes in OpenView's database. If you omit this field, *xnmgraph* takes the list of nodes from the final argument on the command line.

The only required field is *object*; however, as we've seen, you must have all eight colons even if you leave some (or most) of the fields empty.

OpenView Data Collection and Thresholds

Once you close the OpenView graphs, the data in them is lost forever. OpenView provides a way to fix this problem with data collection. Data collection allows the user to poll and record data continuously. It can also look at these results and trigger events. One benefit of data collection is that it can watch the network for you while you're not there; you can start collecting data on Friday then leave for the weekend knowing that any important events will be recorded in your absence.

You can start OpenView's Data Collection and Thresholds function from the command line, using the command *$OV_BIN/xnmcollect*, or from NNM under the Options menu. This brings you to the "Data Collection and Thresholds" window, shown in Figure 9-7, which displays a list of all the collections you have configured and a summary of the collection parameters.

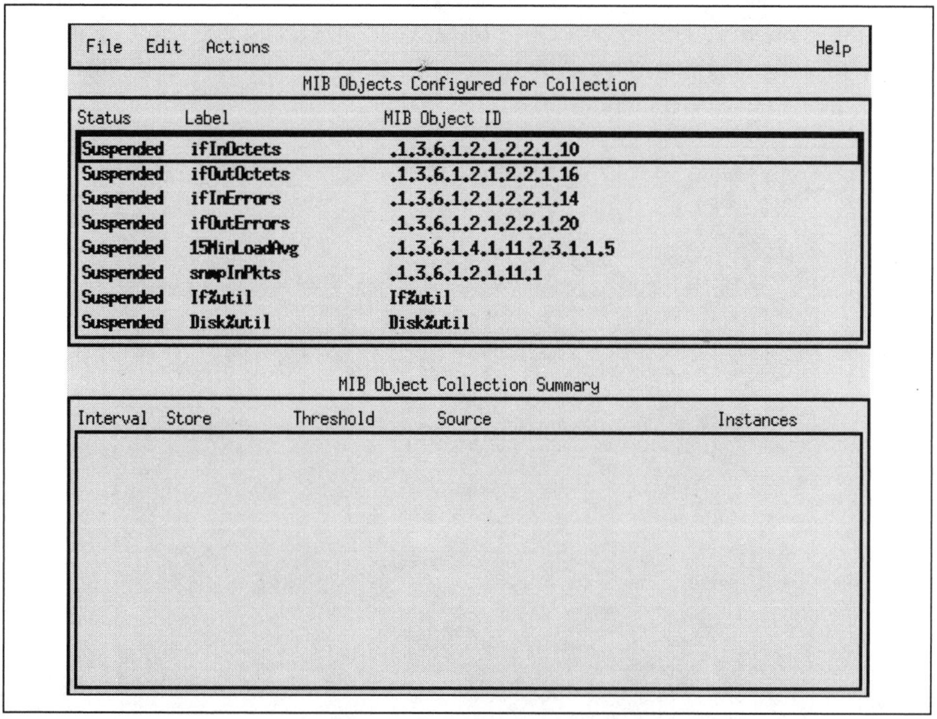

```
File   Edit   Actions                                              Help
                    MIB Objects Configured for Collection

Status       Label              MIB Object ID

Suspended    ifInOctets         .1.3.6.1.2.1.2.2.1.10
Suspended    ifOutOctets        .1.3.6.1.2.1.2.2.1.16
Suspended    ifInErrors         .1.3.6.1.2.1.2.2.1.14
Suspended    ifOutErrors        .1.3.6.1.2.1.2.2.1.20
Suspended    15MinLoadAvg       .1.3.6.1.4.1.11.2.3.1.1.5
Suspended    snmpInPkts         .1.3.6.1.2.1.11.1
Suspended    If%util            If%util
Suspended    Disk%util          Disk%util


                    MIB Object Collection Summary

Interval  Store      Threshold      Source              Instances




```

Figure 9-7. OpenView's Data Collection and Thresholds window

Configured collections that are in "Suspended" mode appear in a dark or bold font. This indicates that OpenView is not collecting any data for these objects. A "Collecting" status indicates that OpenView is polling the selected nodes for the given object and saving the data. To change the status of a collection, select the object, click on "Actions," and then click on either "Suspend Collection" or "Resume Collection." (Note that you must save your changes before they will take effect.)

Designing collections

To design a new collection, click on "Edit → Add MIB Object." This takes you to a new screen. At the top, click on "MIB Object"[*] and click down through the tree

---

[*] You can collect the value of an expression instead of a single MIB object. The topic of expressions is out of the scope of this book but is explained in the *mibExpr.conf*(4) manpage.

until you find the object you would like to poll. To look at the status of our printer's paper tray, for example, we need to navigate down to *.iso.org.dod. internet.private.enterprises.hp.nm.system.net-peripheral.net-printer.generalDevice-Status.gdStatusEntry.gdStatusPaperOut (.1.3.6.1.4.1.11.2.3.9.1.1.2.8).* The object's description suggests that this is the item we want: it reads "This indicates that the peripheral is out of paper." (If you already know what you're looking for, you can enter the name or OID directly.) Once there, you can change the name of the collection to something that is easier to read. Click "OK" to move forward. This brings you to the menu shown in Figure 9-8.

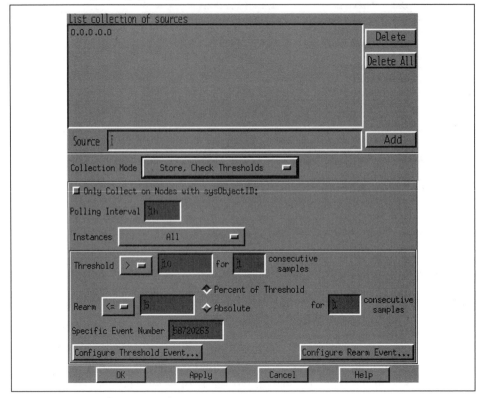

Figure 9-8. OpenView poll configuration menu

The "Source" field is where you specify the nodes from which you would like to collect data. Enter the hostnames or IP addresses you want to poll. You can use wildcards like *198.27.6.** in your IP addresses; you can also click "Add Map" to add any nodes currently selected. We suggest that you start with one node for

---

* This object is in HP's private MIB, so it won't be available unless you have HP printers and have installed the appropriate MIBs. Note that there is a standard printer MIB, RFC 1759, but HP's MIB has more useful information.

testing purposes. Adding more nodes to a collection is easy once you have everything set up correctly; you just return to the window in Figure 9-8 and add the nodes to the Source list.

"Collection Mode" lets you specify what to do with the data NNM collects. There are four collection modes: "Exclude Collection," "Store, Check Thresholds," "Store, No Thresholds," and "Don't Store, Check Thresholds." Except for "Exclude Collection," which allows us to turn off individual collections for each device, the collection modes are fairly self-explanatory. ("Exclude Collection" may sound odd, but it is very useful if you want to exclude some devices from collection without stopping the entire process; for example, you may have a router with a hardware problem that is bombarding you with meaningless data.) Data collection without a threshold is easier than collection with a threshold, so we'll start there. Set the Collection Mode to "Store, No Thresholds." This disable (grays out) the bottom part of the menu, which is used for threshold parameters. (Select "Store, Check Thresholds" if you want both data collection and threshold monitoring.) Then click "OK" and save the new collection. You can now watch your collection grow in the *$OV_DB/snmpCollect* directory. Each collection consists of a binary datafile, plus a file with the same name preceded by an exclamation mark (!); this file stores the collection information. The data-collection files will grow without bounds. To trim these files without disturbing the collector, delete all files that do not contain an "!" mark.

Clicking on "Only Collect on Nodes with sysObjectID:" allows you to enter a value for *sysObjectID*. *sysObjectID* (*iso.org.dod.internet.mgmt.mib-2.system.sysObjectID*) lets you limit polling to devices made by a specific manufacturer. Its value is the enterprise number the device's manufacturer has registered with IANA. For example, Cisco's enterprise number is 9, and HP's is 11 (the complete list is available at *http://www.isi.edu/in-notes/iana/assignments/enterprise-numbers*); therefore, to restrict polling to devices manufactured by HP, set the *sysObjectID* to 11. RFC 1213 formally defines *sysObjectID* (*1.3.6.1.2.1.1.2*) as follows:

```
sysObjectID OBJECT-TYPE
    SYNTAX   OBJECT IDENTIFIER
    ACCESS   read-only
    STATUS   mandatory
    DESCRIPTION
        "The vendor's authoritative identification of the network
        management subsystem contained in the entity. This value
        is allocated within the SMI enterprises subtree (1.3.6.1.4.1)
        and provides an easy and unambiguous means for determining
        what kind of box' is being managed. For example, if vendor
        'Flintstones, Inc.' was assigned the subtree 1.3.6.1.4.1.4242,
        it could assign the identifier 1.3.6.1.4.1.4242.1.1 to its
        'Fred Router'."
    ::= { system 2 }
```

The polling interval is the period at which polling occurs. You can use one-letter abbreviations to specify units: "s" for seconds, "m" for minutes, "h" for hours, "d" for days. For example, 32s indicates 32 seconds; 1.5d indicates one and a half days. When I'm designing a data collection, I usually start with a very short polling interval—typically 7s (7 seconds between each poll). You probably wouldn't want to use a polling interval this short in practice (all the data you collect is going to have to be stored somewhere), but when you're setting up a collection, it's often convenient to use a short polling interval. You don't want to wait a long time to find out whether you're collecting the right data.

The next option is a drop-down menu that specifies what instances should be polled. The options are "All," "From List," and "From Regular Expression." In this case we're polling a scalar item, so we don't have to worry about instances; we can leave the setting to "All" or select "From List" and specify instance "0" (the instance number for all scalar objects). If you're polling a tabular object, you can either specify a comma-separated list of instances or choose the "From Regular Expression" option and write a regular expression that selects the instances you want. Save your changes ("File → Save"), and you're done.

Creating a threshold

Once you've set all this up, you've configured NNM to periodically collect the status of your printer's paper tray. Now for something more interesting: let's use thresholds to generate some sort of notification when the traffic coming in through one of our network interfaces exceeds a certain level. To do this, we'll look at a Cisco-specific object, *locIfInBitsSec* (more formally *iso.org.dod.internet.private.enterprises. cisco.local.linterfaces.lifTable.lifEntry.locIfInBitsSec*), whose value is the five-minute average of the rate at which data arrives at the interface, in bits per second. (There's a corresponding object called *locIfOutBitsSec*, which measures the data leaving the interface.) The first part of the process should be familiar: start Data Collection and Thresholds by going to the Options menu of NNM; then click on "Edit → Add MIB Object." Navigate through the object tree until you get to *locIfInBitsSec*; click "OK" to get back to the screen shown in Figure 9-8. Specify the IP addresses of the interfaces you want to monitor and set the collection mode to "Store, Check Thresholds"; this allows you to retrieve and view the data at a later time. (I typically turn on the "Store" function so I can verify that the collector is actually working and view any data that has accumulated.) Pick a reasonable polling interval—again, when you're testing it's reasonable to use a short interval— then choose which instances you'd like to poll, and you're ready to set thresholds.

The "Threshold" field lets you specify the point at which the value you're monitoring becomes interesting. What "interesting" means is up to you. In this case, let's assume that we're monitoring a T1 connection, with a capacity of 1.544 Mbits/

second. Let's say somewhat arbitrarily that we'll start worrying when the incoming traffic exceeds 75% of our capacity. So, after multiplying, we set the threshold to "> 1158000". Of course, network traffic is fundamentally bursty, so we won't worry about a single peak—but if we have two or three consecutive readings that exceed the threshold, we want to be notified. So let's set "consecutive samples" to 3: that shields us from getting unwanted notifications, while providing ample notification if something goes wrong.

Setting an appropriate consecutive samples value will make your life much more pleasant, though picking the right value is something of an art. Another example is monitoring the */tmp* partition of a Unix system. In this case, you may want to set the threshold to ">= 85", the number of consecutive samples to 2, and the poll interval to 5m. This will generate an event when the usage on */tmp* exceeds 85% for two consecutive polls. This choice of settings means that you won't get a false alarm if a user copies a large file to */tmp* and then deletes the file a few minutes later. If you set consecutive samples to 1, NNM will generate a Threshold event as soon as it notices that */tmp* is filling up, even if the condition is only temporary and nothing to be concerned about. It will then generate a Rearm event after the user deletes the file. Since we are really only worried about */tmp* filling up and staying full, setting the consecutive threshold to 2 can help reduce the number of false alarms. This is generally a good starting value for consecutive samples, unless your polling interval is very high.

The rearm parameters let us specify when everything is back to normal or is, at the very least, starting to return to normal. This state must occur before another threshold is met. You can specify either an absolute value or a percentage. When monitoring the packets arriving at an interface, you might want to set the rearm threshold to something like 926,400 bits per second (an absolute value that happens to be 60% of the total capacity) or 80% of the threshold (also 60% of capacity). Likewise, if you're generating an alarm when */tmp* exceeds 85% of capacity, you might want to rearm when the free space returns to 80% of your 85% threshold (68% of capacity). You can also specify the number of consecutive samples that need to fall below the rearm point before NNM will consider the rearm condition met.

The final option, "Configure Threshold Event," asks what OpenView events you would like to execute for each state. You can leave the default event, or you can refer to Chapter 10 for more on how to configure events. The "Threshold" state needs a specific event number that must reside in the HP enterprise. The default Threshold event is *OV_DataCollectThresh – 58720263*. Note that the Threshold event is always an odd number. The Rearm event is the next number after the Threshold event: in this case, 58720264. To configure events other than the default, click on "Configure Threshold Event" and, when the new menu comes up, add one event (with an odd number) to the HP section and a second event for the corresponding Rearm. After making the additions, save and return to the Collection windows to enter the new number.

When you finish configuring the data collection, click "OK." This brings you back to the Data Collection and Thresholds menu. Click "File → Save" to make your current additions active. On the bottom half of the "MIB Object Collection Summary" window, click on your new object and then on "Actions → Test SNMP." This brings up a window showing the results of an SNMP test on that collection. After the test, wait long enough for your polling interval to have expired once or twice. Then click on the object collection again, but this time click on "Actions → Show Data." This window shows the data that has been gathered so far. Try blasting data through the interface to see if you can trigger a Threshold event. If the Threshold events are not occurring, verify that your threshold and polling intervals are set correctly. After you've seen a Threshold event occur, watch how the Rearm event gets executed. When you're finished testing, go back and set up realistic polling periods, add any additional nodes you would like to poll, and turn off storing if you don't want to collect data for trend analysis. Refer to the *$OV_LOG/ snmpCol.trace* file if you are having any problems getting your data collection rolling. Your HP OpenView manual should describe how to use this trace file to troubleshoot most problems.

Once you have collected some data, you can use *xnmgraph* to display it. The *xnmgraph* command to use is similar to the ones we saw earlier; it's an awkward command that you'll want to save in a script. In the following script, the *−browse* option points the grapher at the stored data:

```
#!/bin/sh
# filename: /opt/OV/local/scripts/graphSavedData
# syntax: graphSavedData <hostname>
/opt/OV/bin/xnmgraph -c public -title Bits_In_n_Out_For_All_Up_Interfaces \
-browse -mib \
 ".1.3.6.1.4.1.9.2.2.1.1.6:::.1.3.6.1.2.1.2.2.1.8:1:.1.3.6.1.2.1.2.2.1.2:::,\
.1.3.6.1.4.1.9.2.2.1.1.8:::.1.3.6.1.2.1.2.2.1.8:1:.1.3.6.1.2.1.2.2.1.2:::" \
$1
```

Once the graph has started, no real (live) data will be graphed; the display is limited to the data that has been collected. You can click on "File → Update Data" to check for and insert any data that has been gathered since the start of the graph. Another option is to leave off *−browse*, which allows the graph to continue collecting and displaying the live data along with the collected data.

Finally, to graph all the data that has been collected for a specific node, go to NNM and select the node you would like to investigate. Then select "Performance → Graph SNMP Data → Select Nodes" from the menus. You will get a graph of all the data that has been collected for the node you selected. Alternately, select the "All" option in "Performance → Graph SNMP Data." With the number of colors limited to 25, you will usually find that you can't fit everything into one graph.

Castle Rock's SNMPc

The workgroup edition of Castle Rock's SNMPc program has similar capabilities to the OpenView package. It uses the term "trend reporting" for its data collection and threshold facilities. The enterprise edition of SNMPc even allows you to export data to a web page. In all our examples we use the workgroup edition of SNMPc.

To see how SNMPc works, let's graph the *snmpOutPkts* object. This object's OID is *1.3.6.1.2.1.11.2* (*iso.org.dod.internet.mgmt.mib-2.snmp.snmpOutPkts*). It is defined in RFC 1213 as follows:

```
snmpOutPkts OBJECT-TYPE
    SYNTAX   Counter
    ACCESS   read-only
    STATUS   mandatory
    DESCRIPTION
        "The total number of SNMP messages which were passed from
        the SNMP protocol entity to the transport service."
    ::= { snmp 2 }
```

We'll use the *orahub* device for this example. Start by clicking on the MIB Database selection tab shown in Figure 9-9; this is the tab at the bottom of the screen that looks something like a spreadsheet—it's the second from the left. Click down the tree until you come to *iso.org.dod.internet.mgmt.mib-2.snmp*. Click on the object you would like to graph (for this example, *snmpOutPkts*). You can select multiple objects with the Ctrl key.

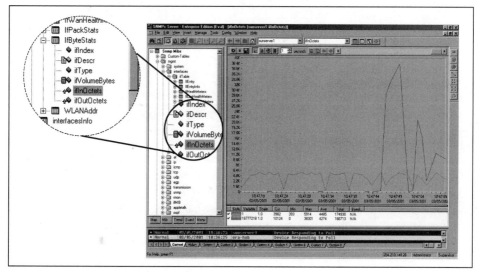

Figure 9-9. SNMPc MIB Database view

SNMPc has a nonstandard way of organizing MIB information. To get to the *snmpOutPkts* object, you need to click down through the following: "Snmp MIBs → mgmt → snmp → snmpInfo." Though this is quicker than the RFC-based organization used by most products, it does get a little confusing, particularly if you work with several products.

Once you have selected the appropriate MIB object, return to the top level of your map by either selecting the house icon or clicking on the Root Subnet tab (at the far left) to select the device you would like to poll. Instead of finding and clicking on the device, you can enter in the device's name by hand. If you have previously polled the device, you can select it from the drop-down box. Figure 9-10 shows what a completed menu bar should look like.

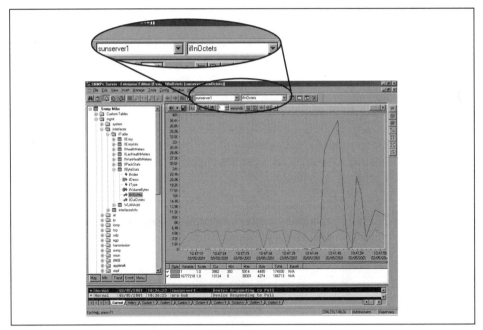

Figure 9-10. SNMPc menu bar graph section

To begin graphing, click the button with the small jagged graph (the third from the right). Another window will appear displaying the graph (Figure 9-11). The controls at the top change the type of graph (line, bar, pie, distribution, etc.) and the polling interval and allow you to view historical data (the horizontal slider bar). Review the documentation on how each of these work or, better yet, play around to learn these menus even faster.

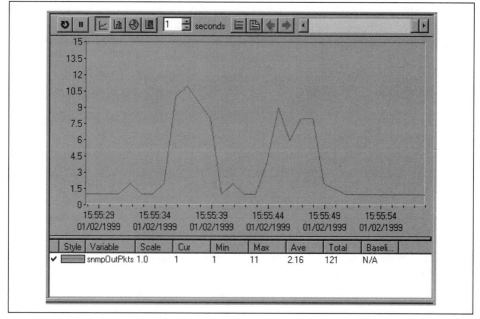

Figure 9-11. SNMPc snmpOutPkts graph section

Once you have a collection of frequently used graphs, you can insert them into the custom menus. Let's insert a menu item in the Tools menu that displays all the information in the *snmpInfo* table as a pie chart. Click on the Custom Menus tab (the last one), right-click on the Tools folder, and then left-click on "Insert Menu". This gets you to the "Add Custom Menu" window (Figure 9-12). Enter a menu name and select "Pie" for the display type. Use the browse button (>>) to click down the tree of MIB objects until you reach the *snmpInfo* table; then click "OK." Back at "Add Custom Menu," use the checkboxes in the "Use Selected Object" section to specify the types of nodes that will be able to respond to this custom menu item. For example, to chart *snmpInfo* a device obviously needs to support SNMP, so we've checked the "Has SNMP" box. This information is used when you (or some other user) try to generate this chart for a given device. If the device doesn't support the necessary protocols, the menu entry for the pie chart will be disabled.

Click "OK" and proceed to your map to find a device to test. Any SNMP-compatible device should suffice. Once you have selected a device, click on "Tools" and then "Show Pie Chart of snmpInfo." You should see a pie chart displaying the data collected from the MIB objects you have configured. (If the device doesn't support SNMP, this option will be disabled.) Alternately, you could have double-clicked your new menu item in the Custom Menu tab.

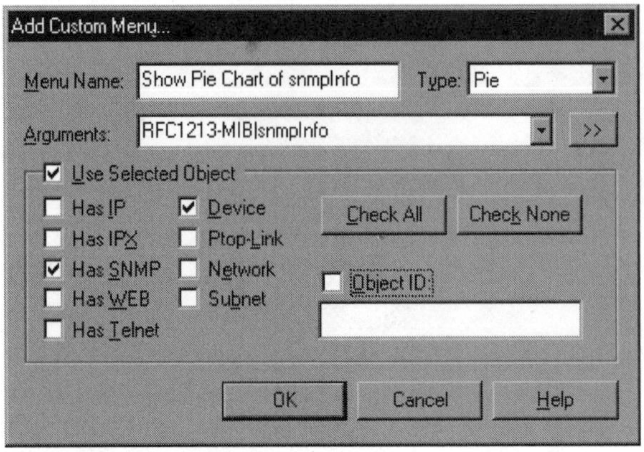

Figure 9-12. SNMPc Add Custom Menu window

SNMPc has a threshold system called Automatic Alarms that can track the value of an object over time to determine its highs and lows (peaks and troughs) and get a baseline. After it obtains the baseline, it alerts you if something strays out of bounds. In the main menu, clicking on "Config → Trend Reports" brings up the menu shown in Figure 9-13.

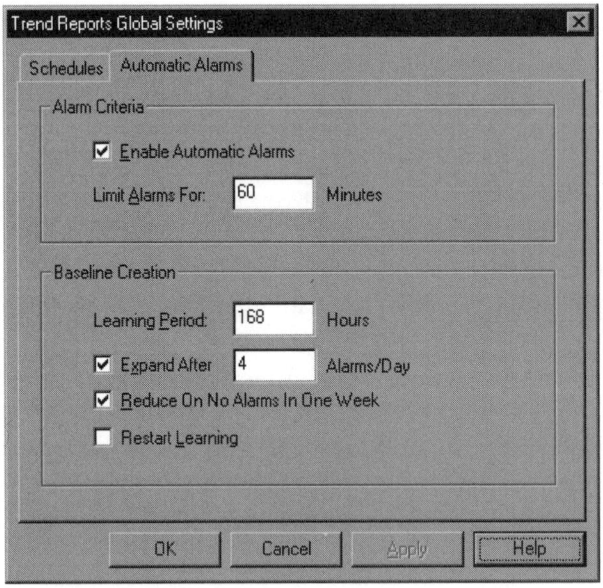

Figure 9-13. SNMPc Trend Reports Global Settings menu

Check the "Enable Automatic Alarms" box to enable this feature. The "Limit Alarms For" box lets you specify how much time must pass before you can receive another alarm of the same nature. This prevents you from being flooded by the same message over and over again. The next section, "Baseline Creation," lets you configure how the baseline will be learned. The learning period is how long SNMPc should take to figure out what the baseline really is. The "Expand After" option, if checked, states how many alarms you can get in one day before SNMPc increases the baseline parameters. In Figure 9-13, if we were to get four alarms in one day, SNMPc would increase the threshold to prevent these messages from being generated so frequently. Checking the "Reduce On No Alarms In One Week" box tells SNMPc to reduce the baseline if we don't receive any alarms in one week. This option prevents the baseline from being set so high that we never receive any alarms. If you check the last option and click "OK," SNMPc will restart the learning process. This gives you a way to wipe the slate clean and start over.

Open Source Tools for Data Collection and Graphing

One of the most powerful tools for data collection and graphing is MRTG, familiar to many in the open source community. It collects statistics and generates graphical reports in the form of web pages. In many respects, it's a different kind of animal than the tools discussed in this chapter. We cover MRTG in Chapter 13.

10

Traps

Traps provide a way for an agent to send a monitoring station asynchronous notification about conditions that the monitor should know about. The traps that an agent can generate are defined by the MIBs it supports; the number of traps can range from zero to hundreds. To see what traps are defined in any MIB file, search for the term "TRAP-TYPE" (SMIv1) or "NOTIFICATION-TYPE" (SMIv2) in the MIB file. This search will quickly get you a list of possible traps.

Of course, just having asynchronous traps arrive at your NMS isn't terribly useful. You can configure the NMS's response to different traps; the response can be anything from discarding the trap to running a script that sends a message to your pager (or even takes some drastic action, such as shutting down your power supplies). In this chapter, we'll show you how to handle incoming traps using Open-View and other tools such as Perl. Then we'll discuss how to read and configure different aspects of trap events. Finally, we'll show you how to define your own traps that report special conditions of particular interest to your network.

Understanding Traps

Before discussing the tools for receiving and generating traps, it's worth reviewing what a trap is. Traps were introduced in Chapter 2. A trap is basically an asynchronous notification sent from an SNMP agent to a network-management station. Like everything else in SNMP, traps are sent using UDP (port 162) and are therefore unreliable. This means that the sender cannot assume that the trap actually arrives, nor can the destination assume that it's getting all the traps being sent its way. Of course, on a healthy network most traps should reach their destinations. But if networks were always healthy, we wouldn't need SNMP.

In somewhat more detail, a trap is a bundle of data that's defined by a MIB. Traps fall into two categories, generic and enterprise-specific. There are seven generic trap numbers (0–6), defined in Table 2-8, for conditions ranging from system reboots (*coldStart*) and interface state changes (*linkUp* and *linkDown*) to generic trap 6 (*enterpriseSpecific*). Enterprise-specific traps are the loophole that makes the trap mechanism so powerful. Anyone with an enterprise number can define enterprise-specific traps for whatever conditions they consider worth monitoring. An enterprise-specific trap is identified by two pieces of information: the enterprise ID of the organization that defined the trap and a specific trap number assigned by that organization. The notion of an enterprise-specific trap is extremely flexible, because organizations are allowed to subdivide their enterprises as much as they like. For example, if your enterprise number is 2789, your enterprise ID is *.1.3.6.1. 4.1.2789*. But you can further subdivide this, defining traps with enterprise IDs such as *.1.3.6.1.4.1.2789.5000*, *.1.3.6.1.4.1.2789.5001*, and so on.

The fact that you've received a trap and therefore know its generic trap number, enterprise ID, and specific trap number is often all you need to diagnose a problem. But traps also carry additional information. In the case of generic traps 0–5, the specific information is predefined and hardwired into the NMS. When you receive a generic trap, the NMS knows how to interpret the information it contains and will be able to display it appropriately, whether it's the time of the reboot or the identity of the interface that just changed state. In contrast, the information carried by an enterprise-specific trap is entirely up to the person who defined the trap. An enterprise-specific trap can contain any number of variable bindings, or MIB object–value pairs. When you define your own traps, you can decide what information is appropriate for them to carry. The objects contained in a trap can be standard MIB objects, vendor-specific objects, or objects of your own devising. It's common to define objects purely for the purpose of including them within a trap.

SNMPv2 Traps

SNMPv2 defines traps in a slightly different way. In a MIB, Version 1 traps are defined as TRAP-TYPE, while Version 2 traps are defined as NOTIFICATION-TYPE. SNMPv2 also does away with the notion of generic traps—instead, it defines many specific traps (properly speaking, notifications) in public MIBs. SNMPv3 traps, which are discussed briefly in Appendix F, are simply SNMPv2 traps with added authentication and privacy capabilities.Most SNMP implementations support only Version 1.

Receiving Traps

Let's start by discussing how to deal with incoming traps. Handling incoming traps is the responsibility of the NMS. Some NMSs do as little as display the incoming traps to standard output (*stdout*). However, an NMS server typically has the ability to react to SNMP traps it receives. For example, when an NMS receives a *linkDown* trap from a router, it might respond to the event by paging the contact person, displaying a pop-up message on a management console, or forwarding the event to another NMS. This procedure is streamlined in commercial packages but still can be achieved with freely available open source programs.

HP OpenView

OpenView uses three pieces of software to receive and interpret traps:

- *ovtrapd*(1M)
- *xnmtrap*
- *xnmevents*

OpenView's main trap-handling daemon is called *ovtrapd*. This program listens for traps generated by devices on the network and hands them off to the Postmaster daemon (*pmd*). In turn, *pmd* triggers what OpenView calls an event. Events can be configured to perform actions ranging from sending a pop-up window to NNM users, forwarding the event to other NMSs, or doing nothing at all. The configuration process uses *xnmtrap*, the Event Configurations GUI. The *xnmevents* program displays the events that have arrived, sorting them into user-configurable categories.

OpenView keeps a history of all the traps it has received; to retrieve that history, use the command *$OV_BIN/ovdumpevents*. Older versions of OpenView kept an event logging file in *$OV_LOG/trapd.log*. By default, this file rolls over after it grows to 4 MB. It is then renamed *trapd.log.old* and a new *trapd.log* file is started. If you are having problems with traps, either because you don't know whether they are reaching the NMS or because your NMS is being bombarded by too many events, you can use *tail –f* to watch *trapd.log* so you can see the traps as they arrive. (You can also use *ovdumpevents* to create a new file.) To learn more about the format of this file, refer to OpenView's manual pages for *trapd.conf*(4) and *ovdumpevents*(1M).

It might be helpful to define what exactly an OpenView event is. Think of it as a small record, similar to a database record. This record defines which trap Open-View should watch out for. It further defines what sort of action (send an email, page someone, etc.), if any, should be performed.

Using NNM's Event Configurations

OpenView uses an internal definition file to determine how to react to particular situations. This definition file is maintained by the *xnmtrap* program. We can start *xnmtrap* by using the menu item "Options → Event Configurations" (on the NNM GUI) or by giving the command *$OV_BIN/xnmtrap*. In the Enterprise Identification

window, scroll down and click on the enterprise name "OpenView .1.3.6.1.4.1.11.2.
17.1." This displays a list in the Event Identification window. Scroll down in this list
until you reach "OV_Node_Down." Double-click on this event to bring up the
Event Configurator (Figure 10-1).

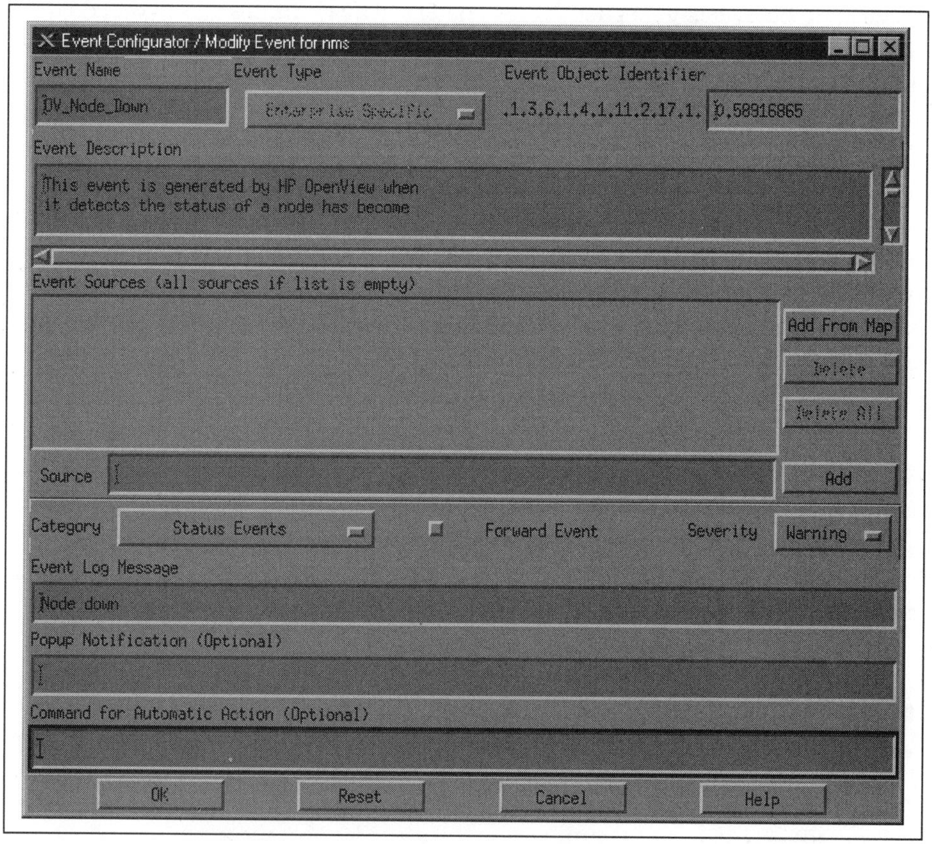

Figure 10-1. OpenView Event Configurator—OV_Node_Down

Figure 10-1 shows the *OV_Node_Down* event in the Event Configurator. When this
event gets triggered, it inserts an entry containing the message "Node down," with
a severity level of "Warning," into the Status Events category. OpenView likes to
have a leading 0 (zero) in the Event Object Identifier, which indicates that this is
an event or trap—there is no way to change this value yourself. The number
before the 0 is the enterprise OID; the number after the 0 is the specific trap
number, in this case 58916865.* Later we will use these numbers as parameters
when generating our own traps.

---

* This is the default number that OpenView uses for this *OV_Node_Down* trap.

Selecting event sources

The Source option is useful when you want to receive traps from certain nodes and ignore traps from other nodes. For example, if you have a development router that people are taking up and down all day, you probably would rather not receive all the events generated by the router's activity. In this case, you could use the Source field to list all the nodes from which you would like to receive traps, and leave out the development router. To do this, you can either type each of the hostnames by hand and click "Add" after each one, or select each node (using the Ctrl and mouse-click sequence) on your OpenView Network Node Map and click "Add From Map." Unfortunately, the resulting list isn't easy to manage. Even if you take the time to add all the current routers to the Event Sources, you'll eventually add a new router (or some other hardware you want to manage). You then have to go back to *all* your events and add your new devices as sources. Newer versions of OpenView allow you to use pattern matching and source files, making it easier to tailor and maintain the source list.

Setting event categories

When NNM receives an event, it sorts the event into an event category. The Categories drop-down box lets you assign the event you're configuring to a category. The list of available categories will probably include the following predefined categories (you can customize this list by adding categories specific to your network and deleting categories, as we'll see later in this section):

- Error events
- Threshold events
- Status events
- Configuration events
- Application alert events
- Don't log or display
- Log only

The last two categories really aren't event categories in the true sense of the word. If you select "Don't log or display," OpenView will not save the event in its database and will not display the Event Log Message in any Event Categories. OpenView will display the Popup Notification in a pop-up window and run the Command for Automatic Action. The "Log only" option tells OpenView not to display the event but to keep a log of the event in its database.*

---

* Again, in earlier releases of OpenView this log was located in *$OV_LOG/trapd.log*. New versions use the OpenView Event Database. This is backward-compatible using the *ovdumpevents* command to produce a *trapd.log* file.

"Log only" is useful if you have some events that are primarily informational; you don't want to see them when they arrive, but you would like to record them for future reference. The Cisco event *frDLCIStatusChange* – *.1.3.6.1.2.1.10.32.0.1* is a good example of such an event. It tells us when a Virtual Circuit has changed its operational state. If displayed, we will see notifications whenever a node goes down and whenever a circuit changes its operational state to down. This information is redundant because we have already gotten a status event of "node down" and a DLCI change.* With this event set to "Log only" we can go to the log file only when we think things are fishy.

Forwarding events and event severities

The "Forward Event" radio button, once checked, allows you to forward an event to other NMSs. This feature is useful if you have multiple NMSs or a distributed network-management architecture. Say that you are based in Atlanta, but your network has a management station in New York in addition to the one on your desk. You don't want to receive all of New York's events, but you would like the *node_down* information forwarded to you. On New York's NMS, you could click "Forward Event" and insert the IP address of your NMS in Atlanta. When New York receives a *node_down* event, it will forward the event to Atlanta.

The Severity drop-down list assigns a severity level to the event. OpenView supports six severity levels: Unknown, Normal, Warning, Minor, Major, and Critical. The severity levels are color-coded to make identification easier; Table 10-1 shows the color associated with each severity level. The levels are listed in order of increasing severity. For example, an event with a severity level of Minor has a higher precedence than an event with a severity of Warning.

Table 10-1. OpenView Severity Levels

Severity	Color
Unknown	Blue
Normal	Green
Warning	Cyan
Minor	Yellow
Major	Orange
Critical	Red

---

* Newer versions of OpenView have a feature called Event Correlation that groups certain events together to avoid flooding the user with redundant information. You can customize these settings with a developer's kit.

The colors are used both on OpenView's maps and in the Event Categories. Parent objects, which represent the starting point for a network, are displayed in the color of the highest severity level associated with any object underneath them.* For example, if an object represents a network with 250 nodes and one of those nodes is down (a Critical severity), the object will be colored red, regardless of how many nodes are up and functioning normally. The term for how OpenView displays colors in relation to objects is *status source*; it is explained in more detail in Chapter 6.

Log messages, notifications, and automatic actions

Returning to Figure 10-1, the Event Log Message and Popup Notification fields are similar, but serve different purposes. The Event Log Message is displayed when you view the Event Categories and select a category from the drop-down list. The Popup Notification, which is optional, displays its message in a window that appears on any server running OpenView's NNM. Figure 10-2 shows a typical pop-up message. The event name, *delme* in this case, appears in the title bar. The time and date at which the event occurred are followed by the event message, "Popup Message Here." To create a pop-up message like this, insert "Popup Message Here" in the Popup Notification section of the Event Configurator. Every time the event is called, a pop-up will appear.

Figure 10-2. OpenView pop-up message

The last section of the Event Configurator is the Command for Automatic Action. The automatic action allows you to specify a Unix command or script to execute when OpenView receives an event. You can run multiple commands by separating them with a semicolon, much as you would in a Unix shell. When configuring an automatic action, remember that *rsh* can be very useful. I like to use *rsh sunserver1 audioplay –v50 /opt/local/sounds/siren.au*, which causes a siren audio file to play. The automatic action can range from touching a file to opening a trouble ticket.

---

* Parent objects can show status (colors) in four ways: Symbol, Object, Compound, or Propagated.

In each Event Log Message, Popup Notification, and Command for Automatic Action, special variables can help you identify the values from your traps or events. These variables provide the user with additional information about the event. Here are some of the variables you can use; the online help has a complete list:

$1

> Print the first passed attribute (i.e., the value of the first variable binding) from the trap.

$2

> Print the second passed attribute.

$n

> Print the *n*th attribute as a value string. Must be in the range of 1–99.

$*

> Print all the attributes as *[seq] name (type)*.

Before you start running scripts for an event, find out the average number of traps you are likely to receive for that event. This is especially true for *OV_Node_Down*. If you write a script that opens a trouble ticket whenever a node goes down, you could end up with hundreds of tickets by the end of the day. Monitoring your network will make you painfully aware of how much your network "flaps," or goes up and down. Even if the network goes down for a second, for whatever reason, you'll get a trap, which will in turn generate an event, which might register a new ticket, send you a page, etc. The last thing you want is "The Network That Cried Down!" You and other people on your staff will start ignoring all the false warnings and may miss any serious problems that arise. One way to estimate how frequently you will receive events is to log events in a file ("Log only"). After a week or so, inspect the log file to see how many events accumulated (i.e., the number of traps received). This is by no means scientific, but it will give you an idea of what you can expect.

Custom Event Categories

OpenView uses the default categories for all its default events. Look through the *$OV_CONF/C/trapd.conf* file to see how the default events are assigned to categories. You can add categories by going to "Event Configuration → Edit → Configure → Event Categories." Figure 10-3 shows this menu, with some custom categories added.

It's worth your while to spend time thinking about what categories are appropriate for your environment. If you plow everything into the default categories you will be bothered by the Critical "Printer Needs Paper" event, when you really want to

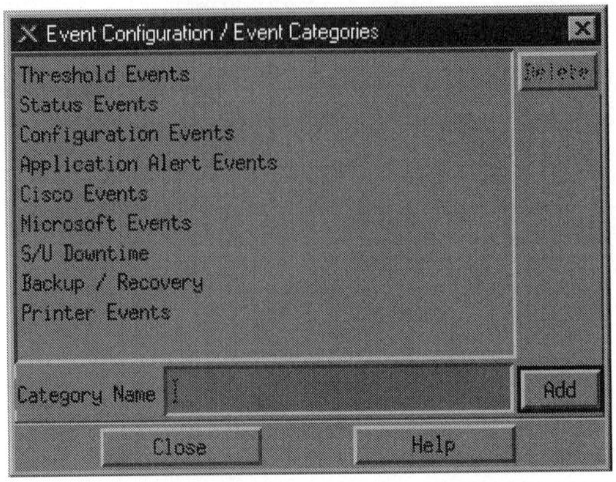

Figure 10-3. Adding event categories in OpenView

be notified of the Critical "Production Server on Fire" event. Either event will turn Status Events red. The categories in Figure 10-3 are a good start, but think about the types of events and activities that will be useful in your network. The Scheduled and Unscheduled (S/U) Downtime category is a great example of a category that is more for human intervention than for reporting network errors. Printer Events is a nice destination for your "Printer Needs Paper" and "Printer Jammed" messages.

Even though none of the default categories are required (except for Error), we recommend that you don't delete them, precisely because they are used for all of the default events. Deleting the default categories without first reconfiguring all the default events will cause problems. Any event that does not have an event category available will be put into the default Error category. To edit the categories, copy the *trapd.conf* file into */tmp* and modify */tmp/trapd.conf* with your favorite editor. The file has some large warnings telling you never to edit it by hand, but sometimes a few simple edits are the best way to reassign events. An entry in the portion of the file that defines event behavior looks like this:

```
EVENT RMON_Rise_Alarm .1.3.6.1.2.1.16.0.1 "Threshold Events" Warning
FORMAT RMON Rising Alarm: $2 exceeded threshold $5; value = $4. (Sample type = \
$3; alarm index = $1)
SDESC
This event is sent when an RMON device exceeds a preconfigured threshold.
EDESC
```

It's fairly obvious what these lines do: they map a particular RMON event into the Threshold Events category with a severity of Warning; they also specify what should happen when the event occurs. To map this event into another category, change Threshold Events to the appropriate category. Once you've edited the file, use the following command to merge in your updates:

```
$ $OV_BIN/xnmevents -l load /tmp/trapd.conf
```

The Event Categories Display

The Event Categories window (Figure 10-4) is displayed on the user's screen when NNM is started. It provides a very brief summary of what's happening on your network; if it is set up appropriately, you can tell at a glance whether there are any problems you should be worrying about.

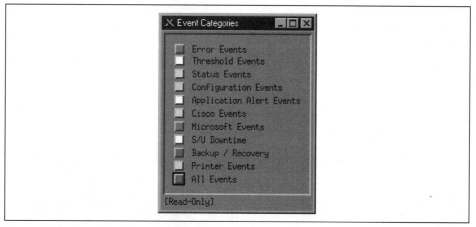

Figure 10-4. OpenView Event Categories

If the window gets closed during an OpenView session, you can restart it using the "Fault → Events" menu item or by issuing the command *$OV_BIN/xnmevents*. The menu displays all the event categories, including any categories you have created. Two categories are special: the Error category is the default category used when an event is associated with a category that cannot be found; the All category is a placeholder for all events and cannot be configured by the Event Configurator. The window shows you the highest severity level of any event in each event category.

The box to the left of Status Events is cyan (a light blue), showing that the highest unacknowledged severity in the Status Events category is Warning. Clicking on that box displays an alarm browser that lists all the events received in the category. A nice feature of the Event Categories display is the ability to restore a browser's state or reload events from the *trapd.log* and *trapd.log.old* files. Reloading events is useful if you find that you need to restore messages you deleted in the past.

Newer versions of OpenView extend the abilities of Event Categories by keeping a common database of acknowledged and unacknowledged events. Thus, when a user acknowledges an event, all other users see this event updated.

At the bottom of Figure 10-4, the phrase "[Read-Only]" means that you don't have
write access to Event Categories. If this phrase isn't present, you have write access.
OpenView keeps track of events on a per-user basis, using a special database
located in *$OV_LOG/xnmevents.username.** With write access, you have the ability
to update this file whenever you exit. By default, you have write access to your
own event category database, unless someone has already started the database by
starting a session with your username. There may be only one write-access Event
Categories per user, with the first one getting write access and all others getting
read-only privileges.

The Alarm Browser

Figure 10-5 shows the alarm browser for the Status Events category. In it we see a
single Warning event, which is causing the Status Events category to show cyan.

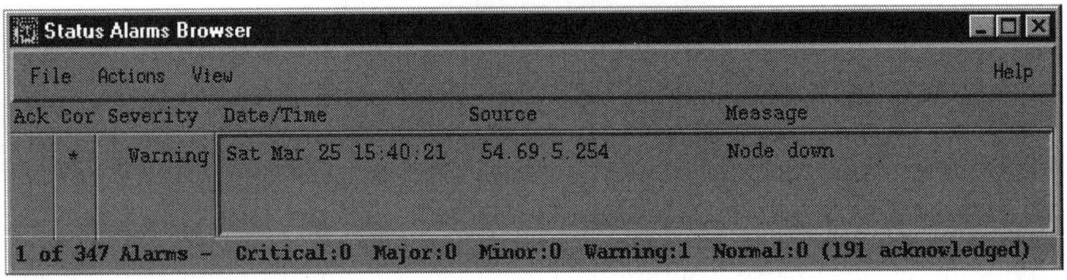

Figure 10-5. OpenView alarm browser

The color of the Status Events box is determined by the highest-precedence event
in the category. Therefore, the color won't change until either you acknowledge
the highest-precedence event or an event arrives with an even higher precedence.
Clicking in the far left column (Ack) acknowledges the message† and sets the
severity to 0.

The Actions menu in the alarm browser allows you to acknowledge, deacknowl-
edge, or delete some or all events. You can even change the severity of an event.
Keep in mind that this does *not* change the severity of the event on other Event
Categories sessions that are running. For example, if one user changes the severity
of an event from Critical to Normal, the event will remain Critical for other users.
The View menu lets you define filters, which allow you to include or discard messages that match the filter.

When configuring events, keep in mind that you may receive more traps than you
want. When this happens, you have two choices. First, you can go to the agent

---

* Again, newer versions of OpenView have only one database that is common for all users.

† Newer versions of OpenView support Event Correlation, which has a column in this window as well.

and turn off trap generation, if the agent supports this. Second, you can configure your trap view to ignore these traps. We saw how to do this earlier: you can set the event to "Log only" or try excluding the device from the Event Sources list. If bandwidth is a concern, you should investigate why the agent is sending out so many traps before trying to mask the problem.

Creating Events Within OpenView

OpenView gives you the option of creating additional (private) events. Private events are just like regular events, except that they belong to your private-enterprise subtree, rather than to a public MIB. To create your own events, launch the Event Configuration window from the Options menu of NNM. You will see a list of all currently loaded events (Figure 10-6).

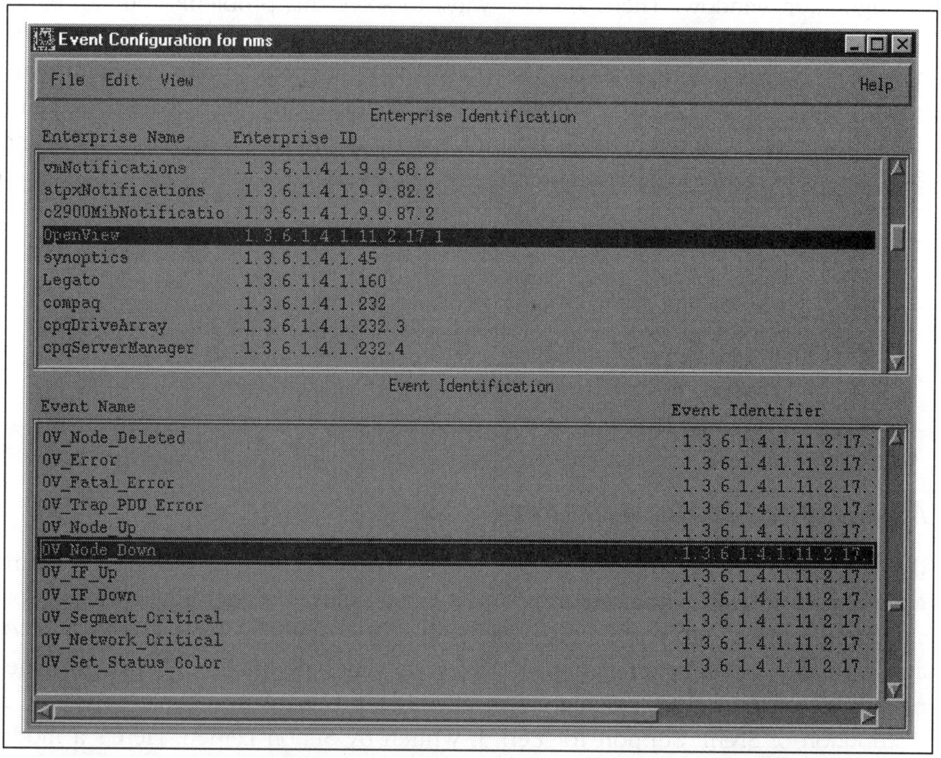

Figure 10-6. OpenView's Event Configuration

The window is divided into two panes. The top pane displays the Enterprise Identification, which is the leftmost part of an OID. Clicking on an enterprise ID displays all the events belonging to that enterprise in the lower pane. To add your own enterprise ID, select "Edit → Add → Enterprise Identification" and insert your enterprise name and a registered enterprise ID.* Now you're ready to create private events. Click on the enterprise name you just created; the enterprise ID you've associated with this name will be used to form the OID for the new event. Click "Edit → Add → Event"; then type the Event Name for your new event, making sure to use Enterprise Specific (the default) for the event type. Insert an Event Object Identifier. This identifier can be any number that hasn't already been assigned to an event in the currently selected enterprise. Finally, click "OK" and save the event configuration (using "File → Save").

To copy an existing event, click on the event you wish to copy and select "Edit → Copy Event"; you'll see a new window with the event you selected. From this point on, the process is the same.

Traps with "no format" are traps for which nothing has been defined in the Event Configuration window. There are two ways to solve this problem: you can either create the necessary events on your own or you can load a MIB that contains the necessary trap definitions, as discussed in Chapter 6. "No format" traps are frequently traps defined in a vendor-specific MIB that hasn't been loaded. Loading the appropriate MIB often fixes the problem by defining the vendor's traps and their associated names, IDs, comments, severity levels, etc.

Before loading a MIB, review the types of traps the MIB supports. You will find that most traps you load come, by default, in LOGONLY mode. This means that you will *not* be notified when the traps come in. After you load the MIB you may want to edit the events it defines, specifying the local configuration that best fits your site.

Monitoring Traps with Perl

If you can't afford an expensive package like OpenView, you can use the Perl language to write your own monitoring and logging utility. You get what you pay for, since you will have to write almost everything from scratch. But you'll learn a lot and probably get a better appreciation for the finer points of network management. One of the most elementary, but effective, programs to receive traps is in a distribution of SNMP Support for Perl 5, written by Simon Leinen. Here's a modified version of Simon's program:

```
#!/usr/local/bin/perl

use SNMP_Session "0.60";
use BER;
use Socket;
```

---

* Refer to Chapter 2 for information about obtaining your own enterprise ID.

```
$session = SNMPv1_Session->open_trap_session ();

while (($trap, $sender, $sender_port) = $session->receive_trap ())
{
    chomp ($DATE=`/bin/date \'+%a %b %e %T\'`);
    print STDERR "$DATE - " . inet_ntoa($sender) . " - port: $sender_port\n";
    print_trap ($session, $trap);
}
1;

sub print_trap ($$) {
    ($this, $trap) = @_;
    ($community, $ent, $agent, $gen, $spec, $dt, @bindings) = \
     $this->decode_trap_request ($trap);
    print "    Community:\t".$community."\n";
    print "    Enterprise:\t".BER::pretty_oid ($ent)."\n";
    print "    Agent addr:\t".inet_ntoa ($agent)."\n";
    print "    Generic ID:\t$gen\n";
    print "    Specific ID:\t$spec\n";
    print "    Uptime:\t".BER::pretty_uptime_value ($dt)."\n";
    $prefix = "    bindings:\t";
    foreach $encoded_pair (@bindings)
        {
        ($oid, $value) = decode_by_template ($encoded_pair, "%{%O%@");
        #next unless defined $oid;
        print $prefix.BER::pretty_oid ($oid)." => ".pretty_print ($value)."\n";
        $prefix = "    ";
        }
}
```

This program displays traps as they are received from different devices in the network. Here's some output, showing two traps:

```
Mon Apr 28 22:07:44 - 10.123.46.26 - port: 63968
    community:  public
    enterprise: 1.3.6.1.4.1.2789.2500
    agent addr: 10.123.46.26
    generic ID: 6
    specific ID: 5247
    uptime:     0:00:00
    bindings:   1.3.6.1.4.1.2789.2500.1234 => 14264026886

Mon Apr 28 22:09:46 - 172.16.51.25 - port: 63970
    community:  public
    enterprise: 1.3.6.1.4.1.2789.2500
    agent addr: 172.16.253.2
    generic ID: 6
    specific ID: 5247
    uptime:     0:00:00
    bindings:   1.3.6.1.4.1.2789.2500.2468 => Hot Swap Now In Sync
```

The output format is the same for both traps. The first line shows the date and time at which the trap occurred, together with the IP address of the device that sent the trap. Most of the remaining output items should be familiar to you. The

bindings output item lists the variable bindings that were sent in the trap PDU. In the example above, each trap contained one variable binding. The object ID is in numeric form, which isn't particularly friendly. If a trap has more than one variable binding, this program displays each binding, one after another.

An ad hoc monitoring system can be fashioned by using this Perl script to collect traps and some other program to inspect the traps as they are received. Once the traps are parsed, the possibilities are endless. You can write user-defined rules that watch for significant traps and, when triggered, send an email alert, update an event database, send a message to a pager, etc. These kinds of solutions work well if you're in a business with little or no budget for commercially available NMS software or if you're on a small network and don't need a heavyweight management tool.

Using the Network Computing Technologies Trap Receiver

The Trap Receiver by Network Computing Technologies is a freely available program that's worth trying.* This program, which currently runs only on Windows-based systems, displays trap information as it's received. It has a standard interface but can be configured to execute certain actions against traps, like OpenView's Command for Automatic Action function. Figure 10-7 shows Trap Receiver's user interface.

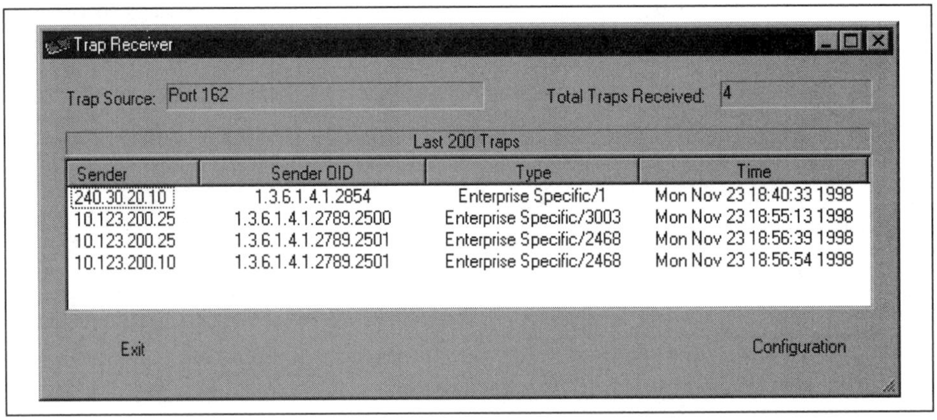

Figure 10-7. Trap Receiver

There are ways to log and forward messages and traps, send email or a page in response to a trap, as well as execute commands. By writing some code in C or C++, you can gain access to an internal trap stream. This program can be a great

---

* This software can be found on their web page at *http://www.ncomtech.com.*

starting place for Windows administrators who want to use SNMP but lack the resources to implement something like OpenView. It's simple to use, extensible, and free.

Receiving Traps Using Net-SNMP

The last trap receiver we'll discuss is part of the Net-SNMP package, which is also freely available. *snmptrapd* allows you to send SNMP trap messages to facilities such as Unix *syslog* or *stdout*. For most applications the program works in the background, shipping messages to *syslog*(8). There are some configuration parameters for the *syslog* side of *snmptrapd*; these tell *snmptrapd* what facility level it should use for the *syslog* messages. The following command forwards traps to standard output (*–P*) rather than to *syslog* as they are received:

```
$ ./snmptrapd -P
2000-12-13 19:10:55 UCD-SNMP Version 4.1.2 Started.
2000-12-13 19:11:14 sunserver2.ora.com [12.1.45.26] enterprises.2789.2500:
     Enterprise Specific Trap (1224) Uptime: 5 days, 10:01:20.42
     enterprises.2789.2500.1224 = 123123

2000-12-13 19:11:53 sunserver2.ora.com [12.1.45.26] enterprises.2789.2500:
     Enterprise Specific Trap (1445) Uptime: 5 days, 10:01:21.20
     enterprises.2789.2500.1445 = "Fail Over Complete"
```

By now the output should look familiar; it's similar to the reports generated by the other programs we've seen in this chapter. The Net-SNMP trap daemon is another great tool for scriptwriters. A simple Perl script can watch the file in which *snmptrapd* logs its traps, looking for important events and reacting accordingly. It's easy to build a powerful and flexible monitoring system at little or no expense.

We have seen several packages that can receive traps and act on them, based on the traps' content. Keep in mind that all of these programs, whether they're free or cost tens of thousands of dollars, are basically doing the same thing: listening on some port (usually UDP port 162) and waiting for SNMP messages to arrive. What sets the various packages apart is their ability to do something constructive with the traps. Some let you program hooks that execute some other program when a certain trap is received. The simpler trap monitors just send a message logging the trap to one or more files or facilities. These packages are generally less expensive than the commercial trap monitors, but can be made to operate like full-fledged systems with some additional programming effort. Programs such as Perl give you the ability to extend these simpler packages.

Sending Traps

By now you should have a mechanism in place for receiving traps. In this section, we'll look at some different utilities that send traps and allow you to develop traps that are appropriate for your own environment. You'll notice that almost all trap utilities are command-line based. This allows you to execute the command from within a script, which is almost always what you want to do. For example, you can write a shell script that checks disk space every five minutes and sends a trap to the NMS if you're running low. You can also use these trap generators within existing programs and scripts. If you have a Perl script that accesses a database, you can use the Perl SNMP module to send a trap from within the script if a database insert fails. The possibilities are almost endless.

Although there are many different *snmptrap* programs, they are all fundamentally similar. In particular, though their command-line syntax may vary, they all expect roughly the same arguments:

Port
> The UDP port to which to send the trap. The default port is 162.

SNMP version
> The SNMP version appropriate to the trap you want to send. Many traps are defined only for Version 2. Note that many SNMP tools support only Version 1.

Hostname or IP address of NMS
> The hostname or IP address of your NMS—i.e., the trap's destination. It is better to use an IP address than a hostname in case you are sending traps during a Domain Name System (DNS) outage. Remember that SNMP is most valuable when your network is failing; therefore, try to avoid assuming that you have a fully functional network when you design traps.

Community name
> The community name to be sent with the trap. Most management stations can be configured to ignore traps that don't have an appropriate community string.

Enterprise OID
> The full enterprise OID for the trap you want to send: everything in the trap's OID from the initial *.1* up to the enterprise number, including any subtrees within the enterprise but not the specific trap number. For example, if your enterprise number is 2789, you've further subdivided your enterprise to include a group of traps numbered 5000, and you want to send specific trap 1234, the enterprise OID would be *.1.3.6.1.4.1.2789.5000.*

> If you have some reason to send a generic trap, you can set the enterprise ID to anything you want—but it's probably best to set the enterprise ID to your own enterprise number, if you have one.

Now for the most confusing case. There are a few specific traps defined in various public MIBs. How do you send them? Basically, you construct something that looks like an enterprise OID. It's best to look at an example. One such trap is *rdbmsOutOfSpace*, which is defined in the RDBMS MIB. Its complete

OID is *.1.3.6.1.2.1.39.2.2* (*.iso.org.dod.internet.mgmt.mib-2.rdbmsMIB.rdbms-Traps.rdbmsOutOfSpace*). To send this trap, which is really an SNMPv2 notification, you would use everything up to *rdbmsTraps* as the enterprise OID, and the entire object ID as the specific trap number.

Hostname or IP address of sender

The IP address of the agent that is sending the trap. Although this may appear to be superfluous, it can be important if there is a proxy server between the agent and the NMS. This parameter allows you to record the actual address of the agent within the SNMP packet; in turn, the NMS will read the agent's address from the trap and ignore the packet's sender address. If you don't specify this parameter, it will almost always default to the address of the machine sending the trap.

Generic trap number

A number in the range 0–6. The true generic traps have numbers 0–5; if you're sending an enterprise-specific trap, set this number to 6. Table 2-8 lists the generic traps.

Specific trap number

A number indicating the specific trap you want to send. If you're sending a generic trap, this parameter is ignored—you're probably better off setting it to zero. If you're sending a specific trap, the trap number is up to you. For example, if you send a trap with the OID *.1.3.6.1.4.1.2500.3003.0*, 3003 is the specific trap number.

Timestamp

The time elapsed between the last initialization of the network entity and the generation of the trap.

OID_1, type_1, value_1

Data bindings to be included in the trap. Each data binding consists of an OID together with a datatype, followed by the value you want to send. Most programs let you include any number of data bindings in a trap. Note that the OIDs for these variable bindings are often specific to the trap and therefore "underneath" the specific OID for the trap. But this isn't a requirement, and it's often useful to send bindings that aren't defined as part of the trap.

Before we start to tackle this section, let's take a moment to review what we learned in Chapter 2 about the various datatypes:

* Each variable that we send has a particular datatype.

* Different datatypes are supported by different versions of SNMP.

* Some common datatypes are `INTEGER`, `OctetString`, `Null`, `Counter`, `Gauge`, and `TimeTicks`.

Be aware that not all programs support all datatypes. For example, the Perl SNMP module supports only the `OctetString`, `INTEGER`, and `OID` types, while the OpenView and Net_SNMP *snmptrap* commands support these three and many more. For each of the packages we use we will list, if applicable, each datatype the program supports.

In the next sections, we'll discuss *snmptrap* programs from OpenView, Network Computing Technologies, and Net-SNMP. We'll also include a script that uses a Perl module to send traps. If you are not using these particular programs in your environment, don't worry. You should still be able to relate these examples to your in-house programs.

Sending Traps with OpenView

OpenView has a command-line program for generating arbitrary traps called *snmptrap*. *snmptrap* supports the `counter`, `counter32`, `counter64`,[*] `gauge`, `gauge32`, `integer`, `integer32`, `ipaddress`, `null`, `objectidentifier`, `octetstring`, `octetstringascii`, `octetstringhex`, `octetstringoctal`, `opaque`, `opaqueascii`, `opaquehex`, `opaqueoctal`, `timeticks`, and `unsigned32` datatypes. Its command-line structure looks like this:

```
snmptrap -c community [-p port] node_addr enterprise_id agent-addr generic \
specific timestamp [OID type value] ...
```

Here's a typical *snmptrap* command. It sends one trap, with three ASCII-string variable bindings for values:

```
$ /opt/OV/bin/snmptrap -c public nms \
.1.3.6.1.4.1.2789.2500 "" 6 3003 "" \
.1.3.6.1.4.1.2789.2500.3003.1 octetstringascii "Oracle" \
.1.3.6.1.4.1.2789.2500.3003.2 octetstringascii "Backup Not Running" \
.1.3.6.1.4.1.2789.2500.3003.3 octetstringascii "Call the DBA Now for Help"
```

It's a complicated command, and it's hard to imagine that you would ever type it on the command line. Let's break it up into pieces. The first line specifies the community string (`public`) and the address to which the trap should be sent (`nms`, though in practice it would be better to use an IP address rather than a node name). The next line is in many respects the most complicated. It specifies the enterprise ID for the trap we're going to send (`.1.3.5.1.6.1.2789.2500`, which is a subtree of the enterprise-specific tree we've devoted to traps); the address of the agent sending the trap (in this case, the null string `""`, which defaults to the agent's address; if you're using a proxy server, it is useful to specify the agent's address explicitly); the generic trap number (6, which is used for all

---

[*] This type will work only on agents that support SNMPv2.

enterprise-specific traps); the specific trap number (3003, which we've assigned); and a timestamp (`""`, which defaults to the current time).

The remaining three lines specify three variable bindings to be included with the trap. For each binding, we have the variable's object ID, its datatype, and its value. The variables we're sending are defined in our private (enterprise-specific) MIB, so their OIDs all begin with *.1.3.6.1.4.1.2789.2500*. All the variables are strings, so their datatype is `octetstringascii`. The trap PDU will be packed with these three strings, among other things. The program that receives the trap will decode the trap PDU and realize that there are three variable bindings in the trap. These variable bindings, like the one that reads "Call the DBA Now for Help," can be used to alert the operator that something bad has happened.

Sending Traps with Perl

In Chapter 8 we learned how to use the *get* and *set* pieces of the SNMP Perl module. In this section we'll see how to use the `snmptrap()` routine to generate traps. Currently, `SNMP_util` supports only three types for traps: `string`, `int`, and `oid`. This can seem limiting, but it covers most needs. Here's how *snmptrap* is called:

```
snmptrap(communityname@host:port_number, enterpriseOID, host_name_from, \
    generic_ID, specific_ID, OID, type, value, [OID, type, value ...])
```

One call to *snmptrap* can include any number of values; for each value, you must specify the object ID, the datatype, and the value you're reporting. The next script generates a trap with only one value:

```perl
#!/usr/local/bin/perl
# Filename: /opt/local/perl_scripts/snmptrap.pl

use SNMP_util "0.54";  # This will load the BER and SNMP_Session for us

snmptrap("public\@nms:162", ".1.3.6.1.4.1.2789", "sunserver1", 6, 1247, \
    ".1.3.6.1.4.1.2789.1247.1", "int", "2448816");
```

The call to `snmptrap()` sends a trap to port 162 on host nms. The trap is sent from host **sunserver1**; it contains a single variable binding, for the object `.1.3.6.1.4.1.2789.1247.1`. The OID's type is `int` and its value is `2448816`.

Now let's try sending a trap with multiple values (multiple variable bindings). The first object we'll report is an integer, to which we give the arbitrary value `4278475`. The second object has a string value and is a warning that our database has stopped. Because we're using OIDs that belong to our own enterprise, we can define these objects to be anything we want:

```perl
snmptrap("public\@nms:162", ".1.3.6.1.4.1.2789", "sunserver2", 6, 3301, \
    ".1.3.6.1.4.1.2789.3301.1", "int",    "4278475", \
    ".1.3.6.1.4.1.2789.3301.2", "string", "Sybase DB Stopped");
```

We can use the Net-SNMP *snmptrapd* program to monitor the traps coming in. We executed the preceding Perl code while running *snmptrapd* in *stdout* mode, and received:

```
$ ./snmptrapd -P
1999-10-12 09:45:08  [12.1.45.26] enterprises.2789.3000:
        Enterprise Specific Trap (3301) Uptime: 0:00:00
        enterprises.2789.3301.1 = 4278475
        enterprises.2789.3301.2 = "Sybase DB Stopped"
```

snmptrapd reported both of the values we sent in the trap: we see the integer value 4278475 and the notification that Sybase has stopped. Although this example is highly artificial, it's not all that different from what you would do when writing your own monitoring software. You would write whatever code is necessary to monitor vital systems such as your database and use the Perl SNMP module to send traps when significant events occur. You can then use any program capable of receiving traps to inform you when the traps arrive. If you want, you can add logic that analyzes the values sent in the trap or takes other actions, such as notifying an operator via a pager.

Sending Traps with Network Computing Technologies Trap Generator

This Windows-based command-line utility gives us the same features as its Unix counterparts. It understands the String, Counter, Gauge, Integer, Address, OID, and TimeTicks datatypes. The command line for *nttrapgen* looks like this:

```
nttrapgen.exe -d DestinationIpAddress:port -c CommunityName
        -o senderOID -i senderIP -g GenericTrapType
        -s SpecificTrapType -t timestamp -v OID TYPE VALUE
```

Here's how to use *nttrapgen* to send a trap notifying us that the UPS battery is running low. We use the String datatype to send an informative message, and we use trap 4025.1 from our private enterprise ID, 2789:

```
C:\tools> nttrapgen.exe -d nms:162 -c public -o ^
1.3.6.1.4.1.2789.4025 -i 10.123.456.4 -g 6 -s 4025 -t 124501 ^
-v 1.3.6.1.4.1.2789.4025.1 STRING 5 Minutes Left On UPS Battery
```

This trap will be sent to our network-management station (which has the hostname nms) on port 162, which is the standard port for SNMP traps. Any management station should be able to receive the trap and act on it appropriately. You can use this command in batch scripts, which are essentially the same as Unix shell scripts. Therefore, you can use *nttrapgen* to generate traps as you need them: you can write scripts that monitor key processes and generate traps when any interesting events take place. As with the earlier Perl example, you can use this simple trap generator in your environment if you don't need a heavy-duty management system.

Sending Traps with Net-SNMP

This *snmptrap* program looks very similar to OpenView's *snmptrap*. This program uses a single letter to refer to datatypes, as shown in Table 10-2.

Table 10-2. Net-SNMP snmptrap Datatypes

Abbreviation	Datatype
a	IP address
c	Counter
d	Decimal string
i	Integer
n	Null
o	Object ID
s	String
t	Time ticks
u	Unsigned integer
x	Hexadecimal string

Here's how the Net-SNMP *snmptrap* program is invoked:

```
snmptrap hostname community enterprise-oid agent \
generic-trap specific-trap uptime [OID type value]...
```

If you use two single quotes (`''`) in place of the time, *snmptrap* inserts the current time into the trap. The following command generates a trap with a single value. The object ID is `2005.1`, within our private enterprise; the value is a string that tells us that the web server has been restarted:

```
$ snmptrap nms public .1.3.6.1.4.1.2789.2005 ntserver1 6 2476317 '' \
.1.3.6.1.4.1.2789.2005.1 s "WWW Server Has Been Restarted"
```

Here's how to send a Version 2 notification with Net-SNMP:[*]

```
$ snmptrap -v2c nms public '' .1.3.6.1.6.3.1.1.5.3 \
ifIndex i 2 ifAdminStatus i 1 ifOperStatus i 1
```

The command is actually simpler than its Version 1 equivalent. There are no generic numbers, specific numbers, or vendor IDs. The `""` argument defaults to the current system uptime. The OID specifies the *linkDown* notification, with three data bindings specifying the link's status. The definition of *linkDown* in the IF-MIB states that the *linkDown* notification must include the *ifIndex*, *ifAdminStatus*, and *ifOperStatus* objects, which report the index of the interface that went down, its administrative status, and its operational status, respectively. For *ifAdminStatus*

---

[*] For information about sending Version 3 notifications with Net-SNMP, see Appendix F.

and *ifOperStatus*, a value of 1 indicates that the link is up. So this notification reports that interface 2 has changed its state from "down" to "up."

Again, the *snmptrap* command-line tool lets you integrate SNMP monitoring into shell scripts and other programs.

Forcing Your Hardware to Generate Traps

When you install a new piece of equipment, you should verify that it generates traps correctly. Testing your equipment's ability to generate traps has the added benefit of testing the behavior of your NMS; you can ensure that it handles traps in the way you want. The best way to test new hardware is to read your vendor's MIB and look for all the TRAP-TYPEs they have defined. This will give you a good feel for what sort of traps your vendor has implemented. For example, I read through our APC MIB and noticed that the unit will send a trap when it goes onto battery power if the AC power goes out. To test this feature, I secured the area in our datacenter and switched off the circuit breaker to simulate a power failure. The trap was generated, but it showed up in the Error event category because I did not have the correct MIB loaded in OpenView. I took the OID from the Error events and searched the APC MIBs for a match. When I found one, I loaded the MIB file into OpenView and repeated the test. This time, when the trap was received OpenView put an informative message in the Event Categories.

Most SNMP-compatible routers, switches, and network devices can generate *linkDown* traps. From RFC 1157, a *linkDown* trap is a "failure in one of the communication links represented in the agent's configuration." This means that if you start unplugging ports on your router you should receive traps, right? Yes, but first make sure you don't start disconnecting production database servers. Furthermore, make sure you don't disconnect the port by which your device would send the trap back to the NMS. Remember, SNMP is designed with the assumption that the network is unreliable—if something sends a trap but there's no way for the trap to reach its destination, no one will find out. By default, a *linkDown* trap won't appear in OpenView's Event Categories, because the default setting for *linkDown* is "Log only"; watch the log file *$OV_LOG/trapd.log* to see these traps arrive. Once you have a mechanism for receiving traps, bringing the link up and down on your device should send some traps your way.

Using Hooks with Your Programs

A *hook* is a convenient interface that lets you integrate your own code into some other product. The *Emacs* text editor is a good example of a program that uses hooks, almost entirely, to allow its users to extend how it operates. Let's look at the following simple program to explain this concept further:

```
# Logical Sample Program NH1
# PROGRAM COMMENTS
# PROGRAM BEGINS

        PROGRAM ADDS              $VAR1 + $VAR2 = $VAR3
        PROGRAM SUBTRACTS         $VAR5 - $VAR6 = $VAR7
        PROGRAM PRINTS RESULTS $VAR3 $VAR7


# PROGRAM ENDS
```

This program simply ADDS, SUBTRACTS, and PRINTS RESULTS; it does not have any hooks. To add a feature, you have to modify the code. For a small program like this that is a trivial exercise, but it would be difficult in a program of any size. The next program contains some hooks that let you add extensions:

```
# Logical Sample Program H1
# PROGRAM COMMENTS
# PROGRAM BEGINS
    PROGRAM RUNS $PATH/start.sh

    PROGRAM ADDS              $VAR1 + $VAR2 = $VAR3
    PROGRAM SUBTRACTS         $VAR5 - $VAR6 = $VAR7
    PROGRAM PRINTS RESULTS $VAR3 $VAR7

    PROGRAM RUNS $PATH/end.sh
# PROGRAM ENDS
```

Notice the two additional RUNS statements. These hooks allow you to run anything you want at the start or end of the program. The first program, *start.sh*, might be as simple as the command *echo "I am starting"*, which sends a simple message to the system or management console. This script could also call one of the trap-generation programs to send a trap to the NMS stating that some program is starting. It would be even more useful to send a message when the program terminates, possibly including information about the program's status. Here's a slightly more complicated program that runs a script, providing a number of arguments so that the script can send useful information back to the NMS when it generates a trap:

```
# Logical Sample Program H2
# PROGRAM COMMENTS
# PROGRAM BEGINS
    PROGRAM RUNS $PATH/start.sh $PROGRAM_NAME

    PROGRAM ADDS              $VAR1 + $VAR2 = $VAR3
    PROGRAM SUBTRACTS         $VAR5 - $VAR6 = $VAR7
    PROGRAM PRINTS RESULTS $VAR3 $VAR7

    PROGRAM RUNS $PATH/end.sh $PROGRAM_NAME $VAR1 $VAR2 $VAR3 $VAR5 $VAR6 $VAR7
# PROGRAM ENDS
```

With the additional arguments available to the hook programs, we can generate messages like "The Program Widget has ended with sales at $4 and YTD at $7." If your hook programs are shell scripts, you can simply add *snmptrap* commands via a text editor. Once you finish adding the *snmptrap* code, you can test your hook program by running it on the command line.

On most systems, many scripts can benefit from *snmptrap* hooks. On Solaris or Linux machines, for example, some of your */etc/init.d* scripts can be retrofitted to make use of *snmptrap* commands. It might be useful to have some kind of notification when important processes such as your web server or DNS server start and stop. Having such information on hand might make life much easier for your help-desk. (The Concord SystemEDGE SNMP agent provides more rigorous process-monitoring capabilities. See Chapter 11 for more information on this product.)

It's harder to add hooks to programs written in languages like C, because you need access to the source code as well as the ability to figure out where to place the hooks. Once you have identified where your hooks go and added them, you must recompile the source code. Some programs have hooks built in, allowing you to run external programs or RPCs. Check your program's documentation for the locations of these hooks. This is much more convenient than trying to build your own hooks into another program. Once you have established what these external programs are called, you can start writing your own traps or adding to existing ones.

11

Extensible SNMP Agents

There will come a time when you want to extend an agent's functionality. Extending an agent usually means adding or changing the MIBs the agent supports. Many agents that claim to support SNMP cover only a minimal number of somewhat useless MIBs—obviously a frustrating situation for someone who is planning on doing lots of automated network management. Upgrading your software to a newer version of SNMP, say Version 2 or 3, won't help; you won't get any more information out of a device than if you were using SNMPv1. The newer versions of SNMP add features to the protocol (such as additional security or more sophisticated options for retrieving and setting values), but the information that's available from any device is defined in the agent's MIBs, which are independent of the protocol itself.

When you are faced with an agent's limitations, you can turn to extensible agents.* These programs, or extensions to existing programs, allow you to extend a particular agent's MIB and retrieve values from an external source (a script, program, or file). In some cases, data can be returned as if it were coming from the agent itself. Most of the time you will not see a difference between the agent's native MIBs and your extensible ones. Many extensible agents give you the ability to read files, run programs, and return their results; they can even return tables of information. Some agents have configurable options that allow you to run external programs and have preset functions, such as disk-space checkers, built in.

The OpenView, Net-SNMP, and SystemEDGE agents are all examples of extensible agents. OpenView provides a separate extensible agent that allows you to extend the master agent (*snmpdm*); requests for the extensible agent won't work unless the master agent is running. You can start and stop the extensible agent

---

* We don't make a distinction between existing agents that can be extended and agents that exist purely to support extensions. We'll call them both "extensible agents."

without disturbing the master agent. To customize the extensible agent you define new objects using the ASN.1 format, as specified by the SMI. The Net-SNMP agent takes an alternate approach. It doesn't make a distinction between the master agent and the extensible agent; there's only one agent to worry about. You can use ASN.1 to define new objects (as with the OpenView extensible agent), but there's also a facility for adding extensions without writing any ASN.1, making this agent significantly more accessible for the novice administrator. SystemEDGE is similar to Net-SNMP in that there is only one agent to worry about. Of the three agents discussed in this chapter, it is the easiest to extend. Figure 11-1 compares the design strategies of the OpenView, Net-SNMP, and SystemEDGE agents.

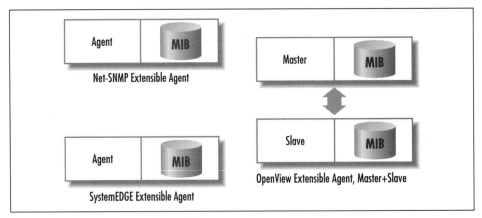

Figure 11-1. Architecture of extensible agents

All three agents have fairly comprehensive configuration options and all allow you to extend the local agent without heavy programming. You may need to write some scripts or a few short C programs, but with the sample programs here and the thousands more that are on the Internet,* nonprogrammers can still get a lot done.

We'll start with the Net-SNMP agent, since it is the simplest, then move to System-EDGE. We'll round out the discussion with OpenView's extensible agent. Be sure to see Chapter 5 for information on where to obtain these agents.

Net-SNMP

When you install the Net-SNMP package, it creates a sample *snmpd.conf* configuration file called *EXAMPLE.conf* in the source directory. This file contains some great examples that demonstrate how to extend your agent. Read through it to see the types of things you can and can't do. We will touch on only a few of Net-SNMP's features: checking for any number of running processes (**proc**), executing

---

* See Chapter 1 for a list of a few web sites that have links to commercial and free SNMP software.

a command that returns a single line of output (**exec**), executing a command that returns multiple lines of output (**exec**), and checking disk-space utilization (**disk**).

The main Net-SNMP configuration file can be found at *$NET_SNMP_HOME/share/ snmp/snmpd.conf*, where $NET_SNMP_HOME is the directory in which you installed Net-SNMP. Here is the configuration file that we will use for the remainder of this section:

```
# Filename: $NET_SNMP_HOME/share/snmp/snmpd.conf
# Check for processes running
# Items in here will appear in the ucdavis.procTable
proc sendmail 10 1
proc httpd

# Return the value from the executed program with a passed parm.
# Items in here will appear in the ucdavis.extTable
exec FileCheck /opt/local/shell_scripts/filecheck.sh /tmp/vxprint.error

# Multiline return from the command
# This needs its own OID
# I have used a subset of my registered enterprise ID (2789) within the OID
exec .1.3.6.1.4.1.2021.2789.51 FancyCheck /opt/local/shell_scripts/fancycheck.sh \
   /core

# Check disks for their mins
disk / 100000
```

Whenever you make changes to the Net-SNMP agent's configuration file, you can have it reread the configuration by sending the process an HUP signal:

```
$ ps -ef | grep snmpd
    root   12345    1  0   Nov 16 ?        2:35 /usr/local/bin/snmpd
$ kill -HUP 12345
```

Now let's look at the file itself. The first **proc** command says to check for the process **sendmail**. The numbers 10 and 1 define how many *sendmail* processes we want running at any given time (a maximum of 10 and a minimum of 1). The second **proc** command says that we want at least one **httpd** process running. To see what effect these commands have on our agent, let's look at an *snmpwalk* of *ucdavis.procTable* (*.1.3.6.1.4.1.2021.2*):

```
$ snmpwalk sunserver2 public .1.3.6.1.4.1.2021.2
enterprises.ucdavis.procTable.prEntry.prIndex.1 = 1
enterprises.ucdavis.procTable.prEntry.prIndex.2 = 2
enterprises.ucdavis.procTable.prEntry.prNames.1 = "sendmail"
enterprises.ucdavis.procTable.prEntry.prNames.2 = "httpd"
enterprises.ucdavis.procTable.prEntry.prMin.1 = 1
enterprises.ucdavis.procTable.prEntry.prMin.2 = 0
enterprises.ucdavis.procTable.prEntry.prMax.1 = 10
enterprises.ucdavis.procTable.prEntry.prMax.2 = 0
enterprises.ucdavis.procTable.prEntry.prCount.1 = 1
enterprises.ucdavis.procTable.prEntry.prCount.2 = 6
enterprises.ucdavis.procTable.prEntry.prErrorFlag.1 = 0
```

```
enterprises.ucdavis.procTable.prEntry.prErrorFlag.2 = 0
enterprises.ucdavis.procTable.prEntry.prErrMessage.1 = ""
enterprises.ucdavis.procTable.prEntry.prErrMessage.2 = ""
enterprises.ucdavis.procTable.prEntry.prErrFix.1 = 0
enterprises.ucdavis.procTable.prEntry.prErrFix.2 = 0
```

The agent returns the contents of the *procTable*. In this table, the *sendmail* and *httpd* process entries occupy instances 1 and 2. prMin and prMax are the minimum and maximum numbers we set for the *sendmail* and *httpd* processes.* The prCount value gives us the number of processes currently running: it looks like we have one *sendmail* process and six *httpd* processes. To see what happens when the number of processes falls outside the range we specified, let's kill all six *httpd* processes and look at the *procTable* again (instead of listing the whole table, we'll walk only instance 2, which describes the *httpd* process):

```
$ snmpwalk sunserver2 public .1.3.6.1.4.1.2021.2
enterprises.ucdavis.procTable.prEntry.prIndex.1 = 1
enterprises.ucdavis.procTable.prEntry.prNames.1 = "httpd"
enterprises.ucdavis.procTable.prEntry.prMin.1 = 0
enterprises.ucdavis.procTable.prEntry.prMax.1 = 0
enterprises.ucdavis.procTable.prEntry.prCount.1 = 0
enterprises.ucdavis.procTable.prEntry.prErrorFlag.1 = 1
enterprises.ucdavis.procTable.prEntry.prErrMessage.1 = "No httpd
process running."
enterprises.ucdavis.procTable.prEntry.prErrFix.1 = 0
```

We had six *httpd* processes running and now, per prCount, we have none. The prErrMessage reports the problem, and the prErrorFlag has changed from 0 to 1, indicating that something is wrong. This flag makes it easy to poll the agent, using the techniques discussed in Chapter 9, and see that the *httpd* processes have stopped. Let's try a variation on this theme. If we set prMin to indicate that we want more than six *httpd* processes running, then restart *httpd*, our prErrMessage is:

```
enterprises.ucdavis.procTable.prEntry.prErrMessage.1 = "Too few
httpd running (# = 0)"
```

The next command in the configuration file is **exec**; this command allows us to execute any program and return the program's results and exit value to the agent. This is helpful when you already have a program you would like to use in conjunction with the agent. We've written a simple shell script called *filecheck.sh* that checks whether the file that's passed to it on the command line exists. If the file exists, it returns a 0 (zero); otherwise, it returns a 1 (one):

```
#!/bin/sh
# FileName: /opt/local/shell_scripts/filecheck.sh

if [ -f $1 ]; then
    exit 0
```

---

* When prMin and prMax are both 0, it says that we want at least one and a maximum of infinity processes running.

```
fi
exit 1
```

Our configuration file uses *filecheck.sh* to check for the existence of the file */tmp/vxprint.error*. Once you have the *filecheck.sh* script in place, you can see the results it returns by walking *ucdavis.extTable (.1.3.6.1.4.1.2021.8)*:

```
$ snmpwalk sunserver2 public .1.3.6.1.4.1.2021.8
enterprises.ucdavis.extTable.extEntry.extIndex.1 = 1
enterprises.ucdavis.extTable.extEntry.extNames.1 = "FileCheck"
enterprises.ucdavis.extTable.extEntry.extCommand.1 =
"/opt/local/shell_scripts/filecheck.sh /tmp/vxprint.error"
enterprises.ucdavis.extTable.extEntry.extResult.1 = 0
enterprises.ucdavis.extTable.extEntry.extOutput.1 = ""
enterprises.ucdavis.extTable.extEntry.extErrFix.1 = 0
```

The first argument to the **exec** command[*] in the configuration file is a label that identifies the command so we can easily recognize it in the *extTable*. In our case we used **FileCheck**—that's not a particularly good name, because we might want to check the existence of several files, but we could have named it anything we deemed useful. Whatever name you choose is returned as the value of the *extTable.extEntry.extNames.1* object. Because the file */tmp/vxprint.error* exists, *filecheck.sh* returns a 0, which appears in the table as the value of *extTable.extEntry.extResult.1*. You can also have the agent return a line of output from the program. Change *filecheck.sh* to perform an *ls –la* on the file if it exists:

```
#!/bin/sh
# FileName: /opt/local/shell_scripts/filecheck.sh

if [ -f $1 ]; then
    ls -la $1
    exit 0
fi

exit 1
```

When we poll the agent, we see the output from the script in the *extOutput* value the agent returns:

```
enterprises.ucdavis.extTable.extEntry.extOutput.1 = \
"  16 -rw-r--r--    1 root     other         2476 Feb 3 17:13 /tmp/vxprint.error."
```

This simple trick works only if the script returns a single line of output. If your script returns more than one line of output, insert an OID in front of the string name in the **exec** command.

Here's the next command from our *snmpd.conf* file:

```
exec .1.3.6.1.4.1.2021.2789.51 FancyCheck /opt/local/shell_scripts/fancycheck.sh \
/core
```

---

[*] See the *EXAMPLE.conf* configuration file introduced at the beginning of this chapter.

This command runs the program *fancycheck.sh*, with the identifying string FancyCheck. We won't bother to list *fancycheck.sh*; it's just like *filecheck.sh*, except that it adds a check to determine the file type. The OID identifies where in the MIB tree the agent will place the result of running the command. It needs to be in the *ucdavis* enterprise (*.1.3.6.1.4.1.2021*). We recommend that you follow the *ucdavis* enterprise ID with your own enterprise number, to prevent collisions with objects defined by other sources and avoid overwriting one of *ucdavis*'s subtrees. Follow your enterprise number with another number to identify this particular command. In this case, our enterprise ID is 2789 and we assign the arbitrary number 51 to this command. Thus, the complete OID is *.1.3.6.1.4.1. 2021.2789.51*.

Here are the results from walking the *.1.3.6.1.4.1.2021.2789.51* subtree:

```
$ snmpwalk sunserver2 public .1.3.6.1.4.1.2021.2789.51
enterprises.ucdavis.2789.51.1.1 = 1
enterprises.ucdavis.2789.51.2.1 = "FancyCheck"
enterprises.ucdavis.2789.51.3.1 =
"/opt/local/shell_scripts/fancycheck.sh /core"
ucdavis.2789.51.100.1 = 0
ucdavis.2789.51.101.1 = "-rw-r--r--   1 root      other
346708 Feb 14 16:30 /core."
ucdavis.2789.51.101.2 = "/core:..ELF 32-bit MSB core file SPARC
Version 1, from 'httpd'."
ucdavis.2789.51.102.1 = 0
```

Notice that we have a few additional lines in our output. *2789.51.100.1* is the exit number, *2789.51.101.1* and *2789.51.101.2* are the output from the command, and *2789.51.102.1* is the *errorFix* value. These values can be useful when you are trying to debug your new extension. (Unfortunately, *snmpwalk* can give you only the numeric OID, not the human-readable name, because *snmpwalk* doesn't know what *2789.51.x* is.)

The last task for Net-SNMP's extensible agent is to perform some disk-space monitoring. This is a great option that lets you check the availability of disk space and return multiple (useful) values. The **disk** option takes a filesystem mount point followed by a number. Here is what our entry looks like in *snmpd.conf*:

```
# Check disks for their mins
disk / 100000
```

The definition of the **disk** option from *UCD-SNMP-MIB.txt* is "Minimum space required on the disk (in kBytes) before the errors are triggered." Let's first take a look on *sunserver2* to see what the common *df* program returns:

```
$ df -k /
Filesystem           kbytes   used   avail capacity  Mounted on
/dev/dsk/c0t0d0s0    432839   93449  296110   24%      /
```

To see what SNMP has to say about the disk space on our server, run *snmpwalk* against the *ucdavis.diskTable* object (*.1.3.6.1.4.1.2021.9*). This returns virtually the same information as the *df* command:

```
$ snmpwalk sunserver2 public .1.3.6.1.4.1.2021.9
enterprises.ucdavis.diskTable.dskEntry.dskIndex.1 = 1
enterprises.ucdavis.diskTable.dskEntry.dskPath.1 = "/" Hex: 2F
enterprises.ucdavis.diskTable.dskEntry.dskDevice.1 =
"/dev/dsk/c0t0d0s0"
enterprises.ucdavis.diskTable.dskEntry.dskMinimum.1 = 100000
enterprises.ucdavis.diskTable.dskEntry.dskMinPercent.1 = -1
enterprises.ucdavis.diskTable.dskEntry.dskTotal.1 = 432839
enterprises.ucdavis.diskTable.dskEntry.dskAvail.1 = 296110
enterprises.ucdavis.diskTable.dskEntry.dskUsed.1 = 93449
enterprises.ucdavis.diskTable.dskEntry.dskPercent.1 = 24
enterprises.ucdavis.diskTable.dskEntry.dskErrorFlag.1 = 0
enterprises.ucdavis.diskTable.dskEntry.dskErrorMsg.1 = ""
```

As you can see, the Net-SNMP agent has many customizable features that allow you to tailor your monitoring without having to write your own object definitions. Be sure to review *$NET_SNMP_HOME/share/snmp/mibs/UCD-SNMP-MIB.txt* for complete definitions of all Net-SNMP's variables. While we touched on only a few customizable options here, you will find many other useful options in the *EXAMPLE. conf* file that comes with the Net-SNMP package.

SystemEDGE

The SystemEDGE agent is also extensible. No other system processes need to be run in order to extend this agent. It comes with three predefined extended objects: Domain Name System (DNS) for Unix, Network Information System (NIS) for Unix, and Remote Pinger for Unix and Windows NT. The first object returns the domain name of the underlying operating system, the second returns the NIS domain name of the underlying operating system, and the third sends ICMP requests to a remote host from the system on which the agent is running. While these are nice scripts to have, what we want to focus on is how to add your own OIDs to the agent.

Extensibility for Unix and Windows NT

The SystemEDGE agent has a private MIB that defines a table called the *extension-Group*. Its full OID is *1.3.6.1.4.1.546.14* (*iso.org.dod.internet.private.enterprises. empire.extensionGroup*). This is where you define your own objects. The first object you define has the OID *extensionGroup.1.0* (*1.3.6.1.4.1.546.14.1.0*), where the *.0* indicates that the object is scalar; the next has the OID *extensionGroup.2.0*, and so on. Note that all the objects defined this way must be scalar. For advanced users, Concord has developed a plug-in architecture for SystemEDGE that allows you to develop complex extended objects (including tables) and full-blown MIBs.

To extend the agent, start by editing the *sysedge.cf* file. This file tells the agent to which extended OIDs it must respond. The format of a command in this file is:

```
extension LeafNumber Type Access 'Command'
```

The keyword `extension` tells the agent that this configuration entry is an extension that belongs to the *extensionGroup*. *LeafNumber* is the extension object number—i.e., the number you assign to the object in the *extensionGroup* table. *Type* is the SNMP type for the OID. Valid types are `Integer`, `Counter`, `Gauge`, `Octetstring`, `TimeTicks`, `Objectid`, and `IPAddress`. *Access* is either `Read-Only` or `Read-Write`. And finally, *Command* is the script or program the agent will execute when this particular OID is queried by an NMS. We'll talk more about this shortly. Here are some examples of extension objects:

```
extension 1 Integer Read-Only '/usr/local/bin/Script.sh'
extension 2 Gauge Read-Only '/usr/local/bin/Script.pl'
extension 33 Counter Read-Write '/usr/local/bin/Program'
```

The first item defines a read-only OID of type `Integer`. The OID is *1.3.6.1.4.1. 546.14.1.0.* The agent will execute the command */usr/local/bin/exampleScript.sh* when this OID is queried. The second entry is similar, except its type is `Gauge` and its numeric OID is *1.3.6.1.4.1.546.14.2.0.* The third example simply shows that *LeafNumber* doesn't have to be sequential; you can use any number you want, provided that it is unique.

Extending the agent allows you to write your own scripts that do whatever you want: you can get information about devices or programs that are not SNMP-capable, as long as you can write a script that queries them for their status. In the example above, */usr/local/bin/Script.sh*, */usr/local/bin/Script.pl*, and */usr/local/bin/ Program* are all examples of scripts the agent will execute when the OID assigned to each script is queried. Two requirements must be met by any script or program:

- All *set*, *get*, and *getnext* requests must generate output. For *get* and *getnext*, the output from the script should be the actual value of the object requested. This means that the script or program that fetches the required information must return a single value. For a *set* request, the script should return the object's new value. The request will fail if there is no output. (Note that for a *set* request, a script may succeed in changing the state of the device even if it produces no output and the agent considers the script to have failed.)

- The script or program should print whatever information it needs to return (based on the type of request), followed by a newline character. The agent parses only up to this character. If a newline is the first character the agent encounters, the agent generates an error and returns this to the NMS or SNMP application.

The agent sends three arguments to the script or program it executes: the *Leaf-Number*, the request type (GET, GETNEXT, or SET, in capital letters), and a string that represents some value to be set (the third argument is used only for SET requests). The following skeletal Perl script, called *skel.pl*, shows how you can use all three arguments:

```perl
#!/usr/local/bin/perl

if ($ARGV[0] == 1) {
    # OID queried is 1.3.6.1.4.1.546.14.1.0
    if ($ARGV[1] eq "SET") {
            # use $ARGV[2] to set the value of something and return the set value,
            # followed by a newline character, to the agent
    } elsif (($ARGV[1] eq "GET") || ($ARGV[1] eq "GETNEXT")) {
            # get the information to which this OID pertains, then return it,
            # followed by a newline character, to the agent
    }
} else {
    return 0;
    # return 0, since I don't know what to do with this OID
}
```

All you have to do is add the logic that takes some action to retrieve (or set) the appropriate value and return the correct value to the agent. The corresponding entry in *sysedge.cf* might look something like this:

```
extension 1 Integer Read-Write '/usr/local/bin/skel.pl'
```

What we've done so far gives the agent the ability to respond to requests for a new kind of data. We still need to solve the other part of the puzzle: telling the management station that some new kind of data is available for it to retrieve. This requires creating an entry in a MIB file.* After adding this entry to the file, you must recompile the MIB into your NMS system so that the NMS will know the access and type of each of the extended objects in the MIB for which it is to perform queries. Here is a MIB entry that corresponds to the previous agent extension:

```
skeletonVariable OBJECT-TYPE
    SYNTAX Integer
    ACCESS Read-Write
    DESCRIPTION
        "This is an example object."
::= { extensionGroup 1 }
```

Once this is compiled into the NMS, you can query the object by specifying its full name (*iso.org.dod.internet.private.enterprises.empire.extensionGroup.skeletonVariable.0*). Alternatively, you can use the numeric OID; for example:

```
$ snmpget server.ora.com public .1.3.6.1.4.1.546.14.1.0
```

---

* Concord recommends that you keep all your extended MIB objects in a separate file, away from the SystemEDGE MIB file. This makes it easier for you to recompile it into your NMS.

Security can be a concern when writing your own extension scripts. On Unix systems, it's a good idea to create a separate user and group to execute your extensions, rather than allowing the root user to run your scripts.

Added Extensibility for Windows NT

While the *extensionGroup* is supported on all platforms, the Windows NT version of SystemEDGE allows you to extend SystemEDGE with objects taken from the registry and performance registry. You can gain access to configuration data and performance data, which are normally viewed using *regedit* and *perfmon*. The Windows NT extension group is defined as *iso.org.dod.internet.private.enterprises. empire.nt.ntRegPerf* (*1.3.6.1.4.1.546.5.7*). As with the Unix extensions, the NT extensions are defined in the *sysedge.cf* file.

To configure a registry extension, add a line with the following syntax to *sysedge.cf*:

```
ntregperf LeafNumber Type Registry 'Key' 'Value'
```

The keyword **ntregperf** defines this as an NT registry or performance extension object. *LeafNumber* and *Type* are the same as for Unix extensions. The keyword **Registry** identifies this entry as a registry extension. Registry extensions are read-only. *Key* is a quoted string that specifies the registry key to be accessed. *Value* is the value you want to read from the key. Here is an example:

```
ntregperf 1 OctetString Registry
'SYSTEM\CurrentControlSet\Control\CrashControl' 'DumpFile'
```

This creates a registry extension object that returns the path to the crash-control dump file. The OID is *1.3.6.1.4.1.546.5.7.1.0* (*iso.org.dod.internet.private.enterprises.empire.nt.ntRegPerf.1.0*).

To configure a performance extension, use the following syntax:

```
ntregperf LeafNumber Type Performance 'Object' 'Counter' 'PerfInstance'
```

Here again, **ntregperf** is the keyword that indicates this is an NT registry/performance extension object. *LeafNumber* and *Type* should be familiar to you. The keyword **Performance** indicates that we're reading a value from the performance registry; performance extensions are read-only. *Object* specifies the performance object to be accessed. *Counter* specifies the object's performance counter value to be accessed. Finally, *PerfInstance* specifies the performance counter instance to be accessed. This should be identical to what's listed with *perfmon*. Here's a typical performance extension:

```
ntregperf 2 Counter Performance 'TCP' 'Segments Sent/sec' '1'
```

You can use this extension to watch the total number of TCP segments transmitted by the system. Its OID is *1.3.6.1.4.1.546.5.7.2.0* (*iso.org.dod.internet.private.enterprises.empire.nt.ntRegPerf.2.0*). Keep in mind that you should create a MIB entry (in a MIB file) for any NT extensions you create, similar to the entry we defined above for *skeletonVariable*.

The examples in this section should be enough to get you up and running with an extended SystemEDGE agent. Be sure to read the SystemEDGE manual for a complete treatment of this topic.

OpenView's Extensible Agent

Before you start playing around with OpenView's extensible agent, make sure that you have its master agent (*snmpdm*) configured and running properly. You must also obtain an enterprise number, because extending the OpenView agent requires writing your own MIB definitions, and the objects you define must be part of the *enterprises* subtree.* Chapter 2 describes how to obtain an enterprise number.

MIBs are written using the SMI, of which there are two versions: SMIv1, defined in RFCs 1155 and 1212; and SMIv2, defined in RFCs 2578, 2579, and 2580. RFC 1155 notes that "ASN.1 constructs are used to define the structure, although the full generality of ASN.1 is not permitted." While OpenView's extensible agent file *snmpd. extend* uses ASN.1 to define objects, it requires some additional entries to create a usable object. *snmpd.extend* also does not support some of the SNMPv2 SMI constructs. In this chapter, we will discuss only those constructs that are supported.

By default, the configuration file for the extensible agent in the Unix version of OpenView is */etc/SnmpAgent.d/snmp.extend*. To jump right in, copy the sample file to this location and then restart the agent:

```
$ cp /opt/OV/prg_samples/eagent/snmpd.extend /etc/SnmpAgent.d/
$ /etc/rc2.d/S98SnmpExtAgt stop
$ /etc/rc2.d/S98SnmpExtAgt start
```

You should see no errors and get an exit code of 0 (zero). If errors occur, check the *snmpd.log* file.† If the agent starts successfully, try walking one of the objects monitored by the extensible agent. The following command checks the status of the mail queue:

```
$ snmpwalk sunserver1  .1.3.6.1.4.1.4242.2.2.0
4242.2.2.0 : OCTET STRING- (ascii):    Mail queue is empty
```

We're off to a good start. We have successfully started and polled the extensible agent.

The key to OpenView's *snmpd.extend* file is the DESCRIPTION. If this seems a little weird, it is! Executing commands from within the DESCRIPTION section is

---

* Do not use my enterprise number. Obtaining your own private enterprise number is easy and free. Using my number will only confuse you and others later in the game.

† On Solaris and HP-UX machines this file is located in */var/adm/snmpd.log*.

peculiar to this agent, not part of the SNMP design. The DESCRIPTION tells the
agent where to look to read, write, and run files. You can put a whole slew of
parameters within the DESCRIPTION, but we'll tackle only a few of the more
common ones. Here's the syntax for the *snmpd.extend* file:

```
your-label-here DEFINITIONS ::= BEGIN

-- insert your comments here

enterprise-name  OBJECT IDENTIFIER ::= { OID-label(1) OID-label{2) 3 }
subtree-name1    OBJECT IDENTIFIER ::= { OID-label(3) 4 }
subtree-name2    OBJECT IDENTIFIER ::= { OID-label(123) 56 }

data-Identifier* OBJECT-TYPE
    SYNTAX Integer | Counter | Gauge | DisplayString†
    ACCESS read-only | read-write
    STATUS mandatory | optional | obsolete | deprecated‡
    DESCRIPTION
        "
        Enter Your Description Here
        READ-COMMAND: /your/command/here passed1 passed2
        READ-COMMAND-TIMEOUT: timeout_in_seconds (defaults to 3)
        FILE-COMMAND: /your/file-command/here passed1 passed2
        FILE-COMMAND-FREQUENCY: frequency_in_seconds (defaults to 10)
        FILE-NAME: /your/filename/here
        "
    ::= { parent-subtree-name subidentifier }

END
```

We can glean some style guidelines from RFC 2578. While there are many guidelines, some more useful than others, one thing stands out: case does matter. Much
of ASN.1 is case sensitive. All ASN.1 keywords and macros should be in upper-
case: OBJECT-TYPE, SYNTAX, DESCRIPTION, etc. Your *data-Identifiers* (i.e., object
names) should start in lowercase and contain no spaces. If you have read any of
the RFC MIBs or done any polling, you should have noticed that all the object
names obey this convention. Try to use descriptive names and keep your names
well under the 64-character limit; RFC 2578 states that anything over 32 characters
is not recommended. If you define an object under an existing subtree, you should
use this subtree-name, or parent-name, before each new object-name you create.
The *ip* subtree in *mib-2* (RFC 1213) provides an example of good practice:

```
ip          OBJECT IDENTIFIER ::= { mib-2 4 }

ipForwarding OBJECT-TYPE
```

---

* This is sometimes called a leaf node, node, object, or MIB.

† These are just to name a few supported datatypes.

‡ For now we will always use mandatory as our STATUS.

```
...
::= { ip 1 }

ipDefaultTTL OBJECT-TYPE
...
::= { ip 2 }
```

This file starts by defining the *ip* subtree. The names of objects within that subtree start with *ip* and use *ip* as the parent-subtree-name. As useful as this recommended practice is, there are times when it isn't appropriate. For example, this practice makes it difficult to move your objects to different parents while you are building a MIB file.

Here's a working *snmpd.extend* file that contains three definitions: *psZombieNum*, *prtDiagExitC*, and *whosOnCall*. I have placed all these objects within my own private enterprise (*2789*, which I have named *mauro*). Figure 11-2 shows this portion of my private subtree.

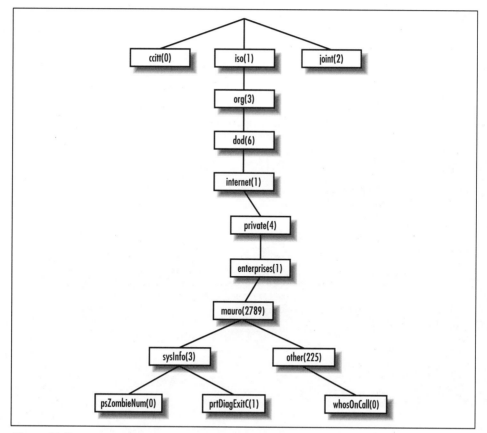

Figure 11-2. mauro subtree

You can now walk the tree and see what my new objects look like; my tree starts at the OID *.1.3.6.1.4.1.2789*, which is equivalent to *.iso.org.dod.internet.private. enterprises.mauro*. I can organize my own subtree any way I want, so I've split it into two branches beneath *mauro*: *mauro.sysInfo* (*2789.3*) will hold information about the status of the system itself (*psZombieNum* and *prtDiagExitC*), and *mauro. other* (*2789.255*) will hold additional information (*whosOnCall*). If you look further down, you can see the three leaf nodes we define in this file:

```
SampleExt DEFINITIONS ::= BEGIN

-- comments appear here behind the dashes

internet        OBJECT IDENTIFIER ::= { iso(1) org(3) dod(6) 1 }
enterprises     OBJECT IDENTIFIER ::= { internet(1) private(4) 1 }
mauro           OBJECT IDENTIFIER ::= { enterprises(1) 2789 }

-- Now that we have defined mauro, let's define some objects

sysInfo         OBJECT IDENTIFIER ::= { mauro 3 }
other           OBJECT IDENTIFIER ::= { mauro 255 }

psZombieNum OBJECT-TYPE
  SYNTAX   INTEGER
  ACCESS   read-only
  STATUS   mandatory
  DESCRIPTION
    "Search through ps and return the number of zombies.
    READ-COMMAND: VALUE=`ps -ef | grep -v grep | grep -c  \<defunct\>`; echo $VALUE
    "
 ::= { sysInfo 0 }

prtDiagExitC OBJECT-TYPE
    SYNTAX   INTEGER
    ACCESS   read-only
    STATUS   mandatory
    DESCRIPTION
        "On Solaris, prtdiag shows us system diagnostic information. The
        manpage states that if this command exits with a non-zero value,
        we have a problem. This is a great polling mechanism for some
        systems.
        READ-COMMAND: /usr/platform/`uname -m`/sbin/prtdiag > /dev/null; echo $?"
    ::= { sysInfo 1 }

whosOnCall OBJECT-TYPE
    SYNTAX   OctetString
    ACCESS   read-write
    STATUS   mandatory
    DESCRIPTION
        "This file contains the name of the person who will be on call
        today. The helpdesk uses this file. Only the helpdesk and
        managers should update this file. If you are sick or unable to
        be on call please contact your manager and/or the helpdesk.
```

```
        FILE-NAME: /opt/local/oncall/today.txt"
    ::= { other 0 }
```

```
END
```

The first two objects, *psZombieNum* and *prtDiagExitC*, both use the READ-COMMAND in the DESCRIPTION. This tells the agent to execute the named command and send any output the command produces to the NMS. By default, the program must complete within three seconds and have an exit value of 0 (zero). You can increase the timeout by adding a READ-COMMAND-TIMEOUT:

```
READ-COMMAND: /some/fs/somecommand.pl
READ-COMMAND-TIMEOUT: 10
```

This tells the agent to wait 10 seconds instead of 3 for a reply before killing the process and returning an error.

The last object, *whosOnCall*, uses a FILE-NAME in the DESCRIPTION. This tells the agent to return the first line of the file, program, script, etc. specified after FILE-NAME. Later we will learn how to manipulate this file.

Now that we've created a MIB file with our new definitions, we need to load the new MIB into OpenView. This step isn't strictly necessary, but it's much more convenient to work with textual names than to deal with numeric IDs. To do this, use *xnmloadmib*, discussed in Chapter 6. After we load the MIB file containing our three new objects, we should see their names in the MIB browser and be able to poll them by name.

Once you have copied the MIB file into the appropriate directory and forced the extensible agent, *extsubagt*, to reread its configuration (by using *kill –HUP*), try walking the new objects using OpenView's *snmpwalk* program:

```
$ snmpwalk sunserver2 -c public .1.3.6.1.4.1.2789
mauro.sysInfo.psZombieNum.0 : INTEGER: 0
mauro.sysInfo.prtDiagExitC.0 : INTEGER: 2
```

Notice anything strange about our return values? We didn't get anything for *whosOnCall*. Nothing was returned for this object because we haven't created the *oncall.txt* file whose contents we're trying to read. We must first create this file and insert some data into the file. There are two ways of doing this. Obviously, you can create the file with your favorite text editor. But the clever way is to use *snmpset*:

```
$ snmpset -c private sunserver2 \
.1.3.6.1.4.1.2789.255.0.0 octetstring "david jones"
mauro.Other.whosOnCall.0 : OCTET STRING- (ascii):        david jones
```

This command tells the SNMP agent to put david jones in the file */opt/local/oncall/today.txt*. The filename is defined by the FILE-NAME: /opt/local/oncall/today.txt command that we wrote in the extended MIB. The additional

.0 at the end of the OID tells the agent we want the first (and only) instance of *whosOnCall*. (We could have used *.iso.org.dod.internet.private.enterprises.mauro. other.whosOnCall.0* instead of the numeric OID.) Furthermore, the *snmpset* command specifies the datatype `octetstring`, which matches the `OctetString` syntax we defined in the MIB. This datatype lets us insert string values into the file. Finally, we're allowed to set the value of this object with *snmpset* because we have `read-write` access to the object, as specified in the MIB.

If you choose to use an editor to create the file, keep in mind that anything after the first line of the file is ignored. If you want to read multiple lines you have to use a table; tables are covered in the next section.

Now let's add another object to the MIB for our extended agent. We'll use a modification of the example OpenView gives us. We'll create an object named *fmailListMsgs* (*2*) that summarizes the messages in the mail queue. This object will live in a new subtree, named *fmail* (*4*), under the private *mauro* subtree. So the name of our object will be *mauro.fmail.fmailListMsgs* or, in numeric form, *.1.3.6. 1.4.1.2789.4.2*. First, we need to define the *fmail* branch under the *mauro* subtree. To do this, add the following line to *snmpd.extend*:

```
fmail          OBJECT IDENTIFIER ::= { mauro 4 }
```

We picked 4 for the branch number, but we could have chosen any number that doesn't conflict with our other branches (3 and 255). After we define *fmail* we can insert the definition for *fmailListMsgs* into *snmpd.extend*, placing it before the `END` statement:

```
fmailListMsgs OBJECT-TYPE
    SYNTAX DisplayString
    ACCESS read-only
    STATUS mandatory
    DESCRIPTION
        "List of messages on the mail queue.
         READ-COMMAND: /usr/lib/sendmail -bp
         READ-COMMAND-TIMEOUT: 10"
    ::= { fmail 2 }
```

When polled, *fmailListMsgs* runs the command *sendmail –bp*, which prints a summary of the mail queue. When all this is done, you can use your management station or a tool such as *snmpget* to read the value of *mauro.fmail.fmailListMsgs* and see the status of the outgoing mail queue.

Tables

Tables allow the agent to return multiple lines of output (or other sets of values) from the commands it executes. At its most elaborate, a table allows the agent to return something like a spreadsheet. We can retrieve this spreadsheet using *snmpwalk*—a process that's significantly easier than issuing separate *get* operations to retrieve the data one value at a time. One table we've already seen is *.iso.org.dod. internet.mgmt.mib-2.interfaces.ifTable*, which is defined in MIB-II and contains information about all of a device's interfaces.

Every table contains an *integer index*, which is a unique key that distinguishes the rows in the table. The index starts with 1, for the first row, and increases by one for each following row. The index is used as an instance identifier for the columns in the table; given any column, the index lets you select the data (i.e., the row) you want. Let's look at a small table, represented by the text file *animal.db*:

```
1       Tweety        Bird    Chirp   2
2       Madison       Dog     Bark    4
3       "Big Ben"     Bear    Grrr    5
```

Our goal is to make this table readable via SNMP, using OpenView's extensible agent. This file is already in the format required by the agent. Each column is delimited by whitespace; a newline marks the end of each row. Data that includes an internal space is surrounded by quotes. OpenView doesn't allow column headings in the table, but we will want to think about the names of the objects in each row. Logically, the column headings are nothing more than the names of the objects we will retrieve from the table. In other words, each row of our table consists of five objects:

animalIndex
> An index that specifies the row in the table. The first row is 1, as you'd expect for SNMP tables. The **SYNTAX** for this object is therefore **INTEGER**.

animalName
> The animal's name. This is a text string, so the **SYNTAX** of this object will be **DisplayString**.

animalSpecies
> The animal's species (another text string, represented as a **DisplayString**).

animalNoise
> The noise the animal makes (another **DisplayString**).

animalDanger
> An indication of how dangerous the animal is. This is another **INTEGER**, whose value can be from 1 to 6. This is called an "enumerated integer"; we're allowed to assign textual mnemonics to the integer values.

At this point, we have just about everything we need to know to write the MIB that allows us to read the table. For example, we know that we want an object named *animalNoise.2* to access the *animalNoise* object in the second row of the table; this object has the value **Bark**. It's easy to see how this notation can be used to locate any object in the table. Now let's write the MIB definition for the table.

```
TableExtExample DEFINITIONS ::= BEGIN

internet        OBJECT IDENTIFIER ::= { iso(1) org(3) dod(6) 1 }
enterprises     OBJECT IDENTIFIER ::= { internet(1) private(4) 1 }
mauro           OBJECT IDENTIFIER ::= { enterprises(1) 2789 }
other           OBJECT IDENTIFIER ::= { mauro 255 }

AnimalEntry ::=
    SEQUENCE {
    animalIndex INTEGER,
    animalName DisplayString,
    animalSpecies DisplayString,
    animalNoise DisplayString,
    animalDanger INTEGER
    }

animalTable OBJECT-TYPE
    SYNTAX SEQUENCE OF AnimalEntry
    ACCESS not-accessible
    STATUS mandatory
    DESCRIPTION
        "This is a table of animals that shows:
         Name
         Species
         Noise
         Danger Level
         FILE-NAME: /opt/local/animal.db"
    ::= { other 247 }

animalEntry OBJECT-TYPE
    SYNTAX AnimalEntry
    ACCESS not-accessible
    STATUS mandatory
    DESCRIPTION
        "List of animalNum"
    INDEX { animalIndex }
    ::= { animalTable 1 }

animalIndex OBJECT-TYPE
    SYNTAX INTEGER
    ACCESS read-only
    STATUS mandatory
    DESCRIPTION
        "The unique index number we will use for each row"
    ::= { animalEntry 1 }

animalName OBJECT-TYPE
    SYNTAX DisplayString
    ACCESS read-only
    STATUS mandatory
    DESCRIPTION
        "My pet name for each animal"
    ::= { animalEntry 2 }
```

```
animalSpecies OBJECT-TYPE
    SYNTAX DisplayString
    ACCESS read-only
    STATUS mandatory
    DESCRIPTION
        "The animal's species"
    ::= { animalEntry 3 }

animalNoise OBJECT-TYPE
    SYNTAX DisplayString
    ACCESS read-only
    STATUS mandatory
    DESCRIPTION
        "The noise or sound the animal makes"
    ::= { animalEntry 4 }

animalDanger OBJECT-TYPE
    SYNTAX INTEGER {
        no-Danger(1),
        can-Harm(2),
        some-Damage(3),
        will-Wound(4),
        severe-Pain(5),
        will-Kill(6)
    }
    ACCESS read-write
    STATUS mandatory
    DESCRIPTION
        "The level of danger that we may face with the particular animal"
    ::= { animalEntry 5 }

END
```

The table starts with a definition of the *animalTable* object, which gives us our DESCRIPTION and tells the agent where the *animal.db* file is located. The SYNTAX is SEQUENCE OF AnimalEntry. *AnimalEntry* (watch the case) gives us a quick view of all our columns. You can leave *AnimalEntry* out, but we recommend that you include it since it documents the structure of the table.

The table is actually built from *animalEntry* elements—because object names are case sensitive, this object is different from *AnimalEntry*. *animalEntry* tells us what object we should use for our index or key; the object used as the key is in brackets after the INDEX keyword.

The definitions of the remaining objects are similar to the definitions we've already seen. The parent-subtree for all of these objects is *animalEntry*, which effectively builds a table row from each of these objects. The only object that's particularly interesting is *animalDanger*, which uses an extension of the INTEGER datatype. As we noted before, this object is an enumerated integer, which allows us to associate textual labels with integer values. The values you can use in an enumerated type should be a series of consecutive integers, starting with 1.* For example, the *animalDanger* object defines six values, ranging from 1 to 6, with strings like **no-danger** associated with the values.

You can save this table definition in a file and use the *xnmloadmib* command to load it into OpenView. Once you've done that and created the *animal.db* file with a text editor, you can walk the table:

```
$ snmpwalk sunserver1 .1.3.6.1.4.1.mauro.other.animalTable
animalEntry.animalIndex.1 : INTEGER: 1
animalEntry.animalIndex.2 : INTEGER: 2
animalEntry.animalIndex.3 : INTEGER: 3
animalEntry.animalName.1 : DISPLAY STRING-(ascii): Tweety
animalEntry.animalName.2 : DISPLAY STRING-(ascii): Madison
animalEntry.animalName.3 : DISPLAY STRING-(ascii): Big Ben
animalEntry.animalSpecies.1 : DISPLAY STRING-(ascii): Bird
animalEntry.animalSpecies.2 : DISPLAY STRING-(ascii): Dog
animalEntry.animalSpecies.3 : DISPLAY STRING-(ascii): Bear
animalEntry.animalNoise.1 : DISPLAY STRING-(ascii): Chirp
animalEntry.animalNoise.2 : DISPLAY STRING-(ascii): Bark
animalEntry.animalNoise.3 : DISPLAY STRING-(ascii): Grrr
animalEntry.animalDanger.1 : INTEGER: can-Harm
animalEntry.animalDanger.2 : INTEGER: will-Wound
animalEntry.animalDanger.3 : INTEGER: severe-Pain
```

snmpwalk goes through the table a column at a time, reporting all the data in a column before proceeding to the next. This is confusing—it would be easier if *snmpwalk* read the table a row at a time. As it is, you have to hop from line to line when you are trying to read a row; for example, to find out everything about Tweety, you need to look at every third line (all the *.1* items) in the output.

Two more things are worth noticing in the *snmpwalk* output. The first set of values that *snmpwalk* reports are the index values (*animalIndex*). It then appends each index value to each OID to perform the rest of the walk. Second, the *animalDanger* output reports strings, such as **can-Harm**, rather than integers. The conversion from integers to strings takes place because we defined the *animalDanger* object as an enumerated integer, which associates a set of possible values with strings.

Of course, just reading a table doesn't do a whole lot of good. Let's say that we need to update this file periodically to reflect changes in the animals' behavior. The *animalDanger* object has an ACCESS of **read-write**, which allows us to set its value and update the database file using our SNMP tools. Imagine that the dog in row 2 turns very mean. We need to turn its danger level to 5 (**severe-Pain**). We could edit the file by hand, but it's easier to issue an *snmpset*:

---

* Some SNMPv1 SMI–compliant MIB compilers will not allow an enumerated type of 0 (zero).

```
$ snmpset -c private sunserver2 \
mauro.other.animalTable.animalEntry.animalDanger.2 integer "5"
mauro.other.animalTable.animalEntry.animalDanger.2 : INTEGER: severe-Pain
```

Now let's go back and verify that the variable has been updated:[*]

```
$ snmpget sunserver2 \
mauro.other.animalTable.animalEntry.animalDanger.2
mauro.other.animalTable.animalEntry.animalDanger.2 : INTEGER: severe-Pain
```

Once the *snmpset* is complete, check the file to see how it has changed. In addition to changing the dog's danger level, it has enclosed all strings within quotes:

```
1 "Tweety" "Bird" "Chirp" 2
2 "Madison" "Dog" "Bark" 5
3 "Big Ben" "Bear" "Grrr" 5
```

There are even more possibilities for keeping the file up-to-date. For example, you could use a system program or application to edit this file. A *cron* job could kick off every hour or so and update the file. This strategy would let you generate the file using a SQL query to a database such as Oracle. You could then put the query's results in a file and poll the file with SNMP to read the results. One problem with this strategy is that you must ensure that your application and SNMP polling periods are in sync. Make sure you poll the file *after* Oracle has updated it, or you will be viewing old data.

An effective way to ensure that the file is up-to-date when you read it is to use FILE-COMMAND within the table's definition. This tells the agent to run a program that updates the table before returning any values. Let's assume that we've written a script named *get_animal_status.pl* that determines the status of the animals and updates the database accordingly. Here's how we'd integrate that script into our table definition:

```
animalTable OBJECT-TYPE
    SYNTAX    SEQUENCE OF AnimalEntry
    ACCESS    not-accessible
    STATUS    mandatory
    DESCRIPTION
        "This is a table of animals that shows:
        Name
        Species
        Noise
        Danger Level
        FILE-COMMAND: /opt/local/get_animal_status.pl
        FILE-NAME: /opt/local/animal.db"
    ::= { other 247 }
```

---

[*] We could already deduce that the *set* was successful when *snmpset* didn't give us an error. This example does, however, show how you can *snmpget* a single instance within a table.

The command must finish within 10 seconds or the agent will kill the process and return the old values from the table. By default, the agent runs the program specified by FILE-COMMAND only if it has not gotten a request in the last 10 seconds. For example, let's say you issue two *snmpget* commands, two seconds apart. For the first *snmpget*, the agent runs the program and returns the data from the table with any changes. The second time, the agent won't run the program to update the data—it will return the old data, assuming that nothing has changed. This is effectively a form of caching. You can increase the amount of time the agent keeps its cache by specifying a value, in seconds, after FILE-COMMAND-FREQUENCY. For example, if you want to update the file only every 20 minutes (at most), include the following commands in your table definition:

```
FILE-COMMAND: /opt/local/get_animal_status.pl
FILE-COMMAND-FREQUENCY: 1200
FILE-NAME: /opt/local/animal.db"
```

This chapter has given you a brief introduction to three of the more popular extensible SNMP agents on the market. While a thorough treatment of every configurable option for each agent is beyond the scope of this chapter, it should help you to understand how to use extensible agents. With an extensible agent, the possibilities are almost endless.

Adapting SNMP to Fit Your Environment

SNMP can make your life as a system administrator a lot easier by performing many of the tasks that you'd either have to do by hand or automate by writing some clever script. It's relatively easy to take care of most everyday system monitoring: SNMP can poll for disk-space utilization, notify you when mirrors are syncing, or record who is logging in or out of the system. The SNMP scripts in this chapter represent just a few of the things SNMP allows you to do; use them as a launching pad for your own ideas.

General Trap-Generation Program

Chapter 10 contained some scripts for collecting SNMP information using Perl, OpenView's *snmptrap* program, and some other tools. Here's how we used *snmptrap* to generate a trap giving us information about some problems with the database:

```
$ /opt/OV/bin/snmptrap -c public nms .1.3.6.1.4.1.2789.2500 "" 6 3003 "" \
.1.3.6.1.4.1.2500.3003.1 octetstringascii "Oracle" \
.1.3.6.1.4.1.2500.3003.2 octetstringascii "Backup Not Running" \
.1.3.6.1.4.1.2500.3003.3 octetstringascii "Call the DBA Now for Help"
```

The way you send a trap in Perl is a little more involved, but it's still easy to use:

```
#!/usr/local/bin/perl
# Filename: /opt/local/perl_scripts/snmptrap.pl

use SNMP_util "0.54";  # This will load the BER and SNMP_Session

snmptrap("public\@nms:162", ".1.3.6.1.4.1.2789", "sunserver1",
        6, 1247, ".1.3.6.1.4.1.2789.1247.1", "int", "2448816");
```

In this chapter, we won't look so much at how to write commands like these, but at how to use them in clever ways. We might want to include commands like these in startup scripts, or invoke them via hooks into other programs. We'll start by writing some code that records successful logins.

Who's Logging into My Machine? (I-Am-in)

When Unix users log in, the system automatically executes a profile; for users of the Bourne, Korn, or *bash* shells, the systemwide profile is named */etc/profile*. There's a similar file for users of *csh* and *tcsh* (*/etc/login*). We can use SNMP to record logins by adding a trap to these profiles. By itself this isn't all that interesting, because Unix already keeps a log of user logins. But let's say that you're monitoring a few dozen machines and don't want to check each machine's log. Adding a trap to the systemwide profile lets you monitor logins to all your systems from one place. It also makes your logging more secure. It's not too difficult for an intelligent user to delete the *wtmp* file that stores Unix login records. Using SNMP to do the logging stores the information on another host, over which you should have better control.[*]

To generate the trap, invoke the external program */opt/local/mib_programs/os/iamin* in */etc/profile* (you can call the same program within */etc/login*). Here is the code for *iamin*:

```perl
#!/usr/local/bin/perl
#
# Filename: /opt/local/mib_programs/os/iamin

chomp ($WHO = `/bin/who am i \| awk \{\'print \$1\'\}`);

exit 123 unless ($WHO ne '');

chomp ($WHOAMI = `/usr/ucb/whoami`);
chomp ($TTY = `/bin/tty`);
chomp ($FROM = `/bin/last \-1 $WHO \| /bin/awk \{\'print \$3\'\}`);

if ($FROM =~ /Sun|Mon|Tue|Wed|Thu|Fri|Sat/) { $FROM = "N/A"; }

# DEBUG BELOW
# print "WHO :$WHO:\n"; print "WHOAMI :$WHOAMI:\n"; print "FROM :$FROM:\n";

if ("$WHOAMI" ne "$WHO") { $WHO = "$WHO\-\>$WHOAMI"; }

# Sending a trap using Net-SNMP
#
```

---

[*] Yes, a clever user could intercept and modify SNMP packets, or rewrite the shell profile, or do any number of things to defeat logging. We're not really interested in making it impossible to defeat logging; we just want to make it more difficult.

```
system "/usr/local/bin/snmptrap nms public .1.3.6.1.4.1.2789.2500 '' 6 1502 ''
.1.3.6.1.4.1.2789.2500.1502.1 s \"$WHO\"
.1.3.6.1.4.1.2789.2500.1502.2 s \"$FROM\"
.1.3.6.1.4.1.2789.2500.1502.3 s \"$TTY\"";

# Sending a trap using Perl
#
#use SNMP_util "0.54";  # This will load the BER and SNMP_Session for us
#snmptrap("public\@nms:162", ".1.3.6.1.4.1.2789.2500", mylocalhostname, 6, 1502,
#".1.3.6.1.4.1.2789.2500.1502.1", "string", "$WHO",
#".1.3.6.1.4.1.2789.2500.1502.2", "string", "$FROM",
#".1.3.6.1.4.1.2789.2500.1502.3", "string", "$TTY");

# Sending a trap using OpenView's snmptrap
#
#system "/opt/OV/bin/snmptrap -c public nms .1.3.6.1.4.1.2789.2500 \"\" 6 1502 \"\"
#.1.3.6.1.4.1.2789.2500.1502.1 octetstringascii \"$WHO\"
#.1.3.6.1.4.1.2789.2500.1502.2 octetstringascii \"$FROM\"
#.1.3.6.1.4.1.2789.2500.1502.3 octetstringascii \"$TTY\"";
#

#
print "\n##############\n";
print "#   NOTICE   \# - You have been logged: :$WHO: :$FROM: :$TTY: \n"; #
print "##############\n\n";
```

This script is a bit meatier than expected because we need to weed out a number of bogus entries. For instance, many programs run within a shell and hence invoke the same shell profiles. Therefore, we have to figure out whether the profile is being invoked by a human user; if not, we quit.* The next step is to figure out more about the user's identity; i.e., where she is logging in from and what her real identity is—we don't want to be confused by someone who uses *su* to switch to another identity. The third part of the program sends the trap with all the newly found information (who the user is, the host from which she is logging in, and what TTY she is on). We've included trap-generation code using the Net-SNMP utilities, the native Perl module, and OpenView's utilities. Take your pick and use the version with which you're most comfortable. The last portion of this program tells the user that she has been logged.

This script isn't without its problems. The user can always break out of the script before it is done, bypassing logging. You can counter this attempt by using *trap*(1), which responds to different signals. This forces the user to complete this program, not letting her stop in midstream. This strategy creates its own problems, since the root user doesn't have any way to bypass the check. In a sense, this is good: we want to be particularly careful about root logins. But what happens if

---

* This will also fail if the user is *su*'ing to another user. In a well-designed environment, users really shouldn't have to *su* all that often—using *sudo* or designing appropriate groups should greatly reduce the need to *su*.

you're trying to investigate a network failure or DNS problem? In this case, the script will hang while DNS tries to look up the host from which you're logging in. This can be very frustrating. Before implementing a script like this, look at your environment and decide which profiles you should lock.

Any of the packages for receiving traps can be used to listen for the traps generated by this program.

Throw Core

Programs frequently leave core dumps behind. A core file contains all the process information pertinent to debugging. It usually gets written when a program dies abnormally. While there are ways to limit the size of a dump or prevent core dumps entirely, there are still times when they're needed temporarily. Therefore, most Unix systems have some sort of *cron* script that automatically searches for core files and deletes them. Let's add some intelligence to these scripts to let us track what files are found, their sizes, and the names of the processes that created them.

The following Perl program is divided into four parts: it searches for a file with a given name (defaults to the name *core*), gets the file's statistics, deletes the file,* and then sends a trap. Most of the processing is performed natively by Perl, but we use the command *ls –l $FILENAME* to include the pertinent core file information within the SNMP trap. This command allows our operators to see information about the file in a format that's easy to recognize. We also use the *file* command, which determines a file's type and its creator. Unless you know who created the file, you won't have the chance to fix the real problem.

```
#!/usr/local/bin/perl

# Finds and deletes core files. It sends traps upon completion and
# errors. Arguments are:
# -path directory    : search directory (and subdirectories); default /
# -lookfor filename  : filename to search for; default core
# -debug value       : debug level

while ($ARGV[0] =~ /^-/)
{
    if     ($ARGV[0] eq "-path")    { shift; $PATH    = $ARGV[0]; }
    elsif  ($ARGV[0] eq "-lookfor") { shift; $LOOKFOR = $ARGV[0]; }
    elsif  ($ARGV[0] eq "-debug")   { shift; $DEBUG   = $ARGV[0]; }
    shift;
}
```

---

* Before you start deleting core files, you should figure out who or what is dropping them and see if the owner wants these files. In some cases this core file may be their only means of debugging.

```
#################################################################
######################## Begin Main ########################
#################################################################

require "find.pl";     # This gives us the find function.

$LOOKFOR = "core" unless ($LOOKFOR); # If we don't have something
                                     # in $LOOKFOR, default to core

$PATH    = "/"    unless ($PATH);     # Let's use / if we don't get
                                      # one on the command line

(-d $PATH) || die "$PATH is NOT a valid dir!";     # We can search
                                                   # only valid
                                                   # directories

&find("$PATH");

#################################################################
##################### Begin SubRoutines #####################
#################################################################

sub wanted
{
    if (/^$LOOKFOR$/)
        {
            if (!(-d $name)) # Skip the directories named core
            {
               &get_stats;
               &can_file;
               &send_trap;
            }
        }
}

sub can_file
{
    print "Deleting :$_: :$name:\n" unless (!($DEBUG));
    $RES = unlink "$name";
    if ($RES != 1) { $ERROR = 1; }
}

sub get_stats
{
    chop ($STATS = `ls -l $name`);
    chop ($FILE_STATS = `/bin/file $name`);

    $STATS =~ s/\s+/ /g;
    $FILE_STATS =~ s/\s+/ /g;
}

sub send_trap
{
    if ($ERROR == 0) { $SPEC = 1535; }
    else             { $SPEC = 1536; }
```

```
        print "STATS: $STATS\n" unless (!($DEBUG));
        print "FILE_STATS: $FILE_STATS\n" unless (!($DEBUG));

    # Sending a trap using Net-SNMP
    #
    #system "/usr/local/bin/snmptrap nms public .1.3.6.1.4.1.2789.2500 '' 6 $SPEC ''
    #.1.3.6.1.4.1.2789.2500.1535.1 s \"$name\"
    #.1.3.6.1.4.1.2789.2500.1535.2 s \"$STATS\"
    #.1.3.6.1.4.1.2789.2500.1535.3 s \"$FILE_STATS\"";

    # Sending a trap using Perl
    #
    use SNMP_util "0.54";  # This will load the BER and SNMP_Session for us
    snmptrap("public\@nms:162", ".1.3.6.1.4.1.2789.2500", mylocalhostname, 6, $SPEC,
    ".1.3.6.1.4.1.2789.2500.1535.1", "string", "$name",
    ".1.3.6.1.4.1.2789.2500.1535.2", "string", "$STATS",
    ".1.3.6.1.4.1.2789.2500.1535.3", "string", "$FILE_STATS");

    # Sending a trap using OpenView's snmptrap
    #
    #system "/opt/OV/bin/snmptrap -c public nms
    #.1.3.6.1.4.1.2789.2500 \"\" 6 $SPEC \"\"
    #.1.3.6.1.4.1.2789.2500.1535.1 octetstringascii \"$name\"
    #.1.3.6.1.4.1.2789.2500.1535.2 octetstringascii \"$STATS\"
    #.1.3.6.1.4.1.2789.2500.1535.3 octetstringascii \"$FILE_STATS\"";
    }
```

The logic is simple, though it's somewhat hard to see since most of it happens implicitly. The key is the call to `find()`, which sets up lots of things. It descends into every directory underneath the directory specified by `$PATH` and automatically sets `$_` (so the `if` statement at the beginning of the `wanted()` subroutine works). Furthermore, it defines the variable **name** to be the full pathname to the current file; this allows us to test whether or not the current file is really a directory, which we wouldn't want to delete.

Therefore, we loop through all the files, looking for files with the name specified on the comand line (or named *core*, if no –*lookfor* option is specified). When we find one we store its statistics, delete the file, and send a trap to the NMS reporting the file's name and other information. We use the variable **SPEC** to store the specific trap ID. We use two specific IDs: 1535 if the file was deleted successfully and 1536 if we tried to delete the file but couldn't. Again, we wrote the trap code to use either native Perl, Net-SNMP, or OpenView. Uncomment the version of your choice. We pack the trap with three variable bindings, which contain the name of the file, the results of *ls* –*l* on the file, and the results of running */bin/file*. Together, these give us a fair amount of information about the file we deleted. Note that we had to define object IDs for all three of these variables; furthermore, although we placed these object IDs under 1535, nothing prevents us from using the same objects when we send specific trap 1536.

Now we have a program to delete core files and send traps telling us about what was deleted; the next step is to tell our trap receiver what to do with these incoming traps. Let's assume that we're using OpenView. To inform it about these traps, we have to add two entries to *trapd.conf,* mapping these traps to events. Here they are:

```
EVENT foundNDelCore .1.3.6.1.4.1.2789.2500.0.1535 "Status Alarms" Warning
FORMAT Core File Found :$1: File Has Been Deleted - LS :$2: FILE :$3:
SDESC
This event is called when a server using cronjob looks for core
files and deletes them.

$1 - octetstringascii    - Name of file
$2 - octetstringascii    - ls -l listing on the file
$3 - octetstringascii    - file $name
EDESC
#
#
#
EVENT foundNNotDelCore .1.3.6.1.4.1.2789.2500.0.1536 "Status Alarms" Minor
FORMAT Core File Found :$1:
File Has Not Been Deleted For Some Reason - LS :$2: FILE :$3:
SDESC
This event is called when a server using cronjob looks for core
files and then CANNOT delete them for some reason.

$1 - octetstringascii    - Name of file
$2 - octetstringascii    - ls -l listing on the file
$3 - octetstringascii    - file $name
EDESC
#
#
#
```

For each trap, we have an **EVENT** statement specifying an event name, the trap's specific ID, the category into which the event will be sorted, and the severity. The **FORMAT** statement defines a message to be used when we receive the trap; it can be spread over several lines and can use the parameters $1, $2, etc. to refer to the variable bindings that are included in the trap.

Although it would be a good idea, we don't need to add our variable bindings to our private MIB file; *trapd.conf* contains enough information for OpenView to interpret the contents of the trap.

Here are some sample traps[*] generated by the *throwcore* script:

```
Core File Found :/usr/sap/HQD/DVEBMGS00/work/core: File Has Been \
Deleted - LS :-rw-rw---- 1 hqdadm sapsys 355042304 Apr 27 17:04 \
/usr/sap/HQD/DVEBMGS00/work/core: \
```

---

[*] We've removed most of the host and date/time information.

```
FILE :/usr/sap/HQD/DVEBMGS00/work/core: ELF 32-bit MSB core file \
SPARC Version 1, from 'disp+work':

Core File Found :/usr/sap/HQI/DVEBMGS10/work/core: File Has Been \
Deleted - LS :-rw-r--r-- 1 hqiadm sapsys 421499988 Apr 28 14:29 \
/usr/sap/HQI/DVEBMGS10/work/core: \
FILE :/usr/sap/HQI/DVEBMGS10/work/core: ELF 32-bit MSB core file \
SPARC Version 1, from 'disp+work':
```

Here is root's *crontab*, which runs the *throwcore* script at specific intervals. Notice that we use the *–path* switch, which allows us to check the development area every hour:

```
# Check for core files every night and every hour on special dirs
27 * * * * /opt/local/mib_programs/scripts/throwcore.pl -path /usr/sap
23 2 * * * /opt/local/mib_programs/scripts/throwcore.pl
```

Veritas Disk Check

The Veritas Volume Manager is a package that allows you to manipulate disks and their partitions. It gives you the ability to add and remove mirrors, work with RAID arrays, and resize partitions, to name a few things. Although Veritas is a specialized and expensive package that is usually found at large data centers, don't assume that you can skip this section. The point isn't to show you how to monitor Veritas, but to show you how you can provide meaningful traps using a typical status program. You should be able to extract the ideas from the script we present here and use them within your own context.

Veritas Volume Manager (*vxvm*) comes with a utility called *vxprint*. This program displays records from the Volume Manager configuration and shows the status of each of your local disks. If there is an error, such as a bad disk or broken mirror, this command will report it. A healthy *vxprint* on the rootvol (/) looks like this:

```
$ vxprint -h rootvol
Disk group: rootdg
```

TY	NAME	ASSOC	KSTATE	LENGTH	PLOFFS	STATE	TUTIL0	PUTIL0
v	rootvol	root	ENABLED	922320	-	ACTIVE	-	-
pl	rootvol-01	rootvol	ENABLED	922320	-	ACTIVE	-	-
sd	rootdisk-B0	rootvol-01	ENABLED	1	0	-	-	Block0
sd	rootdisk-02	rootvol-01	ENABLED	922319	1	-	-	-
pl	rootvol-02	rootvol	ENABLED	922320	-	ACTIVE	-	-
sd	disk01-01	rootvol-02	ENABLED	922320	0	-	-	-

The KSTATE (kernel state) and STATE columns give us a behind-the-scenes look at our disks, mirrors, etc. Without explaining the output in detail, a KSTATE of ENABLED is a good sign; a STATE of ACTIVE or – indicates that there are no problems. We can take this output and pipe it into a script that sends SNMP traps when errors are encountered. We can send different traps of an appropriate severity,

based on the type of error that *vxprint* reported. Here's a script that runs *vxprint*
and analyzes the results:

```perl
#!/usr/local/bin/perl -wc

$VXPRINT_LOC     = "/usr/sbin/vxprint";
$HOSTNAME        = `/bin/uname -n`; chop $HOSTNAME;

while ($ARGV[0] =~ /^-/)
{
    if    ($ARGV[0] eq "-debug")        { shift; $DEBUG = $ARGV[0]; }
    elsif ($ARGV[0] eq "-state_active") { $SHOW_STATE_ACTIVE = 1; }
    shift;
}


#################################################################
######################### Begin Main ##########################
#################################################################

&get_vxprint;  # Get it, process it, and send traps if errors found!

#################################################################
###################### Begin SubRoutines ######################
#################################################################

sub get_vxprint
{

    open(VXPRINT,"$VXPRINT_LOC |") || die "Can't Open $VXPRINT_LOC";
    while($VXLINE=<VXPRINT>)
    {
        print $VXLINE unless ($DEBUG < 2);
        if ($VXLINE ne "\n")
        {
            &is_a_disk_group_name;
            &split_vxprint_output;

            if (($TY ne "TY")   &&
                ($TY ne "Disk") &&
                ($TY ne "dg")   &&
                ($TY ne "dm"))
            {
                if (($SHOW_STATE_ACTIVE) && ($STATE eq "ACTIVE"))
                {
                    print "ACTIVE: $VXLINE";
                }
                if (($STATE ne "ACTIVE") &&
                    ($STATE ne "DISABLED") &&
                    ($STATE ne "SYNC") &&
                    ($STATE ne "CLEAN") &&
                    ($STATE ne "SPARE") &&
                    ($STATE ne "-")     &&
                    ($STATE ne ""))
                {
```

```
                    &send_error_msgs;
               }
               elsif (($KSTATE ne "ENABLED") &&
                      ($KSTATE ne "DISABLED") &&
                      ($KSTATE ne "-")         &&
                      ($KSTATE ne ""))
               {
                    &send_error_msgs;
               }
          } # end if (($TY
       }       # end if ($VXLINE
    }          # end while($VXLINE
}              # end sub get_vxprint


sub is_a_disk_group_name
{
    if ($VXLINE =~ /^Disk\sgroup\:\s(\w+)\n/)
    {
        $DISK_GROUP = $1;
        print "Found Disk Group :$1:\n" unless (!($DEBUG));
        return 1;
    }
}


sub split_vxprint_output
{
($TY, $NAME, $ASSOC, $KSTATE,
    $LENGTH, $PLOFFS, $STATE, $TUTIL0,
    $PUTIL0) = split(/\s+/,$VXLINE);

    if ($DEBUG) {
        print "SPLIT: $TY $NAME $ASSOC $KSTATE ";
        print "$LENGTH $PLOFFS $STATE $TUTIL0 $PUTIL0:\n";
            }
}


sub send_snmp_trap
{
    $SNMP_TRAP_LOC          = "/opt/OV/bin/snmptrap";
    $SNMP_COMM_NAME         = "public";
    $SNMP_TRAP_HOST         = "nms";

    $SNMP_ENTERPRISE_ID     = ".1.3.6.1.4.1.2789.2500";
    $SNMP_GEN_TRAP          = "6";
    $SNMP_SPECIFIC_TRAP     = "1000";

    chop($SNMP_TIME_STAMP        = "1" . `date +%H%S`);
    $SNMP_EVENT_IDENT_ONE   = ".1.3.6.1.4.1.2789.2500.1000.1";
    $SNMP_EVENT_VTYPE_ONE   = "octetstringascii";
    $SNMP_EVENT_VAR_ONE     = "$HOSTNAME";

    $SNMP_EVENT_IDENT_TWO   = ".1.3.6.1.4.1.2789.2500.1000.2";
    $SNMP_EVENT_VTYPE_TWO   = "octetstringascii";
    $SNMP_EVENT_VAR_TWO     = "$NAME";
```

```perl
    $SNMP_EVENT_IDENT_THREE = ".1.3.6.1.4.1.2789.2500.1000.3";
    $SNMP_EVENT_VTYPE_THREE = "octetstringascii";
    $SNMP_EVENT_VAR_THREE   = "$STATE";


    $SNMP_EVENT_IDENT_FOUR  = ".1.3.6.1.4.1.2789.2500.1000.4";
    $SNMP_EVENT_VTYPE_FOUR  = "octetstringascii";
    $SNMP_EVENT_VAR_FOUR    = "$DISK_GROUP";


    $SNMP_TRAP = "$SNMP_TRAP_LOC \-c $SNMP_COMM_NAME $SNMP_TRAP_HOST
    $SNMP_ENTERPRISE_ID \"\" $SNMP_GEN_TRAP $SNMP_SPECIFIC_TRAP $SNMP_TIME_STAMP
    $SNMP_EVENT_IDENT_ONE   $SNMP_EVENT_VTYPE_ONE    \"$SNMP_EVENT_VAR_ONE\"
    $SNMP_EVENT_IDENT_TWO   $SNMP_EVENT_VTYPE_TWO    \"$SNMP_EVENT_VAR_TWO\"
    $SNMP_EVENT_IDENT_THREE $SNMP_EVENT_VTYPE_THREE \"$SNMP_EVENT_VAR_THREE\"
    $SNMP_EVENT_IDENT_FOUR  $SNMP_EVENT_VTYPE_FOUR  \"$SNMP_EVENT_VAR_FOUR\"";


    # Sending a trap using Net-SNMP
    #
    #system "/usr/local/bin/snmptrap $SNMP_TRAP_HOST $SNMP_COMM_NAME
    #$SNMP_ENTERPRISE_ID '' $SNMP_GEN_TRAP $SNMP_SPECIFIC_TRAP ''
    #$SNMP_EVENT_IDENT_ONE s \"$SNMP_EVENT_VAR_ONE\"
    #$SNMP_EVENT_IDENT_TWO s \"$SNMP_EVENT_VAR_TWO\"
    #$SNMP_EVENT_IDENT_THREE s \"$SNMP_EVENT_VAR_THREE\"
    #$SNMP_EVENT_IDENT_FOUR s \"$SNMP_EVENT_VAR_FOUR\"";


    # Sending a trap using Perl
    #
    #use SNMP_util "0.54";  # This will load the BER and SNMP_Session for us
    #snmptrap("$SNMP_COMM_NAME\@$SNMP_TRAP_HOST:162", "$SNMP_ENTERPRISE_ID",
    #mylocalhostname, $SNMP_GEN_TRAP, $SNMP_SPECIFIC_TRAP,
    #"$SNMP_EVENT_IDENT_ONE", "string", "$SNMP_EVENT_VAR_ONE",
    #"$SNMP_EVENT_IDENT_TWO", "string", "$SNMP_EVENT_VAR_TWO",
    #"$SNMP_EVENT_IDENT_THREE", "string", "$SNMP_EVENT_VAR_THREE",
    #"$SNMP_EVENT_IDENT_FOUR", "string", "$SNMP_EVENT_VAR_FOUR");


    # Sending a trap using OpenView's snmptrap (using VARs from above)
    #
    if($SEND_SNMP_TRAP) {
        print "Problem Running SnmpTrap with Result ";
        print ":$SEND_SNMP_TRAP: :$SNMP_TRAP:\n";
    }

sub send_error_msgs
{
    $TY =~ s/^v/Volume/;
    $TY =~ s/^pl/Plex/;
    $TY =~ s/^sd/SubDisk/;

    print "VXfs Problem: Host:[$HOSTNAME] State:[$STATE] DiskGroup:[$DISK_GROUP]
        Type:[$TY] FileSystem:[$NAME] Assoc:[$ASSOC] Kstate:[$KSTATE]\n"
        unless (!($DEBUG));

    &send_snmp_trap;
}
```

Knowing what the output of *vxprint* should look like, we can formulate Perl statements that figure out when to generate a trap. That task makes up most of the
`get_vxprint` subroutine. We also know what types of error messages will be
produced. Our script tries to ignore all the information from the healthy disks and
sort the error messages. For example, if the STATE field contains NEEDSYNC, the
disk mirrors are probably not synchronized and the volume needs some sort of
attention. The script doesn't handle this particular case explicitly, but it is caught
with the default entry.

The actual mechanism for sending the trap is tied up in a large number of variables. Basically, though, we use any of the trap utilities we've discussed; the enterprise ID is *.1.3.6.1.4.1.2789.2500*; the specific trap ID is *1000*; and we include
four variable bindings, which report the hostname, the volume name, the volume's
state, and the disk group.

As with the previous script, it's a simple matter to run this script periodically and
watch the results on whatever network-management software you're using. It's
also easy to see how you could develop similar scripts that generate reports from
other status programs.

Disk-Space Checker

OpenView's agent has a *fileSystemTable* object that contains statistics about disk
utilization and other filesystem parameters. At first glance, it looks extremely
useful: you can use it to find out filesystem names, blocks free, etc. But it has
some quirks, and we'll need to play a few tricks to use this table effectively.
Walking *fileSystemTable.fileSystemEntry.fileSystemDir* (*.1.3.6.1.4.1.11.2.3.1.2.2.1.*
10) lists the filesystems that are currently mounted:*

```
[root][nms] /opt/OV/local/bin/disk_space> snmpwalk spruce \
.1.3.6.1.4.1.11.2.3.1.2.2.1.10
fileSystem.fileSystemTable.fileSystemEntry.fileSystemDir.14680064.1
: DISPLAY STRING- (ascii):  /
fileSystem.fileSystemTable.fileSystemEntry.fileSystemDir.14680067.1
: DISPLAY STRING- (ascii):  /var
fileSystem.fileSystemTable.fileSystemEntry.fileSystemDir.14680068.1
: DISPLAY STRING- (ascii): /export
fileSystem.fileSystemTable.fileSystemEntry.fileSystemDir.14680069.1
: DISPLAY STRING- (ascii): /opt
fileSystem.fileSystemTable.fileSystemEntry.fileSystemDir.14680070.1
: DISPLAY STRING- (ascii): /usr
fileSystem.fileSystemTable.fileSystemEntry.fileSystemDir.41156608.1
: DISPLAY STRING- (ascii): /proc
```

---

* We've truncated the leading *.iso.org.dod.internet.private.enterprises.hp.nm.system.general* to the *walk*
results for space reasons.

```
fileSystem.fileSystemTable.fileSystemEntry.fileSystemDir.41680896.1
: DISPLAY STRING- (ascii): /dev/fd
fileSystem.fileSystemTable.fileSystemEntry.fileSystemDir.42991617.1
: DISPLAY STRING- (ascii): /net
fileSystem.fileSystemTable.fileSystemEntry.fileSystemDir.42991618.1
: DISPLAY STRING- (ascii): /home
fileSystem.fileSystemTable.fileSystemEntry.fileSystemDir.42991619.1
: DISPLAY STRING- (ascii): /xfn
```

Let's think about how we'd write a program that checks for available disk space. At first glance, it looks like this will be easy. But this table contains a number of objects that aren't filesystems in the normal sense; */proc*, for example, provides access to the processes running on the system and doesn't represent storage. This raises problems if we start polling for free blocks: */proc* isn't going to have any free blocks, and */dev/fd*, which represents a floppy disk, will have free blocks only if a disk happens to be in the drive. You'd expect */home* to behave like a normal filesystem, but on this server it's automounted, which means that its behavior is unpredictable; if it's not in use, it might not be mounted. Therefore, if we polled for free blocks using the *fileSystem.fileSystemTable.fileSystemEntry.fileSystem-Bavail* object, the last five instances might return 0 under normal conditions. So the results we'd get from polling all the entries in the filesystem table aren't meaningful without further interpretation. At a minimum, we need to figure out which filesystems are important to us and which aren't. This is probably going to require being clever about the instance numbers.

When I discovered this problem, I noticed that all the filesystems I wanted to check happened to have instance numbers with the same leading digits; i.e., *fileSystemDir.14680064.1*, *fileSystemDir.14680067.1*, *fileSystemDir.14680068.1*, etc. That observation proved to be less useful than it seemed—with time, I learned that not only do other servers have different leading instance numbers, but that on any server the instance numbers could change. Even if the instance number changes, though, the leading instance digits seem to stay the same for all disks or filesystems of the same type. For example, disk arrays might have instance numbers like *fileSystemDir.12312310.1*, *fileSystemDir.12312311.1*, *fileSystemDir. 12312312.1*, and so on. Your internal disks might have instance numbers like *fileSystemDir.12388817.1*, *fileSystemDir.12388818.1*, *fileSystemDir.12388819.1*, and so on.

So, working with the instance numbers is possible, but painful—there is still nothing static that can be easily polled. There's no easy way to say "Give me the statistics for all the local filesystems," or even "Give me the statistics for */usr.*" I was forced to write a program that would do a fair amount of instance-number processing, making guesses based on the behavior I observed. I had to use *snmp-walk* to figure out the instance numbers for the filesystems I cared about before doing anything more interesting. By comparing the initial digits of the instance numbers, I was able to figure out which filesystems were local, which were networked, and which were "special purpose" (like */proc*). Here's the result:

```perl
#!/usr/local/bin/perl
# filename: polling.pl
# options:
#     -min n    : send trap if less than n 1024-byte blocks free
#     -table f  : table of servers to watch (defaults to ./default)
#     -server s : specifies a single server to poll
#     -inst n   : number of leading instance-number digits to compare
#     -debug n  : debug level

$|++;

$SNMPWALK_LOC  = "/opt/OV/bin/snmpwalk -r 5";
$SNMPGET_LOC   = "/opt/OV/bin/snmpget";
$HOME_LOC      = "/opt/OV/local/bin/disk_space";
$LOCK_FILE_LOC = "$HOME_LOC/lock_files";
$GREP_LOC      = "/bin/grep";
$TOUCH_LOC     = "/bin/touch";
$PING_LOC      = "/usr/sbin/ping";        # Ping Location
$PING_TIMEOUT  = 7;                       # Seconds to wait for a ping

$MIB_C = ".1.3.6.1.4.1.11.2.3.1.2.2.1.6";      # fileSystemBavail
$MIB_BSIZE = ".1.3.6.1.4.1.11.2.3.1.2.2.1.7";  # fileSystemBsize
$MIB_DIR = ".1.3.6.1.4.1.11.2.3.1.2.2.1.10";   # fileSystemDir

while ($ARGV[0] =~ /^-/)
{
    if     ($ARGV[0] eq "-min")    { shift; $MIN = $ARGV[0]; }  # In 1024 blocks
    elsif ($ARGV[0] eq "-table")   { shift; $TABLE = $ARGV[0]; }
    elsif ($ARGV[0] eq "-server")  { shift; $SERVER = $ARGV[0]; }
    elsif ($ARGV[0] eq "-inst")    { shift; $INST_LENGTH = $ARGV[0]; }
    elsif ($ARGV[0] eq "-debug")   { shift; $DEBUG = $ARGV[0]; }
    shift;
}

###############################################################
######################### Begin Main #########################
###############################################################

$ALLSERVERS  = 1 unless ($SERVER);
$INST_LENGTH = 5 unless ($INST_LENGTH);

$TABLE = "default" unless ($TABLE);

open(TABLE,"$HOME_LOC/$TABLE") || die "Can't Open File $TABLE";
while($LINE=<TABLE>)
{
    if ($LINE ne "\n")
    {
    chop $LINE;
    ($HOST,$IGNORE1,$IGNORE2,$IGNORE3) = split(/\:/,$LINE);
```

```
if (&ping_server_bad("$HOST")) { warn "Can't Ping Server
   :$HOST:" unless (!($DEBUG)); }
else
{
    &find_inst;

    if ($DEBUG > 99)
    {
    print "HOST:$HOST: IGNORE1 :$IGNORE1: IGNORE2 :$IGNORE2:
        IGNORE3 :$IGNORE3:\n";
    print "Running :$SNMPWALK_LOC $HOST $MIB_C \| $GREP_LOC
        \.$GINST:\n";
    }

    $IGNORE1 = "C1ANT5MAT9CHT4HIS"
            unless ($IGNORE1); # If we don't have anything then let's set
    $IGNORE2 = "CA2N4T6M8A1T3C5H7THIS"
            unless ($IGNORE2); # to something that we can never match.
    $IGNORE3 = "CAN3TMA7TCH2THI6S" unless ($IGNORE3);

    if (($SERVER eq "$HOST") || ($ALLSERVERS))
    {
      open(WALKER,"$SNMPWALK_LOC $HOST $MIB_C \| $GREP_LOC
        \.$GINST |") || die "Can't Walk $HOST $MIB_C\n";
      while($WLINE=<WALKER>)
      {
          chop $WLINE;
          ($MIB,$TYPE,$VALUE) = split(/\:/,$WLINE);
          $MIB =~ s/\s+//g;
          $MIB =~ /(\d+\.\d+)$/;

          $INST = $1;

          open(SNMPGET,"$SNMPGET_LOC $HOST $MIB_DIR`$INST |");
          while($DLINE=<SNMPGET>)
          {
              ($NULL,$NULL,$DNAME) = split(/\:/,$DLINE);
          }

          $DNAME =~ s/\s+//g;

          close SNMPGET;

          open(SNMPGET,"$SNMPGET_LOC $HOST $MIB_BSIZE`$INST |");
          while($BLINE=<SNMPGET>)
          {
          ($NULL,$NULL,$BSIZE) = split(/\:/,$BLINE);
          }

          close SNMPGET;

          $BSIZE =~ s/\s+//g;

          $LOCK_RES = &inst_found; $LOCK_RES = "\[ $LOCK_RES \]";
```

```perl
        print "LOCK_RES :$LOCK_RES:\n" unless ($DEBUG < 99);

        $VALUE = $VALUE * $BSIZE / 1024; # Put it in 1024 blocks

        if (($DNAME =~ /.*$IGNORE1.*/) ||
            ($DNAME =~ /.*$IGNORE2.*/) ||
            ($DNAME =~ /.*$IGNORE3.*/))
        {
            $DNAME = "$DNAME <ignored>";
        }

        else
        {
            if (($VALUE <= $MIN) && ($LOCK_RES eq "\[ 0 \]"))
            {
                &write_lock;
                &send_snmp_trap(0);
            }

            elsif (($VALUE > $MIN) && ($LOCK_RES eq "\[ 1 \]"))
            {
                &remove_lock;
                &send_snmp_trap(1);
            }
        }

        $VALUE = $VALUE / $BSIZE * 1024; # Display it as the
                                         # original block size

        write unless (!($DEBUG));

      } # end while($WLINE=<WALKER>)
    }       # end if (($SERVER eq "$HOST") || ($ALLSERVERS))
  }         # end else from if (&ping_server_bad("$HOST"))

    }               # end if ($LINE ne "\n")
}                   # end while($LINE=<TABLE>)

##############################################################
##################### Begin SubRoutines ######################
##############################################################

format STDOUT_TOP =
Server     MountPoint          BlocksLeft     BlockSize     MIB         LockFile
---------  ----------------    ------------   -----------   ---------   ----------
.


format STDOUT =
@<<<<<<<<  @<<<<<<<<<<<<<<<    @<<<<<<<<<<<    @<<<<<<<<<<    @<<<<<<<<   @<<<<<<<<<
$HOST,     $DNAME,             $VALUE,        $BSIZE,       $INST,      $LOCK_RES
.


sub inst_found
{
```

```
        if (-e "$LOCK_FILE_LOC/$HOST\.$INST") { return 1; }
        else { return 0; }
    }

    sub remove_lock
    {
        if ($DEBUG > 99) { print "Removing Lockfile $LOCK_FILE_LOC/$HOST\.$INST\n"; }
        unlink "$LOCK_FILE_LOC/$HOST\.$INST";
    }

    sub write_lock
    {
        if ($DEBUG > 99) { print "Writing Lockfile
            $TOUCH_LOC $LOCK_FILE_LOC/$HOST\.$INST\n"; }
        system "$TOUCH_LOC $LOCK_FILE_LOC/$HOST\.$INST";
    }


    ################################################################
    ## send_snmp_trap ##
    ####################
    ##
    # This subroutine allows you to send diff traps depending on the
    #  passed parm and gives you a chance to send both good and bad
    #  traps.
    #
    # $1 - integer - This will be added to the specific event ID.
    #
    # If we created two traps:
    #  2789.2500.0.1000 = Major
    #  2789.2500.0.1001 = Good
    #
    # If we declare:
    #  $SNMP_SPECIFIC_TRAP      = "1000";
    #
    # We could send the 1st by using:
    #  send_snmp_trap(0);  # Here is the math (1000 + 0 = 1000)
    #  And to send the second one:
    #  send_snmp_trap(1);  # Here is the math (1000 + 1 = 1001)
    #
    # This way you could set up multiple traps with diff errors using
    #  the same function for all.
    #
    ##
    ################################################################

    sub send_snmp_trap
    {
        $TOTAL_TRAPS_CREATED    = 2;  # Let's do some checking/reminding
                                      # here. This number should be the
                                      # total number of traps that you
                                      # created on the nms.

        $SNMP_ENTERPRISE_ID     = ".1.3.6.1.4.1.2789.2500";
        $SNMP_SPECIFIC_TRAP     = "1500";
```

```
$PASSED_PARM            = $_[0];
$SNMP_SPECIFIC_TRAP     += $PASSED_PARM;

$SNMP_TRAP_LOC          = "/opt/OV/bin/snmptrap";
$SNMP_COMM_NAME         = "public";
$SNMP_TRAP_HOST         = "nms";

$SNMP_GEN_TRAP          = "6";

chop($SNMP_TIME_STAMP        = "1" . `date +%H%S`);

$SNMP_EVENT_IDENT_ONE   = ".1.3.6.1.4.1.2789.2500.$SNMP_SPECIFIC_TRAP.1";
$SNMP_EVENT_VTYPE_ONE   = "octetstringascii";
$SNMP_EVENT_VAR_ONE     = "$DNAME";

$SNMP_EVENT_IDENT_TWO   = ".1.3.6.1.4.1.2789.2500.$SNMP_SPECIFIC_TRAP.2";
$SNMP_EVENT_VTYPE_TWO   = "integer";
$SNMP_EVENT_VAR_TWO     = "$VALUE";

$SNMP_EVENT_IDENT_THREE = ".1.3.6.1.4.1.2789.2500.$SNMP_SPECIFIC_TRAP.3";
$SNMP_EVENT_VTYPE_THREE = "integer";
$SNMP_EVENT_VAR_THREE   = "$BSIZE";

$SNMP_EVENT_IDENT_FOUR  = ".1.3.6.1.4.1.2789.2500.$SNMP_SPECIFIC_TRAP.4";
$SNMP_EVENT_VTYPE_FOUR  = "octetstringascii";
$SNMP_EVENT_VAR_FOUR    = "$INST";

$SNMP_EVENT_IDENT_FIVE  = ".1.3.6.1.4.1.2789.2500.$SNMP_SPECIFIC_TRAP.5";
$SNMP_EVENT_VTYPE_FIVE  = "integer";
$SNMP_EVENT_VAR_FIVE    = "$MIN";

$SNMP_TRAP = "$SNMP_TRAP_LOC \-c $SNMP_COMM_NAME $SNMP_TRAP_HOST
  $SNMP_ENTERPRISE_ID \"$HOST\" $SNMP_GEN_TRAP $SNMP_SPECIFIC_TRAP
  $SNMP_TIME_STAMP
  $SNMP_EVENT_IDENT_ONE    $SNMP_EVENT_VTYPE_ONE    \"$SNMP_EVENT_VAR_ONE\"
  $SNMP_EVENT_IDENT_TWO    $SNMP_EVENT_VTYPE_TWO    \"$SNMP_EVENT_VAR_TWO\"
  $SNMP_EVENT_IDENT_THREE $SNMP_EVENT_VTYPE_THREE \"$SNMP_EVENT_VAR_THREE\"
  $SNMP_EVENT_IDENT_FOUR  $SNMP_EVENT_VTYPE_FOUR  \"$SNMP_EVENT_VAR_FOUR\"
  $SNMP_EVENT_IDENT_FIVE  $SNMP_EVENT_VTYPE_FIVE  \"$SNMP_EVENT_VAR_FIVE\"";

if (!($PASSED_PARM < $TOTAL_TRAPS_CREATED))
{
   die "ERROR SNMPTrap with a Specific Number \>
       $TOTAL_TRAPS_CREATED\nSNMP_TRAP:$SNMP_TRAP:\n";
}

# Sending a trap using Net-SNMP
#
#system "/usr/local/bin/snmptrap $SNMP_TRAP_HOST $SNMP_COMM_NAME
#$SNMP_ENTERPRISE_ID '' $SNMP_GEN_TRAP $SNMP_SPECIFIC_TRAP ''
#$SNMP_EVENT_IDENT_ONE s \"$SNMP_EVENT_VAR_ONE\"
#$SNMP_EVENT_IDENT_TWO i \"$SNMP_EVENT_VAR_TWO\"
#$SNMP_EVENT_IDENT_THREE i \"$SNMP_EVENT_VAR_THREE\"
#$SNMP_EVENT_IDENT_FOUR s \"$SNMP_EVENT_VAR_FOUR\"";
#$SNMP_EVENT_IDENT_FIVE i \"$SNMP_EVENT_VAR_FIVE\"";
```

```perl
    # Sending a trap using Perl
    #
    #use SNMP_util "0.54";  # This will load the BER and SNMP_Session for us
    #snmptrap("$SNMP_COMM_NAME\@$SNMP_TRAP_HOST:162", "$SNMP_ENTERPRISE_ID",
    #mylocalhostname, $SNMP_GEN_TRAP, $SNMP_SPECIFIC_TRAP,
    #"$SNMP_EVENT_IDENT_ONE", "string", "$SNMP_EVENT_VAR_ONE",
    #"$SNMP_EVENT_IDENT_TWO", "int", "$SNMP_EVENT_VAR_TWO",
    #"$SNMP_EVENT_IDENT_THREE", "int", "$SNMP_EVENT_VAR_THREE",
    #"$SNMP_EVENT_IDENT_FOUR", "string", "$SNMP_EVENT_VAR_FOUR",
    #"$SNMP_EVENT_IDENT_FIVE", "int", "$SNMP_EVENT_VAR_FIVE");

    # Sending a trap using OpenView's snmptrap (using VARs from above)
    #
    if($SEND_SNMP_TRAP) {
        print "ERROR Running SnmpTrap Result ";
        print ":$SEND_SNMP_TRAP: :$SNMP_TRAP:\n"
    }

sub find_inst
{
    open(SNMPWALK2,"$SNMPWALK_LOC $HOST $MIB_DIR |") ||
                            die "Can't Find Inst for $HOST\n";
    while($DLINE=<SNMPWALK2>)
    {
      chomp $DLINE;
      ($DIRTY_INST,$NULL,$DIRTY_NAME) = split(/\:/,$DLINE);
      $DIRTY_NAME =~ s/\s+//g;  # Lose the whitespace, folks!
      print "DIRTY_INST :$DIRTY_INST:\nDIRTY_NAME :$DIRTY_NAME:\n"
                        unless (!($DEBUG>99));
        if ($DIRTY_NAME eq "/")
        {
            $DIRTY_INST =~ /fileSystemDir\.(\d*)\.1/;
            $GINST = $1;
            $LENGTH = (length($GINST) - $INST_LENGTH);
            while ($LENGTH--) { chop $GINST; }
            close SNMPWALK;
            print "Found Inst DIRTY_INST :$DIRTY_INST: DIRTY_NAME\
                :$DIRTY_NAME: GINST :$GINST:\n"
                        unless (!($DEBUG > 99));
            return 0;
        }
    }

    close SNMPWALK2;
    die "Can't Find Inst for HOST :$HOST:";
}

sub ping_server_bad
{
    local $SERVER  = $_[0];
    $RES = system "$PING_LOC $SERVER $PING_TIMEOUT \> /dev/null";
    print "Res from Ping :$RES: \- :$PING_LOC $SERVER:\n"
                                    unless (!($DEBUG));
    return $RES;
}
```

The script contains a handful of useful features:

- We use an external ASCII file for a list of servers to poll. We specify the file by using the switch *–table FILENAME*. If no *–table* switch is given, the file named *default* in the current directory is used.

- We can specify a single server name (which must appear in the file above) to poll using the switch *–server SERVER_NAME*.

- We can ignore up to three filesystems per server. For example, we might want to ignore filesystems that are being used for software development.

- The script polls only servers that respond to a *ping*. We don't want to get filesystem traps from a server that is down or not on the network.

- We can set the minimum threshold for each list of servers in 1024-byte blocks using the *–min blocks* option.

- The script sends a trap when a server's threshold has been met and sends another trap when the state goes back to normal.

- We use lockfiles to prevent the server from sending out too many redundant traps.* When a threshold has been met, a file named *hostname.instance* is created. We send a trap only if the lockfile doesn't exist. When the space frees up, we delete the lockfile, allowing us to generate a trap the next time free storage falls below the threshold.

- We can set the number of leading instance digits used to grab the appropriate filesystem with the *–inst* switch. Unfortunately, the number of instance digits you can safely use to isolate a local filesystem varies from installation to installation. The default is five, but a lower value may be appropriate.

- The script displays a useful table when we invoke it with the *–debug* flag.

The script starts by reading the table of servers in which we're interested. It *pings* the servers and ignores those that don't respond. It then calls the subroutine `find_inst`, which incorporates most of the instance-number logic. This subroutine walks the filesystem table to find a list of all the filesystems and their instance numbers. It extracts the entry for the root filesystem (/), which we know exists, and which we assume is a local disk. (We can't assume that the root filesystem will be listed first; we do assume that you won't use a script like this to monitor diskless workstations). We then store the first `INST_LENGTH` digits of the instance number in the variable `GINST`, and return.

Back in the main program, we ask for the number of blocks available for each filesystem; we compare the instance number to `GINST`, which selects the local

---

* There have been a few times that we have missed the fact that a system has filled up because a trap was lost during transmission. Using *cron*, we frequently delete everything in the *lock* directory. This resubmits the entries, if any, at that time.

filesystems (i.e., the filesystems with an instance number whose initial digits match the instance number for /). We then ask for the total number of blocks, which allows us to compare the space available against our threshholds. If the value is less then our minimum we send one of the two enterprise-specific traps we've defined for this program, 1500, which indicates that the filesystem's free space is below the threshold. If the free space has returned to a safe level we send trap 1501, which is an "out of danger" notification. Some additional logic uses a lockfile to prevent the script from bombarding the NMS with repeated notifications; we send at most one warning a day and send an "out of danger" only if we've previously sent a warning. In either case, we stuff the trap with useful information: a number of variable bindings specifying the filesystem, the available space, its total capacity, its instance number, and the threshold we've set. Later, we'll see how to map these traps into OpenView categories.

Let's put the program to work by creating a table called *default* that lists the servers we are interested in watching:

```
db_serv0
db_serv1
db_serv2
```

Now we can run the script with the *–debug* option to show us a table of the results. The following command asks for all filesystems on the server *db_serv0* with fewer than 50,000 blocks (50 MB) free:

```
$ /opt/OV/local/bin/disk_space/polling.pl -min 50000 -server db_serv0 -debug 1
Res from Ping :0: - :/usr/sbin/ping db_serv0:
Server       MountPoint         BlocksLeft  BlockSize  MIB               LockFile
----------   -----------------  ----------  ---------  ----------------  --------
db_serv0     /                  207766      1024       38010880.1        [ 0 ]
db_serv0     /usr               334091      1024       38010886.1        [ 0 ]
db_serv0     /opt               937538      1024       38010887.1        [ 0 ]
db_serv0     /var               414964      1024       38010888.1        [ 0 ]
db_serv0     /db1               324954      1024       38010889.1        [ 0 ]
```

Notice that we didn't need to specify a table explicitly; because we omitted the *–table* option, the *polling.pl* script used the default file we put in the current directory. The *–server* switch let us limit the test to the server named *db_serv0*; if we had omitted this option the script would have checked all servers within the default table. If the free space on any of the filesystems falls under 50,000 1024-byte blocks, the program sends a trap and writes a lockfile with the instance number.

Because SNMP traps use UDP, they are unreliable. This means that some traps may never reach their destination. This could spell disaster—in our situation, we're sending traps to notify a manager that a filesystem is full. We don't want those traps to disappear, especially since we've designed our program so that it doesn't send duplicate notifications. One workaround is to have *cron* delete some or all of the files in the *lock* directory. We like to delete everything in the *lock* directory every hour; this means that we'll get a notification every hour until some free storage appears in the filesystem. Another plausible policy is to delete only the production-server lockfiles. With this policy, we'll get hourly notification about filesystem capacity problems on the server we care about most; on other machines (e.g., development machines, test machines), we will get only a single notification.

Let's say that the filesystem */db1* is a test system and we don't care if it fills up. We can ignore this filesystem by specifying it in our table. We can list up to three file-systems we would like to ignore after the server name (which must be followed by a ":"):

```
db_serv0:db1
```

Running the *polling.pl* script again gives these results:

```
$ /opt/OV/local/bin/disk_space/polling.pl -min 50000 -server db_serv0 -debug 1
Res from Ping :0: - :/usr/sbin/ping db_serv0:
Server      MountPoint        BlocksLeft  BlockSize  MIB              LockFile
----------  ----------------  ----------  ---------  ---------------  --------
db_serv0    /                 207766      1024       38010880.1       [ 0 ]
db_serv0    /usr              334091      1024       38010886.1       [ 0 ]
db_serv0    /opt              937538      1024       38010887.1       [ 0 ]
db_serv0    /var              414964      1024       38010888.1       [ 0 ]
db_serv0    /db1 (ignored)    324954      1024       38010889.1       [ 0 ]
```

When the */db1* filesystem drops below the minimum disk space, the script will not send any traps or create any lockfiles.

Now let's go beyond experimentation. The following *crontab* entries run our program twice every hour:

```
4,34 * * * * /opt/OV/bin/polling.pl -min 50000
5,35 * * * * /opt/OV/bin/polling.pl -min 17000 -table stocks_table
7,37 * * * * /opt/OV/bin/polling.pl -min 25000 -table bonds_table -inst 3
```

Next we need to define how the traps *polling.pl* generates should be handled when they arrive at the NMS. Here's the entry in OpenView's *trapd.conf* file that shows how to handle these traps:

```
EVENT DiskSpaceLow .1.3.6.1.4.1.2789.2500.0.1500 "Threshold Alarms" Major
FORMAT Disk Space For FileSystem :$1: Is Low With :$2:
1024 Blocks Left - Current FS Block Size :$3: - Min Threshold
:$5: - Inst :$4:
SDESC
$1 - octetstringascii   - FileSystem
$2 - integer            - Current Size
$3 - integer            - Block Size
$4 - octetstringascii   - INST
$5 - integer            - Min Threshold Size
EDESC
#
#
#
```

```
EVENT DiskSpaceNormal .1.3.6.1.4.1.2789.2500.0.1501 "Threshold Alarms" Normal
FORMAT Disk Space For FileSystem :$1: Is Normal With :$2:
1024 Blocks Left - Current FS Block Size :$3: - Min Threshold
:$5: - Inst :$4:
SDESC
$1 - octetstringascii   - FileSystem
$2 - integer            - Current Size
$3 - integer            - Block Size
$4 - octetstringascii   - INST
$5 - integer            - Min Threshold size
EDESC
```

These entries define two OpenView events: a *DiskSpaceLow* event that is used when a filesystem's capacity is below the threshold, and a *DiskSpaceNormal* event. We place both of these in the Threshold Alarms category; the low disk space event has a severity of Major, while the "normal" event has a severity of Normal. If you're using some other package to listen for traps, you'll have to configure it accordingly.

Port Monitor

Most TCP/IP services use static ports to listen for incoming requests. Monitoring these ports allows you to see whether particular servers or services are responding or not. For example, you can tell whether your mail server is alive by periodically poking port 25, which is the port on which an SMTP server listens for requests. Some other ports to monitor are FTP (23), HTTP (80) and POP3 (110).* A freely available program called *netcat* can connect to and interact with a specific port on any device. We can write a wrapper for this program to watch a given port or service; if something happens outside of its normal operation, then we can send a trap. In this section, we'll develop a wrapper that checks the SMTP port (25) on our mail server. The program is very simple, but the results are outstanding!

Before we start to write the program, let's establish what we want to do. Telnet to port 25 of your SMTP server. Once you're connected, you can issue the command *HELO mydomain.com*. This should give you a response of 250. After you get a response from the mail server, issue the *QUIT* command, which tells the server you are done. Your session should look something like this:

```
$ telnet mail.ora.com 25
220 smtp.oreilly.com ESMTP O'Reilly & Associates Sendmail 8.11.2 ready
HELO mydomain.com
250 OK
QUIT
221 closing connection
```

---

* Check your *services* file for a listing of port numbers and their corresponding services. On Unix systems, this file is usually in the directory */etc*; on Windows it is usually in a directory such as *C:\WINNT\ System32\drivers\etc*, though its location may vary depending on the version of Windows you are using.

The *netcat* program needs to know what commands you want to send to the port you are monitoring. We will be sending only two commands to our mail server, so we'll create a file called *input.txt* that looks like this:

```
HELO mydomain.com
QUIT
```

Next, we should test this file and see what output we get from the server. The actual *netcat* executable is named *nc*; to test the file, run it like this:

```
$ /opt/OV/local/bin/netcat/nc -i 1 mailserver 25 < input.txt
```

This command produces the same results as the telnet session. You won't see the commands in your *input.txt* file echoed, but you should see the server's responses. Once you have verified that *netcat* works and gives the same response each time, save a copy of its output to the file *mail_good*. This file will be used to determine what a normal response from your mail server looks like. You can save the output to a file with the following command:

```
$ /opt/OV/local/bin/netcat/nc -i 1 mailserver 25 < input.txt > mail_good
```

An alternate approach is to search for the line numbered 250 in the mail server's output. This code indicates that the server is up and running, though not necessarily processing mail correctly. In any case, searching for 250 shields you from variations in the server's response to your connection.

Here's a script called *mail_poller.pl* that automates the process. Edit the appropriate lines in this script to reflect your local environment. Once you have customized the script, you should be ready to go. There are no command-line arguments. The script generates an output file called *mail_status* that contains a 0 (zero) if the server is okay (i.e., if the output of *netcat* matches $GOOD_FILE); any number other than 0 indicates that an error has occurred:

```perl
#!/usr/local/bin/perl
# filename: mail_poller.pl

$HOME_LOC      = "/opt/OV/local/bin/netcat";
$NC_LOC        = "/opt/netcat/nc";
$DIFF_LOC      = "/bin/diff";
$ECHO_LOC      = "/bin/echo";

$MAIL_SERVER   = "mail.exampledomain.com";
$MAIL_PORT     = 25;
$INPUT_FILE    = "$HOME_LOC\/input.txt";
$GOOD_FILE     = "$HOME_LOC\/mail_good";
$CURRENT_FILE  = "$HOME_LOC\/mail_current";
$EXIT_FILE     = "$HOME_LOC\/mail_status";

$DEBUG = 0;

print "$NC_LOC -i 1 -w 3 $MAIL_SERVER $MAIL_PORT
    \< $INPUT_FILE \> $CURRENT_FILE\n" unless (!($DEBUG));
```

```
$NETCAT_RES = system "$NC_LOC -i 1 -w 3 $MAIL_SERVER $MAIL_PORT
    \< $INPUT_FILE \> $CURRENT_FILE";
$NETCAT_RES = $NETCAT_RES / 256;

if ($NETCAT_RES)
{
    # We had a problem with netcat... maybe a timeout?
    system "$ECHO_LOC $NETCAT_RES > $EXIT_FILE";
    &cleanup;
}


$DIFF_RES = system "$DIFF_LOC $GOOD_FILE $CURRENT_FILE";
$DIFF_RES = $DIFF_RES / 256;

if ($DIFF_RES)
{
    # looks like things are different!
    system "$ECHO_LOC $DIFF_RES > $EXIT_FILE";
    &cleanup;
}
else
{
    # All systems go!
    system "$ECHO_LOC 0 > $EXIT_FILE";
    &cleanup;
}

sub cleanup
{
    unlink "$CURRENT_FILE";
    exit 0;
}
```

After you run the program, review the results in *mail_status*. If you can, try shutting down the mail server and running the script again. Your file should now contain a nonzero error status.

Once you have made sure the script works in your environment, you can insert an entry in *crontab* to execute this program at whatever interval you would like. In our environment, we use a 10-minute interval:

```
# Check the mail server and create a file that we can poll via OpenView
1,11,21,31,41,51 * * * * /opt/OV/local/bin/netcat/mail_poller.pl
```

Notice we staggered the polling so that we don't check on the hour, half hour, or quarter hour. Once *cron* has started updating *mail_status* regularly, you can use tools such as the extensible OpenView agent to check the file's contents. You can configure the agent to poll the file regularly and send the results to your management console. The entry in my */etc/SnmpAgent.d/snmpd.extend* looks like this:

```
serviceInfo     OBJECT IDENTIFIER ::= { mauro 5 }

-- BEGIN - serviceInfo
--
```

```
serMailPort  OBJECT-TYPE
    SYNTAX   INTEGER
    ACCESS   read-only
    STATUS   mandatory
    DESCRIPTION
        "This file is updated via crontab. It uses netcat to check the
        port and push a value into this file.
        FILE-NAME: /opt/OV/local/bin/netcat/mail_status"
    ::= { serviceInfo 0 }
```

We discuss the syntax of this file in Chapter 11. Basically, this entry just defines a MIB object in the *serviceInfo* tree, which is node 5 under my private-enterprise tree. In other words, this object's OID is *mauro.serviceInfo.serMailPort* (*2789.5.0*). The object can be read by any program that can issue an SNMP *get* operation. The DESCRIPTION, as we saw in Chapter 11, specifies a filename from which the agent will read an integer value to use as the value of this object. This program can easily be modified to monitor any port on any number of machines. If you're ambitious, you might want to think about turning the *serMailPort* object into an array that reports the status of all your mail servers.

Our goal in this chapter hasn't been to provide you with scripts you can immediately place in your environment. More to the point, we have wanted to show you what's possible, and get you thinking about how you might be able to write scripts that provide elaborate custom monitoring features. If you're thinking creatively about what you can do with SNMP, we've succeeded.

13

MRTG

The *Multi Router Traffic Grapher* (MRTG) is a freely available and fully configurable trend-analysis tool that's easy to configure and use. It's a surprisingly small, lightweight package because it doesn't implement a heavyweight user interface. Instead, it generates graphs in the form of GIF or PNG images; these graphs are embedded in standard HTML pages. Therefore, you can view MRTG's output using any graphical web browser and even make its reports visible across your network by using a web server.

Although MRTG is best at displaying usage graphs for router interfaces, it can be configured to graph things like memory usage, load average, and disk usage on server equipment. MRTG is particularly useful for determining when something "peaks out" for an extended period of time, which indicates that you have a capacity problem and need to upgrade. For example, you might find that your T1 interface is maxed out during your peak business hours and you need to upgrade to a bigger circuit, or you might find that you need to add more memory to a server. Likewise, MRTG may let you know that your network connections are operating at a fraction of the available bandwidth and that you can therefore eliminate a few T1 circuits and reduce your telecommunications costs.

Many sites that use MRTG use its default graphing capabilities for capacity planning and provisioning. MRTG doesn't provide the fine-grained statistical tools you need to calculate baseline information or project when your network will need to be upgraded. However, it can be a very useful tool for businesses that don't have the resources necessary to purchase a full-fledged trend-analysis package. Baselines and projections are invaluable, but MRTG's graphs can give you similar behavior at a glance; your eyes are very good at spotting typical behavior and trends, even if they can't give you the statistical analysis that your management might like.

MRTG has many options that allow you to customize how it operates. It is beyond the scope of this chapter to discuss every option; instead, we will discuss how to install MRTG and use its default graphing capabilities. We'll also outline how you can configure MRTG to gather system information from a server.

It's important to understand that MRTG is not an NMS solution. Although its graphing capabilities make it look superficially like an NMS, it's really a simple polling engine that's very clever about the output it generates. It performs the same *get* functions that an NMS would, but its job isn't problem detection and resolution. It doesn't have a facility for generating alarms or processing traps, nor does it have the ability to set objects. It's simply designed to provide a graphical view of how your network is performing. If you're interested in an open source NMS package, you should investigate Bluebird (*http://www.opennms.org*).

Using MRTG

Before using MRTG, you have to download and install the software. The primary MRTG web site is *http://www.mrtg.org*. The download link takes you to a directory maintained by MRTG's inventor and primary developer, Tobias Oetiker (*http://ee-staff.ethz.ch/~oetiker/webtools/mrtg/pub/*). This directory contains some older MRTG releases, as well as the current one. We downloaded the file *mrtg-2.9.10.tar.gz* (the Unix version) from the list. We will focus on that version in this chapter.

MRTG requires four third-party packages in order to run: Perl Version 5.004_5 (at least), and the *gd*, *libpng*, and *zlib* libraries. MRTG comes with a Perl-based implementation of SNMP, so you don't have to worry about getting and installing any SNMP libraries. You can determine what version of Perl you have (and whether it's installed) by typing the command *perl –v*. This may or may not spit out a bunch of information. If it does, the first line will be the version of Perl you have installed. If you get some sort of "command not found" error, Perl may not be installed. In any event, go to *http://www.perl.com* to get the latest version of Perl.

The *gd* library is used to generate the GIF images that MRTG displays. You can download it from *http://www.boutell.com/gd/*. The other two packages, *libpng* and *zlib*, are also used for various aspects of graphic image creation. They are available from *http://www.libpng.org/pub/png/* and *http://www.info-zip.org/pub/infozip/zlib/*.

Once you have ensured that Perl, *gd*, *libpng*, and *zlib* are installed on your machine, download and unpack the Unix version of MRTG with the following commands:

```
[root][linuxserver] > cd /usr/local
[root][linuxserver] > tar -zxvf mrtg-2.9.10.tar.gz
```

Once it's unpacked, *cd* into the directory it created (which should be *mrtg-2.9.10*) and read the installation hints from the *README* file. To build MRTG, you execute three commands:

```
[root][linuxserver] ~/mrtg-2.9.10> ./configure
[root][linuxserver] ~/mrtg-2.9.10> make
[root][linuxserver] ~/mrtg-2.9.10> make install
```

All three of these commands produce a lot of output, which we have omitted. The *configure* command inspects your system for tools it needs to build MRTG. It will tell you which items are missing and where to go to get them. Running *make* builds MRTG, but don't bother running this if the *configure* command failed; MRTG will not build unless everything has been installed and configured properly. Finally, *make install* installs MRTG and its associated files in the appropriate places. Again, don't bother running *make install* if the previous *make* command terminated with errors. The default location for the MRTG executables is */usr/local/ mrtg-2/bin*. You may want to add this directory to your search path.

Once you've built MRTG, you need to decide where to put the graphs it generates. Since MRTG's graphs are designed to be viewed by a web browser, they're often stored in a directory that's visible to a web server. However, it really doesn't matter where they go. What's more important is who you want to view the graphs. You probably don't want the world to see your network statistics. On a small network, you can place the graphs in a directory that is out of view of the web server and then use a web browser to view the HTML reports in the local filesystem. In a larger network, other people (e.g., other network staff or management) may need to access the reports; to allow access without publishing your network statistics to the rest of the world, you may want to set up some kind of a secure web server. At any rate, the next set of commands you'll want to execute is something like this:

```
[root][linuxserver] ~/mrtg-2.9.10> mkdir /mrtg/images
[root][linuxserver] ~/mrtg-2.9.10> cp ./images/mrtg*.gif /mrtg/images/
```

The first command creates a directory for storing the graphs MRTG creates. The second command copies some MRTG images into the newly created directory for later use in HTML files. For the remainder of this chapter, we will assume that graphs are stored in */mrtg/images*.

You're now ready to set up your first device to poll, which is called a *target* in MRTG. MRTG uses a configuration file to tell it what devices to poll, what options to apply to the creation of the graphs it will generate, etc. The syntax of the configuration file is complex, but MRTG provides a tool called *cfgmaker* to help you build it. You'll probably need to edit the file by hand, but it's much easier to start with a working template. Here's how to execute *cfgmaker*:

```
[root][linuxserver] ~/mrtg-2.9.10> setenv PATH /usr/local/mrtg-2/bin:$PATH
[root][linuxserver] ~/mrtg-2.9.10> cfgmaker --global 'WorkDir: /mrtg/images' \
--output /mrtg/run/mrtg.cfg public@router
```

The first argument to *cfgmaker* sets the WorkDir variable in the configuration file. This tells MRTG where to store any data it gathers from the devices it's going to poll. The second argument specifies where we want *cfgmaker*'s output sent; in this case it's */mrtg/run/mrtg.cfg*. The last argument specifies the device we want to poll and the community string to use when polling that device; its format is *community_string@device*.

The output from *cfgmaker* is a mix of commands and HTML. It performs *get-next* commands on the device you specified on the command line, in order to get an idea of how many interfaces your device has, which ones are up, which are down, etc. It walks the *iso.org.dod.internet.mgmt.mib-2.interfaces* (*1.3.6.1.2.1.2*) tree to discover the total number of interfaces in this table. It then creates logical entries that represent a list of devices to poll, except the list of devices is actually one device with each interface number specified as a target. For example, *Ethernet0* is in the fourth row of the *interfaces* table on our Cisco router, so *cfgmaker* created a `Target` entry called *cisco.4*. If this interface occupied the second row in the *interfaces* table, the `Target` entry would be called *cisco.2*.

Here's a shortened version of our *mrtg.cfg* file:

```
WorkDir: /mrtg/images/

Target[cisco.4]: 4:public@cisco
MaxBytes[cisco.4]: 1250000
Title[cisco.4]: cisco (cisco): Ethernet0
PageTop[cisco.4]: <H1>Traffic Analysis for Ethernet0
  </H1>
  <TABLE>
    <TR><TD>System:</TD><TD>cisco in Atlanta, Ga</TD></TR>
    <TR><TD>Maintainer:</TD><TD></TD></TR>
    <TR><TD>Interface:</TD><TD>Ethernet0 (4)</TD></TR>
    <TR><TD>IP:</TD><TD>cisco ()</TD></TR>
    <TR><TD>Max Speed:</TD>
        <TD>1250.0 kBytes/s (ethernetCsmacd)</TD></TR>
  </TABLE>
```

It's worth learning a bit about the format of the configuration file. Comment lines begin with #; in a real configuration file, you'll see many of them. Most of the lines in the file are either commands or snippets of HTML that will be used in MRTG's output files. MRTG commands take the form of *command[key]: options*. For example, the command for the third line is `Target`, the key is `cisco.4`, and the options are `4:public@cisco`. The key is an identifying string that groups entries in the configuration file and provides a base filename for MRTG to use when generating graphs and HTML files. At a complex site, MRTG might be used to monitor dozens of pieces of equipment, with hundreds of interfaces; the key keeps the configuration file in some semblance of order. The options provide the actual parameters to the command.

This should help you understand the configuration file. The first line specifies the working directory in which MRTG will place its graphs and HTML files. This is a global command, so no key is needed. The working directory is typically somewhere under a web server tree, so that MRTG's reports can be visible from a web browser. We've set ours to `/mrtg/images/`. The third line (`Target`) tells MRTG which device it should poll. The format for this option is *interface: community_string@device*, or in our case `4:public@cisco`. The device is specified by its hostname or IP address; we already know about community strings. Since MRTG is only a data-collection tool, the read-only community string will suffice. `Interface` specifies which interface on the device to poll, according to the device's *ifTable*. In this case, we're polling interface 4 in the *ifTable*.

The `MaxBytes` line sets up the maximum value for the parameters MRTG is going to read from this interface. By default, MRTG reads *ifInOctets* and *ifOutOctets*. It tries to pick a reasonable maximum value depending on the interface's type, which it should be able to read from the device itself. Since this is an Ethernet interface, MRTG sets `MaxBytes` to `1250000`. The `Title` specifies the title for the HTML page generated for the graph. Finally, `PageTop` and the following lines tell MRTG what kind of information to place at the top of the HTML page containing the usage graphs. The command contains actual HTML code, which was generated by *cfgmaker*.

Altogether, this entry tells MRTG to poll for the default objects (*ifInOctets* and *ifOutOctets*) on entry 4 in the interface table for the device *cisco*. Therefore, MRTG will issue *get* commands for the OIDs *.1.3.6.1.2.1.2.2.1.10.4* (*iso.org.dod.internet. mgmt.mib-2.interfaces.ifTable.ifEntry.ifInOctets.4*) and *.1.3.6.1.2.1.2.2.1.16.4* (*iso. org.dod.internet.mgmt.mib-2.interfaces.ifTable.ifEntry.ifOutOctets.4*). By default, MRTG will generate the following graphs:

- Daily graph with 5-minute averages
- Weekly graph with 30-minute averages
- Monthly graph with 2-hour averages
- Yearly graph with 1-day averages

Once you've finished, try running MRTG by hand to see if there are any problems with the configuration script:

```
[root][linuxserver] ~/mrtg-2.9.10> mrtg /mrtg/run/mrtg.cfg
```

If MRTG has no problems with your configuration file, it will run with no configuration-file errors. If it does have problems, it will give you a fairly verbose description of the problem. The first time you run MRTG, it will complain about not being able to find any log files. If you run MRTG three times you'll see messages similar to these:

```
[root][linuxserver] ~/mrtg-2.9.10> mrtg /mrtg/run/mrtg.cfg
Rateup WARNING: /mrtg/run//rateup could not read the primary log file for cisco.4
Rateup WARNING: /mrtg/run//rateup The backup log file for cisco.4 was invalid as
well
```

```
Rateup WARNING: /mrtg/run//rateup Can't remove cisco.4.old updating log file
Rateup WARNING: /mrtg/run//rateup Can't rename cisco.4.log to cisco.4.old
updating log file

[root][linuxserver] ~/mrtg-2.9.10> mrtg /mrtg/run/mrtg.cfg
Rateup WARNING: /mrtg/run//rateup Can't remove cisco.4.old updating log file

[root][linuxserver] ~/mrtg-2.9.10> mrtg /mrtg/run/mrtg.cfg
[root][linuxserver] ~/mrtg-2.9.10>
```

As you can see, the first time we ran the program it spat out some errors. The second run produced only one error, and the last time it ran with no errors. These errors are normal when you run MRTG for the first time; don't worry about them.

The next step is to make sure MRTG runs every five minutes. There's no need for MRTG to be run by root; any user will do. Add a line like the following to the *crontab* entry for the appropriate user:

```
*/5 * * * * /usr/local/mrtg-2/bin/mrtg /mrtg/run/mrtg.cfg
```

This runs MRTG every five minutes of every day. Note that the */5 notation is Linux-specific; on other Unix systems you'll have to specify the times explicitly (0,5,10,15,20,25,30,35,40,45,50,55). If your network is fairly large, you might run into problems if MRTG does not finish all its polling duties before the next polling cycle starts. If this is the case, setting a five-minute poll interval may not be a good idea. You may have to experiment to determine a good interval for your environment.

Viewing Graphs

Once you've generated some graphs, you will want to look at them to see the results. To make it easier to view the graphs, MRTG comes with an *indexmaker* script that generates HTML index pages. Here's how to run *indexmaker* for a typical set of graphs:

```
[root][linuxserver] ~/mrtg-2.9.10> indexmaker --title "Cisco to Internet" \
--filter name=~'cisco' --output /mrtg/images/cisco.html /mrtg/run/mrtg.cfg
```

This command creates one index page with the five-minute average graph for each target you've specified in your *mrtg.cfg* file. Keep in mind that the target is the interface from which you're gathering data. If you have four targets for your router, there will be four graphs in the index file, all pointing to the daily, weekly, monthly, and yearly summary graphs for that target. The *—title* option tells *indexmaker* what title to use for the index file. *—filter name=~cisco* allows you to select some of the targets in the *mrtg.cfg* file by using a regular expression: we told *indexmaker* to find all targets that include the string cisco. The *—output* option is the name of the index file. The final argument on the command line is the full path to the configuration file. Table 13-1 gives a synopsis of these options as well as some other useful options to *indexmaker*.

Table 13-1. Command-Line Options to indexmaker

Option	Description
——title	Specify a title for the HTML page.
——filter	Specify the regular expression that will be used to find a specific target from the *mrtg.cfg* file. These matched targets are used to create the HTML report files.
——output	Indicate the full pathname for the HTML file that is to be generated. The default is standard output.
——sort	Sort how the graphs show up on the index page.
——columns	Arrange the graphs on the index page by *x* columns. The default is 2.
——width	Set the width of the graphs. This is not set by default.
——height	Set the height of the graphs. This is not set by default.
——show	Pick which graph to show on the index page. The default is `day`. Other options include `week`, `month`, `year`, and `none`.

To display the entire list of options to *indexmaker*, run the command without any options. Figure 13-1 shows how the *cisco.html* file generated by *indexmaker* looks when it's loaded into a web browser.

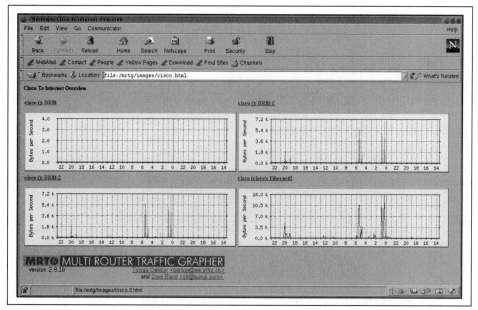

Figure 13-1. Cisco graph overview

There are four graphs on the page, one for each of the operational interfaces (interfaces that were up and running when we ran *cfgmaker*) on our router. This page includes links to other pages that have more detailed information about individual interfaces; Figure 13-2 shows the daily, weekly, monthly, and yearly traffic graphs for the *Ethernet0* interface.

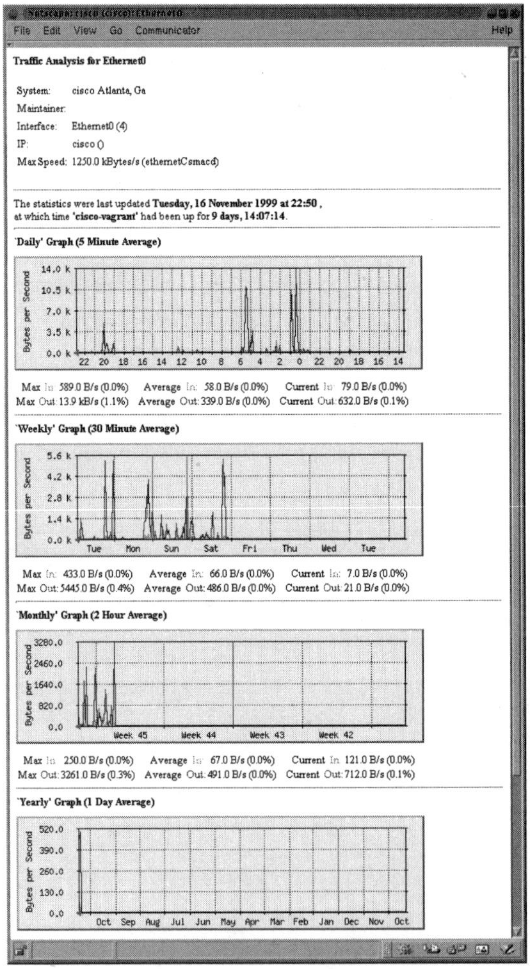

Figure 13-2. Daily, weekly, monthly, and yearly graphs for Etherenet0

The daily graph (which actually represents a 32-hour period) is the one that most people are interested in viewing. It shows the five-minute average of the traffic on this particular interface. Incoming traffic (*ifInOctets*) is represented by a green line; outgoing traffic (*IfOutOctets*) is represented by a blue line. If we had clicked on

one of the other interfaces on the Cisco index page (Figure 13-1), we would have
seen a similar graph.

That's all there is to viewing the graphs. MRTG stores the raw data it collects in
flat-text-file format but, due to its intelligent log rolling capabilities, the log files
don't grow out of control; their sizes remain quite manageable even if you use
MRTG extensively.

Graphing Other Objects

MRTG polls and graphs the MIB variables *ifInOctets* and *ifOutOctets* by default,
but it is possible to poll and graph the values of other objects, in addition to
polling different kinds of devices. Let's first get MRTG collecting input and output
octets from a server. To do this, run the following command:

```
[root][linuxserver] ~/mrtg-2.9.10> cfgmaker public@linuxserver >> \
/mrtg2/run/mrtg.cfg
```

This is almost identical to the command we ran earlier in the chapter, except for
the community string and target* (*public@linuxserver*). We appended the output to
the *mrtg.cfg* file, as opposed to specifying an output file with the *--output* option;
this lets us add a new host to the existing configuration file, rather than starting a
new file. Because the existing file already specifies a working directory, we also
omitted the working directory option (*--global 'WorkDir: .. '*). This *cfgmaker* command adds a number of lines like the following to the configuration file:

```
Target[linuxserver]: 2:public@localhost
MaxBytes[linuxserver]: 1250000
Title[linuxserver]: linuxserver(linuxserver): eth0
PageTop[linuxserver]: <H1>Traffic Analysis for eth0
  </H1>
  <TABLE>
    <TR><TD>System:</TD><TD>linuxserver</TD></TR>
    <TR><TD>Maintainer:</TD><TD></TD></TR>
    <TR><TD>Interface:</TD><TD>eth0 (2)</TD></TR>
    <TR><TD>IP:</TD><TD>linuxserver()</TD></TR>
    <TR><TD>Max Speed:</TD>
        <TD>1250.0 kBytes/s (ethernetCsmacd)</TD></TR>
  </TABLE>
```

These lines tell MRTG how to poll the server's Ethernet interface. The key used for
this interface is `linuxserver`, and the target number is 2. Why 2? Remember that
cfgmaker walks the interface table to determine what entries to add to the configuration file. Therefore, you'll see a set of lines like this for each interface on the

---

* Make sure that your target is running an SNMP agent. See Chapter 7 for a discussion of how to configure
  several SNMP agents for Unix and Windows NT.

device, including the loopback interface. The target numbers are actually indexes into the interface table; on this server, the loopback interface has the index 1.

Now let's create an entry to graph the number of users logged onto the server and the total number of processes running. MRTG is capable of graphing these parameters, but you have to specify explicitly which MIB variables to graph. Furthermore, you have to specify two variables—MRTG won't graph just one. (This is a rather strange limitation, but at least it's consistent: remember that the default graphs show both input and output octets.)

First, let's look at the MIB variables we plan to graph. The two variables, *hrSystemNumUsers* and *hrSystemProcesses*, are defined as OIDs *1.3.6.1.2.1.25.1.5.6.0* and *1.3.6.1.2.1.25.1.6.0*, respectively. The *.0* at the end of each OID indicates that these two objects are both scalar variables, not part of a table. Both come from the Host Resources MIB (RFC 2790), which defines a set of managed objects for system administration. (Some agents that run on server systems implement this MIB but, unfortunately, the Microsoft and Solaris agents do not.) The definitions for these objects are:

```
hrSystemNumUsers OBJECT-TYPE
    SYNTAX Gauge
    ACCESS read-only
    STATUS mandatory
    DESCRIPTION
        "The number of user sessions for which this host is storing state
        information. A session is a collection of processes requiring a
        single act of user authentication and possibly subject to collective
        job control."
    ::= { hrSystem 5 }

hrSystemProcesses OBJECT-TYPE
    SYNTAX Gauge
    ACCESS read-only
    STATUS mandatory
    DESCRIPTION
        "The number of process contexts currently loaded or running on
        this system."
    ::= { hrSystem 6 }
```

The entry we added to our configuration file looks like this:

```
Target[linuxserver.users]:1.3.6.1.2.1.25.1.5.0&1.3.6.1.2.1.25.1.6.0:
public@linuxserver
MaxBytes[linuxserver.users]: 512
Options[linuxserver.users]: gauge
Title[linuxserver.users]: linuxserver (linuxserver): Number of users and processes
YLegend[linuxserver.users]: Users/Processes
LegendI[linuxserver.users]:  Users:
LegendO[linuxserver.users]:  Processes:
PageTop[linuxserver.users]: <H1>Number of users and processes</H1>
```

```
<TABLE>
  <TR><TD>System:</TD><TD>linuxserver<TD></TR>
  <TR><TD>Maintainer:</TD><TD></TD></TR>
  <TR><TD>IP:</TD><TD>linuxserver()</TD></TR>
</TABLE>
```

We've highlighted the changes and additions to the configuration file in bold. The first line specifies the device we want MRTG to poll, along with the two OIDs (*hrSystemNumUsers* and *hrSystemProcessess*) we want to graph. This statement is obviously more complex than the `Target` statement we looked at earlier; its syntax is *OID1&OID2:community_string@device*. The OIDs must be separated by an ampersand character (&). Using this syntax, you can convince MRTG to graph any two scalar-valued MIB variables.

In the next line, we set `MaxBytes` to 512. This is the maximum value for the graph; values greater than 512 are set to 512. (Forget about bytes; `MaxBytes` simply defines a maximum value.) For the number of users logged in, this is a high number; there should never be this many people logged onto our system at once. The same goes for the total number of processes running on the system. You can choose values that make sense for your particular environment. If you need separate maximum values for each object, replace `MaxBytes` with two lines setting `MaxBytes1` and `MaxBytes2`.

The `Options` command is a new one; it allows you to change how MRTG treats the data it gathers. The only option we have specified is `gauge`. This instructs MRTG to treat the gathered data as `Gauge` data, not `Counter` data. Recall that `Counter` data is monotonically increasing, while `Gauge` data is not. Since the MIB definitions for both objects specify the `Gauge` datatype, this option makes sense.

The `YLegend`, `LegendI`, and `LegendO` options are also new. `YLegend` simply changes the label that is placed on the Y-axis of the graph itself. Since we're graphing the number of users and processes, we set the legend to `Users/ Processes`. It's important for the legend to be short; if it's too long, MRTG silently ignores it and doesn't print anything for the label. `LegendI` changes the legend used below the graph for the so-called "input variable" (in this case the number of users logged into the system—remember that MRTG expects to be graphing input and output octets). `LegendO` changes the legend for the "output variable" (the total number of processes running on the system). The terminology is unfortunate; just remember that MRTG always graphs a pair of objects and that the input legend always refers to the first object, while the output legend refers to the second.

Once you have added this entry to your configuration file and saved it, MRTG will start gathering data from the device every time it runs. If you have added the appropriate entry in your *crontab* file, you're all set. Now we'll use *indexmaker* to create intuitive index files for the server graphs, just as we did for the router graphs. The command to create a new index file is similar to the one we used to create the Cisco index file:

```
[root][linuxserver] ~/mrtg-2.9.10> indexmaker --title "Linux Server" \
--filter name=~'linuxserver' --output /mrtg/images/linux.html /mrtg/run/mrtg.cfg
```

Figure 13-3 shows the index page for the server graphs. It contains only two graphs: one shows traffic on the Ethernet interface and the other shows the number of running processes versus the number of users logged onto the system.

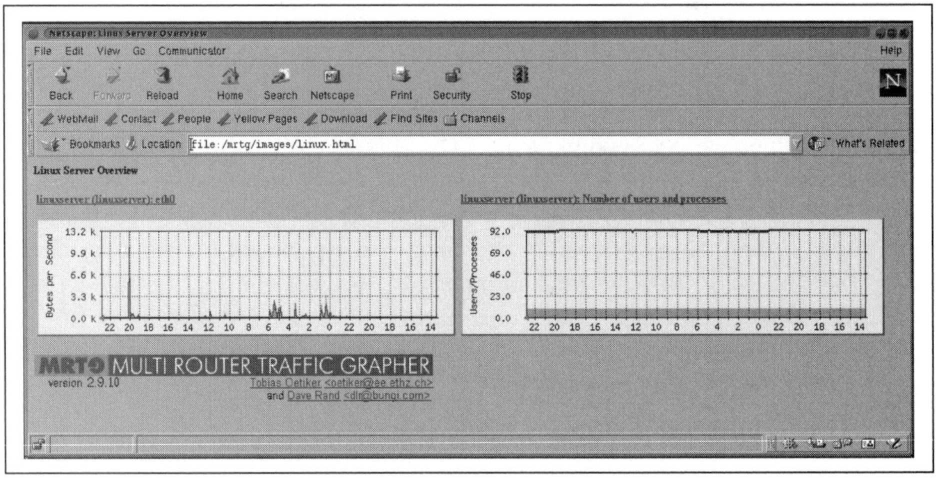

Figure 13-3. Linux Server overview graphs

Figure 13-4 shows the daily, weekly, monthly, and yearly graphs for the number of users and processes logged into the system.

Other Data-Gathering Applications

What if you need to monitor devices on your network that don't support SNMP? MRTG is up to the task. For example, you may have a Perl script that gathers usage statistics from some device that doesn't support SNMP. How can you collect and graph this data? Let's make this more concrete. Assume that you have the following script, */usr/local/scripts/hostinfo.pl*, which reports the number of users and the number of processes on the system:

```perl
#!/usr/bin/perl

$who = "/usr/bin/who | wc -l";
$ps = "/bin/ps -ef | wc -l";

chomp($numUsers = int(`$who`));
# We subtract two because ps generates a header and the ps process
# is counted as running.
```

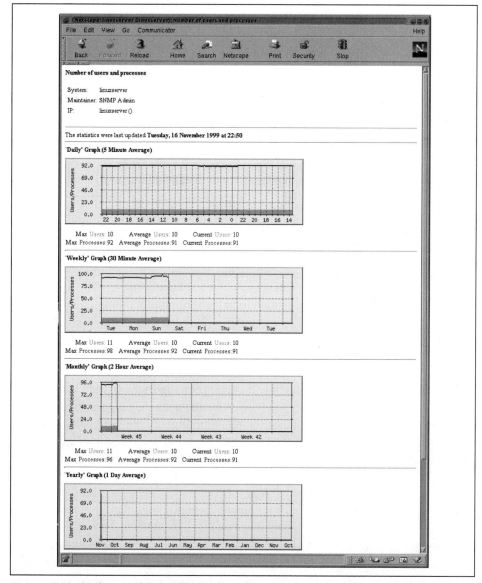

Figure 13-4. Daily, monthly, weekly, and yearly graphs for number of users and processes

```
chomp($numProcesses = int(`$ps`) - 2);
print "$numUsers\n";
print "$numProcesses\n";

#
# The following code prints the system uptime and the hostname. These two
# items need to be included in every script that you write and should be the
# very last thing that is printed.
#
```

```
chomp($uptime = `/usr/bin/uptime`);
print "$uptime\n";

chomp($hostname = `/bin/hostname`);
print "$hostname\n";
```

This script prints four variables: the number of users and the number of processes (the data we want MRTG to collect) and the system uptime and hostname (required by MRTG). To get MRTG to run this script, we'll have to edit *mrtg.cfg* by hand. The modification is actually simpler than our previous example. Here's the new entry to *mrtg.cfg*, with the changes shown in bold:

```
Target[linuxserver.users]: `/usr/bin/perl /usr/local/bin/hostinfo.pl`
MaxBytes[linuxserver.users]: 512
Options[linuxserver.users]: gauge
Title[linuxserver.users]: linuxserver (linuxserver): Number of
users and processes
YLegend[linuxserver.users]: Users/Processes
LegendI[linuxserver.users]:  Users:
LegendO[linuxserver.users]:  Processes:
PageTop[linuxserver.users]: <H1>Number of users and processes
  </H1>
  <TABLE>
    <TR><TD>System:</TD><TD>linuxserver<TD></TR>
    <TR><TD>Maintainer:</TD><TD></TD></TR>
    <TR><TD>IP:</TD><TD>linuxserver()</TD></TR>
  </TABLE>
```

Note the addition of `/usr/bin/perl /usr/local/bin/hostinfo.pl` to the `Target` command. This line tells MRTG to run the script or program between the backticks. The rest should be familiar. MRTG interprets the first value that the script prints (the number of users) as its input data; the second value (the number of processes) is the output data. When it generates graphs, it applies the appropriate input and output legends (`LegendI` and `LegendO`).

Pitfalls

Many SNMP-capable devices change the order of interfaces in the *interfaces* table whenever a new interface card is inserted or an old one is removed. If you run a fairly static router environment (i.e., you hardly ever add or remove cards from your routers), the configuration examples we've shown should work well for you. But in today's fast-paced network environments, stability is rare. MRTG's *cfgmaker* command provides a command-line option, *—ifref,* to help with this problem. It doesn't solve the problem, but it does allow you to generate graphs in which interfaces are labeled with their addresses, descriptions, or names; with this information, you don't have to remember whether interface 1 is your local network interface or your T1 connection. Table 13-2 summarizes the usage of *—ifref.*

Table 13-2. Summary of —ifref Options

Option	Description
—ifref=ip	Identify each interface by its IP address.
—ifref=eth	Use the Ethernet address to identify the interface.
—ifref=descr	Use the interface description to identify the interface.
—ifref=name	Use the interface name to identify the interface.

Thus, to label interfaces with their IP addresses, run *cfgmaker* like so:

```
[root][linuxserver] ~/mrtg-2.9.10> cfgmaker --global 'WorkDir: /mrtg/images' \
--output /mrtg/run/mrtg.cfg --ifref=ip public@router
```

Be sure to read the *cfgmaker* manual that comes with the MRTG documentation.

Getting Help

The MRTG web site, *http://www.mrtg.org*, offers a great deal of information and help. You can subscribe to the MRTG mailing list from this page. MRTG is also discussed frequently in the Usenet newsgroup *comp.dcom.net-management*. Finally, don't ignore MRTG's documentation, which is located in the *doc* subdirectory of the MRTG distribution. The documentation is included in both text and HTML form and is fairly complete and comprehensive.

A

Using Input and Output Octets

To be SNMP-compatible, an IP device must support MIB-II (*iso.org.dod.internet. mgmt.mib-2*) objects. MIB-II contains the *interfaces* table (*mib-2.interfaces.ifTable. ifEntry*), which is one of the most useful objects for network monitoring. This table contains information about the system's network interfaces. Some of its objects are:

ifDescr
> A user-provided description of the interface

ifType
> The interface's type (token ring, Ethernet, etc.)

ifOperStatus
> Whether the interface is up, down, or in some kind of test mode

ifMtu
> The size of the largest packet that can be sent over the interface

ifSpeed
> The maximum bandwidth of the interface

ifPhysAddress
> The low-level (hardware) address of the interface

ifInOctets
> The number of octets received by the interface

ifOutOctets
> The number of octets sent by the interface

We explored various parts of this table in other chapters, but avoided saying too much about *ifInOctets* and *ifOutOctets*. RFC 1213 states that *ifOutOctets* and *ifInOctets* are the total number of octets sent and received on an interface, including framing characters.

In many environments, this information is crucial. Companies such as Internet service providers (ISPs) make their livelihoods by providing usable bandwidth to their customers, and thus spend huge amounts of time and money monitoring and measuring their interfaces, circuits, etc. When these pipes fill up or get clogged, customers get upset. So the big question is, how can you monitor bandwidth effectively? Being able to answer this question is often a life and death issue.

The information you need to answer this question comes in a few parts. First, you must know what type of line you are trying to monitor. Without this information, the numbers don't mean much. Then you must find the line's maximum speed and determine whether it is used in full- or half-duplex mode. In most cases, you can find both of these pieces of information using SNMP. The *ifSpeed* object defined in MIB-II's *interfaces* table provides "an estimate of the interface's current bandwidth in bits per second." You can poll this object to find the line's maximum speed, or at least what the agent thinks the line's maximum speed should be. Note, though, that you must watch for some pitfalls. For example, Cisco routers have default maximum bandwidths for various types of links, but these defaults may not have much to do with reality: for instance, the default bandwidth for a serial line is 1.544 Mbps, regardless of the actual line speed. To get meaningful data, you must configure the router to report the maximum bandwidth correctly. (Sometimes, network administrators intentionally set the interface bandwidth to an incorrect number to nudge routing paths a different way. If this is the case, you're going to have trouble getting meaningful data out of SNMP.)

It's easier to get reliable information about the line's duplex mode. Serial lines operate in full-duplex mode. This means they can send and receive information at the same time (e.g., a 56 Kbps serial line can upload and download at 56 Kbps simultaneously, for a total of 112 Kbps). Other types of lines, such as 10BaseT Ethernet, can handle only half duplex. In a typical 10BaseT environment, the distinction between uploading and downloading data is meaningless; total bandwidth through the line is limited to 10 Mbps of input and output combined. Some devices have 10/100 cards in them, which makes identification even harder.

Many vendors have private MIBs that return the duplex state. For example, the following Cisco object returns the duplex state for an interface on the model 2900 switch: *iso.org.dod.internet.private.enterprises.cisco.ciscoMgmt.ciscoC2900MIB. c2900MIBObjects.c2900Port.c2900PortTable.c2900PortEntry.c2900PortDuplexStatus.*

The table to which this object belongs also contains an object that can be used to switch an interface's duplex state. This object is useful if you have a device that is incorrectly negotiating half duplex instead of full duplex; you can use it to force the port into the correct duplex state.

Once you find the line's maximum speed and duplex mode, you can calculate its utilization percentage. Many NMS products let you create *expressions*, which are named formulas that use MIB objects as variables. OpenView allows you to define expressions in the file *$OV_CONF/mibExpr.conf.* The syntax used in this file is complicated. Expressions are written in postfix notation.* The file contains some entries by default; these expressions are often useful, and may not need any tweaking† to work for your environment. Here is the default definition of the expression `If%util`:

```
If%util \
"Percent of available bandwidth utilized on an interface\n\
Computed by:\n\
    (Received byte rate + transmitted byte rate) * 8\n\
    ------------------------------------------------\n\
                    interface link speed\n\
then converted to a percentage."\
.1.3.6.1.2.1.2.2.1.10. \
.1.3.6.1.2.1.2.2.1.16. \
+ \
8 \
* \
.1.3.6.1.2.1.2.2.1.5. \
/ \
100 \
*
```

This expression is broken up into three parts: an expression name, comments, and the expression itself. We will use the expression name within *xnmgraph* for our data-collection definitions. The comments will help us understand what this expression really does. The syntax of the expression is defined in the *mibExpr.conf*(4) manpage. In short, it adds the values of two MIB objects (*ifInOctets* and *ifOut-Octets*), multiplies by 8 to get the number of bits traveling through the interface, divides by the interface speed (*ifSpeed*), and converts the result to a percentage. As you can see here, you can break expressions into several lines by using the familiar Unix backslash-escape at the end of each line.

Once we have defined `If%util`, we can use it to plot utilization with *xnmgraph*:

```
$ /opt/OV/bin/xnmgraph -monochrome -c public -poll 5 -title Ifutil_Formula -mib \
If%util:CiscoRouter1a:::.1.3.6.1.2.1.2.2.1.2:::" CiscoRouter14a
```

This displays a graph of the percent utilization for every interface on the device *CiscoRouter14a*. Note that you can use an expression name as the first of the colon-separated arguments in the *xnmgraph* command.

Before you start using `If%util` to measure your entire organization, notice that this expression measures only half-duplex lines—that is, it compares the sum of the input and output octets to the line's capacity. Any full-duplex line graphed

---

* Also referred to as "reverse Polish notation." Instead of writing "1 + 2", you would write "1 2 +".

† The recommended way to modify *$OV_CONF/mibExpr.conf* is to use *xnmcollect* with the *–delExpr* or *–loadExpr* switch.

with this calculation will look wrong. To prove this point, consider a full-duplex serial line with a maximum speed of 500 Kbps in each direction that is currently sending 125 Kbps and receiving 125 Kbps. The formula for `If%util` gives us a utilization of 50%, which is incorrect: the line is really at 25% of capacity. For a full-duplex line, it makes more sense to make separate computations for incoming and outgoing data. This gives you a better representation of what your network is doing, since in full-duplex mode the incoming data rate isn't affected by the outgoing data. Here are revised expressions for send utilization (`WANIF%SendUtil`) and receive utilization (`WANIF%RecvUtil`):

```
WANIf%SendUtil \
"% interface utilization from (ifOutOctets * 8 * 100) / ifSpeed"\
.1.3.6.1.2.1.2.2.1.16. \
8 \
* \
100 \
* \
.1.3.6.1.2.1.2.2.1.5. \
/

WANIf%RecvUtil \
"% interface utilization from (ifInOctets * 8 * 100) / ifSpeed"\
.1.3.6.1.2.1.2.2.1.10. \
8 \
* \
100 \
* \
.1.3.6.1.2.1.2.2.1.5. \
/
```

Now let's take a look at some actual graphs. We graphed different expressions and MIB objects at the same time for a 10BaseT (half-duplex) Ethernet interface. We then created some traffic on the interface and captured the results. Here is the script that generates the graphs:

```
/opt/OV/bin/xnmgraph -monochrome -c public -poll 5 -title \
Cisco_Private_Local_Mib -mib \
".1.3.6.1.4.1.9.2.2.1.1.6:CiscoRouter1a:4:::.1.3.6.1.2.1.2.2.1.2:::,\
.1.3.6.1.4.1.9.2.2.1.1.8:CiscoRouter1a:4:::.1.3.6.1.2.1.2.2.1.2:::" \
CiscoRouter1a &

/opt/OV/bin/xnmgraph -monochrome -c public -poll 5 -title Ifutil_Formula \
-mib "If%util:CiscoRouter1a:4:::.1.3.6.1.2.1.2.2.1.2:::" CiscoRouter1a &

/opt/OV/bin/xnmgraph -monochrome -c public -poll 5 -title \
WANIfRecvUtil_Formula -mib \
"WANIf%RecvUtil:CiscoRouter1a:4:::.1.3.6.1.2.1.2.2.1.2:::" CiscoRouter1a &

/opt/OV/bin/xnmgraph -monochrome -c public -poll 5 -title
WANIfSendUtil_Formula -mib \
"WANIf%SendUtil:CiscoRouter1a:4:::.1.3.6.1.2.1.2.2.1.2:::" CiscoRouter1a &
```

```
/opt/OV/bin/xnmgraph -monochrome -c public -poll 5 -title ifInOctets -mib \
".1.3.6.1.2.1.2.2.1.10:CiscoRouter1a:4::::.1.3.6.1.2.1.2.2.1.2:::" \
CiscoRouter1a &

/opt/OV/bin/xnmgraph -monochrome -c public -poll 5 -title ifOutOctets -mib \
".1.3.6.1.2.1.2.2.1.16:CiscoRouter1a:4::::.1.3.6.1.2.1.2.2.1.2:::" \
CiscoRouter1a &
```

Figure A-1 shows the MIB objects *.iso.org.dod.internet.private.enterprises.cisco.local.linterfaces.lifTable.lifEntry.locIfInBitsSec* and *.iso.org.dod.internet.private.enterprises.cisco.local.linterfaces.lifTable.lifEntry.locIfOutBitsSec*. These are private Cisco MIB objects that report the data rate in and out of an interface, in bits per second.

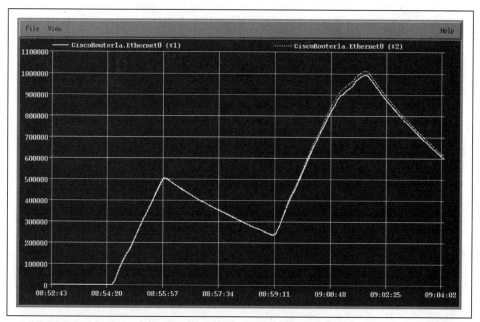

Figure A-1. Graph of Cisco private MIB objects

The next graph, shown in Figure A-2, shows the expression `If%util`. It's surprisingly different. The difference arises because Cisco uses a five-minute decaying average for these two objects. This can be both good and bad. The decaying average can prevent you from seeing local peaks and valleys in usage. In this example, we see two usage peaks, which the decaying average smears over a longer period of time. When using vendors' private MIBs, be sure to find out how they calculate their numbers.

Figures A-3 and A-4 show the `WANIf%RecvUtil` and `WANIf%SendUtil` expressions. Since this is a half-duplex interface we don't need to look at each direction (in and out) separately, but it may help to verify whether the receive path or the send path is maxed out. Comparing Figure A-3 with Figure A-4 shows that we are sending a bit more traffic than we are receiving.

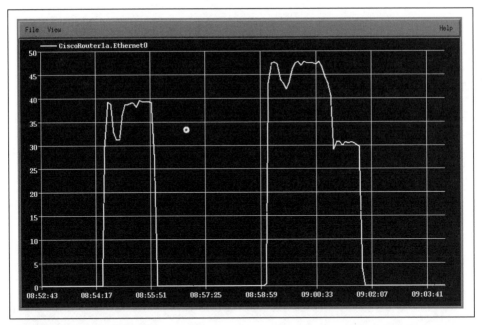

Figure A-2. Graph of If%util

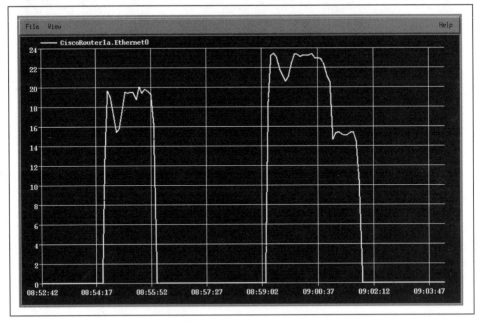

Figure A-3. Graph of WANIf%RecvUtil

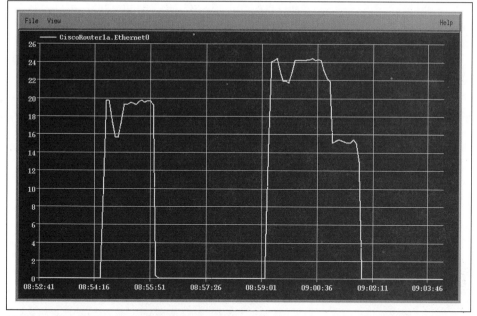

Figure A-4. Graph of WANIf%SendUtil

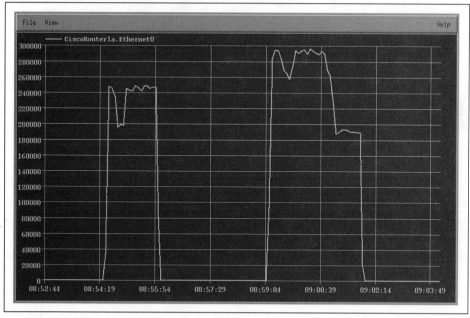

Figure A-5. Graph of ifInOctets

The standard MIB-II objects *ifInOctets* and *ifOutOctets* are graphed in Figure A-5 and Figure A-6. Remember that these do not show bits per second. Again, these graphs show that we are sending more traffic than we are receiving. The octet graphs in Figures A-5 and A-6 show a real-time picture, like the WAN expressions but unlike Cisco's private MIB objects.

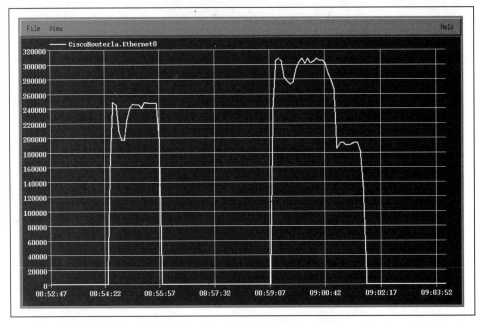

Figure A-6. Graph of ifOutOctets

Try to get a feel for what you are looking for before you start writing expressions. Are you trying to find someone who is flooding the network, or just looking for a weekly average? No matter what you are graphing, be sure to research the device's MIB objects before you start generating graphs that may look good but contain meaningless data. Recheck the variables each time you create new graphs.

Keep in mind that some devices have the ability to switch from full to half duplex automatically. You should be aware of your interface's saturation point, which is the point at which no more traffic can be sent or received. This saturation point is indicated in your graphs by a sustained horizontal ceiling line and can really be seen only over extended periods of time. Thus, while there are some horizontal lines in the graphs in this appendix, we are obviously not close to the interface's capacity.

If you plan to use graphs like these, be sure to plan for the average and not for the exceptions (peaks). All networks have traffic spikes here and there; unless you like spending a lot more on telecommunications than you need to, you should plan your network so that it is geared toward servicing your average day-to-day activities, not the occasional peak.

B

More on OpenView's NNM

By now you should be familiar with OpenView's NNM and its supporting utilities. Even though many network administrators can get by with the basic OpenView information provided in this book, there is much more to learn. Configuring NNM with your own custom tools makes using it that much better.

While we can't cover all the features of NNM in this appendix, we'll discuss each of the following:

- Using external data with *xnmgraph*

- Inserting additional menu items into NNM's menu

- Creating NNM profiles for different users

- Using NNM as a centralized communication device

Using External Data

Chapter 9 introduced the *xnmgraph* command, but only touched on its features. One particularly useful feature is the ability to graph data from external sources. To see how you might graph external data, first generate a graph of any type—one of the graphs we created in Chapter 9 will do—and save the data to a file. Then examine the contents of the file. Each output file contains a short tutorial showing how to reshow the graph. Be sure to look at *$APP_DEFS/Xnmgraph*, which contains *xnmgraph*'s default settings.

Here's a table we created by hand, copying the format of a standard *xnmgraph* datafile. The data points are organized into streams. A *stream* is a set of data that will be plotted as a single curve on the graph. All the streams in the file will be combined into a single graph with multiple curves. The **StartTime** is ignored.

The `StopTime` provides the value for the X (horizontal) axis and the `Value` provides the value for the Y (vertical) axis:

```
# /tmp/data1
#
# Stream Number StartTime     StopTime                     Value
# ------------- ---------     -------------------          -----
#
# Start of Stream 1
#
   1             0            04.28.2001-12:32:16          7
   1             0            04.28.2001-12:32:20          3
   1             0            04.28.2001-12:32:24          23
   1             0            04.28.2001-12:32:28          4
   1             0            04.28.2001-12:32:31          7
   1             0            04.28.2001-12:32:35          12
   1             0            04.28.2001-12:32:39          1
#
# Start of Stream 2
#
   2             0            04.28.2001-12:32:16          17
   2             0            04.28.2001-12:32:20          21
   2             0            04.28.2001-12:32:24          8
   2             0            04.28.2001-12:32:28          28
   2             0            04.28.2001-12:32:31          2
   2             0            04.28.2001-12:32:35          22
   2             0            04.28.2001-12:32:39          9
```

The following *xnmgraph* command displays our datafile. Notice that we use stream numbers, preceded by minus signs, instead of object IDs. The minus sign indicates that the stream can take on negative values. If the stream number is preceded by a + or = sign, *xnmgraph* will take the absolute value of all negative numbers in the datafile.

```
cat /tmp/data1 | xnmgraph -mib "-1:Stream One:::::::,-2:Stream Two:::::::"
```

Figure B-1 shows the result of this command. If your graph looks squished, right-click on it and then left-click on "Show All." An option under the View menu lets you generate a black-and-white graph, which is often more effective if you have only a small number of streams.

Now that we can get data into a format that *xnmgraph* can display, let's see if we can generate some graphs from the output of the Unix *vmstat* utility. *vmstat* should be familiar to all Unix administrators; it provides a lot of information about your memory system, in a cumbersome format. Here's the kind of output *vmstat* produces:

```
 procs     memory            page            disk          faults      cpu
 r b w   swap  free  re  mf pi po fr de sr s6 s2 s2 sd   in   sy   cs us sy id
 0 4 0 5431056 33672  1 2371 0  8  8  0  0  0 18 18  2 2161 5583 4490 17 14 69
 0 2 0 5430912 33576  1 2499 0 20 20  0  0  0  1  1  0 2997 8374 7030 25 18 58
```

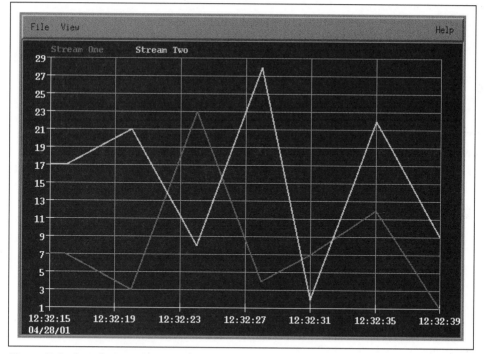

Figure B-1. Sample OpenView graph

```
0 2 0 5431296 33824  0  179  4  0    0    0  0  0  0  0  1 2587 3990 6379 18  8 74
0 0 0 5431240 33792  1 2460  4  8    8    0  0  0  1  1  0 2909 7768 7080 25 18 57
0 3 0 5431216 33768  1 2359  0 12   12    0  0  0  2  2  0 1934 5057 3818 18 13 70
0 0 0 5431288 33824  0  136  0  0    0    0  0  0  0  0  1 1842 2190 3803 13  5 82
0 2 0 5431216 32920  2 1189  0 3196 3176  0  0  0  0  0  4 2734 9980 5642 24 11 65
0 4 0 5431032 32352  8 1571  0 3100 3044  0  0  0  2  2  5 2763 7767 5817 22 15 63
```

Imagine taking 10,000 lines of this output and trying to figure out the trends (min/avg/max) in any given parameter. It's not easy. But with some help from a Perl script, we can massage this data into an *xnmgraph* input file. Here is what our Perl script looks like:

```perl
#!/usr/local/bin/perl
# Filename: /usr/local/bin/perl_scripts/cputimes

$|++; # Unbuffer the output!

open(VMSTAT,"/bin/vmstat 2 |") || die "Can't Open VMStat";
while($CLINE=<VMSTAT>)
{
    ($null,$r,$b,$w,$swap,$free,$re,$mf,$pi,$po,$fr,$de,$sr,$aa,$dd1,\
$dd2,$f0,$in,$sy,$cs,$us,$sycpu,$id) = split(/\s+/,$CLINE);

    if (($id) && ($id ne "id"))
```

```
    {
        $DATE = `date +%m.%d.%y-%H:%M:%S`;
        chomp $DATE;
        print "1 0 $DATE $us \n";
        print "2 0 $DATE $sycpu \n";
        print "3 0 $DATE $id \n";
    }
    sleep 2;
}
```

This script prints the current CPU usage, as a percentage, in the User ($us),
System ($sycpu), and Idle ($ide) states; stream 1 is the User percentage, stream 2
is the System percentage, and stream 3 is the Idle percentage. The first item on
each line is the stream number; note that we can interleave the data from the three
streams:

```
[root][nms] /> /usr/local/bin/perl_scripts/cputimes
1 0 8.14.99-21:00:22 6
2 0 8.14.99-21:00:22 3
3 0 8.14.99-21:00:22 92
1 0 8.14.99-21:00:24 0
2 0 8.14.99-21:00:24 0
3 0 8.14.99-21:00:24 100
1 0 8.14.99-21:00:26 1
2 0 8.14.99-21:00:26 0
3 0 8.14.99-21:00:26 98
1 0 8.14.99-21:00:28 1
2 0 8.14.99-21:00:28 0
3 0 8.14.99-21:00:28 99
```

The following command generates a graph from the script's output:

```
/usr/local/bin/perl_scripts/cputimes | xnmgraph -title "CPU Time"  -mib \
"+1:User:::::::,+2:System:::::::,+3:Idle:::::::"
```

While this graph is based on live data, it's trivial to save data in an appropriate
format and write a script that pulls historical data from your logs and plots it with
xnmgraph.

Adding a Menu to NNM

Once you have a toolbox of scripts, adding them to an NNM menu makes them
easier to access and execute. This trick can be especially useful if you prefer to
use NNM's graphical interface.

The key to adding custom menus is the directory *$OV_REGISTRATION/C*. (*$OV_
REGISTRATION* contains directories for all the languages available on your system;
C is the directory for the default language and is probably where you should start.)
The *C* directory contains all the files that make up the menu system you see when
you run NNM. For example, the file *ovw* contains the familiar options from the
main window (New, Open, Refresh, etc.).

Let's look at the *$OV_REGISTRATION/C/ovsnmp/xnmloadmib* file. It's fairly easy to see how to hook an external command into a menu. Let's jump right in and create a menu that is two levels deep with two menu choices:

```
Application "Graph Menu"
{
        Menubar <100> "Local_Graphs" _p
        {
          <100> "Network"        _N f.menu "network_menu";
        }

        Menu "network_menu"
        {
          <90> "5 Minute CPU"    _M f.action "5mincpu";
          <90> "Bits In and Out For All Up Interfaces"  \
                             _B f.action "bit_for_all_up";
        }

        Action "5mincpu" {
          Command "/opt/OV/local/scripts/Cisco_5min_cpu \
                                \"${OVwSelections}\"";
          MinSelected    1;
          MaxSelected    7;
          SelectionRule  (isSNMPSupported || isSNMPProxied) ;
        }

        Action "bit_for_all_up" {
          Command "/opt/OV/local/scripts/Cisco_Line_Up_Bits \
                                \"${OVwSelections}\"";
          MinSelected    1;
          MaxSelected    3;
          SelectionRule  (isSNMPSupported || isSNMPProxied) ;
        }
}
```

Create a file within *$OV_REGISTRATION/C* and insert the previous code listing. Once this is done, run *ovw* with the *–verify* switch, which checks for errors.* You may see errors or warnings about your new menu item but, if you're successful, you'll see an item that looks like the menu in Figure B-2.

NNM can be picky with registration files. If you can't see your menu, try the *ovw –verify* trick. If it reveals no errors, take some entries out and restart *ovw*. Keep doing this until your items appear. You should also break up your menu items into multiple files. Do not put all your menus and actions into one file. The more files you have, the easier it will be to diagnose and troubleshoot your new menu items.

---

* Do not leave any backup files within any of the directories, because NNM takes each file seriously. Backup or redundant files will produce warnings when you run *ovw*.

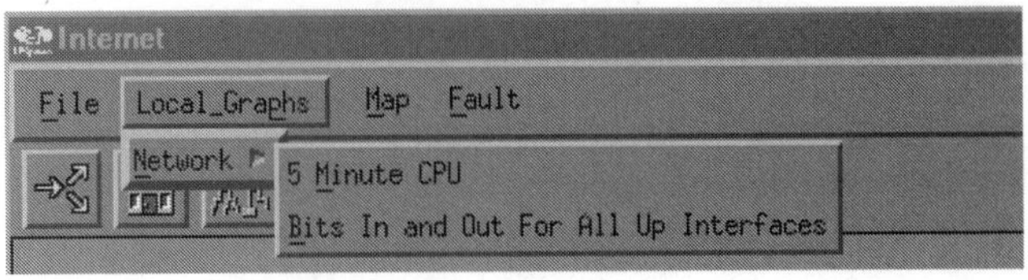

Figure B-2. A new menu

Let's talk about some commonalties within our registration file:

- Each menu and menu item is associated with a keyboard shortcut that allows the user to access it. The trigger character is preceded by an underscore. For example, from the "Local_Graphs → Network" menu, you can hit "M" to go to the "5 Minute CPU" item.

- Each menu item has a precedence number within angle brackets. This allows you to control the order in which items appear. Items with the highest precedence appear first in a menu; items with the same precedence are listed in the order in which they appear in the file. For example, if we reduce the precedence of "5 Minute CPU" from <90> to <80> it will appear after the "Bits In and Out" menu item, because the higher-precedence item comes first.

The `Menubar` entry contains the menus that will appear in the top NNM menu bar. We used the function `f.menu` to call a submenu. The following code shows how we could have used `f.action` to call an action directly:

```
Menubar <precedence> "menubar Label" _MnemonicChar
    {
        <precedence> "SubMenu Label" _MnemonicChar f.menu "menu-name"
        <precedence> "Action Name" _MnemonicChar f.action "action-name"
    }
```

A `Menu` looks and behaves like the menu bar (or menu) that contains it, with a few differences. `Menus` don't declare mnemonic characters or precedence; these are defined by the containing menu or menu bar. The *menu-name* is the linking name that appears after `f.menu`.

```
Menu "menu-name"
    {
        <precedence> "SubMenu Label" _MnemonicChar f.menu   "menu-name"
        <precedence> "Action Name" _MnemonicChar f.action "action-name"
    }
```

`Actions` are called just like `Menus`. The *action-name* is the linking name of an action that gets called when selected from a previous item (either a `Menu` or a `Menubar`):

```
Action "action-name"
    {
```

```
            Command "/opt/OV/local/scripts/Cisco_5min_cpu \"${OVwSelections}\"";
            MinSelected     1;
            MaxSelected     7;
            SelectionRule   (isSNMPSupported || isSNMPProxied) ;
       }
```

There are a few additional parameters in our **Action** declaration:

- **Command** specifies which program or script should be executed. The `\"${OVwSelections}\"` at the end of the command string passes all currently selected objects to the program as arguments.

- **MinSelected** declares how many nodes must be selected before this item becomes available. If nothing is selected, the corresponding menu choice will be grayed out and unclickable.

- **MaxSelected** works the same way, but declares the maximum number of objects that can be selected.

- **SelectionRule** uses capability fields* within a logical statement. These rules declare what is necessary for the selection to be deemed a "good selection."

Action declarations can contain many additional parameters, as can registration files. The examples we've given should be enough to get you going in the right direction. The *OVwRegIntro(5)* manpage defines the syntax of the registration files in detail; read this page carefully if you're serious about adding custom menu items.

Profiles for Different Users

Some users may have specific ways in which they want to use NNM. For example, an operator who is watching the network for problems may need a fairly limited set of menus and tools; a senior network engineer might want a substantially larger set of options. You can use the *$OV_REGISTRATION* directory and the $OVwRegDir environment variable to customize NNM on a per-user basis.

The previous section shows how to add menus by modifying files in the *$OV_REGISTRATION/C* directory. By default, this is the directory NNM uses when it starts. However, you can create as many profiles as you need under the *$OV_REGISTRATION* directory. Once you have created another profile directory, you can change the $OVwRegDir environment variable to point to that new directory. Then, when NNM starts, it will use the new profile.

One way to set up user-specific profiles is to create an account that anyone can use for starting an NNM session. With this account, the network map is opened

---

* Check out $OV_FIELDS for more definitions of capability fields.

read-only* and has only the minimal menus ("File → Exit," "Map → Refresh," "Fault → Alarms," etc.). Create a new profile for this account in the directory *$OV_REGISTRATION/skel* by copying all the files in the default profile *$OV_REGISTRATION/C* to the new *skel* directory. Then modify this profile by removing most of the menu choices, thus preventing the operator from being able run any external commands.† To start NNM using this profile, you must point the $OVwRegDir environment variable to the new profile directory. To test the new profile, give the following Bourne shell commands:

```
[root][nms] /> OVwRegDir=/etc/opt/OV/share/registration/skel
[root][nms] /> export OVwRegDir
[root][nms] /> $OV_BIN/ovw
```

Once you're confident that this new profile works, create an account for running NNM with minimal permissions and, in the startup script for that account, set $OVwRegDir appropriately (i.e., to point to your skeleton configuration). Then make sure that users can't run NNM from their normal accounts—perhaps by limiting execute access for NNM to a particular group, which will force users not in that group to use the special account when they want to run NNM. You should also make sure that the users you don't trust can't modify the *$OV_REGISTRATION* directory or its subdirectories.

Using NNM for Communications

One of the more exotic ways to use SNMP is as a tool for passing messages back and forth. For example, it's certainly useful to know that the Oracle database has gone down, but it's even more useful to send messages to key users notifying them that the database has crashed or that it's going down for maintenance at the end of the day. In a small environment, it's easy to come up with hacks that provide various kinds of notification. But in a large company with many offices, it's useful to have a standard way for communicating with other departments. NNM's Event Categories is the perfect tool to use as a centralized communication device.

Imagine a web interface that allows you to send traps to Event Categories. Filling out a simple form in a browser automatically generates a trap that is posted to the appropriate categories. Figure B-3 shows such an interface.

---

* When starting NNM via the command line, use *$OV_BIN/ovw –ro* to open the default map in read-only mode. This will prevent the user from making any map changes (moves, add, deletes, etc.).

† Just because a map is opened read-only does *not* mean that users cannot make changes to the backend of NNM. A user who has the ability to launch the menu items can make changes just like the superuser can. The best way to prevent these changes is to take out any/all configuration menu options.

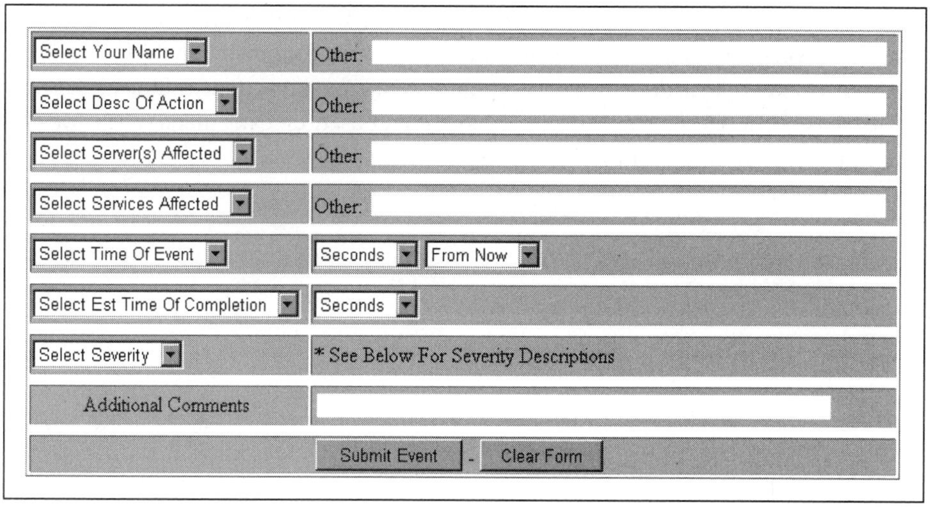

Figure B-3. SNMP web interface

What types of questions does everyone (you, managers, users, etc.) ask when there's a problem? The most typical ones are:

Who is in charge? Name, phone, pager

What is going on? Reboot, upgrade, failure

What servers are affected? Production, test, development

What services are affected? Mail, news, database, web server

When did this happen? E.g., 10 minutes ago, 4 days from now

When will this be fixed? E.g., immediately, tomorrow

What is the severity? Normal, Warning, Minor, Major, Critical

All these questions can be answered using the HTML form in Figure B-3. The CGI script or Java servlet that processes the form can refuse to accept the form until the user has filled in all the fields, guaranteeing that you have complete and consistent information.

Setting up a reporting system like this is not very difficult. You can use any standard web server,* a little HTML, and your favorite language for processing the form. Once you parse the output from the form, you can use any of the trap-generation programs we've discussed to send the trap. This trap will then show up in one of NNM's Event Categories. (If you're not using NNM, we've discussed other trap daemons that can be used to receive the trap and notify users. However, NNM is convenient because it will do everything for you.)

---

* Check out *http://www.apache.org* for more information on a free Unix or NT web server.

The key to this whole setup is getting people to use and watch NNM. If it isn't used by everyone, this mechanism really doesn't accomplish anything. Training users in nontechnical departments to watch NNM for important notifications may not be easy, but if you succeed you'll have created an elegant mechanism for getting important information to users.

C

Net-SNMP Tools

This appendix provides brief summaries of the command-line tools included in Version 4.2 of the Net-SNMP package (available from *http://net-snmp.sourceforge.net*).

Rather than trying to describe all the options to all the commands, we've focused on those that are most important and useful. We have also pointed out a few cases in which the behavior of the commands differs from the behavior that's described in the manual pages. Unfortunately, there are many discrepancies. The current situation is obviously far from ideal, but hopefully either the documentation or the commands will be fixed in some later release.

Net-SNMP and MIB Files

By default, Net-SNMP reads the MIB files in the directory */usr/local/share/snmp/mibs*. When you install Net-SNMP it populates this directory with a few dozen MIB files, including the UCD MIB (Net-SNMP used to be called UCD-SNMP) and RFC 1213 MIB (MIB-II). Net-SNMP uses the MIB files to translate between numeric object IDs and their textual representations. The MIB files also give the tools access to information about each object (its syntax, the type of access allowed, its description, etc.). Adding a vendor-specific MIB file to Net-SNMP is as simple as placing it in the *mibs* directory and setting the environment variable $MIBS to *ALL*, as discussed in the next section.

Common Command-Line Arguments

For the most part, the Net-SNMP commands follow a similar command structure; they share many options and use roughly the same syntax. For example, in the abstract, an *snmpget* command looks like this:

```
snmpget options hostname community objectID...
```

In other words, the command name is followed by a series of options, the hostname of the system you want to poll, the community string, and one or more object IDs. (Note that you can use the *−c* community option instead of placing the community string after the hostname. You can also provide a default hostname in your *snmp.conf* file.) The syntax of *snmpset* is only slightly different; because *snmpset* changes object values, it requires you to specify the object's datatype and the new value:

```
snmpset options hostname community objectID type value...
```

Table C-1 summarizes some of the most useful options that are common to all Net-SNMP commands. See the *snmpcmd*(1) manpage for a complete list.

Table C-1. Summary of Command-Line Options

Option	Description
−m	Specifies which MIB modules you would like the command to load. If you want the command to parse the MIB file for a particular vendor, copy the MIB file to */usr/local/share/snmp/mibs* and invoke the command with the option *−m ALL*. The argument *ALL* forces the command to read all the MIB files in the directory. Setting the environment variable $MIBS to *ALL* achieves the same thing. If you don't want the command to read all the MIB files, you can follow the *−m* option with a colon-separated list of the MIB files you want parsed.
−M	Allows you to specify a colon-separated list of directories to search for MIB files. This option is useful if you don't want to copy MIB files into the default MIB location. Setting the shell variable $MIBDIRS has the same effect.
−IR	Performs a random-access search through the MIB database for an OID label. By default, the commands assume that you specify an object ID relative to *.iso.org.dod.internet.mgmt.mib-2*. In practice, this option allows you to avoid typing long OIDs for objects that aren't under the *mib-2* subtree. For example, there's a group of objects in the Cisco MIB named *lcpu*. If you use the *−IR* option, you can retrieve objects in this group without typing the entire OID; the following command is sufficient: `snmpget -IR hostname community lcpu.2` If there is more than one object with the given name, the Net-SNMP tools will access the first object they find. Since this feature is billed as a random-access search, there's no way to predict which object the tools will find first. Within the standard MIBs, objects rarely (if ever) have the same name, but there's no guarantee that any name will be unique, particularly if you're using vendor-specific MIBs.
−On	Prints OIDs numerically (e.g., *.1.3.6.1.2.1.1.3.0*). Note that the *−O* options can be combined, as long as the combination makes sense.
−Of	Prints the entire OID (i.e., starting with *.1*).
−Os	Displays only the final part of the OID, in symbolic form (e.g., *sysUpTime.0*).
−OS	Same as *−Os*, but prefixes the object name with the name of the MIB file from which the object is taken (e.g., *SNMPv2-MIB::sysUpTime.0*).
−T	Specifies whether the command should use TCP or UDP as the transport-layer protocol. UDP is the default; *−T tcp* uses TCP.

Table C-1. Summary of Command-Line Options (continued)

Option	Description
−*v*	Specifies which version of SNMP to use. By default, the commands use Version 1. Valid options are −*v 1*, −*v 2c*, and −*v 3*. Note that some commands, such as *snmpbulkget*, are available only for Versions 2c and 3.
−*h*	Displays help information for the command.
−*c*	Specifies the community string for the command. Alternately, you can place the community string after the hostname and omit the −*c* option.

Net-SNMP Command-Line Tools

This section briefly describes each of the Net-SNMP tools. By default, installing Net-SNMP places all these commands in */usr/local/bin*. All the examples in this section assume that */usr/local/bin* is in your path.

snmpwalk

snmpwalk performs the *get-next* operation. We've used it throughout the book, so it should be familiar; in this section, we'll use it to demonstrate some of the options introduced in Table C-1.

Let's say you want to perform an *snmpwalk* against a Cisco router. If you don't have any Cisco MIBs installed, here's what you will see:

```
$ snmpwalk cisco.ora.com public .1.3.6.1.4.1.9
enterprises.9.2.1.1.0 = "..System Bootstrap, Version 11.2(17)GS2, [htseng 180]
EARLY DEPLOYMENT RELEASE SOFTWARE (fc1)..Copyright (c) 1999 by Cisco Systems,
Inc..."
enterprises.9.2.1.2.0 = "reload"
enterprises.9.2.1.3.0 = "cisco"
enterprises.9.2.1.4.0 = "ora.com"
enterprises.9.2.1.5.0 = IpAddress: 127.45.23.1
enterprises.9.2.1.6.0 = IpAddress: 0.0.0.0
enterprises.9.2.1.8.0 = 131890952
enterprises.9.2.1.9.0 = 456
enterprises.9.2.1.10.0 = 500
enterprises.9.2.1.11.0 = 17767568
enterprises.9.2.1.12.0 = 0
enterprises.9.2.1.13.0 = 0
enterprises.9.2.1.14.0 = 104
enterprises.9.2.1.15.0 = 600
...
```

Recall that *.1.3.6.1.4.1* is *.iso.org.dod.internet.private.enterprises*, and 9 is Cisco's private enterprise number. Therefore, the previous command is walking the entire Cisco subtree, which is very large; we've deleted most of its output. The output you see isn't very readable because we haven't yet installed the Cisco MIBs, so the *snmpwalk* command has no way of providing human-readable object names. We just have to guess what these objects are.

This problem is easy to solve. Copy the Cisco MIBs[*] to the main Net-SNMP repository (*/usr/local/share/snmp/mibs*) and use the *-m ALL* command-line option. With this option, *snmpwalk* parses all the files in the MIB repository. As a result we get the object IDs in string (human-readable) form, and we can walk the *cisco* subtree by name rather than specifying its complete numeric object ID (*.1.3.6.1.4.1.9*):

```
$ snmpwalk -m ALL cisco.ora.com public cisco
enterprises.cisco.local.lcpu.1.0 = "..System Bootstrap, Version 11.2(17)GS2,
[htseng 180] EARLY DEPLOYMENT RELEASE SOFTWARE (fc1)..Copyright (c) 1999 by Cisco
Systems, Inc..."
enterprises.cisco.local.lcpu.2.0 = "reload"
enterprises.cisco.local.lcpu.3.0 = "cisco"
enterprises.cisco.local.lcpu.4.0 = "ora.com"
enterprises.cisco.local.lcpu.5.0 = IpAddress: 127.45.23.1
enterprises.cisco.local.lcpu.6.0 = IpAddress: 0.0.0.0
enterprises.cisco.local.lcpu.8.0 = 131888844
enterprises.cisco.local.lcpu.9.0 = 456
enterprises.cisco.local.lcpu.10.0 = 500
enterprises.cisco.local.lcpu.11.0 = 17767568
enterprises.cisco.local.lcpu.12.0 = 0
enterprises.cisco.local.lcpu.13.0 = 0
enterprises.cisco.local.lcpu.14.0 = 104
enterprises.cisco.local.lcpu.15.0 = 600
...
```

Now let's trim the output by adding the *-Os* option, which omits the initial part of each OID:

```
$ snmpwalk -m ALL -Os cisco.ora.com public cisco
lcpu.1.0 = "..System Bootstrap, Version 11.2(17)GS2, [htseng 180] EARLY
DEPLOYMENT RELEASE SOFTWARE (fc1)..Copyright (c) 1999 by Cisco Systems, Inc..."
lcpu.2.0 = "reload"
lcpu.3.0 = "cisco"
lcpu.4.0 = "ora.com"
lcpu.5.0 = IpAddress: 127.45.23.1
lcpu.6.0 = IpAddress: 0.0.0.0
lcpu.8.0 = 131888844
lcpu.9.0 = 456
lcpu.10.0 = 500
lcpu.11.0 = 17767568
lcpu.12.0 = 0
lcpu.13.0 = 0
lcpu.14.0 = 104
lcpu.15.0 = 600
...
```

---

[*] You can find many Cisco MIBs at *ftp://ftp.cisco.com/pub/mibs/*.

This output is a little easier to read, since it cuts off the redundant part of each OID. Let's take this command one step further:

```
$ snmpwalk -OsS cisco.ora.com public system
RFC1213-MIB::sysDescr.0 = "Cisco Internetwork Operating System Software ..IOS (tm)
GS Software (GSR-K4P-M), Version 12.0(15)S, EARLY DEPLOYMENT RELEASE SOFTWARE
(fc1)..TAC Support: http://www.cisco.com/cgi-bin/ibld/view.pl?i=support..
Copyright (c) 1986-2001 by Cisco Systems, Inc..."
RFC1213-MIB::sysObjectID.0 = OID: DTRConcentratorMIB::catProd.182
EXPRESSION-MIB::sysUpTimeInstance = Timeticks: (344626986) 39 days, 21:17:49.86
RFC1213-MIB::sysContact.0 = "O'Reilly Data Center"
RFC1213-MIB::sysName.0 = "cisco.ora.com"
RFC1213-MIB::sysLocation.0 = "Atlanta, GA"
RFC1213-MIB::sysServices.0 = 6
RFC1213-MIB::system.8.0 = Timeticks: (0) 0:00:00.00
```

This command walks the *system* subtree. Since the *system* group falls under *mib-2*, there is no need to use *–m ALL*; *mib-2* is one of the MIBs the Net-SNMP tools load automatically. Adding *S* to the *–O* option instructs the command to prefix each line of output with the name of the MIB file; we see that each line begins with *RFC1213-MIB*, which is the name of the file that defines *mib-2*.

snmpget

The *snmpget* command issues a single *get* operation. Its syntax is:

```
snmpget options hostname community objectID...
```

snmpbulkget

SNMPv2 provides an operation called *get-bulk*, which is implemented by the *snmpbulkget* command. *get-bulk* allows you to retrieve a chunk of information in one operation, as opposed to a single *get* or sequence of *get-next* operations. The syntax of *snmpbulkget* is:

```
snmpbulkget -v 2c options hostname community objectID
```

–v 2c is required because *get-bulk* is defined by SNMP Version 2.

There is one command-specific option, *–B nonrep rep*. *nonrep* is the number of scalar objects that this command will return; *rep* is the number of instances of each nonscalar object that the command will return. If you omit this option the default values of *nonrep* and *rep*, 1 and 100, respectively, will be used.

snmpbulkwalk

The *snmpbulkwalk* command uses the *get-bulk* command sequence to retrieve parts of a MIB. This command differs from *snmpbulkget* in that it does not need the −*B* option set; it walks the entire tree until it reaches the end or retrieves all the requested objects. Its syntax is:

```
snmpbulkwalk -v 2c options hostname community objectID
```

snmpset

The *snmpset* command is used to change, or set, the value of a MIB object. The command looks like this:

```
snmpset options hostname community objectID type value...
```

You can provide any number of objectID/type/value triples; the command will execute *set* operations for all the objects you give it. *type* is a single-character abbreviation that indicates the datatype of the object you're setting. Table C-2 lists the valid types.

Table C-2. snmpset Object Types

Abbreviation	Type
a	IP address
b[a]	Bits
d	Decimal string
D	Double
F	Float
i	Integer
I	Signed int64
n	Null
o	Object ID
s	String
t	Time ticks
u	Unsigned integer
U	Unsigned int64
x	Hexadecimal string

[a] While the manpages show this as a valid datatype, the help output from the command does not.

snmptrap

To send a trap, use the *snmptrap* command. The syntax for this command is:

```
snmptrap options hostname community trap parameters...
```

For Version 1, the following trap parameters are required:

```
enterprise-oid agent trap-type specific-type uptime objectID type value...
```

This command is discussed in detail in Chapter 10. Each object ID/type/value triplet specifies a variable binding to be included with the trap; you may include any number of variable bindings. Note that the agent and the uptime are not optional; however, if you provide an empty string (`""`) as a placeholder they default to the IP address of the system sending the trap and the system's current uptime.

The parameters are simpler for Version 2 traps, largely because traps (now called *notifications*) are full-fledged MIB objects in their own right. The following parameters are required:

```
snmptrap -v 2c options hostname community uptime trapoid objectID type value...
```

snmpdelta

The *snmpdelta* command monitors OIDs and tracks changes in OID values over time. Its syntax is:

```
snmpdelta options hostname community objectID...
```

snmpdelta requires you to specify the OID of an integer-valued scalar object—it can't monitor tables. For example, if you want to want to watch the octets arriving on an interface, you can't just specify *ifInOctets*; you must specify the interface number in addition to the object name (e.g., *ifInOctets.3*). By default, *snmpdelta* polls the given object every second.

Table C-3 lists some of the *snmpdelta*-specific options. There are many problems with the documentation for this command, but if you stick to the options listed below you should be on firm ground.

Table C-3. snmpdelta Options

Option	Description
−t	The documentation says "Determine time interval from the monitored entity." It's not clear what this means, but you seem to need this entry to get nonzero readings.
−s	Display a timestamp with every set of results.
−m	Print the maximum value obtained.
−l	Write the output to a file. The filename is in the form *hostname-OID*. For example, if you want to monitor the variables *ifInOctets.3* and *ifOutOctets.3* on the host router, the −l option will create two files, *hostname-ifInOctets.3* and *hostname-ifOutOctets.3*, where the output of *snmpdelta* will be written. (Note that this output has no apparent connection to the configuration, as the documentation claims.)
−p	Specify the polling interval (the default is 1 second).
−T	Print output in tabular format.

snmpdf

snmpdf works exactly like the Unix *df* command, except it uses SNMP to query hosts on a network. Its syntax is:

```
snmpdf -Cu options... hostname community
```

The *–Cu* option tells the command to consult the Net-SNMP private MIB. The Host Resources MIB is used by default.

snmpgetnext

The *snmpgetnext* command uses the *get-next* operation to retrieve the next object from a host. For example, if you ask it to perform a *get-next* for *ifOutOctets.4* it will retrieve the next object in the MIB tree, which will probably be *ifOutOctets.5*. (If the machine you're polling has only four interfaces, you'll get the next object in the MIB, whatever that happens to be. You should also be aware that there are some obscure situations that create a "hole" in the interface table, so the interface following *.4* might be *.6* or *.7.*) You can use this command to implement your own version of *snmpwalk*. The syntax is:

```
snmpgetnext options... hostname community objectID...
```

There are no options specific to *snmpgetnext.*

snmpstatus

The *snmpstatus* command retrieves status information from a host. It prints the following information:

- The IP address of the entity
- A textual description of the entity (*sysDescr.0*)
- The uptime of the entity (*sysUpTime.0*)
- The sum of received packets on all interfaces (*ifInUcastPkts.** + *ifInNUcastPkts.**)
- The sum of transmitted packets on all interfaces (*ifOutUcastPkts.** + *ifOutNUcastPkts.**)
- The number of IP input packets (*ipInReceives.0*)
- The number of IP output packets (*ipOutRequests.0*)

The syntax of *snmpstatus* is straightforward, and there are no command-specific options:

```
snmpstatus options... hostname community
```

snmptable

The *snmptable* command uses *get-next* commands to print the contents of a table in tabular form. Its syntax is:

```
snmptable options... hostname community objectID
```

The *objectID* must be the ID of a table (e.g., *ifTable*), not of an object within a table. Table C-4 lists some of the *snmptable*-specific options.

Table C-4. snmptable Options

Option	Description
−*Cf F*	Separate table columns with the string *F.* For example, −*Cf :* separates columns with a colon, which might make it easier to import the output from *snmptable* into another program.
−*Cw W*	Set the maximum width of the table to *W.* If the lines are longer than *W,* the table is split into sections. Since tables can have many columns, you almost certainly want to use this option.
−*Ci*	Prepend the index of the entry to all printed lines.
−*Cb*	Display a brief heading.
−*Cb*	Print only column headers.
−*CH*	Suppress column headers.

snmpusm

The *snmpusm* command provides simple access to the agent's *User-based Security Model* (USM) table. This is primarily used for configuring the agent's SNMPv3 features (managing users, setting and changing passphrases, etc.). This command is discussed in Appendix F.

snmpconf

This command is an interactive Perl script used to create and maintain the Net-SNMP configuration files, *snmp.conf* and *snmpd.conf.* Its syntax is:

```
snmpconf filename
```

filename must be either *snmp.conf* or *snmpd.conf.*

snmpinform

This command can be used to send an SNMPv2 trap. If you send a trap with *snmpinform,* it will wait for a response from the recipient. Note that you can send an *inform* using the *snmptrap* command if you specify −*Ci.* The options to *snmpinform* are identical to those for *snmptrap.*

snmptranslate

The Net-SNMP package comes with a handy tool called *snmptranslate* that translates between numerical and human-readable object names. More generally, it can be used to look up information from MIB files. Its syntax is:

```
snmptranslate options objectID
```

snmptranslate does not perform queries against any device, so it doesn't need the *hostname* or *community* parameters. Its sole purpose is to read MIB files and produce output about specific objects. Before looking at examples, it's worth noting that *snmptranslate*'s interpretations of the *−O* options are, to be kind, interesting. To speak more plainly, they're just plain wrong. The following examples show what actually happens when you use these options—we'll leave the rationalization to you. We expect these problems to be fixed in some later version of Net-SNMP.

Let's say you want to know the enterprise OID for Cisco Systems. The following command does the trick:

```
$ snmptranslate -m ALL -IR -Of cisco
.1.3.6.1.4.1.9
```

This tells us that Cisco's enterprise OID is *.1.3.6.1.4.9*. Note the use of the *−IR* option, which tells *snmptranslate* to do a random-access search for an object named *cisco*. If you leave this option out, *snmptranslate* will fail because it will try to locate *cisco* under the *mib-2* tree.

Let's say you want to take *.1.3.6.1.4.1.9* and convert it to its full symbolic name. That's easy:

```
$ snmptranslate -m ALL -Ofn .1.3.6.1.4.1.9
.iso.org.dod.internet.private.enterprises.cisco
```

In this case, *−IR* isn't needed because we're not performing a random-access search. *−Ofn* ensures that we print the full object ID, in symbolic (text) form. Here's what happens if we use *−Of* by itself:

```
$ snmptranslate -m ALL -Of .1.3.6.1.4.1.9
enterprises.cisco
```

As we said earlier, this is not how you'd expect *−Ofn* and *−Of* to behave. If you're writing scripts, you shouldn't count on this behavior staying the same in future versions.

Now, let's say you want to know a little bit more information about a particular object. The *−Td* option displays the object's definition as it appears in the MIB file:

```
$ snmptranslate -Td system.sysLocation
.1.3.6.1.2.1.1.6
sysLocation OBJECT-TYPE
  -- FROM              SNMPv2-MIB, RFC1213-MIB
```

```
-- TEXTUAL CONVENTION DisplayString
SYNTAX              OCTET STRING (0..255)
DISPLAY-HINT        "255a"
MAX-ACCESS          read-write
STATUS              current
DESCRIPTION         "The physical location of this node (e.g., 'telephone
                    closet, 3rd floor'). If the location is unknown, the
                    value is the zero-length string."
 ::= { iso(1) org(3) dod(6) internet(1) mgmt(2) mib-2(1) system(1) 6 }
```

—Td can save you a lot of work poking through MIB files to find an appropriate definition, particularly when combined with *—IR*. Furthermore, the last line shows you the entire object ID in both numeric and string forms, not just the object's parent. Note that the other Net-SNMP commands have an unrelated *—T* option; don't get confused. *—T* is meaningless for this command, because *snmptranslate* only looks up a local file and doesn't need to access the network.

The *—Tp* option prints an entire OID tree. The best way to understand this is to see it:

```
$ snmptranslate -Tp system
+--system(1)
   |
   +-- -R-- String     sysDescr(1)
   |         Textual Convention: DisplayString
   |         Size: 0..255
   +-- -R-- ObjID      sysObjectID(2)
   +-- -R-- TimeTicks sysUpTime(3)
   +-- -RW- String     sysContact(4)
   |         Textual Convention: DisplayString
   |         Size: 0..255
   +-- -RW- String     sysName(5)
   |         Textual Convention: DisplayString
   |         Size: 0..255
   +-- -RW- String     sysLocation(6)
   |         Textual Convention: DisplayString
   |         Size: 0..255
   +-- -R-- Integer    sysServices(7)
   +-- -R-- TimeTicks sysORLastChange(8)
   |         Textual Convention: TimeStamp
   |
   +--sysORTable(9)
      |
      +--sysOREntry(1)
         |
         +-- ---- Integer    sysORIndex(1)
         +-- -R-- ObjID      sysORID(2)
         +-- -R-- String     sysORDescr(3)
         |         Textual Convention: DisplayString
         |         Size: 0..255
         +-- -R-- TimeTicks sysORUpTime(4)
                   Textual Convention: TimeStamp
```

We displayed the *system* subtree because it's fairly short. From this output it's relatively easy to see all the objects underneath *system*, together with their types and textual conventions. This is a great way to see what objects are defined in a MIB, as well as their relationships to other objects. The output can be voluminous, but it's still a convenient way to get a map and figure out what objects are likely to be useful.

D

SNMP RFCs

This appendix provides a brief list of all the SNMP RFCs, along with the status of each RFC. This list (often referred to as the Standards Summary) was taken from *The Simple Times*, an online publication that should be familiar to anyone working with SNMP. It is used with their permission and can be found in each quarterly edition of the magazine. Please go to *http://www.simple-times.org* for information on how to subscribe to this free publication.

SMIv1 Data Definition Language

Full Standards:

> *RFC 1155*—Structure of Management Information
> *RFC 1212*—Concise MIB Definitions

Informational:

> *RFC 1215*—A Convention for Defining Traps

SMIv2 Data Definition Language

Full Standards:

> *RFC 2578*—Structure of Management Information
> *RFC 2579*—Textual Conventions
> *RFC 2580*—Conformance Statements

SNMPv1 Protocol

Full Standards:

> *RFC 1157*—Simple Network Management Protocol

Proposed Standards:

>   *RFC 1418*—SNMP over OSI
>   *RFC 1419*—SNMP over AppleTalk
>   *RFC 1420*—SNMP over IPX

SNMPv2 Protocol

Draft Standards:

>   *RFC 1905*—Protocol Operations for SNMPv2
>   *RFC 1906*—Transport Mappings for SNMPv2
>   *RFC 1907*—MIB for SNMPv2

Experimental:

>   *RFC 1901*—Community-based SNMPv2
>   *RFC 1909*—Administrative Infrastructure
>   *RFC 1910*—User-based Security Model

SNMPv3 Protocol

Draft Standards:

>   *RFC 2571*—Architecture for SNMP Frameworks
>   *RFC 2572*—Message Processing and Dispatching
>   *RFC 2573*—SNMP Applications
>   *RFC 2574*—User-based Security Model
>   *RFC 2575*—View-based Access Control Model
>   *RFC 1905*—Protocol Operations for SNMPv2
>   *RFC 1906*—Transport Mappings for SNMPv2
>   *RFC 1907*—MIB for SNMPv2

Proposed Standards:

>   *RFC 2576*—Coexistence between SNMP Versions

Informational:

>   *RFC 2570*—Introduction to SNMPv3

Experimental:

>   *RFC 2786*—Diffie-Hellman USM Key Management

SNMP Agent Extensibility

Proposed Standards:

>   *RFC 2741*—AgentX Protocol Version 1
>   *RFC 2742*—AgentX MIB

SMIv1 MIB Modules

Full Standards:

> *RFC 1213*—Management Information Base II
> *RFC 1643*—Ethernet-Like Interface Types MIB

Draft Standards:

> *RFC 1493*—Bridge MIB
> *RFC 1559*—DECnet phase IV MIB

Proposed Standards:

> *RFC 1285*—FDDI Interface Type (SMT 6.2) MIB
> *RFC 1381*—X.25 LAPB MIB
> *RFC 1382*—X.25 Packet Layer MIB
> *RFC 1414*—Identification MIB
> *RFC 1461*—X.25 Multiprotocol Interconnect MIB
> *RFC 1471*—PPP Link Control Protocol MIB
> *RFC 1472*—PPP Security Protocols MIB
> *RFC 1473*—PPP IP NCP MIB
> *RFC 1474*—PPP Bridge NCP MIB
> *RFC 1512*—FDDI Interface Type (SMT 7.3) MIB
> *RFC 1513*—RMON Token Ring Extensions MIB
> *RFC 1515*—IEEE 802.3 MAU MIB
> *RFC 1525*—Source Routing Bridge MIB
> *RFC 1742*—AppleTalk MIB

SMIv2 MIB Modules

Full Standards:

> *RFC 2819*—Remote Network Monitoring MIB

Draft Standards:

> *RFC 1657*—BGP Version 4 MIB
> *RFC 1658*—Character Device MIB
> *RFC 1659*—RS-232 Interface Type MIB
> *RFC 1660*—Parallel Printer Interface Type MIB
> *RFC 1694*—SMDS Interface Type MIB
> *RFC 1724*—RIP Version 2 MIB
> *RFC 1748*—IEEE 802.5 Interface Type MIB
> *RFC 1850*—OSPF Version 2 MIB
> *RFC 1907*—SNMPv2 MIB
> *RFC 2115*—Frame Relay DTE Interface Type MIB
> *RFC 2571*—SNMP Framework MIB

RFC 2572—SNMPv3 MPD MIB

RFC 2573—SNMP Applications MIBs

RFC 2574—SNMPv3 USM MIB

RFC 2575—SNMP VACM MIB

RFC 2790—Host Resources MIB

RFC 2863—Interfaces Group MIB

Proposed Standards:

RFC 1611—DNS Server MIB

RFC 1612—DNS Resolver MIB

RFC 1666—SNA NAU MIB

RFC 1696—Modem MIB

RFC 1697—RDBMS MIB

RFC 1747—SNA Data Link Control MIB

RFC 1749—802.5 Station Source Routing MIB

RFC 1759—Printer MIB

RFC 2006—Internet Protocol Mobility MIB

RFC 2011—Internet Protocol MIB

RFC 2012—Transmission Control Protocol MIB

RFC 2013—User Datagram Protocol MIB

RFC 2020—IEEE 802.12 Interfaces MIB

RFC 2021—RMON Version 2 MIB

RFC 2024—Data Link Switching MIB

RFC 2051—APPC MIB

RFC 2096—IP Forwarding Table MIB

RFC 2108—IEEE 802.3 Repeater MIB

RFC 2127—ISDN MIB

RFC 2128—Dial Control MIB

RFC 2206—Resource Reservation Protocol MIB

RFC 2213—Integrated Services MIB

RFC 2214—Guaranteed Service MIB

RFC 2232—Dependent LU Requester MIB

RFC 2238—High Performance Routing MIB

RFC 2266—IEEE 802.12 Repeater MIB

RFC 2287—System-Level Application Mgmt MIB

RFC 2320—Classical IP and ARP over ATM MIB

RFC 2417—Multicast over UNI 3.0/3.1 / ATM MIB

RFC 2452—IPv6 UDP MIB

RFC 2454—IPv6 TCP MIB

RFC 2455—APPN MIB

RFC 2456—APPN Trap MIB

RFC 2457—APPN Extended Border Node MIB

RFC 2465—IPv6 Textual Conventions and General Group MIB
RFC 2466—ICMPv6 MIB
RFC 2493—15 Minute Performance History TCs
RFC 2494—DS0, DS0 Bundle Interface Type MIB
RFC 2495—DS1, E1, DS2, E2 Interface Type MIB
RFC 2496—DS3/E3 Interface Type MIB
RFC 2512—Accounting MIB for ATM Networks
RFC 2513—Accounting Control MIB
RFC 2514—ATM Textual Conventions and OIDs
RFC 2515—ATM MIB
RFC 2558—SONET/SDH Interface Type MIB
RFC 2561—TN3270E MIB
RFC 2562—TN3270E Response Time MIB
RFC 2564—Application Management MIB
RFC 2576—SNMP Community MIB
RFC 2584—APPN/HPR in IP Networks
RFC 2591—Scheduling MIB
RFC 2592—Scripting MIB
RFC 2594—WWW Services MIB
RFC 2605—Directory Server MIB
RFC 2613—RMON for Switched Networks MIB
RFC 2618—RADIUS Authentication Client MIB
RFC 2619—RADIUS Authentication Server MIB
RFC 2667—IP Tunnel MIB
RFC 2662—ADSL Line MIB
RFC 2665—Ethernet-Like Interface Types MIB
RFC 2668—IEEE 802.3 MAU MIB
RFC 2669—DOCSIS Cable Device MIB
RFC 2670—DOCSIS RF Interface MIB
RFC 2677—Next Hop Resolution Protocol MIB
RFC 2720—Traffic Flow Measurement Meter MIB
RFC 2737—Entity MIB
RFC 2742—AgentX MIB
RFC 2787—Virtual Router Redundancy Protocol MIB
RFC 2788—Network Services Monitoring MIB
RFC 2789—Mail Monitoring MIB
RFC 2837—Fibre Channel Fabric Element MIB
RFC 2851—Internet Network Address TCs
RFC 2856—High Capacity Data Type TCs
RFC 2864—Interfaces Group Inverted Stack MIB
RFC 2895—RMON Protocol Identifier Reference
RFC 2925—Ping, Traceroute, Lookup MIBs

RFC 2932—IPv4 Multicast Routing MIB

RFC 2933—IGMP MIB

RFC 2940—COPS Client MIB

RFC 2954—Frame Relay Service MIB

RFC 2955—Frame Relay/ATM PVC MIB

RFC 2959—Real-Time Transport Protocol MIB

Informational:

RFC 1628—Uninterruptible Power Supply MIB

RFC 2620—RADIUS Accounting Client MIB

RFC 2621—RADIUS Accounting Server MIB

RFC 2666—Ethernet Chip Set Identifiers

RFC 2707—Print Job Monitoring MIB

RFC 2896—RMON Protocol Identifier Macros

RFC 2922—Physical Topology MIB

Experimental:

RFC 2758—SLA Performance Monitoring MIB

RFC 2786—Diffie-Hellman USM Key MIB

RFC 2934—IPv4 PIM MIB

IANA-Maintained MIB Modules

Interface Type Textual Convention
ftp://ftp.iana.org/mib/ianaiftype.mib

Address Family Numbers Textual Convention
ftp://ftp.iana.org/mib/ianaaddressfamilynumbers.mib

TN3270E Textual Conventions
ftp://ftp.iana.org/mib/ianatn3270etc.mib

Language Identifiers
ftp://ftp.iana.org/mib/ianalanguage.mib

IP Routing Protocol Textual Conventions
ftp://ftp.iana.org/mib/ianaiprouteprotocol.mib

Related Documents

Informational:

RFC 1270—SNMP Communication Services

RFC 1321—MD5 Message-Digest Algorithm

RFC 1470—Network Management Tool Catalog

RFC 2039—Applicability of Standard MIBs to WWW Server Management

RFC 2962—SNMP Application Level Gateway for Payload Address Translation

Experimental:

RFC 1187—Bulk Table Retrieval with the SNMP
RFC 1224—Techniques for Managing Asynchronously Generated Alerts
RFC 1238—CLNS MIB
RFC 1592—SNMP Distributed Program Interface
RFC 1792—TCP/IPX Connection MIB Specification
RFC 2593—Script MIB Extensibility Protocol

E

SNMP Support for Perl

This appendix summarizes Mike Mitchell's `SNMP_util` module, which we have used in our Perl scripts throughout this book. This module is distributed with Simon Leinen's SNMP Perl module; Mike's module, together with Simon's, can make SNMP programming a snap. You can get these modules from *http://www.switch.ch/misc/ leinen/snmp/perl/* or *http://www.cpan.org.*

Perl scripts need two **use** statements to take advantage of the SNMP Perl module:

```
use BER;
use SNMP_Session;
```

The `BER` and `SNMP_Session` modules make up the core of Simon's package. The `SNMP_util` module discussed in this appendix makes using this package a little easier. It requires only one **use** statement:

```
use SNMP_util;
```

Mike's package uses the other two modules, so it's not necessary to include all three in your scripts.

MIB Management Routines

The following sections describe a set of routines for working with MIBs.

snmpmapOID()

The MIB objects in RFC 1213 (MIB-II) and RFC 2955 (Frame Relay) are preloaded by the routines in this package. This means that you can refer to a symbolic name like *sysLocation.0* rather than to its numeric OID (*.1.3.6.1.2.1.1.6*). The snmpmapOID() routine allows you to add name-OID pairs to this map. The routine is used as follows:

```
snmpmapOID(text, OID, [text, OID...])
```

All the parameters are strings. *text* is the textual (or symbolic) name that you want to use and *OID* is the numeric object ID of the object to which the name refers. A single call to this routine may specify any number of name-OID pairs.

If **snmpmapOID()** fails it returns **undef**, so you can test for errors like this:

```
@return = snmpmapOID(..);
if(!@return) {
    # error
}
```

snmpMIB_to_OID()

This routine takes the filename of a MIB as an argument. It reads and parses the MIB file and associates the object IDs defined by the MIB with their textual names. It returns the number of mappings it created. A return value of zero means that no mappings were created; –1 means an error occurred (i.e., it was unable to open the file). The routine is used as follows:

```
snmpMIB_to_OID(filename)
```

snmpLoad_OID_Cache()

This routine allows you to map textual names to object IDs using a file. The file should consist of a number of lines in the form:

```
textual_name OID
```

This is much faster than calling **snmpMIB_to_OID()** because it doesn't require parsing a MIB file. The only argument to this routine is the name of the file that contains the preparsed data:

```
snmpLoad_OID_Cache(filename)
```

snmpLoad_OID_Cache() returns –1 if it can't open the file; a return value of 0 indicates success.

snmpQueue_MIB_File()

This routine specifies a list of MIB files that will be used for mapping textual names to object IDs. If a name or OID can't be found in the internal map, each MIB file is parsed in turn until a match is found. The routine is used as follows:

```
snmpQueue_MIB_File(filename, [filename])
```

SNMP Operations

The routines for performing SNMP operations correspond to the standard SNMP Version 1 operations[*] and have the following parameters in common:

community (optional)
> The community string. If no community string is specified, *public* is used.

host (required)
> The hostname or IP address of the device you want to query.

port (optional)
> The port number to which to send the query or trap. The default for all routines except **snmptrap()** is 161. The default for **snmptrap()** is 162.

timeout (optional)
> The timeout in seconds; if no response is received within this period, the operation is considered to have failed and is retried. The default is 2 seconds.

retries (optional)
> The number of retries before the routine returns failure. The default is 5.

backoff (optional)
> The backoff value; for each successive retry, the new timeout period is obtained by multiplying the current timeout with the backoff. The default is 1.

OID (required)
> The object ID or textual name of the object you are querying.

snmpget()

The syntax of the **snmpget()** routine is:

```
snmpget(community@host:port:timeout:retries:backoff, OID, [OID...])
```

If **snmpget()** fails, it returns **undef**.

Recall that all the MIB-II objects are preloaded into this Perl module, so the following code is legal:

```
@sysDescr = snmpget("public\@cisco.ora.com", "sysDescr");
```

We did not specify any of the optional parameters (*timeout, backoff,* etc.); the default values will be used. This routine lets us request **"sysDescr"** as shorthand for *sysDescr.0.* When the Perl module builds its mappings of names to object IDs, it automatically appends the trailing *.0* to any scalar objects it finds.

---

[*] Simon Leinen's package supports both SNMP v1 and v2; Mike Mitchell's **SNMP_util** module supports only v1.

Because *sysDescr* is a scalar object defined by MIB-2, and because the MIB-2 objects are pre-loaded, *sysDescr* is mapped to *.1.3.6.1.2.1.1.1.0*. If you request a scalar object from a private MIB, you must append *.0* to the OID.

Since one call to **snmpget()** can retrieve many objects, the return values are stored in an array. For example:

```
@oids = snmpget("public\@cisco.ora.com", "sysDescr", "sysName");
```

When this function call executes, the value for *sysDescr* will be stored in **$oids[0]**; the value for *sysName* will be stored in **$oids[1]**. All the routines in this package share this behavior.

snmpgetnext()

The **snmpgetnext()** routine performs a *get-next* operation to retrieve the value of the MIB object that follows the object you pass to it. Its syntax is:

```
snmpgetnext(community@host:port:timeout:retries:backoff, OID, [OID...])
```

If **snmpgetnext()** fails, it returns **undef**.

As with **snmpget()**, you can request many OIDs; the return value from **snmpgetnext()** is an array, with the result of each *get-next* operation in each successive position in the array. The array you get back from **snmpgetnext()** differs from the array returned by **snmpget()** in that the value of each object is preceded by the object's ID, in the form:

```
OID:value
```

This routine returns both the OID and the value because with the *get-next* operation you don't necessarily know what the next object in the MIB tree is.

snmpwalk()

The **snmpwalk()** routine could easily be implemented with repeated calls to **snmpgetnext()**; it traverses the entire object tree, starting with the object passed to it. Its syntax is:

```
snmpwalk(community@host:port:timeout:retries:backoff, OID)
```

If **snmpwalk()** fails, it returns **undef**.

Unlike many of the routines in this module, **snmpwalk()** allows only one OID as an argument. Like the other routines, it returns an array of values; each element of the array consists of an object's ID followed by its value, separated by a colon. For example, after executing the following code:

```
@system = snmpwalk("public\@cisco.ora.com","system");
```

The contents of the array **@system** would be something like:

```
1.0:cisco.ora.com Cisco
2.0:1.3.6.1.4.1.0
3.0:23 days, 11:01:57
4.0:Ora Network Admin Staff
5.0:cisco.ora.com
6.0:Atlanta, GA
7.0:4
```

Note that the array doesn't include the entire object ID. We've told **snmpwalk()** to walk the tree starting at the *system* object, which has the OID *.1.3.6.1.2.1.1.* The first child object, and the first item in the array, is *sysName*, which is *.1.3.6.1.2.1.1.* *1.0.* **snmpwalk()** returns **1.0:cisco.ora.com** because it omits the generic part of the OID (in this case, *system*) and prints only the instance-specific part (**1.0**). Similarly, the next item in the array is *system.2.0*, or *system.sysObjectID.0*; its value is Cisco's enterprise ID.

snmpset()

The **snmpset()** routine allows you to set the value of an object on an SNMP-managed device. In addition to the standard arguments (hostname, community, etc.), this routine expects three arguments for each object you want it to set: the object's ID, datatype, and value. The syntax for this routine is:

```
snmpset(community@host:port:timeout:retries:backoff,
        OID, type, value, [OID, type, value...])
```

The *type* argument must be one of the following strings:

string
>   Represents the string type

int
>   Represents the 32-bit integer type

ipaddr
>   Represents the IP address type

oid
>   Represents the object identifier (OID) type

If **snmpset()** fails, it returns **undef**.

Performing a *set* from a script is straightforward. The following code sets the value of *sysContact* to **"Joe@Ora"**. If the operation succeeds, **snmpset()** returns the new value for *sysContact*. If the operation fails, the **fs** variable is not set and **snmpset()** prints an error message:

```
$setResponse =
    snmpset("private\@cisco.ora.com", sysContact,"string","Joe\@Ora");
```

```
if ($setResponse) {
    print "SET: sysContact: $setResponse\n";
} else {
    print "No response from cisco.ora.com\n";
}
```

The most common reasons for an **snmpset()** to fail are that the host isn't up, the host isn't running an SNMP agent, or the community string is wrong.

snmptrap()

The **snmptrap()** routine generates an SNMPv1 trap. Most of the arguments are familiar:

```
snmptrap(community@host:port:timeout:retries:backoff,
         enterpriseOID, agent, generalID, specificID,
         OID, type, value, [OID, type, value...])
```

The *enterpriseOID, agent, generalID*, and *specificID* arguments are discussed in Chapter 10. Each OID/type/value triplet defines a data binding to be included in the trap. *OID* is the object ID of the variable you want to send, *value* is the value you want to send for this object, and *type* is the object's datatype. *type* must be one of the following three strings:

string
   Represents the string type

int
   Represents the 32-bit integer type

oid
   Represents the object identifier (OID) type

If **snmptrap()** fails, it returns **undef**. See Chapter 10 for a more detailed discussion of SNMP traps.

F

SNMPv3

Security has been the biggest weakness of SNMP since the beginning. Authentication in SNMP Versions 1 and 2 amounts to nothing more than a password (community string) sent in clear text between a manager and agent. Any security-conscious network or system administrator knows that clear-text passwords provide no real security at all. It is trivial for someone to intercept the community string, and once he has it, he can use it to retrieve information from devices on your network, modify their configuration, and even shut them down.

The *Simple Network Management Protocol Version 3* (SNMPv3) addresses the security problems that have plagued both SNMPv1 and SNMPv2. For all practical purposes, security is the only issue SNMPv3 addresses; there are no other changes to the protocol. There are no new operations; SNMPv3 supports all the operations defined by Versions 1 and 2. There are several new textual conventions, but these are really just more precise ways of interpreting the datatypes that were defined in earlier versions.

This appendix provides an introduction to SNMPv3 and covers SNMPv3 configuration for a Cisco router and the Net-SNMP agent. Although SNMPv3 is not yet a full standard, a few vendors sell products with SNMPv3 support. We chose to cover two popular SNMPv3 implementations for our configuration examples.

Changes in SNMPv3

Although SNMPv3 makes no changes to the protocol aside from the addition of cryptographic security, its developers have managed to make things look much different by introducing new textual conventions, concepts, and terminology. The changes to the terminology are so radical that it's hard to believe the new terms essentially describe the same software as the old ones, but they do. However, they do differ in terms of how they relate to each other and in that they specify much more precisely the pieces that an SNMP implementation needs.

The most important change is that Version 3 abandons the notion of managers and agents. Both managers and agents are now called SNMP *entities*. Each entity consists of an SNMP engine and one or more SNMP applications, which are discussed in the following sections. These new concepts are important because they define an architecture, rather than simply defining a set of messages; the architecture helps to separate different pieces of the SNMP system in a way that makes a secure implementation possible. Let's look at what these concepts mean, starting with the RFCs that define them (Table F-1).

Table F-1. RFCs for SNMPv3

Name	Number	Status	Last Activity Date
Architecture for SNMP Frameworks	RFC 2571	Draft	April 1999
Message Processing and Dispatching	RFC 2572	Draft	April 1999
SNMP Applications	RFC 2573	Draft	April 1999
User-based Security Model	RFC 2574	Draft	April 1999
View-based Access Control Model	RFC 2575	Draft	April 1999
Protocol Operations for SNMPv2	RFC 1905	Draft	January 1996
Transport Mappings for SNMPv2	RFC 1906	Draft	January 1996
MIB for SNMPv2	RFC 1907	Draft	January 1996
Coexistence Between SNMP Versions	RFC 2576	Proposed	March 2000
Introduction to SNMPv3	RFC 2570	Informational	April 1999
Diffie-Hellman USM Key Management	RFC 2786	Experimental	March 2000

The SNMPv3 Engine

The engine is composed of four pieces: the Dispatcher, the Message Processing Subsystem, the Security Subsystem, and the Access Control Subsystem. The Dispatcher's job is to send and receive messages. It tries to determine the version of each received message (i.e., v1, v2, or v3) and, if the version is supported, hands the message off to the Message Processing Subsystem. The Dispatcher also sends SNMP messages to other entities.

The Message Processing Subsystem prepares messages to be sent and extracts data from received messages. A message processing system can contain multiple message processing modules. For example, a subsystem can have modules for processing SNMPv1, SNMPv2, and SNMPv3 requests. It may also contain a module for other processing models that are yet to be defined.

The Security Subsystem provides authentication and privacy services. Authentication uses either community strings (SNMP Versions 1 and 2) or SNMPv3 user-based authentication. User-based authentication uses the MD5 or SHA algorithms to authenticate users without sending a password in the clear. The privacy service uses the DES algorithm to encrypt and decrypt SNMP messages. Currently, DES is the only algorithm used, though others may be added in the future.

The Access Control Subsystem is responsible for controlling access to MIB objects. You can control what objects a user can access as well what operations she is allowed to perform on those objects. For example, you might want to limit a user's read-write access to certain parts of the *mib-2* tree, while allowing read-only access to the entire tree.

SNMPv3 Applications

Version 3 divides most of what we have come to think of as SNMP into a number of applications:

Command generator
> Generates *get*, *get-next*, *get-bulk*, and *set* requests and processes the responses. This application is implemented by a Network Management Station (NMS), so it can issue queries and *set* requests against entities on routers, switches, Unix hosts, etc.

Command responder
> Responds to *get*, *get-next*, *get-bulk*, and *set* requests. This application is implemented by an entity on a Cisco router or Unix host. (For Versions 1 and 2, the command responder is implemented by the SNMP agent.)

Notification originator
> Generates SNMP traps and notifications. This application is implemented by an entity on a router or Unix host. (For Versions 1 and 2, the notification originator is part of an SNMP agent. Freestanding utilities for generating traps are also available.)

Notification receiver
> Receives traps and inform messages. This application is implemented by an NMS.

Proxy forwarder
> Facilitates message-passing between entities.

RFC 2571 allows additional applications to be defined over time. This ability to extend the SNMPv3 framework is a significant advantage over the older SNMP versions.

What Does an Entity Look Like?

Thus far we've talked about the SNMPv3 entity in terms of abstract definitions. Figure F-1 (taken from RFC 2571) shows how the components that make up an entity fit together.

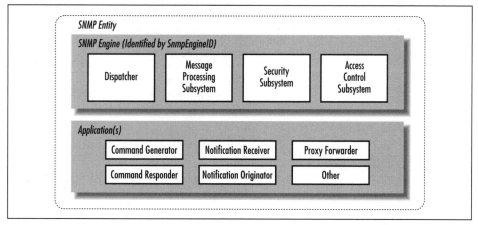

Figure F-1. SNMPv3 entity

SNMPv3 Textual Conventions

SNMPv3 defines a number of additional textual conventions, outlined in Table F-2.

Table F-2. SNMPv3 Textual Conventions

Textual Convention	Description
SnmpEngineID	An administratively unique identifier for an SNMP engine. Objects of this type are for identification, not for addressing, even though an address can be used in the generation of a specific value. RFC 2571 provides a detailed discussion of how SnmpEngineIDs are created.
SnmpSecurityModel	An SNMP securityModel (SNMPv1, SNMPv2, or USM). USM stands for User-based Security Model, which is the security method used in SNMPv3.
SnmpMessageProcessingModel	A Message Processing Model used by the Message Processing Subsystem.
SnmpSecurityLevel	The level of security at which SNMP messages can be sent, or the level of security at which operations are being processed. Possible values are noAuthNoPriv (without authentication and without privacy), authNoPriv (with authentication but without privacy), and authPriv (with authentication and with privacy). These three values are ordered such that noAuthNoPriv is less than authNoPriv and authNoPriv is less than authPriv.

Table F-2. SNMPv3 Textual Conventions (continued)

Textual Convention	Description
SnmpAdminString	An octet string containing administrative information, preferably in human-readable form. The string can be up to 255 bytes in length.
SnmpTagValue	An octet string containing a tag value. Tag values are preferably in human-readable form. According to RFC 2573, valid tags include `acme`, `router`, and `host`.
SnmpTagList	An octet string containing a list of tag values. Tag values are preferably in human-readable form. According to RFC 2573, valid examples of a tag list are the empty string, `acme router`, and `host managerStation`.
KeyChange	An object used to change authentication and privacy keys.

Configuring SNMPv3

Now we get to put the SNMPv3 concepts to use. We'll look at two examples: configuring a Cisco router and setting up the Net-SNMP tools on a system running Unix. The concepts are the same for both entities; the only difference is how you configure SNMPv3.

Most of the work in administering SNMPv3 has to do with managing users and their passwords. It shouldn't be surprising that the table of users, passwords, and other authentication information is just another SNMP table, called *usmUser*. The table's full object ID is *.iso.org.dod.internet.snmpV2.snmpModules.snmpUsmMIB. usmMIBObjects usmUser*; the numeric form is *.1.3.6.1.6.3.15.1.2*.

Configuring SNMPv3 for a Cisco Router

Chapter 7 describes how to configure SNMP on a Cisco router. This section assumes that you're already familiar with IOS and that we don't have to tell you the basics, such as how to log into the router and get to privileged mode. It also assumes that you've read Chapter 7 and have configured basic SNMP on your router.

The first task in configuring SNMPv3 is to define a view. To simplify things, we'll create a view that allows access to the entire *internet* subtree:

```
router(config)#snmp-server view readview internet included
```

This command creates a view called *readview*. If you want to limit the view to the *system* tree, for example, replace `internet` with `system`. The `included` keyword states that the specified tree should be included in the view; use `excluded` if you wanted to exclude a certain subtree.

Next, create a group that uses the new view. The following command creates a group called *readonly*; v3 means that SNMPv3 should be used. The `auth` keyword specifies that the entity should authenticate packets without encrypting them; `read readview` says that the view named *readview* should be used whenever members of the *readonly* group access the router.

```
router(config)#snmp-server group readonly v3 auth read readview
```

Now let's create a user. The following command creates a user called *kschmidt*, who belongs to the *readonly* group. `auth md5` specifies that the router should use MD5 to authenticate the user (the other possibility is `sha`). The final item on the command line is the user's password or passphrase, which may not exceed 64 characters.

```
router(config)#snmp-server user kschmidt readonly v3 auth md5 mysecretpass
```

This configuration uses encryption only to prevent passwords from being transferred in the clear. The SNMP packets themselves, which may contain information that you don't want available to the public, are sent without encryption and can therefore be read by anyone who has a packet sniffer and access to your network. If you want to go a step further and encrypt the packets themselves, use a command like this:

```
router(config)#snmp-server user kschmidt readonly v3 auth md5 mysecretpass \
priv des56 passphrase
```

The additional keywords on this command specify privacy (i.e., encryption for all SNMP packets), use of DES 56-bit encryption, and a passphrase to use when encrypting packets.

The encrypted passwords and passphrases depend on the engine ID, so if the engine ID changes you'll need to delete any users you have defined (with the familiar IOS *no* command), and recreate them (with *snmp-server user* commands). Why would the engine ID change? It's possible to set the engine ID on the IOS command line. You shouldn't ever need to set the engine ID explicitly, but if you do, you'll have to delete and recreate your users.

This has been the briefest of introductions to configuring SNMPv3 on a Cisco router. For more information see Cisco's documentation, which is available at *http://www.cisco.com/univercd/cc/td/doc/product/software/ios120/120newft/120t/120t3/snmp3.htm.*

Configuring SNMPv3 for Net-SNMP

Chapter 7 describes basic configuration for Net-SNMP. In this section, we discuss how to configure Net-SNMP's Version 3 features. First, we will discuss how to configure SNMPv3 by editing the *snmpd.conf** files. Note that you must install OpenSSL before editing the files if you want to use either DES or SHA. OpenSSL is available from *http://www.openssl.org.*

To create a user named *kschmidt* who has read-write access to the *system* subtree, add the following line to your *snmpd.conf* file:

```
rwuser  kschmidt auth system
```

To create a user with read-only access, use the command **rouser** instead of **rwuser**. The **auth** keyword requests secure authentication, but not privacy: the SNMP packets themselves aren't encrypted. The other possibilities are **noauth** (no authentication and no privacy) and **priv** (authentication and privacy). Now add the following line to */var/ucd-snmp/snmpd.conf:*

```
createUser kschmidt MD5 mysecretpass
```

This creates an MD5 password for the user *kschmidt.* The password assigned to *kschmidt* is **mysecretpass.** To create a user with a DES passphrase in addition to an MD5 password, add the following line to */var/ucd-snmp/snmpd.conf:*

```
createUser kschmidt MD5 mysecretpass DES mypassphrase
```

If you omit **mypassphrase,** Net-SNMP sets the DES passphrase to be the same as the MD5 password. The RFCs for SNMPv3 recommend that passwords and passphrases be at least eight characters long; Net-SNMP enforces this recommendation and won't accept shorter passwords.

After making these changes, stop and restart the agent. When the agent is started, it reads the configuration file, computes secret keys for the users you have added, and deletes the **createUser** commands from the file. It then places the secret key in the configuration file. This behavior has a number of consequences. The secret key is based on the engine ID, which for Net-SNMP is based on the IP address. Therefore, you can't copy configuration files from one machine to another. Furthermore, if you change a machine's IP address, you will have to reconfigure Net-SNMP: stop the agent, edit */var/ucd-snmp/snmpd.conf,* delete any entries Net-SNMP has added for your users, add **createUser** commands to recreate your users, and start the agent again.

Now we can perform an *snmpwalk* using Version 3 authentication. The following command specifies Version 3, with the username **kschmidt,** requesting authentication without privacy using the MD5 algorithm. The password is **mysecretpass:**

```
$ snmpwalk -v 3 -u kschmidt -l authNoPriv -a MD5 -A mysecretpass \
server.ora.com
system.sysDescr.0 = Linux server 2.2.14-VA.2.1 #1 Mon Jul 31 21:58:22 PDT 2000 i686
```

---

* There are two *snmpd.conf* files in play here: the normal */usr/share/snmp/snmpd.conf* file and the persistent */var/ucd-snmp/snmpd.conf* file. The persistent file will be discussed momentarily.

```
system.sysObjectID.0 = OID: enterprises.ucdavis.ucdSnmpAgent.linux
system.sysUpTime.0 = Timeticks: (1360) 0:00:13.60
system.sysContact.0 = "Ora Network Admin"
system.sysName.0 = server
system.sysLocation.0 = "Atlanta, Ga"
system.sysServices.0 = 0
system.sysORLastChange.0 = Timeticks: (0) 0:00:00.00
system.sysORTable.sysOREntry.sysORID.1 = OID: ifMIB
...
system.sysORTable.sysOREntry.sysORUpTime.9 = No more variables left in this MIB
View
```

Note that we see only objects from the *system* subtree, even though the command tries to walk the entire tree. This limitation occurs because we have given *kschmidt* access only to the *system* subtree. If *kschmidt* tries to query a subtree he is not allowed to access, he gets the following result:

```
$ snmpwalk -v 3 -u kschmidt -l authNoPriv -a MD5 -A mysecretpass \
server.ora.com interfaces
interfaces = No more variables left in this MIB View
```

If you want privacy in addition to authentication, use a command like this:

```
$ snmpwalk -v 3 -u kschmidt -l authPriv -a MD5 -A mysecretpass -x DES -X \
mypassphrase server.ora.com
```

Remember that to use DES privacy, you must install the OpenSSL library.

Using snmpusm to manage users

The Net-SNMP utility *snmpusm* is used to maintain SNMPv3 users. The following command creates the user *kjs* by cloning the *kschmidt* user:

```
$ snmpusm -v 3 -u kschmidt -l authNoPriv -a MD5 -A mysecretpass localhost create \
kjs kschmidt
```

Since *kjs* was cloned from *kschmidt*, the two users now have the same authorization, password, and passphrase. It's obviously essential to change *kjs*'s password. To do so, use *snmpusm* with the *–Ca* option. Similarly, to change the privacy passphrase, use *–Cx*. The following two commands change the password and passphrase for the new user *kjs*:

```
$ snmpusm -v3 -l authNoPriv -u kjs -a MD5 -A mysecretpass localhost passwd \
-Co -Ca mysecretpass mynewpass
$ snmpusm -v3 -l authPriv -u kjs -a MD5 -A mysecretpass localhost passwd \
-Co -Cx mypassphrase mynewphrase
```

There are many things to note about this seemingly simple operation:

- You must know both the password and passphrase for *kschmidt* to set up a new password and passphrase for *kjs*.

- According to the documentation, Net-SNMP allows you to clone any given user only once. It's not clear whether this means that you can create only one clone of a user or that once you have created a clone, you can't create a clone of that clone. In any case, this restriction doesn't appear to be enforced.

- *snmpusm* can only clone users; it can't create them from scratch. Therefore, you must create the initial user by hand, using the process described above. (This isn't quite true. *snmpusm* can create a user, but once you've done so you have to assign it a password by changing its previous password. So you're in a catch-22: the new user doesn't have a password, so you can't change its password.)

For the user to be written to the persistent *snmpd.conf* file, you must either stop and restart the agent or send an HUP signal to the *snmpd* process. This forces the agent to write the current state of the user table to disk, so the agent can reread it upon startup. Note that *kill –9* does not produce the desired result.

The *snmpusm* command exists primarily to allow end users to manage their own passwords and passphrases. As the administrator, you may want to change your users' passwords and passphrases periodically. This is possible only if you keep a master list of users and their passwords and passphrases.

If the engine ID changes, you will have to regenerate all the usernames, passwords, and passphrases. (Remember that the engine ID depends in part on the host's IP address and therefore changes if you have to change the address.) To do this, stop the agent and edit the */var/ucd-snmp/snmpd.conf* file. Remove all the persistent usmUser entries and add new createUser commands (as described previously) for your users. A usmUser entry looks something like this:

```
usmUser 1 3 0x800007e580e134af77b9d8023b 0x6b6a7300 0x6b6a7300 NULL
.1.3.6.1.6.3.10.1.1.2 0xb84cc525635a155b6eb5fbe0e3597873
.1.3.6.1.6.3.10.1.2.2 0x1cfd8d3cadd95abce8efff7962002e24 ""
```

Simplifying commands by setting defaults

At this point you may be wondering why anyone would use SNMPv3, because the commands are so painfully long and complex that it's practically impossible to type them correctly. Fortunately, there's a way around this problem. Net-SNMP allows you to set configuration variables that the commands pick up when they execute. Create a directory in your home directory called *.snmp*, then edit the *snmp.conf* file. Add entries that look like this:

```
defSecurityName    kschmidt
defAuthType        MD5
defSecurityLevel   authPriv
defAuthPassphrase  mysecretpass
defPrivType        DES
defPrivPassphrase  mypassphrase
defVersion         3
```

The fields in this file are:

`defSecurityName`
> The SNMPv3 username.

`defAuthType`
> The authentication method (either MD5 or SHA).

`defSecurityLevel`
> The security level for the user. Valid levels are `noAuthNoPriv`, `authNoPriv`, and `authPriv`.

`defAuthPassphrase`
> Your password; must be at least eight characters long.

`defPrivType`
> The privacy protocol to use. Only DES is supported at this time.

`defPrivPassphrase`
> Your privacy passphrase; not needed if the security level is `noAuthNoPriv` or `authNoPriv`. Must be at least eight characters long.

`defVersion`
> The SNMP version to use (in this case, SNMPv3).

You can also use the *snmpconf* command to set up this file. *snmpconf* prompts you for the various passwords and keywords that need to be in the file. In our opinion, it's easier to write the file yourself.

Once you've created *snmp.conf*, you can use defaults to simplify your commands. For example, the following command:

```
$ snmpwalk -v3 -u kschmidt -l authPriv -a MD5 -A mysecretpass -x DES -X \
mypassphrase localhost
```

becomes:

```
$ snmpwalk localhost
```

These defaults apply to all Net-SNMP commands, including *snmpusm*.

Sending SNMPv3 traps with Net-SNMP

Sending an SNMPv3 trap with Net-SNMP is easy.* Simply run *snmptrap* with the normal SNMPv2 trap options combined with SNMPv3 options. For example:

```
$ snmptrap -v3 -l authPriv -u kjs -a MD5 -A mysecretpass -x DES -X mypassphrase \
localhost '' .1.3.6.1.6.3.1.1.5.3 ifIndex i 2 ifAdminStatus i 1 ifOperStatus i 1
```

---

* SNMPv3 traps are simply SNMPv2 traps with added authentication and privacy capabilities.

Setting the appropriate configuration options in *~/.snmp/snmp.conf* greatly reduces the complexity of the command:

```
$ snmptrap localhost '' .1.3.6.1.6.3.1.1.5.3 ifIndex i 2 ifAdminStatus i 1 \
ifOperStatus i 1
```

Final Words on SNMPv3

While vendors have begun to support SNMPv3 in their products, keep in mind that it is still a draft standard, not a full standard. If you would like to keep track of SNMPv3 happenings, you can visit the Internet Engineering Task Force's (IETF) SNMPv3 working group site at *http://www.ietf.org/html.charters/snmpv3-charter.html.*

Index

We'd like to hear your suggestions for improving our indexes. Send email to *index@oreilly.com.*

About the Authors

Douglas R. Mauro (*doug@mauro.com*) lives outside of Rochester, New York, with his wife Amy, daughter Kari, and cat Megabyte (a.k.a. Meg). He received a bachelor's degree at the University of Albany, New York, and worked as a system administrator for several years before becoming a project engineer with Sun Microsystems, Inc. In addition to his consulting duties with Sun, he authors their internal OneStop Sun Management Center page and has also published several InfoDocs with them.

Computers are not just a way of life for Douglas, but a profound passion. He feels extremely fortunate to be working in a field he truly loves.

Kevin J. Schmidt (*kevin@vagrant.org*) currently lives in Decatur, Georgia. He shares a home with his significant other Callie, their loving cats Chester and Twiggy, two Peruvian guinea pigs, two *Litoria* species White's tree frogs, and several poison dart frogs.

Originally from Pensacola, Florida, Kevin spent several years studying computer science at the University of West Florida. In late 1996 he was recruited by Mind-Spring Enterprises (now known as Earthlink, Inc.), a national ISP based in Atlanta, and subsequently left school to pursue his career. He spent four years in network management and was the senior network management architect for Earthlink. He then left Earthlink to work at Netrail, a tier-1 Internet backbone provider. While at Netrail, Kevin was in charge of the company's network management architecture. These days Kevin works as a software engineer for GuardedNet, a network security start-up in Atlanta.

Kevin's first computer was a Commodore 64. He began running Bulletin Board Systems (BBSs) at age 11 and later became interested in computer networking in general. His other computing interests include Linux, MySQL, and programming in C, Java, Perl, and PHP. Kevin will soon have his private pilot's license and plans to become instrument- and multiengine-rated soon thereafter. He recently discovered the LEGO™ MINDSTORMS® Robotics Invention System, and he uses Dave Baum's Not Quite C (NQC) for Linux to control his robotic creations.

Colophon

Our look is the result of reader comments, our own experimentation, and feedback from distribution channels. Distinctive covers complement our distinctive approach to technical topics, breathing personality and life into potentially dry subjects.

The animals on the cover of *Essential SNMP* are red deer (*Cervus elaphus*). Male red deer, also known as *stags* or *harts*, can grow to over 400 lbs. and stand 42–54 inches tall at the shoulder. Females, or *hinds*, are more slightly built and usually reach a weight of only about 200 lbs. The color of the red deer's coat ranges from a warm reddish-brown in the summer to a darker grayish-brown in winter. Calves are spotted at birth, but the spots fade after about two months.

The typical family group consists of a hind, a new calf, a yearling calf, and perhaps a 2–3 year old stag. Mature stags and hinds live in separate groups for most of the year, with the hinds tending to monopolize the better, more grassy habitats. At the start of the mating season (the rut) in the early fall, the stags split up and join the females. Each eligible stag establishes a harem of up to 20 or more hinds, which he defends vigorously during the rut. During this period, which typically lasts 6–8 weeks, the stags often forego eating and can lose as much as 15% of their body mass.

Red deer are one of the most widely distributed deer species: though they are native to Europe, today they can be found everywhere from New Zealand to North America. They are herbivores, feeding mainly on rough grasses, young tree shoots, and shrubs. Forest-dwellers by nature, they can adapt easily to different climates and terrain. In many of the areas in which they were introduced red deer are commercially farmed for venison and antler velvet, which has been used in traditional Chinese medicine for over 2,000 years to treat a broad range of ailments including anemia, arthritic pain and rheumatism, kidney disorders, and stress.

Rachel Wheeler was the production editor and copyeditor for *Essential SNMP*. Colleen Gorman was the proofreader and Catherine Morris provided quality control. Sada Preisch provided production assistance. Jan Wright wrote the index.

Ellie Volckhausen designed the cover of this book, based on a series design by Edie Freedman. The cover image is a 19th-century engraving from the Dover Pictorial Archive. Emma Colby produced the cover layout with QuarkXPress 4.1 using Adobe's ITC Garamond font.

David Futato designed the interior layout based on a series design by Nancy Priest. Neil Walls converted the files from Microsoft Word to FrameMaker 5.5.6 using tools created by Mike Sierra. The text and heading fonts are ITC Garamond Light and Garamond Book; the code font is Constant Willison. The illustrations that appear in the book were produced by Robert Romano and Jessamyn Read using Macromedia FreeHand 9 and Adobe Photoshop 6. This colophon was written by Rachel Wheeler.

Whenever possible, our books use a durable and flexible lay-flat binding. If the page count exceeds this binding's limit, perfect binding is used.

More Titles from O'Reilly

Network Administration

DNS and BIND, 4th Edition

By Paul Albitz & Cricket Liu
4th Edition April 2001
622 pages, ISBN 0-596-00158-4

DNS and BIND, 4th Edition, covers the new 9.1.0 and 8.2.3 versions of BIND as well as the older 4.9 version. There's also more extensive coverage of NOTIFY, IPv6 forward and reverse mapping, transaction signatures and the new DNS Security Extensions; and a section on accommodating Windows 2000 clients, servers, and Domain Controllers.

Internet Core Protocols: The Definitive Guide

By Eric Hall
1st Edition February 2000
472 pages, Includes CD-ROM
ISBN 1-56592-572-6

Internet Core Protocols: The Definitive Guide provides the nitty-gritty details of TCP, IP, and UDP. Many network problems can only be debugged by working at the lowest levels—looking at all the bits traveling back and forth on the wire. This guide explains what those bits are and how to interpret them. It's the only book on Internet protocols written with system and network administrators in mind.

Network Troubleshooting Tools

By Joseph D. Sloan
1st Edition August 2001
364 pages, ISBN 0-596-00186-X

Network Troubleshooting Tools helps you sort through the thousands of tools that have been developed for debugging TCP/IP networks and choose the ones that are best for your needs. It also shows you how to approach network troubleshooting using these tools, how to document your network so you know how it behaves under normal conditions, and how to think about problems when they arise so you can solve them more effectively.

TCP/IP Network Administration, 2nd Edition

By Craig Hunt
2nd Edition December 1997
630 pages, ISBN 1-56592-322-7

A complete guide to setting up and running a TCP/IP network for practicing system administrators. Beyond basic setup, this new second edition discusses the Internet routing protocols and provides a tutorial on how to configure important network services. It also includes Linux in addition to BSD and System V TCP/IP implementations.

Managing NFS and NIS, 2nd Edition

By Hal Stern, Mike Eisler & Ricardo Labiaga
2nd Edition July 2001
510 pages, ISBN 1-56592-510-6

This long-awaited new edition of a classic, now updated for NFS Version 3 and based on Solaris 8, shows how to set up and manage a network filesystem installation. Managing NFS and NIS is the only practical book devoted entirely to NFS and the distributed database NIS; it's a "must-have" for anyone interested in Unix networking.

sendmail, 2nd Edition

By Bryan Costales & Eric Allman
2nd Edition January 1997
1050 pages, ISBN 1-56592-222-0

sendmail, 2nd Edition, covers sendmail Version 8.8 from Berkeley and the standard versions available on most systems. This cross-referenced edition offers an expanded tutorial and solution-oriented examples, plus topics such as the #error delivery agent, sendmail's exit values, MIME headers, and how to set up and use the user database, mailertable, and smrsh.

Network Administration

Cisco IOS Access Lists

By Jeff Sedayao
1st Edition June 2001
272 pages, ISBN 1-56592-385-5

This book focuses on a critical aspect of the
Cisco IOS—access lists, which are central to
securing routers and networks. Administrators cannot implement access control or traffic routing policies without them. The book
covers intranets, firewalls, and the Internet.
Unlike other Cisco router titles, it focuses on practical instructions for setting router access policies rather than the details of
interfaces and routing protocol settings.

Server Load Balancing

By Tony Bourke
1st Edition August 2001
192 pages, ISBN 0-596-00050-2

Load balancing distributes traffic efficiently
among network servers so that no individual
server is overburdened. This vendor-neutral
guide to the concepts and terminology of
load balancing offers practical guidance to
planning and implementing the technology in
most environments. It includes a configuration guide with diagrams and sample configurations for installing, configuring, and
maintaining products from the four major server load balancing
vendors.

Cisco IOS in a Nutshell

By James Boney
1st Edition December 2001
606 pages, ISBN 1-56592-942-X

This two-part reference covers IOS configuration for the TCP/IP protocol family. The
first part includes chapters on the user interface, configuring lines and interfaces, access
lists, routing protocols, and dial-on-demand
routing and security. The second part is a
classic O'Reilly-style quick reference to all the commands you
need to work with TCP/IP and the lower-level protocols on which
it relies, with lots of examples of the most common configuration
steps for the routers themselves.

Unix Backup & Recovery

By W. Curtis Preston
1st Edition November 1999
734 pages, Includes CD-ROM
ISBN 1-56592-642-0

This guide provides a complete overview of
all facets of Unix backup and recovery and
offers practical, affordable backup and
recovery solutions for environments of all
sizes and budgets. It explains everything from
freely available backup systems to large-scale commercial utilities.

T1: A Survival Guide

By Matthew Gast
1st Edition August 2001
304 pages, ISBN 0-596-00127-4

This practical, applied reference to T1 for
system and network administrators brings
together in one place the information you
need to set up, test, and troubleshoot T1.
You'll learn what components you need to
build a T1 line; how the components interact
to transmit data; how to adapt the T1 to work with data networks
using standardized link layer protocols; troubleshooting strategies; and working with vendors.

Unix System Administration

Using Samba

By Bob Eckstein, David Collier-Brown
& Peter Kelly
1st Edition November 1999
416 pages, Includes CD-ROM
ISBN 1-56592-449-5

Samba turns a Unix or Linux system into a
file and print server for Microsoft Windows
network clients. This complete guide to
Samba administration covers basic 2.0 configuration, security, logging, and troubleshooting. Whether you're
playing on one note or a full three-octave range, this book will
help you maintain an efficient and secure server. Includes a
CD-ROM of sources and ready-to-install binaries.

O'REILLY®

TO ORDER: **800-998-9938** • *order@oreilly.com* • *www.oreilly.com*
ONLINE EDITIONS OF MOST O'REILLY TITLES ARE AVAILABLE BY SUBSCRIPTION AT **safari.oreilly.com**
ALSO AVAILABLE AT MOST RETAIL AND ONLINE BOOKSTORES

Unix System Administration

Using & Managing PPP

By Andrew Sun
1st Edition March 1999
444 pages, ISBN 1-56592-321-9

This book is for network administrators and others who have to set up computer systems to use PPP. It covers all aspects of the protocol, including how to set up dial-in servers, authentication, debugging, and PPP options. In addition, it contains overviews of related areas, like serial communications, DNS setup, and routing.

UNIX Power Tools, 2nd Edition

By Jerry Peek, Tim O'Reilly & Mike Loukides
2nd Edition August 1997
1120 pages, Includes CD-ROM
ISBN 1-56592-260-3

Loaded with practical advice about almost every aspect of Unix, this second edition of *UNIX Power Tools* addresses the technology that Unix users face today. You'll find thorough coverage of POSIX utilities, including GNU versions, detailed bash and tcsh shell coverage, a strong emphasis on Perl, and a CD-ROM that contains the best freeware available.

The UNIX CD Bookshelf, 2nd Edition

By O'Reilly & Associates, Inc.
2nd Edition February 2000
624 pages, Features CD-ROM
ISBN 0-596-00000-6

The second edition of *The UNIX CD Bookshelf* contains six books from O'Reilly, plus the software from *UNIX Power Tools*—all on a convenient CD-ROM. Buyers also get a bonus hard-copy book, *UNIX in a Nutshell*, 3rd Edition. The CD-ROM contains *UNIX in a Nutshell*, 3rd Edition; *UNIX Power Tools*, 2nd Edition (with software); *Learning the UNIX Operating System*, 4th Edition; *Learning the vi Editor*, 6th Edition; *sed & awk*, 2nd Edition; and *Learning the Korn Shell*.

Essential System Administration, 2nd Edition

By AEleen Frisch
2nd Edition September 1995
788 pages, ISBN 1-56592-127-5

Covering all major versions of Unix, this second edition of *Essential System Administration* provides a compact, manageable introduction to the tasks faced by everyone responsible for a Unix system. Whether you use a standalone Unix system, routinely provide administrative support for a larger shared system, or just want an understanding of basic administrative functions, this book is for you. Offers extensive sections on networking, electronic mail, security, and kernel configuration.

The Perl CD Bookshelf, Version 2.0

By O'Reilly & Associates, Inc.
May 2001
672 pages, Features CD-ROM
ISBN 0-596-00164-9

We've updated the *Perl CD Bookshelf* with the third edition of *Programming Perl* and our new *Perl for System Administration*. Our Perl powerhouse of O'Reilly guides also includes *Perl in a Nutshell*, *Perl Cookbook*, and *Advanced Perl Programming*, all unabridged and searchable.

Volume 8: X Window System Administrator's Guide

By Linda Mui & Eric Pearce
1st Edition October 1992
372 pages, ISBN 0-937175-83-8

This book focuses on issues of system administration for X and X-based networks—not just for Unix system administrators, but for anyone faced with the job of administering X (including those running X on standalone workstations).

How to stay in touch with O'Reilly

1. Visit Our Award-Winning Web Site

http://www.oreilly.com/

★ "Top 100 Sites on the Web" —PC Magazine
★ "Top 5% Web sites" —Point Communications
★ "3-Star site" —The McKinley Group

Our web site contains a library of comprehensive product information (including book excerpts and tables of contents), downloadable software, background articles, interviews with technology leaders, links to relevant sites, book cover art, and more. File us in your Bookmarks or Hotlist!

2. Join Our Email Mailing Lists

New Product Releases

To receive automatic email with brief descriptions of all new O'Reilly products as they are released, send email to:
ora-news-subscribe@lists.oreilly.com
Put the following information in the first line of your message (not in the Subject field):
subscribe ora-news

O'Reilly Events

If you'd also like us to send information about trade show events, special promotions, and other O'Reilly events, send email to:
ora-news-subscribe@lists.oreilly.com
Put the following information in the first line of your message (not in the Subject field):
subscribe ora-events

3. Get Examples from Our Books via FTP

There are two ways to access an archive of example files from our books:

Regular FTP

• ftp to:
  ftp.oreilly.com
  (login: anonymous
  password: your email address)
• Point your web browser to:
  ftp://ftp.oreilly.com/

FTPMAIL

• Send an email message to:
  ftpmail@online.oreilly.com
  (Write "help" in the message body)

4. Contact Us via Email

order@oreilly.com
To place a book or software order online. Good for North American and international customers.

subscriptions@oreilly.com
To place an order for any of our newsletters or periodicals.

books@oreilly.com
General questions about any of our books.

cs@oreilly.com
For answers to problems regarding your order or our products.

booktech@oreilly.com
For book content technical questions or corrections.

proposals@oreilly.com
To submit new book or software proposals to our editors and product managers.

international@oreilly.com
For information about our international distributors or translation queries. For a list of our distributors outside of North America check out:
http://www.oreilly.com/distributors.html

5. Work with Us

Check out our website for current employment opportunites:
http://jobs.oreilly.com/

O'Reilly & Associates, Inc.
1005 Gravenstein Hwy North
Sebastopol, CA 95472 USA
TEL 707-829-0515 or 800-998-9938
(6am to 5pm PST)
FAX 707-829-0104

Titles from O'Reilly

International Distributors

http://international.oreilly.com/distributors.html • *international@oreilly.com*

UK, EUROPE, MIDDLE EAST, AND AFRICA (EXCEPT FRANCE, GERMANY, AUSTRIA, SWITZERLAND, LUXEMBOURG, AND LIECHTENSTEIN)

INQUIRIES
O'Reilly UK Limited
4 Castle Street
Farnham
Surrey, GU9 7HS
United Kingdom
Telephone: 44-1252-711776
Fax: 44-1252-734211
Email: information@oreilly.co.uk

ORDERS
Wiley Distribution Services Ltd.
1 Oldlands Way
Bognor Regis
West Sussex PO22 9SA
United Kingdom
Telephone: 44-1243-843294
UK Freephone: 0800-243207
Fax: 44-1243-843302 (Europe/EU orders)
or 44-1243-843274 (Middle East/Africa)
Email: cs-books@wiley.co.uk

FRANCE

INQUIRIES & ORDERS
Éditions O'Reilly
18 rue Séguier
75006 Paris, France
Tel: 33-1-40-51-71-89
Fax: 33-1-40-51-72-26
Email: france@oreilly.fr

GERMANY, SWITZERLAND, AUSTRIA, LUXEMBOURG, AND LIECHTENSTEIN

INQUIRIES & ORDERS
O'Reilly Verlag
Balthasarstr. 81
D-50670 Köln, Germany
Telephone: 49-221-973160-91
Fax: 49-221-973160-8
Email: anfragen@oreilly.de (inquiries)
Email: order@oreilly.de (orders)

CANADA

(FRENCH LANGUAGE BOOKS)
Les Éditions Flammarion ltée
375, Avenue Laurier Ouest
Montréal (Québec) H2V 2K3
Tel: 1-514-277-8807
Fax: 1-514-278-2085
Email: info@flammarion.qc.ca

HONG KONG

City Discount Subscription Service, Ltd.
Unit A, 6th Floor, Yan's Tower
27 Wong Chuk Hang Road
Aberdeen, Hong Kong
Tel: 852-2580-3539
Fax: 852-2580-6463
Email: citydis@ppn.com.hk

KOREA

Hanbit Media, Inc.
Chungmu Bldg. 210
Yonnam-dong 568-33
Mapo-gu
Seoul, Korea
Tel: 822-325-0397
Fax: 822-325-9697
Email: hant93@chollian.dacom.co.kr

PHILIPPINES

Global Publishing
G/F Benavides Garden
1186 Benavides Street
Manila, Philippines
Tel: 632-254-8949/632-252-2582
Fax: 632-734-5060/632-252-2733
Email: globalp@pacific.net.ph

TAIWAN

O'Reilly Taiwan
1st Floor, No. 21, Lane 295
Section 1, Fu-Shing South Road
Taipei, 106 Taiwan
Tel: 886-2-27099669
Fax: 886-2-27038802
Email: mori@oreilly.com

INDIA

Shroff Publishers & Distributors Pvt. Ltd.
12, "Roseland", 2nd Floor
180, Waterfield Road, Bandra (West)
Mumbai 400 050
Tel: 91-22-641-1800/643-9910
Fax: 91-22-643-2422
Email: spd@vsnl.com

CHINA

O'Reilly Beijing
SIGMA Building, Suite B809
No. 49 Zhichun Road
Haidian District
Beijing, China PR 100080
Tel: 86-10-8809-7475
Fax: 86-10-8809-7463
Email: beijing@oreilly.com

JAPAN

O'Reilly Japan, Inc.
Yotsuya Y's Building
7 Banch 6, Honshio-cho
Shinjuku-ku
Tokyo 160-0003 Japan
Tel: 81-3-3356-5227
Fax: 81-3-3356-5261
Email: japan@oreilly.com

SINGAPORE, INDONESIA, MALAYSIA, AND THAILAND

TransQuest Publishers Pte Ltd
30 Old Toh Tuck Road #05-02
Sembawang Kimtrans Logistics Centre
Singapore 597654
Tel: 65-4623112
Fax: 65-4625761
Email: wendiw@transquest.com.sg

AUSTRALIA

Woodslane Pty., Ltd.
7/5 Vuko Place
Warriewood NSW 2102
Australia
Tel: 61-2-9970-5111
Fax: 61-2-9970-5002
Email: info@woodslane.com.au

NEW ZEALAND

Woodslane New Zealand, Ltd.
21 Cooks Street (P.O. Box 575)
Waganui, New Zealand
Tel: 64-6-347-6543
Fax: 64-6-345-4840
Email: info@woodslane.com.au

ARGENTINA

Distribuidora Cuspide
Suipacha 764
1008 Buenos Aires
Argentina
Phone: 54-11-4322-8868
Fax: 54-11-4322-3456
Email: libros@cuspide.com

ALL OTHER COUNTRIES

O'Reilly & Associates, Inc.
1005 Gravenstein Hwy North
Sebastopol, CA 95472 USA
Tel: 707-829-0515
Fax: 707-829-0104
Email: order@oreilly.com

O'REILLY®